The End

At the time appointed the end shall be
(Daniel 8:19)

Percy Fairwater

Kingdom Publishers

The End
At the time appointed the end shall be
Copyright© Percy Fairwater

All rights reserved. No part of this book may be reproduced in any form by photocopying or any electronic or mechanical means, including information storage or retrieval systems, without permission in writing from both the copyright owner and the publisher of the book. The right of Percy Fairwater to be identified as the author of this work has been asserted by him in accordance with the Copyright, Designs and Patents Act 1988 and any subsequent amendments thereto.
A catalogue record for this book is available from the British Library.

All Scripture Quotations have been taken from the New International Version and the King James Version of the Bible.

ISBN: 978-1-911697-00-8

1st Edition by Kingdom Publishers
Kingdom Publishers
London, UK.

You can purchase copies of this book from any leading bookstore or email **contact@kingdompublishers.co.uk**

Contents

Introduction	7
Chapter 1: Daniel Opening chapters	9
Chapter 2: Daniel's dream	35
Chapter 3: Daniel's Vision and Daniel's Supplications	57
Chronological Sequence of significant dates	75
Chapter 4: Daniel's Revelation	76
Chapter 5: Jeremiah	88
Chapter 6: Ezekiel	96
Ezekiel Summary of contents	107
Chapter 7: Haggai & Zechariah	109
Zechariah summary of contents	115
Chapter 8: New Testament Teachings	118
Chapter 9: The LORD's Teachings in Mark and Luke	137
Comparison of gospel accounts of the LORD's Last days teachings	160
Chapter 10: Paul's teachings in Thessalonians & Timothy	162
The DOCTRINES OF DEMONS OR FALSE DOCTRINES	178
Paul's teachings in 2 Timothy	

Chapter 11: The Revelation (Introduction and the Seven Churches)   183

Chapter 12: The Revelation (Heavenly Vision and Seven Seals)   201

Chapter 13: The Revelation (The Seven Trumpets)   219

Chapter 14: The Revelation (The Woman, Dragon, Beast and False Prophet)   234

Chapter 15 The Revelation (The Seven Vials and the Whore of Babylon)   248

Chapter 16: The Revelation (Marriage, Millennium, New Jerusalem)   268

Chapter 17: Summary   282

Chapter 18: The LORD's Comings   290

Chapter 19: The Events of the LAST DAYS   309

Chapter 20: CONCLUSION the LORD's Coming for His People   331

APPENDIX 1 The Babylonian Captivity Periods   337

APPENDIX 2 The Lunar Year, The Seventy Year Period, Years of Servitude   340

APPENDIX 3 The Final Week   344

APPENDIX 4 Scriptural titles and References to the Beast and the False Prophet   356

APPENDIX 5 The Scriptural Gospels   359

APPENDIX 6 ARMAGEDDON   366

APPENDIX 7 Daniel's Supplications and the Persian Kings   373

Introduction

Any study of the scriptures concerning the last days cannot be too brief or over simplified, if it is to be of any real value. Those, who lightly esteem prophetical study, should recognise that Daniel the prophet (whose prophecies are the foundation of eschatology,) and the Apostle John (who received the wonderful New Testament Revelation,) were men, who were greatly loved by the LORD and the revelations given to them are indeed a measure of that love. Such was the calibre of men like these that their writings make nothing of what they endured in terms of fleshly suffering, as opposition to their efforts to follow the will of God and to seek understanding and guidance concerning the revelations they were given. They merely recorded what happened to them in passing, ensuring that others, who might follow in their steps, would expect the same opposition. (Compare Daniel 7:28, 8:27, 10: 2, 3 and Revelation 1:9.) There are several unique references in the writings of Daniel and John that unmistakably link these prophecies (to which attention will be drawn in every case, as this study proceeds.)

When considering the scriptural foundations of last days prophecies, bible students should be particularly wary that they avoid approaching the subject with preconceived ideas or thoughts; for difficulties follow, when no further support is found for these views and opinions. For example, many attempt to introduce the Church into Old Testament writings, completely disregarding dispensational divisions and in particular the place in the divine plan of GOD's chosen nation, Israel. Others, especially in the days when the British Empire held a more conspicuous place in the world, allowed their patriotism to distort and stretch their scriptural interpretations to a ridiculous extreme; neglecting the fact that Britain cannot be readily, or positively, identified in scriptures. This was especially true of some of the prominent bible commentators of the Nineteenth century and earlier, who could not exclude their observations of the increasing British influence and later, the disintegration of the Ottoman Empire, from their bible interpretations. Nevertheless their works are a tribute to their scholarship and research; this is evident by the fact that some are still in print until mid 20th Century.

These notes were commenced in 1957 and have been amended, corrected, updated and revised constantly; I still consider it to be my favourite study and my personal experience has benefitted enormously from my studies of Bible prophecies. I shall continue in His grace as long as possible.

Scriptural prophecy has not been given to enable men to prophesy, but to enable those believers, who are interested, to recognise when the awesome events of the last days are coming to pass under GOD's overall control and to give them hope, when these things begin to happen. Those who reject the truth inevitably believe the lie. This may be illustrated from the experience of the Jews, for whom their captivity and the judgments of the nations surrounding them was prophesied repeatedly. In their failure to believe such prophets the Jewish nation lost their land and they were taken into captivity, from whence (as prophesied) they were delivered eventually and restored. But in their failure to learn from these lessons, they fell short in not accepting their Messiah, when He came in the Person of the LORD Jesus Christ; and until they accept Him, their nation will never enjoy the blessings promised or see the establishment of the Kingdom that only He can accomplish.

This study is intended to help those, who seek a better understanding of the last days, by presenting a scriptural examination of the prophecies involved and allowing the scriptures to reveal the truth.

Anon

Chapter 1 : DANIEL The Opening Chapters.

[1] Every effort made to understand Daniel's prophecy is amply rewarded, for the book of Daniel lays the basic foundation for all prophetical teaching concerning the last days. This foundation affords a reliable means of recognising erroneous teachings, for any doctrines can be ignored immediately that contradict this fundamental teaching.

Daniel is considered particularly in relation to the last days and such portions of it are studied in detail. Other chapters are examined, inasmuch as they provide the background to the experiences of Daniel and also have some relevance to the last days, as will become evident. But obviously, there is a wealth of real spiritual blessing and wisdom to be found in Daniel, which is beyond the scope of these considerations. The value of Daniel's writings, and other scriptures considered, are in no way confined, limited or diminished, by looking in particular at their last day application.

Daniel 1. The background to Daniel's captivity in Babylon.

(1:1, 2) *In the third year of the reign of Jehoiakim king of Judah came Nebuchadnezzar king of Babylon unto Jerusalem, and besieged it. And the Lord gave Jehoiakim king of Judah into his hand, with part of the vessels of the house of God; which he carried into the land of Shinar to the house of his god; and he brought the vessels into the treasure house of his god.*

Rejoicing in the success of his defeat of Pharaoh Necho at

Carchemish, Nebuchadnezzar could afford to be magnanimous in his *first* siege of Jerusalem. The critics chose to ignore this siege, because it is not mentioned in great detail in Kings; Nebuchadnezzar plundered the temple of GOD in Jerusalem and took away some of the vessels (of gold and silver etc.) This siege cannot be discounted (compare 2 Kings 24:1 and 2 Chronicles 36:7.)

(1:3-7) *And the king spake unto Ashpenaz the master of his eunuchs, that he should bring certain of the children of Israel, and of the king's seed, and of the princes; children in whom was no blemish, but well favoured, and skilful in all wisdom, and cunning in knowledge, and understanding science, and such as had ability in them to stand in the king's palace, and whom they might teach the learning and the tongue of the Chaldeans. And the king appointed them a daily provision of the king's meat, and of the wine which he drank: so nourishing them three years, that at the end thereof they might stand before the king. Now among these were of the children of Judah, Daniel, Hananiah, Mishael, and Azariah: unto whom the prince of the eunuchs gave names: for he gave unto Daniel the name of Belteshazzar; and to Hananiah of Shadrach; and to Mishael, of Meshach; and to Azariah, of Abed-nego.*

Also on this first invasion Nebuchadnezzar took away of some the seed royal (Daniel, Hananiah, Mishael, and Azariah,) who were most likely made eunuchs in Babylon (see 2 Kings 20:18). These royal subjects would have been the best educated class in Israel, and conquerors knew the value of educated people to help in their affairs.

(1:8-16) *But Daniel purposed in his heart that he would not defile himself with the portion of the king's meat, nor with the wine which he drank: therefore he requested of the prince of the eunuchs that he might not defile himself. Now God had brought Daniel into favour* and tender love with the prince of the eunuchs. And the prince of the eunuchs said unto Daniel, "I fear my lord the king, who hath appointed your meat and your drink: for why should he see your faces worse liking than the children which are of your sort? Then shall ye make me endanger my head to the king." Then said Daniel to Melzar, whom the prince of the eunuchs had set over Daniel, Hananiah, Mishael, and Azariah, "Prove thy servants, I beseech thee, ten days; and let them give us pulse to eat, and water to drink. Then let our countenances be looked upon before thee, and the countenance of the children that eat of the portion of the king's meat: and as thou seest, deal with thy servants." So he consented to them in this matter, and proved them ten days. And at the end of ten days their countenance appeared fairer and fatter in flesh than all the children which did eat the portion of the king's meat. Thus Melzar took away the portion of their meat, and the wine that they should drink; and gave them pulse.

(1:17-21) *As for these four children, God gave them knowledge and skill in all learning and wisdom: and Daniel had understanding in all visions and dreams. Now at the end of the days that the king had said he should bring them in, then the prince of the eunuchs brought them in before Nebuchadnezzar. And the king communed with them; and among them all was found none like Daniel, Hananiah, Mishael, and Azariah: therefore stood they before the king. And in all matters of wisdom and understanding that the king inquired of them, he found them ten times better than all the magicians and astrologers that were in all his realm. And Daniel continued even unto the first year of King Cyrus.*

Daniel was taken into captivity by Nebuchadnezzar the King of Babylon in the third year of Jehoiakim (BC 605) and Daniel's life span extended through his reign and that of Belshazzar, who lost the kingdom to Darius the Mede[1]. From the Medes, the kingdom passed to the Persians and it is believed that Daniel died in the third year of the reign of Cyrus (BC 519) when his age has been estimated, (assuming he was fifteen when taken into captivity,) at about one hundred and one.

Particularly noteworthy in the opening of Daniel's writings, was the heart displayed by Daniel and his friends, all of them young men, who were not prepared to conform to Babylonian ways at the expense of their spiritual experience. The steward (or eunuch) appointed to take care of them recognised the danger of their action, which could have incurred the wrath of Nebuchadnezzar, but they were blessed of God for their faith.

[The so-called Higher Criticism, (which originated in Germany in mid nineteenth century, but later embraced academics and scholars throughout Europe and America,) targeted Daniel's prophecy in particular, to undermine the credibility of the Bible. They insisted for example that; his prophecy was written after the events that are prophesied and to justify such absurd suggestions, claimed, that a later Daniel wrote those prophecies. Church leaders, who should have spoken out loudly against such nonsense, mildly succumbed for

---

[1] The 3rd year of Jehoiakim (BC 605) was the commencement of The Servitude. Cyrus took the Persian throne after Darius the Mede in BC 536 and his proclamation was BC 535. Daniel lived to the third year of Darius Hystaspes (BC 519 the latest date mentioned in Daniel 10:1) so if he was 15 (approximately) when he went into captivity (BC 605) he would have died at 101. [The Servitude, The Captivity and The Desolations need to be distinguished, see Appendix 1.] Daniel's total captivity is scripturally recorded (1:1 & v21.) It is reasonable to assume that Daniel (and his friends) would have been eligible as young men (from age 13,) to join in worship in the Temple. After the captivity, when synagogue worship was established, young Hebrew males were given Bar Mitzvah (making them, Sons of The Commandment) but they were being prepared for this from twelve years of age, from which time they were entitled to take part, speak, during their synagogue worship. Characteristically, their views were invited first, so they might not be intimidated by the more experienced older males; the point being, they were encouraged to take part in worship. Spiritually speaking, this was a shrewd investment.

fear of being labelled non-academic or whatever. Likewise these Critics attacked Isaiah, inventing a second Isaiah, (called Pseudo-Isaiah, or even Deutero-Isaiah,) for which there is not the slightest scriptural support. Their pernicious doctrines prevailed in far too many cases; but some stalwarts responded vigorously against the Higher Criticism (Sir Robert Anderson, Dr E.W. Bullinger and others) and destroyed their arguments. The effects of Darwin's theory of Evolution, seemingly strengthened the Critics' case and the Church (through Europe and Britain too,) has never fully recovered from the damage inflicted.

(See also footnote 4 page 35.]

[2] Daniel 2. The Image of Nebuchadnezzar's Dream (see figure 1.)

(2:1-9) *And in the second year of the reign of Nebuchadnezzar, Nebuchadnezzar dreamed dreams, wherewith his spirit was troubled, and his sleep brake from him. Then the king commanded to call the magicians, and the astrologers, and the sorcerers, and the Chaldeans, for to shew the king his dreams. So they came and stood before the king. And the king said unto them, "I have dreamed a dream, and my spirit was troubled to know the dream." Then spake the Chaldeans to the king in Syriak, "O king, live for ever: tell thy servants the dream, and we will shew the interpretation." The king answered and said to the Chaldeans, "The thing is gone from me: if ye will not make known unto me the dream, with the interpretation thereof, ye shall be cut in pieces, and your houses shall be made a dunghill. But if ye shew the dream, and the interpretation thereof, ye shall receive of me gifts and rewards and great honour: therefore shew me the dream, and the interpretation thereof." They answered again and said, "Let the king tell his servants the dream, and we will shew the interpretation of it." The king answered and said, "I know of certainty that ye would gain the time, because ye see the thing is gone from me. But if ye will not make known unto me the dream, there is but one decree for you: for ye have prepared lying and corrupt words to speak before me, till the* time be changed: therefore tell me the dream, and I shall know that ye can shew me the interpretation thereof."

(2:10-13) The Chaldeans answered before the king, and said, "There is not a man upon the earth that can shew the king's matter: therefore there is no king, lord, nor ruler, that asked such things at any magician, or astrologer, or Chaldean. And it is a rare thing that the king requireth, and there is none other that can shew it before the king, except the gods, whose dwelling is not with flesh." For this cause the king was angry and very furious, and commanded to destroy all the wise men of Babylon. And the decree went forth that the wise men should be slain; and they sought Daniel and his fellows to be slain.

(2:14-18) Then Daniel answered with counsel and wisdom to Arioch the captain of the king's guard, which was gone forth to slay the wise men of Babylon: he answered and said to Arioch the king's captain, "Why is the decree so hasty from the king?" Then Arioch made the thing known to Daniel. Then Daniel went in, and desired of the king that he would give him time, and that he would shew the king the interpretation. Then Daniel went to his house, and made the thing known to Hananiah, Mishael, and Azariah, his companions: that they would desire mercies of the God of heaven concerning this secret; that Daniel and his fellows should not perish with the rest of the wise men of Babylon.

(2:19-23) Then was the secret revealed unto Daniel in a night vision. Then Daniel blessed the God of heaven. Daniel answered and said, "Blessed be the name of God for ever and ever: for wisdom and might are His: and He changeth the times and the seasons: He removeth kings, and setteth up kings: He giveth wisdom unto the wise, and knowledge to them that know understanding: He revealeth the deep and secret things: He knoweth what is in the darkness, and the light dwelleth with Him. I thank Thee, and praise Thee, O Thou God of my fathers, Who hast given me wisdom and might, and hast made known unto me now what we desired of Thee: for Thou hast now *made known unto us the king's matter."*

(2:24-30) Therefore Daniel went in unto Arioch, whom the king had ordained to destroy the wise men of Babylon: he went and said thus unto him; "Destroy not the wise men of Babylon: bring me in before the king, and I will shew unto the king the interpretation." Then Arioch brought in Daniel before the king in haste, and said thus unto him, "I have found a man of the captives of Judah, that will make known unto the king the interpretation." The king answered and said to Daniel, whose name was Belteshazzar, "Art thou able to make known unto me the dream which I have seen, and the interpretation thereof?" Daniel answered in the presence of the king, and said, "The secret which the king hath demanded cannot the wise men, the astrologers, the magicians, the soothsayers, shew unto the king; but there is a God in heaven that revealeth secrets, and maketh known to the king Nebuchadnezzar what shall be in the latter days. Thy dream, and the visions of thy head upon thy bed, are these; as for thee, O king, thy thoughts came into thy mind upon thy bed what should come to pass hereafter: and He that revealeth secrets maketh known to thee what shall come to pass. But as for me, this secret is not revealed to me for any wisdom that I have more than any living, but for their sakes that shall make known the interpretation to the king, and that thou mightest know the thoughts of thy heart

(2:31-35) Thou, O King, sawest, and behold a great image. This great image, whose brightness was excellent, stood before thee; and the form thereof was terrible. This image's head was of fine gold, his breast and his arms of silver, his belly and his thighs of brass, his legs of iron, his feet part of iron and part of clay. Thou sawest till that a stone was cut out without hands, which smote the image upon his feet that were of iron and clay, and brake them to pieces. Then was the iron, the clay, the brass, the silver, and the gold, broken to pieces together, and became like the chaff of the summer threshingfloors; and the wind carried them away, that no place was found for them; and the stone that smote the image became a great mountain, and filled the whole earth.

(2:36-45) *This is the dream; and we will tell the interpretation thereof before the King. Thou, O king, art a king of kings: for the God of heaven hath given thee a kingdom, power, and strength, and glory. And wheresoever the children of men dwell, the beasts of the field and the fowls of the heaven hath He given into thine hand, and hath made thee ruler over them all. Thou art this head of gold. And after thee shall arise another kingdom inferior to thee, and another third kingdom of brass, which shall bear rule over all the earth. And the fourth kingdom shall be strong as iron: forasmuch as iron breaketh in pieces and subdueth all things: and as iron that breaketh all these, shall it break in pieces and bruise. And whereas thou sawest the feet and toes, part of potters' clay, and part of iron, the kingdom shall be divided; but there shall be in it of the strength of the iron, forasmuch as thou sawest the iron mixed with miry clay. And as the toes of the feet were part of iron, and part of clay, so the kingdom shall be partly strong, and partly broken. And whereas thou sawest iron mixed with miry clay, they shall mingle themselves with the seed of men: but they shall not cleave one to another, even as iron is not mixed with clay. And in the days of these kings shall the God of heaven set up a kingdom, which shall never be destroyed: and the kingdom shall not be left to other people, but it shall break in pieces and consume all these kingdoms, and it shall stand for ever. Forasmuch as thou sawest that the stone was cut out of the mountain without hands, and that it brake in pieces the iron, the brass, the clay, the silver, and the gold; the great God hath made known to the king what shall come to pass hereafter: and the dream is certain, and the interpretation thereof sure."*

(2:46-49) *Then the king Nebuchadnezzar fell upon his face, and worshipped Daniel, and said, "Of a truth it is, that your God is a God of gods, and a Lord of kings, and a revealer of secrets, seeing thou couldest reveal this secret." Then the king made Daniel a great man, and gave him many great gifts, and made him ruler over the whole province of Babylon. Then Daniel requested of the king, and he set Shadrach, Meshach, and Abed-nego over the affairs of the province of Babylon: but Daniel sat in the gate of the king.*

[3] Daniel and his friends knew nothing of this dream, until the king's guards came to slay them, because of Nebuchadnezzar's fury that none of his wise men could tell him, what he had dreamed and give him the interpretation of it. Any lesser character would have promptly given up all hope that such an unreasonable demand could ever be satisfied. But Daniel was of a different calibre and he merely asked Nebuchadnezzar for time, then with his companions he sought God for the answer. Understandably, when God graciously gave Daniel the dream and its interpretation, Daniel was most grateful and very quickly he was standing before Nebuchadnezzar, to whom Daniel revealed the dream and its meaning. Such was the impact of what Daniel revealed to him that Nebuchadnezzar fell on his face to worship Daniel, for the king realised at once that he was in the presence of a young man highly favoured by God. The generous way that Nebuchadnezzar rewarded Daniel was not merely gratitude, it was shrewd insurance. Even in the height of such spectacular success, Daniel for his part did not forget his friends, who had loyally supported him.

The account given shows how the image of Nebuchadnezzar's dream was miraculously described to him by Daniel and the interpretation given by the prophet revealed that the image and its component parts in various metals, depicted the four successive gentile empires, which would rule in turn over Jerusalem, from that time. Thus:

1. Head	Gold	Babylon	(see figures 1 & 2)
2. Breast & Arms	Silver	Medo-Persian	(" " 1 & 3)
3. Belly & Thighs	Brass	Greece	(" " 1 & 4)
4. Legs & Feet	Iron	Rome	(" " 1 & 5)

Daniel's comments were quite straight forward and there should be no difficulties considering this image and the interpretation of it as given by Daniel. The following points are noted:

1. Head of Gold   Babylon

In Daniel's description the head was mentioned quite briefly, *"this image's head was of fine gold"* and in his interpretation Daniel left no room to doubt that this represented the Babylonian kingdom under the absolute rule of Nebuchadnezzar, *"thou art this head of gold."* The kingdom of Babylon, the power, the strength, the wealth and the glory of it, were all given to Nebuchadnezzar, he was the God ordained ruler[2].

2. Breast & Arms of Silver   Medo-Persia

Although the metal silver was named in the description of the image, it was not mentioned in the interpretation given by Daniel, he referred to *"another kingdom inferior to thee."* This inferiority was not in geographical size, for this was a larger kingdom (compare Figures 2 and 3.) The inferiority was in the power of the ruler; Nebuchadnezzar was sole ruler in Babylon, but the Medes and Persians split their kingdom up and appointed local princes and governors as rulers (see Daniel 6:1-8.) The kingdom, which actually replaced Babylon was the Mede (see Daniel 5:31,) this was succeeded by the Persian (Daniel 6:28.) But in addition to the similarities of their languages, the Medes and Persians considered themselves also to be associated in their laws and rule (Daniel 6:8, 12 & 15,) and further, subsequent revelations to Daniel treated them as

---

[2] Nebuchadnezzar was not the first king of Babylon, which was in fact one of the most ancient of kingdoms (see Genesis 10:10.) But Nebuchadnezzar's conquest and rule of Judah commenced a succession of various gentile dominions, which ruled over Jerusalem. The faithfulness to the LORD of Daniel and his friends in captivity was not maintained in Judah, where the king Jehoiakim highhandedly burnt the written roll from the prophet Jeremiah (compare Jeremiah 36:1-32 with Daniel 1:1 and 2:1.) The divine response was the revelation of Gentile supremacy through the dream given to Nebuchadnezzar. This revelation has continued through the LORD's times to the present day. *The End* refers to the time when this gentile domination of Jerusalem is terminated in the last days. (Compare also Deuteronomy 32:8 and Jeremiah 15:4, 24:9 and 29:18.)

one kingdom scripturally (see Daniel 8:20.) The duality can of course be seen typified in the *silver* arms of the image, so that it is reasonable to attribute the silver of the image to the Medes and Persians as one kingdom.

3. Belly & Thighs of Brass   Greece

Daniel's interpretation was very brief "*another kingdom of brass which shall bear rule over all the earth.*" The Greek Empire founded by Alexander the Great replaced the Medo-Persian Kingdom. Alexander's empire was subsequently divided on his death, as Daniel's later writings prophesied (see Daniel 8:21, 22 [31].)

[Throughout the scriptures, *brass* should always be translated as *bronze* (an early alloy of copper and tin,) the ancients did not have the technology to extract zinc (brass is an alloy of copper and zinc, it appeared sometime during the Roman era).]

4. Legs & Feet of Iron   Rome

Prophetically and historically this was the most remote kingdom from Daniel's time and yet in the description of the image by Daniel and in his interpretation, this kingdom was given more attention than the previous three kingdoms together. The completely autocratic rule of Nebuchadnezzar in Babylon, typified in the "*fine gold*", had now degenerated to the more democratic system, typified by the *iron* in the legs and feet of the image, yet the inherent strength in the metal was much greater. It is obviously true, that if everything Is invested in one man, it is easier by comparison to overthrow or replace him than a system appointed by governments, which collectively supports a recognised succession or election of rulers. The "legs" (plural) imply a duality (as in the case of the arms) and it usually suggested that in the later stages of this empire, this could refer to religious divisions, possibly Byzantine and Roman (which was how the Roman Empire became divided) or possibly, Catholic and Protestant. Perhaps another suggestion would be Christian and Muslim; but this division must apply within the boundaries of the Roman Empire.

But this neglects the duality throughout this empire, (in the upper legs so to speak,) in which case the duality could perhaps represent the Jewish believers and the religion of the Roman nation controlling Israel or Judea (Palestine.) However, it was in the last stages of this kingdom (i.e. in the feet) that a completely new constituent was found in the non-metallic "*miry clay,*" which resulted in the kingdom being "*partly strong and partly broken*" (or "*brittle*" as margin references allow.) This weakness was not a characteristic in the image as a whole, which in its metallic structure was getting continually stronger (gold, silver, brass and iron). From Daniel's explanation, it was learned that the weakness typified in the miry clay, applied to "*the seed of men.*" It must follow from this, that "*they that mingle themselves*" (i.e. with the seed of men) cannot be of mankind and scripturally this leaves spirits as the candidates for this role[3].

This weakness, this involvement of men (influenced by, or controlled by, the ruling spirits to some extent,) in the government and rule of nations, will be a definite feature of the last stages of the fourth kingdom. (This was a truth evident to the apostle Paul, who also recognised, that such spiritual influences were a last day sign already being made manifest in his days. Ephesians 6:12 compare 1Timothy 4:1-3 see [103] [104].)

Notice also "*and in the days of these kings... which in its context referred to the ten toes of the feet ....shall the God of Heaven set up a kingdom.*" The ten toes typified ten kings or kingdoms and in their days shall the kingdom of God be established. The eventual establishment of the Kingdom of God will destroy all traces of the previous earthly kingdoms and using none of their methods or

---

[3] The involvement of evil or disobedient spirits with men "*as in the days of Noah*" is a characteristic feature of the last days, which is to be expected from the LORD's Own teachings (see Matthew 24:37 compare Genesis 6.) That this involvement of spirits with mankind is so clearly typified in the miry clay in the feet of Nebuchadnezzar's image is remarkable scriptural confirmation. Later in Daniel (chapters 4 and 11) it is plainly established that spirits and spiritual forces control nations and rulers, under the overall divine sovereignty of GOD Himself.

means; it will extend throughout the whole world in its glory and power.

Nebuchadnezzar's image and the interpretation of it given by Daniel must be regarded as the basis on which prophecies concerning the last days are interpreted. In this respect it is invaluable.

[4] Daniel 3. Shadrach, Meshach and Abed-nego.

(3:1-7) *Nebuchadnezzar the king made an image of gold, whose height was threescore cubits, and the breadth thereof six cubits: he set it up in the plain of Dura, in the province of Babylon. Then Nebuchadnezzar the king sent to gather together the princes, the governors, and the captains, the judges, the treasurers, the counsellors, the sheriffs, and all the rulers of the provinces, to come to the dedication of the image which Nebuchadnezzar the king had set up. Then the princes, the governors, and captains, the judges, the treasurers, the counsellers, the sheriffs, and all the rulers of the provinces, were gathered together unto the dedication of the image that Nebuchadnezzar the king had set up; and they stood before the image that Nebuchadnezzar had set up. Then an herald cried aloud, "To you it is commanded, O people, nations, and languages, that at what time ye hear the sound of the cornet, flute, harp, sackbut, psaltery, dulcimer, and all kinds of musick, ye fall down and worship the golden image that Nebuchadnezzar the king hath set up: and whoso falleth not down and worshippeth shall the same hour be cast into the midst of a burning fiery furnace." Therefore at that time, when all the people heard the sound of the cornet, flute, harp, sackbut, psaltery, and all kinds of musick, all the people, the nations, and the languages, fell down and worshipped the golden image that Nebuchadnezzar the king had set up.*

(3:8-12) *Wherefore at that time certain Chaldeans came near, and accused the Jews. They spake and said to the king Nebuchadnezzar, "O king, live for ever. Thou, O king, hast made a decree, that every man that shall hear the sound of the cornet, flute, harp, sackbut,* psaltery, and dulcimer, and all kinds of musick, shall fall down, and worship the golden image: and whoso falleth not down and worshippeth, that he should be cast into the midst of a burning fiery furnace. There are certain Jews whom thou hast set over the affairs of the province of Babylon, Shadrach, Meshach, and Abed-nego; these men, O king, have not regarded thee: they serve not thy gods, nor worship the golden image which thou hast set up."

(3:13-18) Then Nebuchadnezzar in his rage and fury commanded to bring Shadrach, Meshach, and Abed-nego. Then they brought these men before the king. Nebuchadnezzar spake and said unto them, "Is it true, O Shadrach, Meshack, and Abed-nego, do not ye serve my gods, nor worship the golden image which I have set up? Now if ye be ready that at what time ye hear the sound of the cornet, flute, harp, sackbut, psaltery, and dulcimer, and all kinds of musick, ye fall down and worship the image which I have made; well: but if ye worship not, ye shall be cast the same hour into the midst of a burning fiery furnace; and who is that God that shall deliver you out of my hands?" Shadrach, Meshach, and Abed-nego answered and said to the king, "O Nebuchadnezzar, we are not careful to answer thee in this matter. If it be so, our God Whom we serve is able to deliver us from the burning fiery furnace, and He will deliver us out of thine hand, O king. But if not, be it known unto thee, O king, that we will not serve thy gods, nor worship the golden image which thou hast set up."

(3:19-25) Then was Nebuchadnezzar full of fury, and the form of his visage was changed against Shadrach, Meshach, and Abed-nego; therefore he spake and commanded that they should heat the furnace one seven times more than it was wont to be heated. And he commanded the most mighty men that were in his army to bind Shadrach, Meshach, and Abed-nego, and to cast them into the burning fiery furnace. Then these men were bound in their coats, their hosen, and their hats, and their other garments, and were cast into the midst of the burning fiery furnace. Therefore because the king's commandment was urgent, and the furnace exceeding hot, the flame of the fire slew those men that took up Shadrach, Meshach, *and Abed-nego. And these three men, Shadrach, Meshach, and Abed-nego, fell down bound into the midst of the burning fiery furnace. Then Nebuchadnezzar the king was astonied, and rose up in haste, and spake, and said unto his counsellors, "Did not we cast three men bound into the midst of the fire?" They answered and said unto the king, "True, O king." He answered and said, "Lo, I see four men loose, walking in the midst of the fire, and they have no hurt; and the form of the fourth is like the Son of God."*

(3:26-30) Then Nebuchadnezzar came near to the mouth of the burning fiery furnace, and spake, and said, "Shadrach, Meshach, and Abed-nego, ye servants of the Most High GOD, come forth and come hither." Then Shadrach, Meshach, and Abed-nego, came forth of the midst of the fire. And the princes, governors, and captains, and the king's counsellors, being gathered together, saw these men, upon whose bodies the fire had no power, nor was an hair of their head singed, neither were their coats changed, nor the smell of fire had passed on them. Then Nebuchadnezzar spake, and said, "Blessed be the God of Shadrach, Meshach, and Abed-nego, Who hath sent His angel, and delivered His servants that trusted in Him, and have changed the king's word, and yielded their bodies, that they might not serve nor worship any god, except their own God. Therefore I make a decree. That every people, nation, and language, which speak any thing amiss against the God of Shadrach, Meshach, and Abed-nego, shall be cut in pieces, and their houses shall be made a dunghill: because there is no other God that can deliver after this sort." Then the king promoted Shadrach, Meshach, and Abed-nego, in the province of Babylon.

[5] One of the most familiar incidents of Daniel's writings, it happened when Nebuchadnezzar set up a golden image and commanded everyone to worship it. Daniel's three friends refused to bow in worship to the image and in his wrath Nebuchadnezzar had them thrown into the fiery furnace, from which God miraculously

delivered them. It is essential to recognise the spirit displayed by Shadrach, Meshach and Abed-nego; which was revealed most wonderfully and significantly, in their words to Nebuchadnezzar, *"O Nebuchadnezzar we are not careful to answer thee in this matter. If it be so, our God Whom we serve is able to deliver us from the burning fiery furnace, and He will deliver us out of thine hand, O king. But if not, be it known unto thee, O king, that we will not serve thy gods, nor worship the golden image which thou hast set up."*

These remarkable men gave God full credit for His ability to deliver them, if He so desired; but they made it equally clear, that even if God chose not to save them, they were not going to worship any idol for anybody.

In the light of the prophetical significance of Daniel's writings, concerning the last days, this sounds a very ominous note. For a feature of the terrible tribulation of the last days will be the fact that initially no deliverance comes for those, who refuse to worship the beast or his image and it will seem that he must prevail, even over God's chosen people. But the underlying scriptural lesson is plain, it is far better to choose to die than submit to such demands. [It might be added that in view of the divine judgments poured out on the worshippers of the beast, death for not worshipping him would be in any case a better alternative.]

A comparison of the meanings of their Hebrew names, and their Chaldee names is included here;

Hebrew		Chaldee	
Daniel	*GOD is his judge*	Belteshazar	*Bel preserve/protect his life*
Hananiah	*JEHOVAH hath been gracious*	Shadrach*	*By the command of AKU (The Chaldean Moon God)*
Mishael	*Who is what GOD is*	Meshach*	*Who is as AKU*
Azariah	*JEHOVAH hath helped*	Abed-nego*	*Servant or worshipper of Nego*

(not Nebo as assumed.)

[*The details on these names provided by Dr Bullinger, (in his *Companion Bible*) who ascribes them to Dr Pinches.
Strong's Concordance and Commentaries seem reluctant to offer translations.]

[6] Daniel 4. Nebuchadnezzar's Madness.

(4:1-4) *Nebuchadnezzar the king, unto all people, nations, and languages, that dwell in all the earth; Peace be multiplied unto you. I thought it good to shew the signs and wonders that the high God hath wrought toward me. How great are His signs! And how mighty are His wonders! His kingdom is an everlasting kingdom, and His dominion is from generation to generation.*

(4:4-7) *I Nebuchadnezzar was at rest in mine house, and flourishing in my palace: I saw a dream which made me afraid, and the thoughts upon my bed and the visions of my head troubled me. Therefore made I a decree to bring in all the wise men of Babylon before me, that they might make known unto me the interpretation of the dream. Then came in the magicians, the astrologers, the Chaldeans, and the soothsayers: and I told the dream before them; but they did not make known unto me the interpretation thereof.*

(4:8-18) *But at the last Daniel came in before me, whose name was Belteshazzar, according to the name of my god, and in whom is the spirit of the holy gods: and before him I told the dream, saying, "O Belteshazzar, master of the magicians, because I know that the spirit of the holy gods is in thee, and no secret troubleth thee, tell me the visions of my dream that I have seen, and the interpretation thereof. Thus were the visions of mine head in my bed; I saw, and behold a tree in the midst of the earth, and the height thereof was great. The tree grew, and was strong, and the height thereof reached unto* heaven, and the sight therof to the end of all the earth: the leaves thereof were fair, and the fruits thereof much, and in it was meat for all: the beasts of the field had shadow under it, and the fowls of the heaven dwelt in the boughs thereof, and all flesh was fed of it. I saw in the visions of my head upon my bed, and behold a watcher and an holy one came down from heaven; he cried aloud, and said thus, 'Hew down the tree, and cut off his branches, shake off his leaves, and scatter his fruit: let the beasts get away from under it, and the fowls from his branches: nevertheless leave the stump of his roots in the earth, even with a band of iron and brass, in the tender grass of the field; and let it be wet with the dew of heaven, and let his portion be with the beasts in the grass of the earth: let his heart be changed from man's, and let a beast's heart be given unto him; and let seven times pass over him. This matter is by the decree of the watchers, and the demand by the word of the holy ones: to the intent that the living may know that the MOST HIGH ruleth in the kingdom of men, and giveth it to whomsoever He will, and setteth up over it the basest of men.' This dream I king Nebuchadnezzar have seen. Now thou, O Belteshazzar, declare the interpretation thereof, forasmuch as all the wise men of my kingdom are not able to make known unto me the interpretation: but thou art able; for the spirit of the holy gods is in thee."

(4:19-27) Then Daniel, whose name was Belteshazzar, was astonied for one hour, and his thoughts troubled him. The king spake, and said, "Belteshazzar, let not the dream, or the interpretation therof, trouble thee." Belteshazzar answered and said, "My lord, the dream be to them that hate thee, and the interpretation thereof to thine enemies. The tree that thou sawest, which grew, and was strong, whose height reached unto the heaven, and the sight thereof to all the earth: whose leaves were fair, and the fruit thereof much, and in it was meat for all, under which the beasts of the field dwelt, and upon whose branches the fowls of the heaven had their habitation: it is thou, O king, that art grown and become strong: for thy greatness is grown, and reacheth unto heaven, and thy dominion to the end of the earth. And whereas the king saw a watcher and an holy one coming down from heaven, and saying, 'Hew the tree down, and destroy it; yet leave the stump of the roots thereof in the earth, even with a band of iron and brass, in the tender grass of the field; and let it be wet with the dew of heaven, and let his portion be with the beasts of the field, till seven times pass over him;' this is the interpretation, O king, and this is the decree of the MOST HIGH GOD, which is come upon my lord the king; that they shall drive thee from men, and thy dwelling shall be with the beasts of the field, and they shall make thee to eat grass as oxen, and they shall wet thee with the dew of heaven, and seven times shall pass over thee, till thou know that the MOST HIGH, ruleth in the kingdom of men, and giveth it to whomsoever He will. And whereas they commanded to leave the stump of the tree roots; thy kingdom shall be sure unto thee, after that thou shalt have known that the heavens do rule. Wherefore, O king, let my counsel be acceptable unto thee, and break off thy sins by righteousness, and thine iniquities by shewing mercy to the poor; if it may be a lengthening of thy tranquillity."

(4:28-37) *All this came upon the king Nebuchadnezzar. At the end of twelve months he walked in the palace of the kingdom of Babylon. The king spake, and said, "Is not this great Babylon, that I have built for the house of the kingdom by the might of my power, and for the honour of my majesty?" While the word was in the king's mouth, there fell a voice from heaven, saying, "O king Nebuchadnezzar, to thee it is spoken, the kingdom is departed from thee. And they shall drive thee from men, and thy dwelling shall be with the beasts of the field: they shall make thee to eat grass as oxen, and seven times shall pass over thee, until thou know that the MOST HIGH ruleth in the kingdom of men, and giveth it to whomsoever He will." The same hour was the thing fulfilled upon Nebuchadnezzar: and he was driven from men, and did eat grass as oxen, and his body was wet with the dew of heaven, till his hairs were grown like eagles' feathers, and his nails like birds' claws. And at the end of the days I Nebuchadnezzar lifted up mine eyes unto heaven, and mine understanding returned unto me, and I blessed the MOST HIGH, and I praised and honoured Him that liveth for ever, Whose dominion, is an everlasting dominion,* and His kingdom is from generation to generation: and all the inhabitants of the earth are reputed as nothing: and He doeth according to His will in the army of heaven, and among the inhabitants of the earth: and none can stay His hand, or say unto Him, 'What doest Thou?' At the same time my reason returned unto me; and for the glory of my kingdom, mine honour and brightness returned unto me; and my counsellors and my lords sought unto me; and I was established in my kingdom, and excellent majesty was added unto me. Now I Nebuchadnezzar praise and extol and honour the King of heaven, all Whose works are truth, and His ways judgment: and those that walk in pride He is able to abase.

[7] This was a personal account by Nebuchadnezzar of the madness with which he was afflicted, to teach him that earthly monarchs are established by heavenly decree. The purpose of the dream, a warning to Nebuchadnezzar of the impending affliction, was explained to him in the dream itself. *"This matter is by the decree of the watchers, and the demand by the word of the holy ones; to the intent that the living may know that the MOST HIGH ruleth in the kingdom of men, and giveth it to whomsoever He will, and setteth up over it the basest of men."*

To ordinary people, who at times despair, that their leaders will ever display plain common sense; these words offer considerable comfort and encouragement. GOD has not lost overall control; He is merely using the folly and stupidity of men, whom He has enabled to rule in high places, to accomplish His will on earth. The significance of this experience of Nebuchadnezzar in relation to the last days will become more apparent and relevant in the course of these considerations.

Interestingly, whilst the conventional English belief is that Nebuchadnezzar suffered from lycanthropy (his being transformed into a wolf) for which view there is manifestly no scriptural support. Voltaire the famous French playright, philosopher, and an atheist, wrote a very successful play *Le aureau blanc* (The White Bull) about Nebuchadnezzar's misfortune in being turned into a bull for seven years. Based on the verse: *they shall make thee to eat grass as oxen, and they shall wet thee with the dew of heaven, and seven times shall pass over thee, till thou know that the MOST HIGH GOD ruleth in the kingdom of men.* [See *Voltaire Almighty* by Roger Pearson, Bloomsbury Publishing, 36 Soho Sq. London W1D 3QY 2005. Chapter 20, page 345.]

[8] Daniel 5. Belshazzar's Feast and the Writing on the Wall.

(5:1-4) *Belshazzar the king made a great feast to a thousand of his lords, and drank wine before the thousand. Belshazzar, whiles he tasted the wine, commanded to bring the golden and silver vessels which his father Nebuchadnezzar had taken out of the temple which was in Jerusalem; that the king, and his princes, his wives and his concubines, might drink therein. Then they brought the golden vessels that were taken out of the temple of the house of God which was at Jerusalem; and the king, and his princes, his wives, and his concubines, drank in them. They drank wine, and praised the gods of gold, and of silver, of brass, of iron, of wood, and of stone.*

(5:5-9) *In the same hour came forth fingers of a man's hand, and wrote over against the candlestick upon the plaister of the wall of the king's palace: and the king saw the part of the hand that wrote. Then the king's countenance was changed, and his thoughts troubled him, so that the joints of his loins were loosed, and his knees smote one against another. The king cried aloud to bring in the astrologers, the Chaldeans, and the soothsayers. And the king spake and said to the wise men of Babylon, "Whosoever shall read this writing, and shew me the interpretation thereof, shall be clothed with scarlet, and have a chain of gold about his neck, and shall be the third ruler in the kingdom." Then came in all the king's wise men, but they could not read the writing, nor make known to the king the interpretation thereof. Then was Belshazzar greatly troubled, and his countenance was changed in him, and his lords were astonied.*

(5:10-16) *Now the queen, by reason of the words of the king and his lords, came into the banquet house: and the queen spake and said, "O king, live for ever: let not thy thoughts trouble thee, nor let thy countenance be changed: there is a man in thy kingdom, in whom is the spirit of the holy gods; and in the days of thy father light and understanding and wisdom, like the wisdom of the gods, was found in him; whom the king Nebuchadnezzar thy father, the king, I say, thy father, made master of the magicians, astrologers, Chaldeans, and soothsayers; forasmuch as an excellent spirit, and knowledge, and understanding, interpreting of dreams, and shewing of hard sentences, and dissolving of doubts, were found in the same Daniel, whom the king named Belteshazzar: now let Daniel be called, and he will shew the interpretation." Then was Daniel brought in before the king. And the king spake and said unto Daniel, "Art thou that Daniel, which art of the children of the captivity of Judah, whom the king my father brought out of Jewry? I have even heard of thee, that the spirit of the gods is in thee, and that light and understanding and excellent wisdom is found in thee. And now the wise men, the astrologers, have been brought in before me, that they should read this writing, and make known unto me the interpretation thereof: but they could not shew the interpretation of the thing: and I have heard of thee, that thou canst make interpretations, and dissolve doubts: now if thou canst read the writing, and make known to me the interpretation thereof, thou shall be clothed with scarlet, and have a chain of gold about thy neck, and shalt be the third ruler in the kingdom."*

(5:17-24) *Then Daniel answered and said before the king, "Let thy gifts be to thyself, and give thy rewards to another; yet I will read the writing unto the king, and make known to him the interpretation. O thou king, the MOST HIGH GOD gave Nebuchadnezzar thy father a kingdom, and majesty, and glory, and honour: and for the majesty that He gave him, all people, nations, and languages, trembled and feared before him: whom he would he slew; and whom he would he kept alive; and whom he would he set up; and whom he would he put down. But when his heart was lifted up, and his mind hardened in pride, he was deposed from his kingly throne, and they took his glory from him: and he was driven from the sons of men, and his heart was made like the beasts, and his dwelling was with the wild asses: they fed him with grass like oxen, and his body was wet with the dew of heaven; till he knew that the MOST HIGH GOD ruled in the kingdom of men, and that He appointeth over it whomsoever He will. And thou his son, O Belshazzar, has not humbled thine heart, though thou knewest all this; but hast lifted up thyself against the Lord of heaven; and they have brought the vessels of His house before thee, and thou, and thy lords, thy wives, and thy concubines, have drunk wine in them; and thou hast praised the gods of silver, and gold, of brass, iron, wood, and stone, which see not, nor hear, nor know: and the God in Whose hand thy breath is, and Whose are all thy ways, hast thou not glorified: then was the part of the hand sent from Him; and this writing was written.*

(5:25-29) *And this is the writing that was written, ME-NE, ME-NE, TE-KEL, UPHARSIN. This is the interpretation of the thing: ME-NE; God hath numbered thy kingdom and finished it. TE-KEL; Thou art weighed in the balances and art found wanting. PE-RES; Thy kingdom is divided, and given to the Medes and Persians." Then commanded Belshazzar, and they clothed Daniel with scarlet, and put a chain of gold about his neck, and made a proclamation concerning him, that he should be the third ruler in the kingdom.*

(5:30, 31) *In that night was Belshazzar the king of the Chaldeans slain. And Darius the Median took the kingdom, being about threescore and two years old.*

Another very familiar story from Daniel's writings, but the significant point in respect of these considerations was (5:22,) *"thou his son, O Belshazzar, hast not humbled thine heart, though thou knewest all this."* The judgment of Belshazzar came because he ignored the facts that he knew regarding the MOST HIGH GOD; for he knew of Nebuchadnezzar's madness and the lessons that Nebuchadnezzar's experience had taught him (5:20, 21.) Belshazzar's folly was that he ignored the warnings and in a festive mood he exceeded a divinely imposed limit. This mentality will be manifested in the *eating and drinking* attitude of the last days, which was one of the points, to which the LORD Himself drew attention in His teachings (see Luke 17:26, 27 [78].)

[9] Daniel 6. Daniel cast into the lions' den.

(6:1-3) *It pleased Darius to set over the kingdom an hundred and twenty princes, which should be over the whole kingdom; and over these three presidents; of whom Daniel was first: that the princes might give accounts unto them, and the king should have no damage. Then this Daniel was preferred above the presidents and princes, because an excellent spirit was in him; and the king thought to set him over the whole realm.*

(6:4-9) *Then the presidents and princes sought to find occasion against Daniel concerning the kingdom; but they could find none occasion nor fault; forasmuch as he was faithful, neither was there any error or fault found in him. Then said these men, "We shall not find any occasion against this Daniel, except we find it against him concerning the law of his God." Then these presidents and princes assembled together to the king, and said thus unto him, "King Darius, live forever. All the presidents of the kingdom, the governors, and the princes, the counsellors, and the captains, have consulted together to establish a royal statute, and to make a firm decree, that whosoever shall ask a petition of any God or man for thirty days, save of thee, O king, he shall be cast into the den of lions. Now, O king, establish the decree, and sign the writing, that it be not changed, according to the law of the Medes and Persians, which altereth not." Wherefore king Darius signed the writing and the decree.*

(6:10-17) *Now when Daniel knew that the writing was signed, he went into his house; and his windows being open in his chamber toward Jerusalem, he kneeled upon his knees three times a day, and prayed, and gave thanks before his God, as he did aforetime. Then these men assembled, and found Daniel praying, and making supplication before his God. Then they came near, and spake before the king concerning the king's decree; "Hast thou not signed a decree,* that every man that shall ask a petition of any God or man within thirty days, save of thee, O king, shall be cast into the den of lions?" The king answered and said, "The thing is true, according to the law of the Medes and Persians, which altereth not." Then answered they and said before the king, "That Daniel, which is of the captivity of Judah, regardeth not thee, O king, nor the decree that thou hast signed, but maketh his petition three times a day." Then the king, when he heard these words, was sore displeased with himself, and set his heart on Daniel to deliver him: and he laboured till the going down of the sun to deliver him. Then these men assembled unto the king, and said unto the king, "Know, O king, that the law of the Medes and Persians is, That no decree nor statute which the king establisheth may be changed." Then the king commanded, and they brought Daniel, and cast him into the den of lions. Now the king spake and said unto Daniel, "Thy GOD Whom thou servest continually, He will deliver thee." And a stone was brought, and laid upon the mouth of the den; and the king sealed it with his own signet, and with the signet of his lords; that the purpose might not be changed concerning Daniel.

(6:18-23) Then the king went to his palace, and passed the night fasting: neither were instruments of musick brought before him: and his sleep went from him. Then the king arose very early in the morning, and went in haste unto the den of lions. And when he came to the den, he cried with a lamentable voice unto Daniel: and the king spake and said to Daniel, "O Daniel, servant of the living GOD, is Thy GOD, Whom thou servest, continually, able to deliver thee from the lions?" Then said Daniel unto the king, "O king live forever. My GOD hath sent His angel, and hath shut the lions' mouths, that they have not hurt me: forasmuch as before Him innocency was found in me; and also before thee, O king, have I done no hurt." Then was the king exceeding glad for him, and commanded that they should take Daniel up out of the den. So Daniel was taken up out of the den, and no manner of hurt was found upon him, because he believed in his GOD.

(6:24) And the king commanded, and they brought those men which had accused Daniel, and they cast them into the den of lions, them, their children, and their wives; and the lions had the mastery of them, and brake all their bones in pieces or ever they came at the bottom of the den.

(6:25-28) *Then king Darius wrote unto all people, nations, and languages, that dwell in all the earth; "Peace be multiplied unto you. I make a decree, That in every dominion of my kingdom men tremble and fear before the GOD of Daniel: for He is the living GOD, and stedfast for ever, and His kingdom that which shall not be destroyed, and His dominion shall be even unto the end. He delivereth and rescueth, and He worketh signs, and wonders in heaven and in earth, Who hath delivered Daniel from the power of the lions." So this Daniel prospered in the reign of Darius, and in the reign of Cyrus the Persian.*

Quite probably Nebuchadnezzar himself would not have been so foolish, where Daniel was concerned; but Darius the Mede was completely deceived by his princes and presidents into signing a decree that he could not alter and as a result Daniel was cast into the lions' den. In the miraculous deliverance of Daniel, Darius himself gave glory to God for His greatness and the king's relief that Daniel survived the ordeal was made plain. The lesson remains, that the most just and righteous of rulers can be manipulated and deceived into perpetrating the most extreme and callous injustices on perfectly innocent people.

[The Jewish historian Josephus claimed that Daniel's accusers protested to Darius that he had fed the lions before casting Daniel into their den; in his fury at their accusation Darius ordered these men and their families to be cast into the den of lions to prove how hungry the lions were. See also Appendix 7 DANIEL'S SUPPLICATIONS and The Persian Kings.]

Chapter 2: DANIEL'S DREAM

[10] The opening chapters of Daniel's prophecy have laid the foundation of this last days study and the relevance of the various things noted will become apparent as the study proceeds. What has been recorded has involved Daniel as the interpreter of things concerning Nebuchadnezzar and Belshazzar and also as the recorder for what happened in the experiences of Shadrach, Meshach and Abed-nego and Darius (Daniel was himself involved in this last case.) The final chapters of Daniel's prophecy manifest the real fruit of that godly man's experience, for these contain the various revelations given to Daniel personally. It will also become evident that there is a harmony between the revelations given to Daniel himself and those revelations already considered, which confirms the inspiration of the whole book[4].

Daniel 7. Daniel's Dream

(7:1-8) *In the first year of Belshazzar king of Babylon Daniel had a dream and visions of his head upon his bed: then he wrote the dream, and told the sum of the matters. Daniel spake and said, "I saw in my vision by night, and behold, the four winds of the heaven strove upon the great sea. And four great beasts came up from the sea, diverse*

---

[4] It is not accepted that the book of Daniel was shared between two prophets named Daniel; this suggestion is as preposterous as it is unfounded, and it has already been more than adequately refuted by competent Bible scholars. The same tactic has also been employed in an effort to discredit Isaiah's prophecy. It might be noted that the LORD Himself referred to Daniel and Isaiah, without the slightest suggestion in either case that their prophecies were revelations to more than one individual. As noted (footnote 1, page 3) Daniel's total time in captivity is scripturally recorded, it is beyond argument therefore that there was *scripturally* only ONE prophet Daniel.

one from another. The first was like a lion, and had eagle's wings: I beheld till the wings thereof were plucked, and it was lifted up from the earth, and made stand upon the feet as a man, and a man's heart was given to it. And behold another beast, a second, like to a bear, and it raised up itself on one side, and it had three ribs in the mouth of it between the teeth of it: and they said thus unto it, 'Arise, devour much flesh.' After this I beheld, and lo another, like a leopard, which had upon the back of it four wings of a fowl; the beast had also four heads; and dominion was given to it. After this I saw in the night visions, and behold a fourth beast, dreadful and terrible, and strong exceedingly; and it had great iron teeth: it devoured and brake in pieces and stamped the residue with the feet of it: and it was diverse from all the beasts that were before it; and it had ten horns. I considered the horns, and behold, there came up among them another little horn, before whom there were three of the first horns plucked up by the roots: and behold, in this horn were eyes like the eyes of man, and a mouth speaking great things.

(7:9-14) I beheld till the thrones were cast down, and the Ancient of days did sit, Whose garment was white as snow, and the hair of His head like the pure wool: His throne was like the fiery flame, and His wheels as burning fire. A fiery stream issued and came forth from before Him: thousand thousands ministered unto Him, and ten thousand times ten thousand stood before Him: the judgment was set, and the books were opened. I beheld then because of the voice of the great words which the horn spake: I beheld even till the beast was slain, and his body destroyed, and given to the burning flame. As concerning the rest of the beasts, they had their dominion taken away: yet their lives were prolonged for a season and time. I saw in the night visions, and behold, one like the Son of man came with the clouds of heaven, and came to the Ancient of days, and they brought Him near before Him. And there was given Him dominion, and glory, and a kingdom, that all people, nations, and languages, should serve Him: His dominion is an everlasting dominion, which shall not pass away, and His kingdom that which shall not be destroyed.

(7:15-28) *I Daniel was grieved in my spirit in the midst of my body, and the visions of my head troubled me. I came near unto one of them that stood by, and asked him the truth of all this. So he told me, and made me know the interpretation of the things. These great beasts, which are four, are four kings, which shall arise out of the earth. But the saints of the MOST HIGH GOD shall take the kingdom and possess the kingdom for ever, even for ever and ever. Then I would know the truth of the fourth beast, which was diverse from all the others, exceeding dreadful, whose teeth were of iron, and his nails of brass; which devoured, brake in pieces, and stamped the residue with his feet: and of the ten horns that were in his head, and of the other which came up, and before whom three fell; even of that horn that had eyes, and a mouth that spake very great things, whose look was more stout than his fellows. I beheld, and the same horn made war with the saints, and prevailed against them; until the Ancient of days came, and judgment was given to the saints of the MOST HIGH; and the time came that the saints possessed the kingdom. Thus he said, 'The fourth beast shall be the fourth kingdom upon earth, which shall be diverse from all kingdoms, and shall devour the whole earth, and shall tread it down, and break it in pieces. And the ten horns out of this kingdom are ten kings that shall arise: and another shall rise after them; and he shall be diverse from the first, and he shall subdue three kings. And he shall speak great words against the Most High, and shall wear out the saints of the Most High, and think to change times and laws: and they shall be given into his hand until a time and times and the dividing of time*. But the judgment shall sit, and they shall take away his dominion, to consume and to destroy it unto the end. And the kingdom and dominion, and the greatness of the kingdom under the whole heaven, shall be given to the people of the saints of the Most High, Whose kingdom is an everlasting kingdom, and all dominions shall serve and obey Him.' Hitherto is the end of the matter. As for me Daniel, my cogitations much troubled me, and my countenance changed in me: but I kept the matter in my heart."* [*(i) *a time, times and the dividing of time* is the first of the unique references (exclusive to Daniel and the Revelation of John and noted in the Introduction;) that link these prophecies. All of these ten references apply to the Final Week of the Seventy Weeks; which is the ultimate foundation for last days' prophecies. See also Appendix 3.]

[11] In the first year of Belshazzar's reign, Daniel had a dream himself (7:2-14,) which troubled him and he asked for the interpretation (7:16.) This was the first account of a revelation given to Daniel personally, but in fact, the rest of Daniel's writings revealed his own experiences and the revelations, which he was given during the reigns of Belshazzar, Darius and Cyrus, the successive rulers in Babylon. The revelations given to Daniel personally are more complicated and detailed than anything in his previous writings, but nevertheless their consideration is most rewarding.

Daniel's Dream and its interpretation are considered only in respect of their last days' application. This does not deny that there are possibly historical partial fulfilments of some of the events, but these are beyond the scope of this study and would detract from its purpose.

However to establish particularly that Daniel's Dream and its interpretation apply to the last days, note:

(1) The beasts appeared following the striving of the four winds on the great sea (The Mediterranean 7:2, 3.)

(2) The descriptions of the four beasts associated them together, but emphasised their differences:

(7:3) *Four great beasts came up .... diverse one from another*

(7:4) *The first ....*

(7:5) *And behold another beast, a second, ...*

(7:6) *And lo another, ...*

(7:7) *And behold a fourth beast, ...*

They appeared together and clearly, they existed together at the judgment of the fourth beast (7:11, 12.)

(3) The establishment of the kingdom of God and casting down of earthly thrones were last days' events and involved the four beasts of Daniel's Dream (7:9-14.)

(4) The assurance that the saints of the Most High shall possess the kingdom for ever and ever was evidently last days' doctrine (7:18, 27.)

(5) The interpretation itself established that these were future events (7:17) *these great beasts, which are four, are four kings, which SHALL arise out of the earth.*

[12] All the evidence in the dream and its interpretation pointed to the conclusion that the whole was intended as a revelation concerning the last days. As these considerations proceed, this conclusion is strengthened and the difficulties are magnified that would be found seeking historical fulfilments or attempting to confine the dream and its interpretation to Israel during the times of these ruling empires.

Returning for the moment, to the Image of Nebuchadnezzar's dream - in that case, a clear succession of kingdoms was revealed to Daniel, which he gave in his interpretation to Nebuchadnezzar (2:39,) "*Thou art this head of gold.... .....and after thee shall arise another kingdom inferior to thee.*" The structure of the image itself also suggested a progression - the head of gold, continuing to the silver of the breast and arms, to the brass of the belly and thighs, to the iron of the legs, down to the miry clay found in the feet. Then the whole image was destroyed, when the stone smote the image in the feet. Quite clearly even though the kingdoms in the image succeeded each other, they all existed together at the end, when they were all destroyed at once (note especially 2:44 *In the days of these kings ...* see [2].)

But in Daniel's Dream, the four beasts appeared together as a result of the striving of the four winds on the great sea and this was all future, relative to Daniel's experience (7:17.) Note also that even in the short account of the first three beasts not one of them was mentioned as being destroyed, in fact (7:12) *they had their dominion taken away. Yet their lives were prolonged for a season and time.* (Again compare with Nebuchadnezzar's image, in which the first three kingdoms were dismissed briefly, but the whole image was destroyed at once.) So the astonishing thing is that whilst the image of Nebuchadnezzar's dream in Daniel's interpretation clearly pointed to a succession of kingdoms, (and their final destruction altogether,) Daniel's Dream portrayed the four kingdoms existing together in the last days. These two revelations do not contradict each other; for both confirm that these four nations shall eventually be destroyed altogether when the kingdom of God is established.

The revelations given to Nebuchadnezzar and Daniel confirmed that these four nations had a successive historical role to play (this was prophetic from Daniel's time of course) and also a collective and prophetic last day role to fulfil together. With this in mind, they may be compared (see also Figure 1.)

Nebuchadnezzar's image		Kingdom	Daniel's Dream	Figure
HEAD	GOLD	BABYLON	WINGED LION	2
CHEST & ARMS	SILVER	MEDO-PERSIA	BEAR	3
BELLY & THIGHS	BRASS	GREECE	LEOPARD	4
LEGS & FEET (Ten toes)	IRON	ROME	DREADFUL BEAST (Ten horns)	5

In this comparison there is an obvious association of the winged lion, (the recognised symbol of Babylon,) with the Head of Nebuchadnezzar's Image (and he was declared to be that head, i.e. the ruler of Babylon). There are also valid associations in the ten toes of Nebuchadnezzar's Image, with the ten horns of the dreadful beast.

These comparisons are made only to emphasise that the identities of the four kingdoms of the Image and the four kingdoms of the Dream are the same. What is important, is that in Nebuchadnezzar's Image these four kingdoms were to be considered more in their successive historical roles (from the way Daniel gave his interpretation) and in Daniel's Dream, they were to be considered as contemporary kingdoms (or nations) appearing together in the last days.

Daniel (7:12) showed clearly, that the first four beasts go on living AFTER the judgment of the little horn, the horn, the beast; which leaves no room for argument that the four exist together in the last days. In actual fact the four beasts go on living after the judgment of the little horn's kingdom and his personal destruction.

[13] To proceed, Daniel's Dream can be considered in more detail.

(7:1) Daniel deserved to be commended for writing down what he dreamed, yet there was no record that he mentioned anything of the dream or its interpretation to Belshazzar, a lesson in wisdom and stewardship.

(7:2, 3) The striving of the four winds of heaven on the great sea (the name given to the Mediterranean) represented some catastrophic disturbance involving either the elements, or more probably, the spiritual forces that control nations. Something like a world war would perhaps answer the question, regarding what this really involved; but the outcome was the emergence of these four kingdoms together, or in rapid succession. In their previous historical and individual appearances, each of these kingdoms was established by war and conquest. It does not seem unreasonable therefore, to suggest that another war could be the basic cause for their collective re-emergence. In the last century, there have been two world wars, which have had profound effects on the countries surrounding the Mediterranean. Some of the territories and borders established by the major powers as a result of agreements, treaties or peace reparations have not always been with the consent, consideration or consultation of the native peoples or inhabitants. This has left many small and large nations in the Middle East with legitimate grievances, at their having to accept conditions imposed by foreign powers, or international corporations, in those times when these peoples had no arms or ability to fight for their rights. Now the situation has changed dramatically, arms are freely available to small countries and the money to purchase them can be found from oil revenues and other legitimate sources. For the unscrupulous, or perhaps the poorer countries with no oil revenues, finances from drug dealing, money laundering, piracy and other illegal activities can be used to buy arms for terrorists, or political extremists and such organisations can cause considerable national or international problems. The nations involved in Daniel's Dream have these territorial, economic, political and religious interests that overlap and extend well beyond their individual boundaries. Who could confidently claim that the forces typified in *the four winds of heaven, strove upon the great sea*, have already been adequately expended and fulfilled in respect of these events?

Daniel saw the emergence of four beasts *"diverse one from another"* and representing four kingdoms and he compared them with each other.

[14] (7:4) *THE LION WITH EAGLE'S WINGS*

The lion had eagle's wings, which were plucked and it was lifted up from the earth and made to stand upon the feet as a man and a man's heart was given to it.

Some hastily assume that because the wings were plucked, that this applied to Nebuchadnezzar, who lost his power for the period of his madness. However Nebuchadnezzar was dead at the time of Daniel's dream! Neither did Nebuchadnezzar obtain Babylon as the result of any striving in the great sea. This dream applied to the future not the past (7:17.) Such attempts to explain this verse do nothing but discredit PROPHECY[5]. To make real sense, this passage has to apply to a Babylon of the last days. In which case (in the light of

---

[5] There is a deplorable tendency by some to attempt to apply subsequent prophetic scriptures to previous scriptural events. This invariably leads to confusion and also leads to the necessity of having to stretch or distort the scriptures to make them fit.

Nebuchadnezzar's madness) the last day kingdom could be initially established by spiritual powers ordained of God (as Nebuchadnezzar was in Babylon.) But when the beast was made to stand on its own feet like a man, it suggested that the kingdom (or its king) was extending itself (or himself) beyond the divinely intended limit. The beast was over-reaching itself. Scripturally the difference between a man and a beast is simply in man's ability to worship. So that when a man's heart was given to this beast, the king (as typified in the beast) was making spiritual demands or claims beyond his divinely appointed rights. This happened previously in the case of Shadrach, Meshach and Abed-nego of course, who refused to conform to Nebuchadnezzar's demands that they worship his image. But this must have last day application from Daniel's Dream; and the Babylon of the last days will provoke God in the worship it introduces. Another historical bell rings, because it was this characteristic that brought His judgment on the place in its very foundation. For God confused the language of men to prevent their building the tower of Babel in their rebellion against Him (see Genesis 11:1-9.) Babel is the Hebrew name, Babylon is the Greek name, their meanings are the same, *confusion*.

[15] (7:5) *THE BEAR RAISED UP ON ONE SIDE WITH THREE RIBS IN ITS MOUTH*

It is reasonable to identify the bear raising itself up on one side, as the Medo-Persian kingdom in which, in its last days appearance, the Persian influence predominates. But some commentators generally claimed the three ribs in the bear's mouth typified the three Persian kings, who succeeded Cyrus. (This resulted from their applying the interpretation of Daniel's Vision to Daniel's Dream, an obvious error – see footnote 21, page 32.)

The commandment *"Arise, devour much flesh"* presents some difficulty and points in its last day fulfilment to the Persian nation's being established in a particularly ruthless fashion with no respect for life. This brings us back to the three ribs - presumably the debris, or residue from whence the flesh has been consumed. These could possibly represent three smaller regions, tribes, ethnic groups etc.

closely akin to (or within the boundary of) Persia, who were engulfed or devoured by Persia, to the extent that only the framework of their identity remained. If not within the national boundary of Persia, could these ribs represent adjacent territories (or small islands) which Persia had claimed and exploited? If within the Persian borders, perhaps these could be smaller ethnic races. Whatever they were, whilst they might be barely recognisable in the jaws of the bear, their substance had certainly nourished the bear.

The last day's fulfilment of these prophecies in Persia must be closely associated with the prophecies concerning Babylon, Greece and other nations within the boundaries of the Roman Empire (manifestly including a particular alliance or group of ten.) Seeking historical fulfilments of these eventualities must not be allowed to distract from, or disguise, the prophetic application to these nations in their last days' reappearance.

[16] (7:6) *THE LEOPARD WITH FOUR WINGS AND FOUR HEADS*

With respect to the Greek Empire, the temptation to seek historical fulfilment is much greater, because of the well-known subdivision of the empire founded by Alexander the Great into the four parts, which were shared eventually by his generals. However recognising the last day concept of Daniel's dream, this beast must also be considered in relation to the other kingdoms so far examined. In which case, the four wings and the four heads, of this beast need not typify division, but rather unity. The wings perhaps represent unity of power and the heads typify unity of rule or authority.

The last day Greek kingdom might involve the re-uniting of the four former divisions of the ancient Greek Empire (but not necessarily so, this is only conjecture.) Such a unity could exercise considerably more power and authority in the last days[6].

The feature concerning the leopard[7] *"dominion was given to it"* allows for its authority or influence to extend considerably beyond its own national boundaries. Daniel's Dream had revealed the appearance of three kingdoms in the last days. Babylon ruled by a man who extended himself beyond the divinely appointed limits. Persia, more down to earth, establishing itself in a brutal manner and possibly exploiting or devouring three territories or regions etc. Greece, becoming dominant, mainly it would seem as a direct result of an alliance (of four perhaps.)

None of the suggestions made concerning the beast, or the bear with three ribs, or the leopard with four heads and four wings need necessarily be correct; what matters is that these characteristics, when they are fulfilled, will enable these kingdoms to be identified beyond any doubt.

There was at this point, a distinct change in Daniel's narrative: (7:7) *after this I saw in the night visions, and behold a fourth beast.* It is this, the fourth beast, which takes the pre-eminence in Daniel's Dream and interpretation. But the first significant point to note is that its appearance is AFTER the appearances of the three preceding beasts. So that in the last days, the establishment of the three can be expected first and then the fourth beast will emerge to play its role.

---

[6] A strong feature of the last days is the revival of nationalism, to which the LORD Himself referred when speaking of the fig tree (Israel) shooting forth (Luke 21:29) *"Behold the fig tree and all the trees"*. There is the possibility of a Greek alliance of four. Also the ten horn alliance in the last days' Roman Empire, and within the ten horned alliance, there appears to be a further association of three which the beast exploits to his advantage. This does not exhaust the list, for other nations outside of the ten appear to form themselves into groups rather than stand individually. Such alliances may reflect the improved means of communication between nations, and also the intense political activity, echoing the involvement of men (the miry clay again) in the last days governments of nations.

[7] The combination of four in the wings and heads of this beast could perhaps point to an internal coalition politically and also an external alliance, which would not necessarily require including the former divisions of the ancient Greek empire. This is suggested however, partly because history tends to repeat itself and also because the animal depicted a leopard (which is Asian or African) points to nations toward the east or south of Greece.

[17] (7:7, 8) THE DREADFUL AND TERRIBLE BEAST.

The emphasis in Daniel's account (7:3, 7, 19 & 23) was on the difference between this beast and the others (which were distinguished scripturally from the outset as being different from each other 7:3). Yet the picture of the fourth beast[8] remained indistinct, it was not a beast that could be identified immediately (like a lion, bear or leopard.) The description *"Dreadful and terrible"* was very ominous, especially when considering how unsociable and dangerous the previous beasts were. It is also worthy of notice that this beast *shall devour the whole earth, and shall tread it down, and break it in pieces.* The wanton destruction and exploitation of the earth and its resources have been particularly extreme in this last century or so and such destruction reaches its climax in this prophecy (compare the judgment prophesied for those that *destroy the earth* - Revelation 11:18 [155].)

The description given *Behold a fourth beast, dreadful and terrible, and strong exceedingly: and it had great iron teeth: it devoured and brake in pieces, and stamped the residue with the feet of it: and it was diverse from all the beasts that were before it; and it had ten horns. I considered the horns, and behold, there came up among them another little horn, before whom there were three of the first horns plucked up by the roots: and behold, in this horn were eyes like the eyes of a man, and a mouth speaking great things.*

The original words in this description reveal far more:

Dreadful - this is a Chaldean word "dechal" which means to slink or crawl and by implication, it can mean "to make afraid, or cause dread". It comes from a root word "zachal" meaning "to crawl" or "serpent, or worm" (the word occurs again 7:19, where the beast is described as "exceeding dreadful" or "very dreadful".)

---

[8] It is difficult to imagine such a beast as a mammal. The figure used in illustration is loosely based on a bas-relief on the Ishtar Gate, excavated in the ruins of Babylon. This seemed a most appropriate image to use and it would have been familiar to Daniel.

Terrible - again a Chaldean word "emtaniy" which means "well-loined or mighty" but it derives from a root word "mothen" meaning "slender loined," as for example in the case of a greyhound, not suggesting weakness, but sleek power.

Strong - Chaldean "taqqiyph" means "strong, mighty, powerful" in the sense of overpowering, or overwhelming (the same word is found in Daniel 2:40 and 42 with respect to the fourth kingdom of Nebuchadnezzar's image).

The description that "*it had great iron teeth*" described its formidable jaws and it devoured and brake in pieces with these jaws and its terrible teeth "*and stamped the residue with the feet of it.*" A most fearsome and ferocious beast, which used every means at its disposal to overcome and destroy any opposition. The fact that this beast was described as having feet, does not contradict the "serpentine" description found in the word "dreadful". For, with the word "terrible," the whole description could apply to a reptile like a dragon. This would certainly agree with the clear distinction made, that this beast was *"diverse from all the beasts that were before it,"* since such a creature would be scaled, cold-blooded, and untameable and yet fascinating, even beautiful, which is the case with many reptiles. Further, the final characteristic *It had ten horns* would be a feature far more likely to be found in reptiles, than in any other species of large animals[9].

[18] Daniel himself *considered the horns*, he realised that these represented something particularly important *and there came up among them another little horn* (notice this, *another little horn* came up among the ten) *before whom there were three of the first horns plucked up by the roots.*

These are significant, recognisable events or happenings. But the most compelling feature of the little horn to Daniel was, BEHOLD *"in this horn were eyes like the eyes of man, and a mouth speaking great*

---

[9] Such conclusions immediately associate this beast with the dragon of Revelation 12 [157] and the beast of Revelation 13 [161] and 17 [184].

things."

Caution is necessary to avoid jumping to any wrong conclusions and to understand what is actually written. Whilst this fourth beast is certainly the most fearful and ferocious, it does not destroy the other beasts in establishing itself. It does not even attack them, at the time it emerges to play its prophetic role. The Roman Empire (typified in the Iron legs of Nebuchadnezzar's image,) in its final stages, concluded with a confederation of ten, among whom this little horn appears. The ten horns were included in the description of this beast from its emergence, so this must point to the time, when this confederation of ten within the boundaries of the Roman Empire fulfils its prophetical role. The little horn, who was not evident in the emergence of the beast but appeared later, will be readily identifiable in this chain of events.

[19] What followed next in Daniel's account was his record of the judgment of the beasts and the establishment of the kingdom of the Son of man. There were some noteworthy points: *The thrones were cast down.* In its context this must refer to earthly thrones, which can no longer rule under the overall authority of the Ancient of days. Daniel's description of His throne (*where millions minister to Him and millions more stand before Him, as the judgment was set up and the books were opened*) expressed in so few words a vivid picture of the greatness of God; to Whom millions can minister, whilst millions more wait for judgment - all completely under His divine control.

Yet, in spite of this, Daniel was compelled to look because of *the voice of the great words which the horn spake.* Even in the presence of the Ancient of days, when earthly thrones had been cast down, this horn continued to pour out these great words that captured the prophet's attention. All his talking made no difference, the beast was slain, his body destroyed and given to the burning flame. The other beasts were allowed to continue, their dominion was taken away and their lives were prolonged for *a season and time.* Finally in Daniel's dream the kingdom of the Son of man was established forever. But the extraordinary feature was *the voice of the great words which the horn spake*, for this character continued to spout out these great words, even as the judgment of God was established. Such defiance, at such a time, was incredible, almost unbelievable and it was no wonder that it so attracted Daniel's attention. But the judgment was inexorable and the great words of the horn counted for nothing in the exercise of divine justice, the beast was slain and his body destroyed. The other beasts were treated differently, their dominion was removed i.e. their authority or rule was ended and their lives prolonged for a *season and time*.

Difficulty is encountered by some, who attempt to add the "*season*" to the "*time*" in an effort to determine the length of the period, for which the lives of these beasts (the nations in typology) are prolonged or continued. But the word "*season*" in Chaldean is "zemawn" and it means "an appointed occasion or a fixed time" i.e. an appointment. Putting this meaning, with *time* in context, it revealed that these beasts were allowed to continue without any power or authority, until their turn came (in their appointed time) for judgment.

The remaining point to emphasise was the absolute dominion given to the Son of man. *"There was given Him dominion, and glory, and a kingdom, that all people, nations, and languages, should serve Him: His dominion is an everlasting dominion, which shall not pass away, and His kingdom that which shall not be destroyed."*

[20] (7:15-18) Daniel was understandably affected by his dream, it troubled him and he asked *One of them that stood by* (presumably, from 7:10, one of those who stand before the Ancient of days) for the interpretation. The answer was quite brief, *"These great beasts, which are four, are four kings, which shall arise out of the earth. But the saints of the Most High shall take the kingdom, and possess the kingdom for ever, even for ever and ever."* Even this short explanation afforded a basic illumination, a foundation that should

be kept in mind, when considering the events in greater detail. *These great beasts, which are four...* the appearance of these four kings (or kingdoms - see 7:23) is the FIRST recognisable event to look for relative to the last days. They were future relative to Daniel's experience and definitely last days, from their association with the establishment of the kingdom of the Son of man.

Regarding His kingdom, note especially *But the saints of the Most High shall take the kingdom and possess the kingdom for ever, even for ever and ever.* When this kingdom has been established, the saints of the Most High will prevail - this assurance was given to Daniel and to claim that it referred to the church (about which Daniel and the other Old Testament prophets were given nothing, by way of revelation) is simply not valid.

[21] Finally Daniel desired to know more, he did not in any way question, who *"the saints"* were or their part in this revelation, so he must have been satisfied that he knew to whom this applied (i.e. his own people, the nation Israel). He asked for further details and there were two issues on which Daniel sought further illumination (7:19) *"I would know the truth of the fourth beast"* (7:20) *"And of the ten horns that were in his head and the other which came up, and before whom three fell."*

The answer was given (7:23) *"The fourth beast shall be the fourth kingdom upon earth, which shall be diverse from all kingdoms, and shall devour the whole earth, and shall tread it down, and break it in pieces."* Respecting the fourth beast, this must mean:

(1) it shall be *diverse from all kingdoms*, it differs from all not just the previous three.

(2) it *shall devour the whole earth, and shall tread it down and break it in pieces*. This must be seen in its perspective i.e. in relation to this fourth kingdom. Within the limits imposed upon this kingdom, it devours, treads down and breaks in

pieces. This is not to be considered in a worldwide sense. For example, it does not destroy the other beasts and this is in accord with Daniel's interpretation of Nebuchadnezzar's dream (2:36-38.) What Daniel said, was perfectly true with respect to Nebuchadnezzar's power in Babylon, but Daniel did not intend nor imply that what he said referred to vast areas outside of that dominion (e.g. India, China, etc.) Returning to this fourth beast of Daniel's Dream, this kingdom is different from the others and is far more ruthless and formidable; but it does not destroy them. They exist together in the last days for some time after the judgment of the fourth beast. It needs to be emphasised that the previous three beasts (nations or kingdoms in the last days,) were (in their previous greatness as empires) gentile powers that ruled over Jerusalem. The kingdom of the beast will be the last of the gentile powers to rule over Jerusalem.

[22] Commentators in the past have seemed to be determined to follow, or apply, the succession of Nebuchadnezzar's image within the interpretation of Daniel's Dream. This is rather amazing, for if Daniel already knew that the interpretation of Nebuchadnezzar's image covered his dream, he would not be asking for the truth of all this (7:16.) Such comment results from not *rightly dividing the word of truth* (2 Tim 2:15 as Paul advised Timothy,) for these two revelations are completely separated in Daniel's writings, which means they merit separate consideration, not association.

But from Daniel's Dream these nations are unmistakably associated together in the last days; this means these former empires (which each ruled Jerusalem in turn,) will re-appear together and play a prominent part in the will of God in the last days. Scripturally speaking, these are the nations to watch to see the commencement of that fulfilment of God's plan. The last days' national reappearances of Babylon, Persia, Greece and Rome are to be expected and within the Roman element or boundary there will be a ten-kingdom confederation.

[23] From Daniel's question (7:20) on *The ten horns that were in his head, and of the other which came up,* this must mean that the ten horns appear as the fourth beast itself rises. So that the ten kingdoms of the last days can be expected within the Roman boundary (see also 7:3) and these ten horns are an immediately identifiable key feature. The explanation of this (7:24-28) *"And the ten horns out of this kingdom are ten kings that shall arise; and another shall rise after them; and he shall be diverse from the first, and he shall subdue three kings. And he shall speak great words against the Most High, and shall wear out the saints of the Most High, and think to change times and laws: and they shall be given into his hand until a time and times and the dividing of time. But the judgment shall sit, and they shall take away his dominion, to consume and destroy it unto the end. And the kingdom and dominion, and the greatness of the kingdom under the whole heaven shall be given to the people of the saints of the Most High, Whose kingdom is an everlasting kingdom, and all dominions shall serve and obey Him. Hitherto is the end of the matter. As for me Daniel, my cogitations much troubled me, and my countenance changed in me: but I kept the matter in my heart."*

In the ten toes of Nebuchadnezzar's Image and the ten horns of Daniel's Dream there were evidently a last days confederation of ten nations within the boundaries or influence of the Roman Empire and this necessarily appeared before the beast, as explained. *"Another shall rise after them* (the ten) *and he shall be diverse from the first* (ten) *and he shall subdue three kings* (of the ten)."

This last one was the remarkable *"little horn"* (7:8) who became predominant and his manifestation involved:

(1) The emergence of the fourth beast (kingdom)

(2) The association of the ten kingdoms which rise with that beast

(3) His overcoming three of the ten kingdoms.

However the little horn himself was NOT one of the ten (nationally) he was completely different from any of them. It was after his manifestation in this fashion, that the little horn went on to speak *"Words against the Most High, and shall wear out the saints of the Most High, and think to change times and laws."* The little horn's blasphemy (*words against the Most High*) and his opposition to the Jews (the saints) came after his rise to power among the ten. His judgment was inevitable and after his destruction the kingdom of the Most High was established forever.

As far as Daniel was concerned, this was the end of the matter and the revelation had a profound effect on him, but in spite of this Daniel displayed superb stewardship; he carefully recorded what he had been privileged to receive, but wisely, he said nothing.

[24] THE LITTLE HORN

The character, who so captured Daniel's attention in his dream, was the little horn and he merits closer examination. His blasphemous outburst in the face of impending judgment amazed Daniel and whilst his initial appearance was almost unnoticeable (from the adjective *little* which compared him to the other ten horns among whom he appears,) but his rise was meteoric.

From the description (7:8) *"eyes like the eyes of man"* his vision or outlook was confined to worldly or natural realms; so that his human ambitions and aims were worldly wealth, power, fame, fleshly acclaim, abilities etc. But *"a mouth speaking great things"* reached beyond human limitations and extended into spiritual realms, a most dangerous practise[10].

At the judgment, when earthly thrones were cast down, it was this *voice of the great words which the horn spake* which compelled Daniel's attention. Note especially the change of noun within this verse – *"I beheld then, because of the voice of the great words which the HORN spake: I beheld even till the BEAST was slain."* Thus, from the *"little horn"* (7:8) this same character becomes *"the horn"* and *"the beast"* (7:11.) This verse embraces the career of the beast from his becoming *"the horn,"* when he had usurped the authority of the three other horns, to his final status as *"the beast"*. Scripturally his power extended to the ten kingdoms, within the boundaries or influence of the Roman Empire. He totally dominated all of them (compare this, with the autocratic Nebuchadnezzar, the head of gold, the solitary ruler with power over the whole of his kingdom). The beast himself personified the ten kingdom confederation in its last day existence as the ruler of everything contained within the ten kingdoms, (this confederation was typified in the ten horns, not the beasts,) and on his destruction, the power of the whole alliance was destroyed forever. But *the rest of the beasts* (typifying Babylon, Persia, Greece, Rome) (v12) *had their dominion taken away: yet their lives were prolonged for a season and time*, so that these nations continued until their time for judgment. Daniel understood that this little horn made war with the saints and prevailed[11]. From the assurance given to Daniel (7:18, 27) this victory of the horn over the saints was disturbing and coupled with his blasphemous outbursts and his wearing down the saints, it could be the cause of many saints

---

[10] Herod Agrippa I (Acts 12:20-23) provides a scriptural example of the truth of this type of folly. Jude (7, 8) pointed to Sodom and Gomorrah as examples of the ungodly men, who crept into the early church to commit the same sort of defiance in their ungodly acts (compare Genesis 18:20, 21 and 19:13.)

[11] This contrasts vividly with the church of The LORD Jesus Christ against whom, in His own words, "the gates of Hell would not prevail" (see Matthew 16:18), which considerably strengthens the argument that the church has no part to play in the last days, But this is discussed later.

abandoning any belief or hope they have in God[12]. But it must be emphasised that the fourth empire, the dragon, the dreadful and terrible beast, (within the boundaries of the former Roman empire,) spawns this ten kingdom confederation and the beast's power and dominion commences and ends within this alliance (see 7:24-28 above.)

Returning to the little horn, (7:25) *He shall think to change times and laws: and they* (the saints) *shall be given into his hand until a time and times and the dividing of time.* The times and laws that the little horn intended to change were part of his action against the Jews and the only possible conclusion from this verse must be his rejection of the Ten Commandments and other Jewish laws. His extreme blasphemy will not allow his recognising the commandments of God, for he will seek to impose his own commandments. However his opposition to their recognised times of feasting, sacrifice etc. will be seen as total treachery, for his initial acceptance by the Jews will be established on his recognition of their religious worship in the covenant he establishes with the Jewish nation. There is a built-in time limit to his activities and the termination of his reign results in the end of gentile domination of Jerusalem and the national dominion being restored by God and given to the saints; this marks the end, within the context of Daniel's Dream, of the little horn.

---

[12] This point might be expanded, in such cases it is God's apparent inactivity or lack of reaction to such blasphemy, and His apparent lack of response to the prayers of His persecuted saints, which cause some of them to give up and the beast prevails. The failure of the saints stems simply from the fact that they imagine that God has to behave or respond in the ways that man imagines, or thinks that God should react in such circumstances. The very fact that God does not respond in accordance with man's imagination shows His absolute divinity. Notice too, that even whilst Daniel himself was awed or captivated by the voice of his blasphemy, none of the beast's words prevailed in the slightest to delay his judgment when God appointed it. In such times it is well to recall the type of spirit displayed by Shadrach, Meshach and Abed-nego, who shrewdly gave God the right to deliver them or not, as He chose. The Lord Himself upheld this attitude, spirit, in His Own teachings(see Matthew 10:28, and compare v23, which confirms this applies in respect of His coming as the Son of man. See also Luke 12:5.)

[25] Summary

"The four winds of the heaven strove upon the great sea" suggested the heavenly or spiritual disturbances and reshuffling that were necessary to accomplish the re-appearances of these former empires in the last days as nations. This also reflected the overall power and control of God, for the scriptures made it abundantly plain that all these eventualities ultimately accomplish His divine will.

The features noted in respect of the four nations will be manifested in their appearance and in the re-emergence of Rome there was also a confederation of ten nations and then the rising of the little horn among them. These were recognisable and unmistakable signs to identify the last days' fulfilment of Daniel's prophetic dream.

It must be stressed that the beast himself was not identified with any of the ten nations of the confederation. But as their ultimate ruler he controlled them all and at the height of his power he demanded not merely subjection but worship, particularly from the Jews, who were the specific target of his attentions, his ultimate purpose being their destruction (as will be shown.)

It might be noted too, that this amazing character, the beast, cannot be easily confined nor categorised, because his ultimate power and involvement in the affairs of the world are so extensive. He fulfils a whole range of scriptures and is extraordinarily versatile as will become apparent.

Chapter 3: DANIEL'S VISION & DANIEL'S SUPPLICATIONS

[26] DANIEL'S VISION

(8:1-12) *In the third year of the reign of king Belshazzar a vision appeared unto me, even unto me Daniel, after that which appeared unto me at the first. And I saw in a vision; and it came to pass, when I saw, that I was at Shushan in the palace, which is in the province of Elam; and I saw in a vision, and I was by the river of Ulai. Then I lifted up mine eyes, and saw, and, behold, there stood before the river a ram which had two horns: and the two horns were high; but one was higher than the other, and the higher came up last. I saw the ram pushing westward, and northward, and southward; so that no beasts might stand before him, neither was there any that could deliver out of his hand; but he did according to his will, and became great. And as I was considering, behold, an he goat came from the west on the face of the whole earth, and touched not the ground: and the goat had a notable horn between his eyes. And he came to the ram that had two horns, which I had seen standing before the river, and ran unto him in the fury of his power. And I saw him come close unto the ram, and he was moved with choler against him, and smote the ram, and brake his two horns: and there was no power in the ram to stand before him, but he cast him down to the ground, and stamped upon him: and there was none that could deliver the ram out of his hand. Therefore the he goat waxed very great: and when he was strong, the great horn was broken; and for it came up four notable ones toward the four winds of heaven. And out of one of them came forth a little horn, which waxed exceeding great, toward the south, and toward the east, and toward the pleasant (land.) And it waxed great even to* the host of heaven; and it cast down (some) of the host and of the stars to the ground, and stamped upon them. Yea, he magnified himself even to the prince of the host, and by him the daily sacrifice was taken away, and the place of his sanctuary was cast down. And an host was given (him) against the daily (sacrifice) by reason of transgression, and it cast down the truth to the ground; and it practised, and prospered.

(8:13, 14) Then I heard one saint speaking, and another saint said unto that certain saint which spake, "How long shall be the vision concerning the daily sacrifice, and the transgression of desolation, to give both the sanctuary and the host to be trodden under foot?" And he said unto me, "Unto two thousand and three hundred days; then shall the sanctuary be cleansed."

(8:15-27) And it came to pass, when I, even I Daniel, had seen the vision, and sought for the meaning, then, behold, there stood before me as the appearance of a man. And I heard a man's voice between the banks of Ulai, which called, and said, "Gabriel, make this man to understand the vision." So he came near where I stood: and when he came, I was afraid, and fell upon my face: but he said unto me, "Understand, O son of man: for at the time of the end shall be the vision." Now as he was speaking with me, I was in a deep sleep on my face toward the ground: but he touched me, and set me upright. And he said, "Behold, I will make thee know what shall be in the last end of the indignation: for at the time appointed the end shall be. The ram which thou sawest having two horns are the kings of Media and Persia. And the rough goat is the king of Grecia: and the great horn that is between his eyes is the first king. Now that being broken, whereas four stood up for it, four kingdoms shall stand up out of the nation, but not in his power. And in the latter time of their kingdom, when the transgressors are come to the full, a king of fierce countenance, and understanding dark sentences, shall stand up. And his power shall be mighty, but not by his own power: and he shall destroy wonderfully, and shall prosper, and practise, and shall destroy the mighty and the holy people. And through his policy also *he shall cause craft to prosper in his hand; and he shall magnify himself in his heart, and by peace shall destroy many: he shall also stand up against the Prince of princes; but he shall be broken without hand. And the vision of the evening and the morning which was told is true: wherefore shut thou up the vision; for it shall be for many days." And I Daniel fainted, and was sick certain days; afterward I rose up, and did the king's business; and I was astonished at the vision, but none understood it.*

[27] Daniel himself made the distinction between this vision and his previous experience. (8:1) *A vision appeared unto me, even unto me Daniel, after that which appeared unto me at the first.* He seemed surprised to have been so privileged, and this was an entirely new revelation involving different animals, so that there was no direct association with Daniel's Dream. The nations involved in his vision were named, which meant there could be no mistaking what was involved. In this respect, the involvement of nations prophetically, the vision reflected the dream, although the nations were not named in the dream.

[Daniel's writings from this vision onwards were in Hebrew, as were his opening words (chapter 1:1-2:3.) Daniel's intervening writings were written in Chaldean (from Daniel 2:4-7:28) and this has caused critics to claim that the writings in the book of Daniel were not exclusively Daniel's own work. Other commentators have dealt quite adequately with this quibble. It seems reasonable to assume, that what was given to Daniel personally, he was perfectly entitled to write in his own tongue, if he felt so inspired or inclined, more especially since his own nation was included.]

Considering the vision given to Daniel (8:3, 4), *"Then I lifted up mine eyes, and saw, and behold, there stood before the river a ram which had two horns: and the two horns were high; and one was higher than the other, and the higher came up last. I saw the ram pushing westward, and northward, and southward; so that no beasts might stand before him, neither was there any that could deliver out of his hand; but he did according to his will, and became great."* This intrigued Daniel, who considered what he had seen but the vision allowed him no time to seriously contemplate anything (8:5-12). *"And as I was considering, behold, an he goat came from the west on the face of the whole earth, and touched not the ground: and the goat had a notable horn between his eyes. And he came to the ram that had two horns, which I had seen standing before the river, and ran unto him in the fury of his power. And I saw him come close unto the ram, and he was moved with choler against him, and smote the ram, and brake his two horns: and there was no power in the ram to stand before him, but he cast him down to the ground, and stamped upon him: and there was none that could deliver the ram out of his hand. Therefore the he goat waxed very great: and when he was strong, the great horn was broken; and for it came up four notable ones toward the four winds of heaven. And out of one of them came forth a little horn, which waxed exceeding great, toward the south, and toward the east, and toward the pleasant land. And it waxed great, even to the host of heaven; and it cast down some of the host and of the stars to the ground, and stamped upon them. Yea, he magnified himself even to the prince of the host, and by him the daily sacrifice was taken away and the place of his sanctuary was cast down. And an host was given him against the daily sacrifice by reason of transgression, and it cast down the truth to the ground; and it practised, and prospered."*

[28] The sequence in the vision was quite straightforward. The ram having two horns was utterly destroyed by the he goat having the great horn, which was then broken and replaced by four notable (horns) toward the four winds of heaven. From one of these came a "little horn" that waxed great toward the south, the east, the pleasant land (Israel.) The little horn's greatness extended even to the host of heaven and eventually he magnified himself against the prince of the host and as a result of this action, the daily sacrifice was

taken away and the place of the sanctuary cast down. The changes occurred in the horns of the he goat - the notable horn became four and out of these sprang the little horn, who featured so prominently in this vision. But there was more:

(8:13, 14) *"Then I heard one saint speaking, and another saint said unto that certain saint which spake, 'How long shall be the vision concerning the daily sacrifice, and the transgression of desolation, to give both the sanctuary and the host to be trodden under foot?' and he said unto me, 'Unto two thousand and three hundred days*; then shall the sanctuary be cleansed.'"*

[(viii) *two thousand and three hundred days* This is the second unique reference (Introduction) linking Daniel and the Revelation. (The Roman numerals in brackets are the references to these scriptures in Appendix 3.)]

[29] Daniel recorded what he had heard, the one saint speaking unto *that certain saint*. The Hebrew word was "PALMONI," which means *the numberer of secrets* or *the wonderful numberer*. This is a most interesting name to appear in Daniel's writings, in which figures and times feature so prominently. It revealed that there is a heavenly being, Palmoni, who is appointed to record and possibly declare such things. (Compare Judges 13:18 and Revelation 10:5, 6.) The first saint asked Palmoni, *"How long shall be the vision .... etc."* Notice the question concerned the daily sacrifice and the transgression (the Hebrew word is "pasha" and refers to revolt or rebellion against lawful authority.) It was revealed concerning the little horn (8:12) *an host* (= a military force) *was given him against the daily sacrifice* (i.e. to oppose or prevent the daily sacrifice) *by reason of transgression* (i.e. revolt or rebellion.) The little horn had attempted to introduce laws, against which there had been a revolt, or rebellion, because these infringed the Hebrew laws of worship or sacrifice. The question that the one saint asked was in effect, "How long will the host be able to prevent the offering of sacrifice in the sanctuary?" and the

61

answer was, "Two thousand three hundred days." [For the record this is 6 years (of 360 days,) plus 140 days = 2,160 + 140 = 2,300 days.]

[30] Daniel sought to understand what the vision meant, the answer was not automatically given to him, he had to show interest and desire to seek for the answer and the whole experience took a physical toll on Daniel (8:27.) The illumination was given to Daniel by command (8:15-19.) *"And it came to pass, when I, even I Daniel, had seen the vision, and sought for the meaning, then, behold, there stood before me as the appearance of a man. And I heard a man's voice between the banks of the Ulai, which called, and said, "Gabriel, make this man to understand the vision." So he came near where I stood: and when he came I was afraid, and fell upon my face: but he said unto me, "Understand, O son of man: for at the time of the end shall be the vision." Now as he was speaking with me, I was in a deep sleep on my face toward the ground: but he touched me, and set me upright. And he said, "Behold I will make thee know what shall be in the last end of the indignation: for at the time appointed the end shall be."*

[31] From Gabriel's words evidently the vision in its main application was for the last days and Gabriel's explanation was remarkably concise (8:20-26.) *"The ram which thou sawest having two horns are the kings of Media and Persia. And the rough goat is the king of Grecia: and the great horn that is between his eyes is the first king. Now that being broken whereas four stood up for it, four kingdoms shall stand up out of the nation, but not in his power. And in the latter time of their kingdom, when the transgressors are come to the full, a king of fierce countenance, and understanding dark sentences, shall stand up. And his power shall be mighty, but not by his own power: and he shall destroy wonderfully, and shall prosper, and practise, and shall destroy the mighty and the holy people. And through his policy*

also he shall cause craft to prosper in his hand; and he shall magnify himself in his heart, and by peace shall destroy many: he shall also stand up against the Prince of princes; but he shall be broken without hand. And the vision of the evening and the morning which was told is true: wherefore shut thou up the vision; for it shall be for many days."

The recognised animal symbols of Persia (the ram) and Greece (the goat) have been used in this vision; but it is in their horns, that the explanation finds its main application. Historically from our times, the fulfilment has been seen, the ram (the two horns representing the kings of Media, and Persia, with Persia the greater coming last) was destroyed by the goat (Greece under the leadership of Alexander the Great, the notable horn broken off in his prime). On Alexander's death his kingdom was divided between his generals into four separate kingdoms (see figure 4.) The king of fierce countenance, who appeared in the latter times of these kingdoms, was Antiochus Epiphanes, a vile man, who fulfilled to some extent what was revealed in the vision. But these historical facts by no means exhaust the purpose or meanings of this vision, for scriptural prophecy can have more than one fulfilment. For example, the prophecies concerning the Lord Jesus Christ can apply in their first instance to Old Testament characters e.g. David and then find further fulfilment in the LORD's life. [Note that Gabriel's explanation does not by any means fully explain the details of Daniel's Vision: *The ram which thou sawest having two horns are the kings of Media and Persia. And the rough goat is the king of Grecia: and the great horn that is between his eyes is the first king.* In the vision the he goat is described: *behold, an he goat came from the west on the face of the whole earth, and touched not the ground: and the goat had a notable horn between his eyes.* Daniel was given no illumination on such details as *and touched not the ground* but these details must be important, in respect of the emergence of Greece as a power to be included in the vision.(Purely speculation, but the possibility of an Air Strike, comes to mind.)]

[32] Gabriel's words, which mention *the end* and must apply to the last days, also mention "the little horn". The previous use of this in Daniel's Dream associated the little horn, (who became the horn and then the beast) with the ten kingdom confederation within the Roman boundaries in the last days. But in Daniel's Vision the same title "the little horn" was unmistakably related to the last stages of the divided Greek Empire. It must be noted too, that the division of the Greek Empire into four (after the death of Alexander the Great) was evidently covered in Daniel's Vision. But the Greek nation of Daniel's Dream, which was undeniably last days, also involved a foursome in two respects (typified in the leopard's having four wings and four heads.).

Such inspired words have not been chosen lightly; so the conclusion must be, that the little horn has last day associations with the ten kingdom confederation within the boundaries of the Roman Empire and somehow, he is also involved with the last day Greek nation. [It deserves notice that under the rule of Augustus, the Roman Empire included large areas of Africa and Asia.] This does not deny nor diminish the possible historical fulfilments of these prophecies (which establish their accuracy so brilliantly in such details). However it deserves emphasis that in the very terminology chosen, the scriptures point to future, last days' significance and to miss this application would lose valuable prophetic teaching, which will be so necessary when the time comes. But before leaving Daniel's Vision: Gabriel concluded, *"And the vision of the evening and the morning which was told is true."* The day in scripture and the Jewish day usually commenced at sundown and the "evening and the morning" effectively mean "a day". It is not unreasonable to suggest that Gabriel was referring to a particular "day" (as a period of time, e.g. the day of judgment etc) in this terminology (which is used in scripture,) and most obviously, THE DAY OF THE LORD. This would conclusively establish that prophetically the whole vision in its primary fulfilment has last day significance[13].

[33] DANIEL'S SUPPLICATIONS

(9:1, 2) *In the first year of Darius the son of Ahasuerus, of the seed of the Medes, which was made king over the realm of the Chaldeans; in the first year of his reign I Daniel understood by books the number of the years, whereof the word of the Lord came to Jeremiah the prophet, that He would accomplish seventy years in the desolations of Jerusalem.*

(9:3-15) *And I set my face unto the Lord God, to seek by prayer and supplications, with fasting, and sackcloth, and ashes: and I prayed unto the Lord my God, and made my confession, and said, "O Lord, the great and dreadful God, keeping the covenant and mercy to them that love Him, and to them that keep His commandments; we have sinned, and have committed iniquity, and have done wickedly, and have rebelled, even by departing from Thy precepts and from Thy judgments: Neither have we hearkened unto Thy servants the prophets, which spake in Thy name to our kings, our princes, and our fathers, and to all the people of the land. O Lord, righteousness belongeth unto Thee but unto us confusion of faces, as at this day; to the men of Judah, and to the inhabitants of Jerusalem, and unto all Israel, that are near, and that are far off, through all the countries whither Thou hast driven them, because of their trespass that they have trespassed against Thee. O Lord, to us belongeth confusion of face, to our kings, to our princes, and to our fathers, because we have sinned against Thee. To the Lord our God belong mercies and*

---

[13] The period *unto two thousand and three hundred days; then shall the sanctuary be cleansed* has always been difficult to apply; it might have had some significance in the times of Antiochus Epiphanes. But the fact that it is included in scripture, points to a last days' fulfilment and it is very difficult to find a place for its satisfactory application historically, for it has not been totally fulfilled. When these *ten unique references* are considered together (Appendix 3, The Final Week) a very satisfactory solution to these difficulties is found.

forgivenesses, though we have rebelled against Him; neither have we obeyed the voice of the Lord our God, to walk in His laws, which He set before us by His servants the prophets. Yea, all Israel have transgressed Thy law, even by departing, that they might not obey Thy voice; therefore the curse is poured upon us, and the oath that is written in the law of Moses the servant of God, because we have sinned against Him. And He hath confirmed His words, which He spake against us, and against our judges that judged us, by bringing upon us a great evil: for under the whole heaven hath not been done as hath been done upon Jerusalem. As it is written in the law of Moses, all this evil is come upon us: yet made we not our prayer before the Lord our God, that we might turn from our iniquities, and understand Thy truth. Therefore hath the Lord watched upon the evil, and brought it upon us: for the Lord our God is righteous in all His works which He doeth: for we obeyed not His voice. And now, O Lord our God, that hast brought Thy people forth out of the land of Egypt with a mighty hand, and hast gotten Thee renown, as at this day; we have sinned, we have done wickedly.

(9:16-19) *O Lord, according to all Thy righteousness, I beseech Thee, let Thine anger and Thy fury be turned away from Thy city Jerusalem, Thy holy mountain: because for our sins, and for the iniquities of our fathers, Jerusalem and Thy people are become a reproach to all that are about us. Now therefore, O our God, hear the prayer of Thy servant, and his supplications, and cause Thy face to shine upon Thy sanctuary that is desolate, for the Lord's sake. O my God, incline Thine ear, and hear; open Thine eyes, and behold our desolations, and the city which is called by Thy name: for we do not present our supplications before Thee for our righteousnesses, but for Thy great mercies. O Lord, hear; O Lord, forgive; O Lord, hearken and do; defer not, for Thine Own sake, O my God: for Thy city and Thy people are called by Thy name."*

(9:20-27) *And whiles I was speaking, and praying, and confessing my sin and the sin of my people Israel, and presenting my supplication before the Lord my God for the holy mountain of my God; Yea, whiles*

I was speaking in prayer, even the man Gabriel, whom I had seen in the vision at the beginning, being caused to fly swiftly, touched me about the time of the evening oblation. And he informed me, and talked with me, and said, "O Daniel, I am now come forth to give thee skill and understanding. At the beginning of thy supplications the commandment came forth, and I am come to shew thee; for thou art greatly beloved: therefore understand the matter, and consider the vision. Seventy weeks are determined upon thy people, and upon thy holy city, to finish the transgression, and to make an end of sins, and to make reconciliation for iniquity, and to bring in everlasting righteousness, and to seal up the vision and prophecy, and to anoint the most Holy. Know therefore and understand, that from the going forth of the commandment to restore and to build Jerusalem unto the Messiah the Prince shall be seven weeks, and threescore and two weeks: the street shall be built again, and the wall, even in troublous times. And after threescore and two weeks shall Messiah be cut off, but not for Himself: and the people of the prince that shall come shall destroy the city and the sanctuary; and the end thereof shall be with a flood, and unto the end of the war desolations are determined. And he shall confirm the covenant with many for one week: and in the midst of the week he shall cause the sacrifice and the oblation to cease, and for the overspreading of abominations he shall make it desolate, even until the consummation, and that determined shall be poured upon the desolate."

[Sir Robert Anderson in *Pseudo-Criticism* (Chapter 2 page 25, footnote 2) adds the following note to Daniel 9:25: "The *Athnah* accent in verse 25 might possibly be explained by the fact that the Jews never read the prophecy of the Seventy Weeks in their synagogues, and any attempt to compute the period is anathema. But to make the Hebrew accent equivalent to our colon is a blunder. We should have to read verse 2: "I, Daniel, understood by the books: the number of years," &c." An interesting point without any doubt, but it makes one wonder why the Jews avoid this prophecy.]

[34] Darius took the kingdom off Belshazzar (Daniel 5:30, 31) in the first year of his reign, but in the opening of the account of Daniel's supplications it is emphasised Darius was *the son of Ahasuerus, of the seed of the Medes* (this would have been the first Ahasuerus (of Esther), because Mordecai and Esther were taken into captivity with Jeconiah by Nebuchadnezzar. However, Daniel (inspired by the writings of the prophet Jeremiah,[14]) made his supplications to the Lord for illumination concerning the seventy years of desolations determined for Jerusalem. Scripturally the Babylonian Captivity covered three overlapping periods of seventy years called The Servitude, The Captivity and The Desolations. [See Appendix 1 also Appendix 7 DANIEL'S SUPPLICATIONS and The Persian Kings, which proves scripturally, which *Ahasuerus* was involved with Esther and Mordecai.]

Daniel had set himself no easy task and in the main the account shows how earnestly Daniel had to seek the LORD, for help in understanding Jeremiah's prophecy and for Him to restore Jerusalem (9:1-19.) Eventually Daniel prevailed (9:20-23) *And whiles I was speaking, and praying, and confessing my sin and the sin of my people Israel, and presenting my supplication before the Lord my GOD for the holy mountain of my GOD; Yea, whiles I was speaking in prayer, even the man Gabriel, whom I had seen in the vision at the beginning, being caused to fly swiftly, touched me about the time of the evening oblation. And he informed me, and talked with me, and said, "O Daniel, I am now come forth to give thee skill and understanding. At the beginning of thy supplications the commandment came forth, and I am come to shew thee; for thou art greatly beloved: therefore understand the matter, and consider the vision."*

---

[14] *Jeremiah 25:11, 12. And this whole land shall be a desolation, and an astonishment; and these nations shall serve the king of Babylon seventy years. And it shall come to pass, when seventy years are accomplished, that I will punish the king of Babylon, and that nation, saith the Lord, for their iniquity, and the land of the Chaldeans, and will make it perpetual desolations.*

[35] Gabriel's reply (in English 196 words,) was the only explanation given to Daniel, these constitute a direct prophecy from a heavenly messenger (which gives them considerably more weight than prophecy through a man - compare Hebrews 2:2,) and Gabriel's words were not challenged or questioned.[15]

Gabriel's words to Daniel were (9:24-27) *"Seventy weeks are determined upon thy people and upon thy holy city, to finish the transgression, and to make an end of sins, and to make reconciliation for iniquity, and to bring in everlasting righteousness, and to seal up the vision and prophecy, and to anoint the most Holy. Know therefore and understand, that from the going forth of the commandment to restore and to build Jerusalem unto the Messiah the Prince shall be seven weeks, and threescore and two weeks: the street shall be built again, and the wall, even in troublous times. And after threescore and two weeks shall Messiah be cut off, but not for Himself: and the people of the prince that shall come shall destroy the city and the sanctuary; and the end thereof shall be with a flood, and unto the end of the war desolations are determined. And he shall confirm the covenant with many for one week: and in the midst of the week he shall cause the sacrifice and the oblation to cease, and for the overspreading of abominations he shall make it desolate, even until the consummation, and that determined shall be poured upon the desolate."*

---

[15] It should be noted in passing here, that this same messenger Gabriel heralded the birth of John the Baptist, and smote Zacharias dumb for his unbelief. When he was sent to Mary her question was not unbelief, but that she might know what her part involved (see Luke 1:5-39.) It was most unusual for angelic messengers of the Lord to reveal their names (in vivid contrast to "familiar spirits," who name themselves readily.) The fact that Gabriel revealed himself to Zacharias, effectively established to the priest that the Messiah was coming. Because Zacharias would have known, that Gabriel was the angel who had spoken of the last days to Daniel, and to any Jew the Messiah's Coming would be the last days major event. [Compare also Hebrews 1:1, 2 a most valuable reference, which established that having spoken through His Son, GOD has Himself commenced the last days.] For the Jews of course this advent is in abeyance, but the times of the Gentiles are rapidly closing. When the Jews seek for their Messiah during their terrible tribulation, their ears and hearts will be opened to prepare them for their phenomenal role in the tremendous events of the last days.

[36] Daniel himself had explained at the outset (9:2,) "*I Daniel understood by books the number of the years .... that he would accomplish seventy years ....* etc." But in the explanation given to Daniel, by Gabriel, in each case the word used was WEEKS not YEARS. The Hebrew word for week, means a period of seven and can apply to days, months or years; from which, the revelation given to Daniel (who was seeking illumination on *seventy years in the desolations of Jerusalem*) by Gabriel, revealed that what was actually involved was not seventy years, but seventy weeks (i.e. sevens) of years; or a total of seven times seventy (= 490) years.[16]

The writings of Jeremiah conveyed nothing beyond the seventy years of desolation (see Jeremiah 25:11, 12 and footnote 14, page 26) and the subsequent judgments of GOD upon Babylon for the sins of that nation. But as Daniel entreated the Lord for the restoration of Jerusalem and proclaimed His righteousness for so judging Israel, the angel Gabriel was sent to reveal to Daniel that what was involved for the nation Israel, was not just a seventy year period of captivity in Babylon, but a 490 year period (seventy weeks of years).

This period as described by Gabriel was divided into three distinct parts.

Seventy Weeks of Years = Seven weeks (49 years) Sixty two weeks (434 years) One Week (7 years) Total Seventy Weeks (490 years)

SEVEN WEEKS	THREESCORE & TWO WEEKS	ONE WEEK
From the going forth of the commandment to restore Jerusalem BC 445 to 397*	After which shall Messiah be cut off BC 397 to AD 32*	Of the covenant of the prince that shall come The final week of 7 years
(9:25) Gabriel associated these two periods. 7 X 7 Weeks (of 7 years) = 49 years 62 weeks (of 7 years) = 434 years		*Dates in Chronological Table p30 1week = 7 years.(49+ 434+7 = 490)

---

[16] The scriptural year is the lunar year of 360 days (12 lunar months of 30 days) and any reckoning has to take this into account. It has also been shown that the period of seventy weeks of years (490 years) is most significant in Jewish history. Appendix 2.

The seventy weeks (or weeks of years) commenced (BC 445) *from the going forth of the commandment to restore and build Jerusalem* (and the seven weeks and threescore and two weeks) i.e. the sixty-nine weeks ended when Messiah the prince was cut off (32 AD on the cross.)

['Now both the "Servitude, BC 606," and the "Captivity BC 598" ended (effectively) with the decree of Cyrus in B.C. 536 permitting the return of the exiles.' "The Desolation, BC 589" ended with Foundation of Temple BC 520. But these separate (but overlapping) *seventy year* punishments of servitude, captivity and desolation must not be confused with the Seventy Weeks of YEARS, (i.e. 490 years) of Jeremiah and Daniel's prophecies, which was the basis for the prophecy concerning the seventy weeks. (See Sir Robert Anderson *The Coming Prince,* Preface to Tenth Edition page iv.) See Chronological Sequence page 30.]

The very manner in which Gabriel presented this to Daniel, *seven weeks, and threescore and two weeks* revealed a combined total (of sixty-nine weeks,) but the periods were all distinct. The commencement was marked by the commandment to restore and build Jerusalem (the command given by the Persian King Artaxerxes see Nehemiah 2 and the date computed for this is BC 445, see Appendix 1.) Seven weeks (of years) later (i.e. 49 years, BC 397) brought the completion of the prophetic ministry of the Old Testament to a close with Malachi's prophecy. Sixty two weeks (434 years) later brings the date to AD 32, which is the year calculated for the LORD's entry into Jerusalem.[17]

---

[17] The apparent inaccuracies, which contradict the angel Gabriel's words [who distinctly spoke of seven weeks, (49 years) and sixty two weeks (434 years) and the remaining week (7 years) i.e. seventy weeks (of seven year weeks) a total of 490 years] are due to the fact that the dates given relate to the Julian calendar. When the days are calculated using the lunar year, the first two periods combined, work out to sixty-nine weeks (i.e. sevens) of years times 360 days for the lunar year. This is 7 X 69 X 360 = 173,880 days. Sir Robert Anderson produced these figures and proved that they coincide perfectly with the actual dates involved - see "*The Coming Prince*".

[37] The remaining week, the final week of the seventy applies to *The prince that shall come* and he *shall confirm the covenant with many for one week.*

Since the cutting off of The Messiah (on the cross), scripturally Israel/Judah has been outside of GOD's will for their rejection of His Son. During the intervening years, roughly speaking from the end of the ministry of the gospel of God, the period covered by the Acts of the Apostles until now, (see Appendix 5) time, in respect of the fulfilment of the prophecies for Israel, does not count.[18]

The fact that the *prince that shall come* will not make, but *shall confirm the covenant with many for one week* suggests that the covenant (or treaty, or agreement) already exists and Israel might have ratified such a thing with other nations, but with which covenant hitherto the beast, or the prince, has rejected any such agreement. When he accepts it and this includes him and the people(s) he represents, (quite possibly the entire ten kingdom confederation,) this act necessarily involves a specific date, which commences the seventieth week, the final seven years (the final week) of the prophecy.

[38] The covenant itself included provision for the resumption of the offerings and sacrifices of the Jews and also, a clause concerning the Holy Place or the Sanctuary, which the gentiles would respect as holy to the Jews. This was revealed (9:24) from the need *to anoint the most Holy,* the word means "holy of holies" i.e. a place, because such terms are never applied to a person. (This also echoes the *cleansing of the sanctuary* (8:14) [28]) The term to *make reconciliation for iniquity* means to make atonement for iniquity, which points to the re-establishment of the Atonement. Realistically, for the Jews to

---

[18] This has been conclusively established from scriptures, for it can be proved that during the various periods of ten Judges, the times of Israel's bondage under the various nations used to oppress them for their disobedience to GOD, the years did not count. This again is explained more fully in Appendix 2.

resume their sacrificial worship on the site of their old temple in Jerusalem, it would be necessary for some agreement to be reached with Islamic nations. This site is now occupied by the Dome of The Rock, the oldest existing Muslim monument built by Caliph Abd-al Malik and completed in AD 691. It is not a mosque, but a shrine over the sacred rock (sakhra) from which Mohammed is believed to have ascended to heaven. Their third most holy shrine it is regarded by Moslems as the navel (omphalos) of the world. If the site were to be used by the Jews, it would be a very delicate issue to negotiate successfully and any suggestion of the use of force would spark a Holy War too horrifying to contemplate. This is all conjecture, but the covenant is prophesied as a means by which such agreement might be reached. However, the matter will be considered again in the light of New Testament scriptures.

Attention should also be given to Gabriel's words (9:26) *"The people of the prince that shall come shall destroy the city and the sanctuary"* for in the context of his remarks, this happens BEFORE the prince confirms the covenant, which he then breaks (9:27.) It would appear that the prince and his people first attack Israel (Jerusalem), then confirm this covenant or agreement (commencing the final week,) which is broken (in the middle of the week) and then he turns on Israel with incredible fury and treachery.

This event marks not only the commencement of the final week, but probably the most important aspect of the events of the last days, the ghastly tribulation.[19] The close of The Final Half of the Week will be when the LORD Himself comes to deliver Israel (Armageddon.)

---

[19] It might be emphasised that the commencement of the seventieth week coincides with the confirmation of the covenant. The crisis occurs when *"in the midst of the week he shall cause the sacrifice and oblations to cease"*, and this divides the final week of seven years into two periods. It would appear that whilst the atonement and sacrificial offerings cannot be made in the holy place, that again the prophetic clock stops for the nation Israel, and power is again given to gentiles - the period involved is limited in GOD's mercy, but it is a time of unbelievable horror. See Appendix 3 The Final Week.

[Daniel's Supplications resulted from his study of the writings of Jeremiah, but Jeremiah's prophecy is not studied in any depth in these considerations, which are not attempting to exhaust every scriptural reference to the last days. Jeremiah did correspond with those in captivity including the prophets (Ezekiel and Daniel, see Jeremiah 29:1-32 and compare Ezekiel 1:1) and Daniel's Supplications followed. It does deserve noting however, that the beast's fury extends beyond Israel and he seeks to destroy other races or nations, the reasons for which are not revealed in scripture. (Possibly because these nations refuse to submit totally to his rule, but this is not scripturally stated, it is speculation.)

The descendants of Lot (Genesis 19: 37, 38) The Moabites and Ammonites, and the descendants of Esau (Genesis 36,) i.e. The Edomites, (Idumeans,) seem to become particular targets of the beast, but their survival is promised – Compare Isaiah 11:14, Jeremiah 48:47, 49:6 (v39 Elam – people dwelling East of the Tigris). Also Daniel 11:41 *"these shall escape out of his* (the beast's) *hand, even Edom, and Moab, and the chief of the children of Ammon."*]

Chronological Sequence of Significant Dates

BC	Event	Remarks
606	Servitude begins	Nebuchadnezzar imposed servitude (taking Daniel and his companions.)
598	Captivity begins	Jehoiachin (Jeconiah) taken to Babylon (also Esther and Mordecai)
597	Zedekiah's reign begins	
594	Ezekiel begins to prophesy	(30th year from Josiah's Passover and 5th year of Captivity)
589	Jerusalem invaded	3rd time by Nebuchadnezzar, commences Desolations
587	Jerusalem taken & burnt	Referred to as *12th year of our Captivity* Ezekiel 33:21
561	Evil-Merodach	(or Iluoradam) commenced his reign
555	Nabonidus	Commenced his reign
541	Belshazzar	Regent during lifetime of his father Nabonidus. [Daniel's vision of 4 beasts in his 1st year, & vision of Ram & Goat in 3rd year.]
538	Babylon taken by Cyrus	Daniel's vision of 70 Weeks in this year.
536	Decree of Cyrus	Authorised Jews to return to Jerusalem (End of Servitude & Captivity)
521	Darius Hystaspes	
520	End of Desolations	Foundation of second Temple laid on 24/9 (Haggai 2:18.)
516	Temple finished (Ezra 6:15)	This was 70 years before the edict to build the city (commencing 70 Weeks of Jeremiah's/ Daniel's prophecy.)
445	21st yr of Artaxerxes	Commandment to rebuild Jerusalem (commenced 1st week of (years))
397	Malachi's Prophecy	Closes Dispensation of Prophets, and ends first week of Daniel's 70 weeks.
4	Nativity	Birth of LORD. Death of Herod the Great.
14	Tiberias Emperor of Rome	
28	15th year Tiberias	LORD's ministry commenced (Luke 3.)
32	The Crucifixion	Cutting off of Messiah end of 69 weeks of Daniel's Prophecy

Chapter 4: DANIEL'S REVELATION

[39] (10:1-9) *In the third year of Cyrus king of Persia a thing was revealed unto Daniel, whose name was called Belteshazzar; and the thing was true, but the time appointed was long: and he understood the thing, and had understanding of the vision. In those days I Daniel was mourning three full weeks. I ate no pleasant bread, neither came flesh nor wine in my mouth, neither did I anoint myself at all, till three whole weeks were fulfilled. And in the four and twentieth day of the first month, as I was by the side of the great river, which is Hiddekel; then I lifted up mine eyes, and looked, and behold a certain man clothed in linen, whose loins were girded with fine gold of Uphaz: his body also was like the beryl, and his face as the appearance of lightning, and his eyes as lamps of fire, and his arms and his feet like in colour to polished brass, and the voice of his words like the voice of a multitude. And I Daniel alone saw the vision: for the men that were with me saw not the vision; but a great quaking fell upon them, so that they fled to hide themselves. Therefore I was left alone, and saw this great vision, and there remained no strength in me: for my comeliness was turned in me into corruption, and I retained no strength. Yet heard I the voice of his words: and when I heard the voice of his words, then was I in a deep sleep on my face, and my face toward the ground.* [Hiddekel = The Tigris, see Genesis 2:10-14.]

(10:10-21) *And, behold, an hand touched me, which set me upon my knees and upon the palms of my hands. And he said unto me, "O Daniel, a man greatly beloved, understand the words that I speak unto thee, and stand upright: for unto thee am I now sent." And when he had spoken this word unto me, I stood trembling. Then said he unto me, "Fear not, Daniel: for from the first day that thou didst set thine heart to understand, and to chasten thyself before thy God, thy words were heard, and I am come for thy words. But the prince of the kingdom of Persia withstood me one and twenty days: but, lo, Michael, one of the chief princes, came to help me; and I remained there with the kings of Persia. Now I am come to make thee understand what shall befall thy people in the latter days: for yet the vision is for many days." And when he had spoken such words unto me, I set my face toward the ground, and I became dumb. And, behold, one like the similitude of the sons of men touched my lips: then I opened my mouth, and spake, and said unto him that stood before me, "O my lord, by the vision my sorrows, are turned upon me, and I have retained no strength. For how can the servant of this my lord, talk with this my lord? For as for me, straightway there remained no strength in me, neither is there breath left in me." Then there came again and touched me one like the appearance of a man, and he strengthened me, and said, "O man greatly beloved, fear not: peace be unto thee, be strong, yea, be strong." And when he had spoken unto me, I was strengthened, and said, "Let my lord speak; for thou hast strengthened me." Then said he, 'Knowest thou wherefore I come unto thee? And now will I return to fight with the prince of Persia: and when I am gone forth, lo, the prince of Grecia shall come. But I will shew thee that which is noted in the scripture of truth: and there is none that holdeth with me in these things, but Michael your prince."*

[40] This revelation covers the remainder of the prophecy (Daniel 10-12) and commenced, in the third year of Cyrus, when Daniel set himself to seek the Lord, for understanding on what was going to happen to His people (Israel) in the last days. An unnamed angelic messenger was sent to give Daniel the revelation and it was stressed that this was given to Daniel in response to his prayers (10:7, 8, 11 and 14.) It was particularly interesting, that it was revealed that Daniel's prayer was heard from the beginning of his supplications, but spiritual opposition in high places had prevented the messenger's coming to Daniel earlier and the angel's eventual success had been enabled by Michael (the guardian of Israel) (10:12-14.)

The opposition, from the prince and kings of Persia (10:13), was in their efforts to frustrate the declaration of the will of God and thereby prevent it happening at all; but it was overcome by the intervention of Michael. He is the chief of the princes, a unique rank, appointed to take spiritual care of the LORD's chosen people and Michael would want the will of God declared and fulfilled for Israel. The messenger himself intended returning to the fray (10:20,) after he had explained things to Daniel, but it was an amazing revelation of the conflict of the spiritual forces involved. The revelation the messenger brought was declared to be last days (10:14,) *"Now I am come to make thee understand what shall befall thy people in the latter days: for yet the vision is for many days*[20]*."*

[41] The messenger referred initially to the first year of Darius the Mede, whom he strengthened to enable him to take over Babylon, and then he brought Daniel to the present time "*Now*" and continued to describe the immediate events to be expected in Persia.[21]

(11:1-4) *"Also I in the first year of Darius the Mede, even I, stood to confirm and to strengthen him. And now will I shew thee the truth. Behold there shall stand up yet three kings in Persia; and the fourth shall be far richer than they all: and by his strength through his riches he shall stir up all against the realm of Grecia. And a mighty king shall stand up, that shall rule with great dominion, and do according to his*

---

[20] There are fourteen references in the Old Testament – Genesis 49:1, Numbers 24:14, Deuteronomy 4:30, 31:29, Isaiah 2:2, Jeremiah 23:20, 30:24, 48:47, 49:39, Ezekiel 38:16, Daniel 2:28, 10:14, Hosea 3:5, Micah 4:1. In eleven of these references the term 'latter days' is used, and in three 'last days' (Genesis 49:1, Isaiah 2 & Micah 4:1.) A comparison of these scriptures shows that in prophetic terms, the last days or the latter days, covers the days of the LORD's earthly ministry, and His Coming as Messiah, to establish the Kingdom of Heaven. The terms 'last days' and 'latter days' are interchangeable, they mean the same. Quite probably the last days applies literally to the last week (seven years of 360 days, = 2520 days.)

[21] It was noted paragraph [15] page 16, that the three ribs in the bear's mouth of Daniel's Dream were considered by some to be types of the three succeeding kings in Persia to Darius. But Daniel's Dream was given in the time of Belshazzar and it is evidently wrong to apply this interpretation to an earlier prophecy.

will. And when he shall stand up, his kingdom shall be broken, and shall be divided toward the four winds of heaven; and not to his posterity, nor according to his dominion which he ruled: for his kingdom shall be plucked up, even for others beside those."

There were three kings to follow in Persia [Darius II Nothus (BC 423-404) Artaxerxes II Mnemon (404-358 another Ahasuerus, but not mentioned in scripture) Ochus Artaxerxes III (359-338)] and a fourth *far richer than they all* [Darius III Codomanus (336-331) his immense wealth attracted the Greeks] who were succeeded by Alexander the Great. Alexander was obviously enabled and intended to rule with great power or dominion; but the clause *and do according to his will* perhaps echoes the possibility that Alexander the Great did not continue in the way that he was intended, or inspired, to follow. His premature demise, at the height of his power, could perhaps be the consequence of his self-determination. On his death his kingdom was divided into four between his generals, who ruled a portion each (Figure 4) and this was prophesied: *his kingdom shall be broken and divided toward the four winds.*

[42] 11:5-30) *And the king of the south shall be strong, and (one) of his princes; and he shall be strong about him, and have dominion; his dominion shall be a great dominion. And in the end of years they shall join themselves together; for the king's daughter of the south shall come to the king of the north to make an agreement: but she shall not retain the power of the arm; neither shall he stand, nor his arm: but she shall be given up, and they that brought her, and he that begat her, and he that strengthened her in these times. But out of a branch of her roots shall one stand up in his estate, which shall come with an army, and shall enter into the fortress of the king of the north, and shall deal against them, and shall prevail: and shall also carry captives into Egypt their gods, with their princes, and with their precious vessels of silver and of gold; and he shall continue more years than the king of the north. So the king of the south shall come into his kingdom, and shall return into his own land. But his sons shall be stirred up, and shall assemble a multitude of great forces: and one* shall certainly come, and overflow, and pass through: then shall he return, and be stirred up, even to his fortress. And the king of the south shall be moved with choler, and shall come forth and fight with him, even with the king of the north: and he shall set forth a great multitude; but the multitude shall be given into his hand. And when he hath taken away the multitude, his heart shall be lifted up; and he shall cast down many ten thousands: but he shall not be strengthened by it. For the king of the north shall return, and shall set forth a multitude greater than the former, and shall certainly come after certain years with a great army and with much riches. And in those times there shall many stand up against the king of the south: also the robbers of thy people shall exalt themselves to establish the vision; but they shall fall. So the king of the north shall come, and cast up a mount, and take the most fenced cities: and the arms of the south shall not withstand, neither his chosen people, neither shall there be any strength to withstand. But he that cometh against him shall do according to his own will, and none shall stand before him: and he shall stand in the glorious land, which by his hand shall be consumed. He shall also set his face to enter with the strength of his whole kingdom, and upright ones with him; thus shall he do: and he shall give him the daughter of women, corrupting her: but she shall not stand on his side, neither be for him. After this shall he turn his face unto the isles, and shall take many: but a prince for his own behalf shall cause the reproach offered by him to cease; without his own reproach he shall cause it to turn upon him. Then he shall turn his face toward the fort of his own land: but he shall stumble and fall, and not be found. Then shall stand up in his estate a raiser of taxes in the glory of the kingdom: but within few days he shall be destroyed, neither in anger, nor in battle. And in his estate shall stand up a vile person, to whom they shall not give the honour of the kingdom: but he shall come in peaceably, and obtain the kingdom by flatteries. And with the arms of a flood shall they be overflown from before him, and shall be broken, yea, also the prince of the covenant. And after the league made with him he shall work deceitfully: for he shall come up, and shall become strong with a small people. He shall enter *peaceably even upon the fattest places of the province; and he shall do that which his fathers have not done, nor his fathers' fathers; he shall scatter among them the prey, and spoil, and riches: yea and he shall forecast his devices against the strong holds, even for a time. And he shall stir up his power and his courage against the king of the south with a great army; and the king of the south shall be stirred up to battle with a very great and mighty army; but he shall not stand: for they shall forecast devices against him. Yea, they that feed of the portion of his meat shall destroy him, and his army shall overflow: and many shall fall down slain. And both these kings' hearts shall be to do mischief, and they shall speak lies at one table; but it shall not prosper: for yet the end shall be at the time appointed. Then shall he return unto his land with great riches; and his heart shall be against the holy covenant; and he shall do exploits, and return to his own land. At the time appointed he shall return, and come toward the south; but it shall not be as the former, or as the latter.*

(11:30-45) *For the ships of Chittim shall come against him: therefore he shall be grieved, and return, and have indignation against the holy covenant: so shall he do; he shall even return, and have intelligence with them that forsake the holy covenant. And arms shall stand on his part, and they shall pollute the sanctuary of strength, and shall take away the daily sacrifice, and they shall place the abomination that maketh desolate. And such as do wickedly against the covenant shall he corrupt by flatteries: but the people that do know their God shall be strong and do exploits. And they that understand among the people shall instruct many: yet they shall fall by the sword, and by flame, by captivity, and by spoil, many days. Now when they shall fall, they shall be holpen with a little help: but many shall cleave to them with flatteries. And some of them of understanding shall fall, to try them, and to purge, and to make them white, even to the time of the end: because it is yet for a time appointed. And the king shall do according to his will; and he shall exalt himself, and magnify himself above every god, and shall speak marvellous things against the God of gods, and shall prosper till the indignation be accomplished: for that that is determined shall be done. Neither shall he regard the God of his fathers, nor the desire of women, nor regard any god: for he shall magnify himself above all*[22]. *But in his estate shall he honour the God of forces: and a god whom his fathers knew not shall he honour with gold, and silver, and with precious stones, and pleasant things. Thus shall he do in the most strong holds with a strange god, whom he shall acknowledge and increase with glory: and he shall cause them to rule over many, and shall divide the land for gain. And at the time of the end shall the king of the south push at him: and the king of the north shall come against him like a whirlwind, with chariots, and with horsemen, and with many ships; and he shall enter into the countries, and shall overflow and pass over. He shall enter also into the glorious land, and many countries shall be overthrown: but these shall escape out of his hand, even Edom, and Moab, and the chief of the children of Ammon. He shall stretch forth his hand also upon the countries: and the land of Egypt shall not escape. But he shall have power over the treasures of gold and of silver, and over all the precious things of Egypt: and the Libyans and the Ethiopians shall be at his steps. But tidings out of the east and out of the north shall trouble him: therefore he shall go forth with great fury to destroy and utterly to make away many. And he shall plant the tabernacles of his palace between the seas in the glorious holy mountain; yet he shall come to his end, and none shall help him.*

---

[22] V37 *Neither shall he regard the God of his fathers, nor the desire of women, nor regard any god: for he shall magnify himself above all.* This is a particularly significant verse in reference to the *abomination of desolation.* For example; in *The Two Babylons* or *The Papal Worship proved to be the worship of Nimrod and his wife* by the Rev. Alexander Hislop (1916, 1921, 1926, 1929 4th edition, reprinted nine times up to 1965) Chapter VII Section IV The Image of the Beast, pages 263-269; the author goes to considerable lengths to prove that the image of the beast is in fact the image of the Madonna, or The Virgin Mary (as the Queen of heaven.) V37 establishes beyond argument that the beast regards not *the god of his fathers, nor the desire of women , nor regard any god.* Ezekiel was shown *women weeping for Tammuz* (the queen of heaven lamenting for her son, Ezekiel 8:14;) and likewise Jeremiah had to contend with the women (and men) worshippers of the queen of heaven (Jeremiah 44:15-19.) The Jewish worship of the queen of heaven is not denied, (for which they suffered the divine judgments of the desolations.) But it blatantly absurd to imagine that if the dragon (Satan) gave all his power to the Beast, in addition to the efforts of the False Prophet, to make the Beast appear to be god and for him to demand the worship of the Jews; that they (the beast, the false prophet or Satan) could consider making any image to the queen of heaven (who does not exist.)

[Compare *"between the seas"* with Zechariah 14:4-11 esp. v8 *"the former (margin = East) sea (i.e. The Dead Sea) and the hinder sea"* (The Mediterranean.)]

(12:1-4) *And at that time shall Michael stand up, the great prince which standeth for the children of thy people: and there shall be a time of trouble, such as never was since there was a nation even to that same time: and at that time thy people shall be delivered, every one that shall be found written in the book. And many of them that sleep in the dust of the earth shall awake, some to everlasting life, and some to shame and everlasting contempt. And they that be wise shall shine as the brightness of the firmament; and they that turn many to righteousness as the stars for ever and ever. But thou, O Daniel, shut up the words, and seal the book, even to the time of the end: many shall run to and fro, and knowledge shall be increased"*.

(12:5-13) *Then I Daniel looked, and, behold, there stood other two, the one on this side of the bank of the river, and the other on that side of the bank of the river. And one said to the man clothed in linen, which was upon the waters of the river, "How long shall it be to the end of these wonders?" And I heard the man clothed in linen, which was upon the waters of the river, when he held up his right hand and his left hand unto heaven, and sware by Him that liveth for ever that it shall be for a time, times, and an half*; and when he shall have accomplished to scatter the power of the holy people, all these things shall be finished. And I heard, but I understood not: then said I, "O my Lord, what shall be the end of these things?" And he said, "Go thy way, Daniel; for the words are closed up and sealed till the time of the end. Many shall be purified, and made white, and tried; but the wicked shall do wickedly: and none of the wicked shall understand; but the wise shall understand. And from the time that the daily sacrifice shall be taken away, and the abomination that maketh desolate set up, there shall be a thousand two hundred and ninety days*. Blessed is he that waiteth, and cometh to the thousand three hundred and five and thirty days*. But go thou thy way till the end be: for thou shalt rest, and stand in thy lot at the end of the days."*

[*(ii) *a time, times and an half;* (ix) *a thousand two hundred and ninety days;* (x) *the thousand three hundred and five and thirty days.* (The Roman numerals refer to these references in Appendix 3.) These are three more of *the ten unique references* that link the prophecies of Daniel and Revelation. Making a total of five in Daniel; the remaining five are in the Revelation.]

This was the messenger's account of the conflict between the king of the north and the king of the south, which were portions of that divided Greek empire (See Figure 4, compare Daniel 8:20-26.)

Whilst a detailed study of Jeremiah's prophecy is beyond these considerations, there is one point worthy of emphasis. Throughout Jeremiah's prophecies the invasions of Israel and Judah were nearly always *from the north,* (the only obvious exception to this being Egypt.) This was because invading armies (even from the East, like Babylon,) tended to follow the East bank of the Euphrates almost to its source (effectively following the *fertile crescen*t) and then descend from the north. The reason was partly the difficulty of fording the Euphrates in its lower reaches, but also to enable the army to feed itself en route to invade Palestine or Israel. For this reason one of the titles of the beast *the king of the north* is perfectly valid. Although he originates geographically east of Israel, his invading Israel from the north must not be overlooked.]

[43] Undeniably the revelation given to Daniel applied in no small measure to this particular historical period (some Bible commentaries will give details on these fulfilments, which are beyond the scope of these considerations.) But it cannot be claimed that, for example, Antiochus Epiphanes fulfilled all that was contained in this prophecy. As noted already, the angel's own words pointed deliberately and definitely to the last days and on the authority of the LORD Jesus Christ Himself (Matthew 24:15, Mark 13:14) this prophecy applies to the last days for its complete fulfilment.

Historically speaking, the facts in the prophecy can be recognised and accepted up to (11:20,) *"Then shall stand up in his estate a raiser of taxes etc"*. But the next verse (11:21) *And in his estate shall stand up a vile person, to whom they shall not give the honour of the kingdom: but he shall come in peaceably, and obtain the kingdom by flatteries*, has not been convincingly and clearly fulfilled. This is however considered especially applicable to the last days' fulfilment of this prophecy (partly because at least in part, it has not been satisfactorily fulfilled to date.) But in particular it points to the appearance of the beast. His career proceeds (11:23-36,) and he becomes powerful and eventually rules. It is interesting that the appearance of this *vile person* is in connection with the divisions of the Greek empire and it accords perfectly with the appearance of the little horn in the divided Greek kingdom of Daniel's Vision (8:20-26. [31])

Since he is shown to be in conflict with the king of the north and the king of the south (11:40,) this leaves either the kingdom of the west or the kingdom of the east (see Figure 4) from which he can arise. But it had been revealed previously (8:9 [28]) that the little horn *Waxed great toward the south, and toward the east, and toward the pleasant land*; which means, that if he is to fulfil this scripture, the beast must be associated with, or rise in, either of the other two divisions of the divided Greek empire (ie Cassander's area of Greece and Macedon, or that of Lysimachus which was Bithynia and Thrace. See Figure 4 with note, also [116].).

[44] The revelation given to Daniel revealed a great deal of the activity and events of the last days; especially concerning the beast and his various conflicts with the king of the north (Syria) and the king of the south (Egypt) and other nations, who unavoidably become involved in the complex situations of that time. Certain aspects of this will be considered later, but before leaving this portion of Daniel, reference should be made in particular to the closing words, because the Lord Himself quoted details from this, a fact of profound significance (12:8-13) *And I heard, but I understood not, then said I, "O my LORD, what shall be the end of these things?"*

and he said, "Go thy way, Daniel: for the words are closed up and sealed till the time of the end. Many shall be purified, and made white, and tried; but the wicked shall do wickedly: and none of the wicked shall understand; but the wise shall understand. And from the time that the daily sacrifice shall be taken away, and the abomination that maketh desolate set up, there shall be a thousand two hundred and ninety days. Blessed is he that waiteth, and cometh to the thousand three hundred and five and thirty days. But go thou thy way till the end be: for thou shalt rest, and stand in thy lot at the end of the days."

It has to be recognised that the prophecies concerning the events of the last days are beyond the understanding of some, for *none of the wicked shall understand*, this has to be accepted as a fact. But

the final sentence is most significant – for it declares that Daniel *shall rest and stand in thy lot at the end of days*. Daniel will undoubtedly be one of *"two witnesses"* in the last days (Revelation 11). The other will most likely be Elijah; who did not die, but was taken up in a chariot to heaven (2 Kings2:11.) It would be difficult to name any other scriptural characters, more suitable for such an assignment!

[45] The *abomination of desolation*[23] was mentioned by the LORD Himself, Who attributed it to Daniel's prophecy (Matthew 24:15, Mark 13:14) and the importance of this reference will be discussed later. The two periods specified (1,290 days and 1,335 days) are mysterious times, which have been the subject of a great deal of conjecture or speculation. Care has to be taken however to confine such considerations to scriptural interpretation, these times have been examined in Appendix 3 The Final Week.)

[46] From Daniel's writings it has become evident, that the basic application of the prophecies to Israel or Judah relates to the gentile domination of Jerusalem and to the eventual re-establishment of

---

[23] The various scriptural titles and useful references to the beast are listed for convenience in Appendix 4.

that nation and its worship as the LORD's Chosen People, when the Kingdom of GOD is established on earth. Daniel had no concept of, or knowledge of, the church of the LORD Jesus Christ, who are His fruits during *the times of the gentiles,* in a period of grace made possible by the Jewish rejection of their Messiah. Daniel's writings revealed that he and his friends were of the tribe of Judah (Daniel 3:12.) But Daniel's entreaties for understanding concerning the writings of Jeremiah, revealed that his whole prophecy in its last day application concerns the nation Israel not merely Judah (see also Daniel 9:7, 11, 20 and compare 10:21 and 12:1.)

Chapter 5: Jeremiah

Daniel, Jeremiah and Ezekiel were contemporaries and Jeremiah ministered to the Jews in Judah and Jerusalem, during the reigns of Josiah, Jehoiakim and Zedekiah; the very brief reigns of Jehoahaz and Jehoiachin would not count in the Jewish reckoning, although Jeremiah's prophecy covers both.

It was Jeremiah' prophecy, which inspired Daniel's supplications to the LORD for understanding (which he was given,) and Daniel's revelations provide the essential key to understanding last days' prophecies. Jeremiah is very much under-estimated as a prophet, although uniquely, the LORD laid His hand on Jeremiah's mouth when He called him (Jeremiah 1:9); this divine touch gives Jeremiah's spoken prophecies an authority beyond any other prophet's and also to his ministry to Israel and Judah, and the kings (although he did not minister to Josiah.)

Essentially, Jeremiah's ministry was to persuade the people (and the kings in succession) to submit themselves (in the revealed will of GOD) to the judgments on the nation for their idolatry and accept the *Servitude, Captivity* and eventually, *the Desolations;* which were imposed by Nebuchadnezzar and the Babylonians (or Chaldeans.) The increasing severity of these impositions came because of the Jews' resistance to, and rejection of, Jeremiah's ministry. Jeremiah had the heart breaking task of prophesying to a rebellious and stubborn generation, who even as the judgments came upon them, preferred to listen to their false prophets. (There were false prophets even in Babylon, who attempted to persuade those in captivity, that deliverance would come. Ezekiel had to contend with these.) What Jeremiah endured in persecution, and rejection (few appreciate he was scourged twice, for example) was terrible; and one can only marvel at the calibre of the man, who endured (in the LORD's strength) even through the ghastly consequences of the sieges imposed (revealed so graphically in Lamentations.)

However this is but the barest outline, but what needs to be appreciated is that Jeremiah was told to write a book of His prophecies (up to that time) for the benefit of Jehoiakim (who reigned for eleven years.) Jehoiakim scorned these written prophecies, and had the audacity to cut up the scroll and burn it on the fire (for it was winter at the time.) This provoked the LORD's anger, Who condemned Jehoiakim to an ignominious end (dying and not being lamented or buried as a king, but his carcase would be consumed by vultures.) Additionally, Jeremiah had to re-write the book Jehoiakim destroyed, (to which even more was added,) and since these writings are largely concerned with the last days, they are noted here.

30:1-3 The LORD to Jeremiah concerning the book *The word that came to Jeremiah from the LORD, saying, "Thus speaketh the LORD GOD of Israel, saying, Write thee all the words that I have spoken unto thee in a book. For, lo, the days come, saith the LORD, that I will bring again the captivity of My people Israel and Judah, saith the LORD: and I will cause them to return to the land that I gave to their fathers, and they shall possess it.'"*

30:4-9 *And these (are) the words that the LORD spake concerning Israel and concerning Judah. For thus saith the LORD; We have heard a voice of trembling, of fear, and not of peace. Ask ye now, and see whether a man doth travail with child? Wherefore do I see every man with his hands on his loins, as a woman in travail, and all faces are turned into paleness? Alas! For that day (is) great, so that none is like it: it is even the time of Jacob's trouble;* (manifestly last days' applications also) *but he shall be saved out of it. For it shall come to pass in that day, saith the LORD of hosts, (that) I will break his yoke* from off thy neck, and will burst thy bonds, and strangers shall no more serve themselves of him: but they shall serve the LORD their GOD, and David their king, whom I will raise up unto them.

30:10 -17 Therefore fear thou not, O My servant Jacob, saith the LORD; neither be dismayed, O Israel: for, lo, I will save thee from afar, and thy seed from the land of their captivity; and Jacob shall return, and shall be in rest, and be quiet, and none shall make him afraid. For I am with thee, saith the LORD, to save thee: though I make a full end of all nations whither I have scattered thee, yet will I not make a full end of thee: but I will correct thee in measure, and will not leave thee altogether unpunished. For thus saith the LORD, Thy bruise (is) incurable, (and) thy wound (is) grievous. (There is) none to plead thy cause, that thou mayest be bound up: thou hast no healing medicines. All thy lovers have forgotten thee; they seek thee not; for I have wounded thee with the wound of an enemy, with the chastisement of a cruel one, for the multitude of thine iniquity; (because) thy sins were increased. Why criest thou for thine affliction? Thy sorrow (is) incurable for the multitude of thine iniquity: (because) thy sins were increased, I have done these things unto thee. Therefore all they that devour thee shall be devoured; and all thine adversaries, every one of them, shall go into captivity; and they that spoil thee shall be a spoil, and all that prey upon thee will I give for a prey. For I will restore health unto thee, and I will heal thee of thy wounds, saith the LORD; because they called thee an Outcast, (saying,) This is Zion, whom no man seeketh after.

30:18-24 Thus saith the LORD; Behold, I will bring again the captivity of Jacob's tents, and have mercy on his dwelling places; and the city shall be builded upon her own heap, and the palace shall remain after the manner thereof. And out of them shall proceed thanksgiving and the voice of them that make merry: and I will multiply them, and they shall not be few; I will also glorify them, and they shall not be small. Their children also shall be as aforetime, and their congregation shall be established before Me, and I will punish all that oppress them. And their nobles shall be of themselves, and their governor shall proceed *from the midst of them; and I will cause him to draw near, and he shall approach unto Me: for who (is) this that engaged his heart to approach unto Me? saith the LORD. And ye shall be My people, and I will be your GOD. Behold the whirlwind of the LORD goeth forth with fury, a continuing whirlwind: it shall fall with pain upon the head of the wicked. The fierce anger of the LORD shall not return, until He have done (it,) and until He have performed the intents of His heart: in the latter days ye shall consider it.*

The latter days (the same as the last days) indicating such fulfilments also possible.

31:1-9 *At the same time, saith the LORD, will I be the GOD of all the families of Israel, and they shall be My people. Thus saith the LORD, The people (which were) left of the sword found grace in the wilderness; (even) Israel, when I went to cause him to rest. The LORD hath appeared of old unto me, (saying,) "Yea, I have loved thee with an everlasting love: therefore with lovingkindness have I drawn thee. Again I will build thee, and thou shalt be built, O virgin of Israel: thou shalt again be adorned with thy tabrets, and shalt go forth in the dances of them that make merry. Thou shalt yet plant vines upon the mountains of Samaria: the planters shall plant, and shall eat them as common things. For there shall be a day, (that) the watchmen upon the mount Ephraim shall cry, 'Arise ye, and let us go up to Zion unto the LORD our GOD.' For thus saith the LORD; 'Sing with gladness for Jacob, and shout among the chief of the nations: publish ye, praise ye, and say, 'O LORD, save Thy people, the remnant of Israel.' Behold, I will bring them from the north country, and gather them from the coasts of the earth, (and) with them the blind and the lame, the woman with child and her that travaileth with child together: a great company shall return thither. They shall come with weeping, and with supplications will I lead them: I will cause thee to walk by the rivers of waters in a straight way, wherein they shall not stumble: for I am a father to Israel, and Ephraim (is) My firstborn.'"* (This is explained in Appendix 7 page 160.)

31:10-14 *Hear the word of the LORD, O ye nations, and declare (it) in the isles afar off, and say, "He that scattered Israel will gather him, and keep him, as a shepherd (doth) his flock. For the LORD hath redeemed Jacob, and ransomed him from the hand of (him that was) stronger than he. Therefore they shall come and sing in the height of Zion, and shall flow together to the goodness of the LORD, for wheat, and for wine, and for oil, and for the young of the flock and of the herd: and their soul shall be as a watered garden; and they shall not sorrow any more at all. Then shall the virgin rejoice in the dance, both young men and old together: for I will turn their mourning into joy, and will comfort them, and make them rejoice from their sorrow. And I will satiate the soul of the priests with fatness, and My people shall be satisfied with My goodness, saith the LORD."*

31:15-17 *Thus saith the LORD: A voice was heard in Ramah, lamentation, (and) bitter weeping; Rahel weeping for her children refused to be comforted for her children, because they (were) not.* [This also fulfilled, Matthew 2:16-18] *Thus saith the LORD; 'Refrain thy voice from weeping, and thine eyes from tears: for thy work shall be rewarded, saith the LORD; and they shall come again from the land of the enemy. And there is hope in thine end, saith the LORD, that thy children shall come again to their own border.*

31:18-21 *I have surely heard Ephraim bemoaning himself (thus;) 'Thou hast chastised me, and I was chastised, as a bullock unaccustomed (to the yoke:) turn Thou me, and I shall be turned; for Thou (art) the LORD my GOD. Surely after that I was turned, I repented; and after that I was instructed, I smote upon (my) thigh: I was ashamed, yea, even confounded, because I did bear the reproach of my youth.' (Is) Ephraim My dear son? (Is he) a pleasant child? For since I spake against him, I do earnestly remember him still: therefore My bowels are troubled for him; I will surely have mercy upon him, saith the LORD. Set thee up waymarks,* (= sign posts, see 2 Kings 23:17, title; Ezekiel 39: *a sign*) *make thee high heaps: set thine heart toward the highway, (even) the way (which) thou wentest: turn again, O virgin of Israel, turn again to these thy cities.*

31:22-26 *How long wilt thou go about, O thou backsliding daughter? For the LORD hath created a new thing in the earth, A woman shall compass a man. Thus saith the LORD of hosts, the GOD of Israel; As yet they shall use this speech in the land of Judah and in the cities thereof, when I shall bring again their captivity; 'The LORD bless thee, O habitation of justice, (and) mountain of holiness.' And there shall dwell in Judah itself, and in all the cities thereof together, husbandmen, and they (that) go forth with flocks. For I have satiated the weary soul and I have replenished every sorrowful soul.'" Upon this I awaked, and beheld; and my sleep was sweet unto me.*

31:27-30 *Behold the days come, saith the LORD, that I will sow the house of Israel and the house of Judah with the seed of man, and with the seed of beast. And it shall come to pass, (that) like as I have watched over them, to pluck up, and to break down, and to throw down, and to destroy, and to afflict; so will I watch over them, to build, and to plant, saith the LORD. In those days they shall say no more, 'The fathers have eaten a sour grape, and the children's teeth are set on edge.' But every one shall die for his own iniquity: every man that eateth the sour grape, his teeth shall be set on edge.*

The new covenant one of the most important doctrines of the New Testament, revealed through Jeremiah.

31:31-34 *Behold, the days come, saith the LORD, that I will make <u>a new covenant</u> with the house of Israel, and with the house of Judah: not according to the covenant that I made with their fathers in the day (that) I took them by the hand to bring them out of the land of Egypt; which My covenant they brake, although I was an husband unto them, saith the LORD: but this (shall be) the covenant that I will make with the house of Israel; after those days, saith the LORD, I will put My law in their inward parts, and write it in their hearts; and will be their GOD, and they shall be My people. And they shall teach no more every man his neighbour, and every man his brother, saying, 'Know the LORD:' for they shall all know Me, from the least* *of them unto the greatest of them, saith the LORD: for I will forgive their iniquity, and I will remember their sin no more.*

The LORD Jesus Christ Himself established this New Covenant (or New Testament,) in His Communion.

31:35-37 Thus saith the LORD, Which giveth the sun for light by day, (and) the ordinances of the moon and of the stars for a light by night, Which divideth the sea when the waves thereof roar; the LORD of Hosts is His name: If those ordinances depart from before Me,' saith the LORD, '(Then) the seed of Israel also shall cease from being a nation before Me for ever.' Thus saith the LORD; 'If heaven above can be measured, and the foundations of the earth searched out beneath, I will also cast off all the seed of Israel for all that they have done.' saith the LORD.

31:38-40 Behold, the days come,' saith the LORD, 'that the city shall be built to the LORD from the tower of Hananeel unto the gate of the corner. And the measuring line shall yet go forth over against it upon the hill Gareb, and shall compass about to Goath. And the whole valley of the dead bodies, and of the ashes, and all the fields unto the brook of Kidron, unto the corner of the horse gate toward the east, (shall be) holy unto the LORD; it shall not be plucked up nor thrown down any more for ever.'

------------the end of the book. The book is distinctly last days' doctrines.

Furthermore, Jeremiah also (like some of the Minor Prophets and also Ezekiel,) had ministry for Gentile nations[24]. Whilst this ministry is

---

[24] Ezekiel (in captivity in Babylon,) was also given ministry to gentile nations; but from a different perspective, and containing (in some cases) vastly different content to Jeremiah's. The following references are offered (for those who might like to make the comparison.) Ezekiel 25:1-7 his prophecy against the Ammonites. 25:8-11 against Moab. 25:12-14

recorded in the book of Jeremiah, after the account of Jeremiah's disastrous experience with the remnant that determined to go to Egypt; it is clear that the ministry was given to Jeremiah much earlier; when pending Nebuchadnezzar's first invasion (about BC 609,) the surrounding nations sent ambassadors, (messengers) to Jehoiakim to see if some alliance could be formed (see Jeremiah 27:1-11 and this ministry was later given to Zedekiah) but the ambassadors or messengers were sent during Jehoiakim's reign (which gave Jeremiah opportunity to minister to these gentiles through their messengers.) As a matter of fact, when Judah was taken captive, most of their "neighbours" betrayed them to the Chaldeans (as they sought escape routes,) and triumphed over the hardships the Jews endured; for which the LORD later judged them severely.

---

against Edom (Seir). 25:15-17 against the Philistines. 26, 27 against Tyrus. 28:1-10 against the prince of Tyrus 28:11-19 against the King of Tyrus (Satan) 28:20-23 against Zidon (sister city to Tyrus). 28:24-26 assurances to Israel. 29:1-16 against Egypt. 29:17-20 Spoils of Egypt given to Nebuchadnezzar as reward for his destroying Tyrus (during his siege the people evacuated the island during the night, and when Nebuchadnezzar took the island, there was nothing for his efforts.) The LORD's compensation was his victory over Egypt (with the spoils.) 29:21 blessing for Israel, in captivity in Babylon 30:1-26 Desolation of Egypt. 31:1, 2 Egypt compared to 31:3-17 Assyrian's greatness and fall. 32:1-32 Desolation of Egypt.
Several of the Minor Prophets also ministered to Gentile Nations: *Obadiah* Edom); *Jonah* (Nineveh); *Micah* (Samaria and Jerusalem); *Nahum* (Nineveh); *Habakkuk* (Chaldeans); *Zephaniah* (Judah, Jerusalem. Philistines, Moab, Ammon, Ethiopians, Assyria, Nineveh.)

Chapter 6: EZEKIEL

[47] (Ezekiel 38:1-7) *And the word of the Lord came unto me, saying, "Son of man, set thy face against Gog, the land of Magog, the chief prince of Meshech and Tubal, and prophesy against him, and say, 'Thus saith the Lord God; Behold, I am against thee, O Gog, the chief prince of Meshech and Tubal: and I will turn thee back, and put hooks into thy jaws, and I will bring thee forth, and all thine army, horses and horsemen, all of them clothed with all sorts of armour, even a great company with bucklers and shields, all of them handling swords; Persia, Ethiopia, and Libya with them; all of them with shield and helmet, Gomer, and all his bands; the house of Togarmah of the north quarters, and all his bands: and many people with thee. Be thou prepared, and prepare for thyself, thou, and all thy company that are assembled unto thee, and be thou a guard unto them.*

(38:8-13) *After many days thou shalt be visited: in the latter years thou shalt come into the land that is brought back from the sword, and is gathered out of many people, against the mountains of Israel, which have been always waste: but it is brought forth out of the nations, and they shall dwell safely all of them. Thou shalt ascend and come like a storm, thou shalt be like a cloud to cover the land, thou and all thy bands, and many people with thee. Thus saith the Lord God; It shall also come to pass, that at the same time shall things come into thy mind, and thou shalt think an evil thought: and thou shalt say, 'I will go up to the land of unwalled villages; I will go to them that are at rest, that dwell safely, all of them dwelling without walls, and having neither bars nor gates.' To take a spoil, and to take a prey; to turn thine hand upon the desolate places that are now inhabited, and upon the people that are gathered out of the nations, which have gotten cattle and goods, that dwell in the midst of the* land. Sheba, and Dedan, and the merchants of Tarshish, with all the young lions thereof, shall say unto thee, 'Art thou come to take a spoil? Hast thou gathered thy company to take a prey? To carry away silver and gold, to take away cattle and goods, to take a great spoil?'

(38:14-23) *Therefore, son of man, prophesy and say unto Gog, Thus saith the Lord God, In that day when My people of Israel dwelleth safely, shalt thou not know it? And thou shalt come from thy place out of the north parts, thou, and many people with thee, all of them riding upon horses, a great company, and a mighty army: and thou shalt come up against My people of Israel, as a cloud to cover the land; it shall be in the latter days, and I will bring thee against My land, that the heathen may know Me, when I shall be sanctified in thee, O Gog, before their eyes. Thus said the Lord God; Art thou he of whom I have spoken in old time by My servants the prophets of Israel, which prophesied in those days many years that I would bring thee against them? And it shall come to pass at the same time when Gog shall come against the land of Israel, saith the Lord God, that My fury shall come up in My face. For in My jealousy and in the fire of My wrath have I spoken, Surely in that day there shall be a great shaking in the land of Israel; so that the fishes of the sea, and the fowls of the heaven, and the beasts of the field, and all creeping things that creep upon the earth, and all the men that are upon the face of the earth, shall shake at My presence, and the mountains shall be thrown down, and the steep places shall fall, and every wall shall fall to the ground. And I will call for a sword against him throughout all My mountains, said the Lord God; every man's sword shall be against his brother. And I will plead against him with pestilence and with blood; and I will rain upon him, and upon his bands, and upon the many people that are with him, an overflowing rain, and great hailstones, fire, and brimstone. Thus will I magnify Myself, and sanctify Myself; and I will be known in the eyes of many nations, and they shall know that I am the Lord.*

(39:1-7) *Therefore, thou son of man, prophesy against Gog, and say, Thus saith the Lord God; Behold, I am against thee, O Gog, the chief prince of Meshech and Tubal: and I will turn thee back, and leave but the sixth part of thee, that will cause thee to come up from the north parts, and will bring thee upon the mountains of Israel: and I will smite thy bow out of thy left hand, and will cause thine arrows to fall out of thy right hand. Thou shalt fall upon the mountains of Israel, thou, and all thy bands, and the people that is with thee: I will give thee unto the ravenous birds of every sort, and to the beasts of the field to be devoured. Thou shalt fall upon the open field: for I have spoken it, saith the Lord God. And I will send a fire on Magog, and among them that dwell carelessly in the isles: and they shall know that I am the Lord. So will I make My holy name known in the midst of My people Israel; and I will not let them pollute My holy name any more: and the heathen shall know that I am the Lord, the Holy One in Israel.*

(Ezekiel 39:8-10) *Behold, it is come, and it is done, saith the Lord God; this is the day whereof I have spoken. And they that dwell in the cities of Israel shall go forth, and shall set on fire, and burn the weapons, both the shields and the bucklers, the bows and the arrows, and the handstaves, and the spears, and they shall burn them with fire seven years: so that they shall take no wood out of the field, neither cut down any out of the forests; for they shall burn the weapons with fire: and they shall spoil those that spoiled them, and rob those that robbed them, saith the Lord God.*

(39:11-16) *And it shall come to pass in that day, that I will give unto Gog a place there of graves in Israel, the valley of the passengers on the east of the sea: and it shall stop the noses of the passengers: and there shall they bury Gog and all his multitude: and they shall call it The valley of Hamon-gog. And seven months shall the house of Israel be burying of them, that they may cleanse the land. Yea, all the people of the land shall bury them; and it shall be to them a renown the day that I shall be glorified, saith the Lord God. And they shall sever out men of continual employment, passing through the land to bury with the passengers those that remain upon the face of the earth, to cleanse it: after the end of seven months shall they search.*

And the passengers that pass through the land, when any seeth a man's bone, then shall he set up a sign by it, till the buriers have buried it in the valley of Hamon-gog. And also the name of the city shall be Hamonah. Thus shall they cleanse the land.

(39:17-22) And thou son of man, thus saith the Lord God; Speak unto every feathered fowl, and to every beast of the field, Assemble yourselves, and come; gather yourselves on every side to My sacrifice that I do sacrifice for you, even a great sacrifice upon the mountains of Israel, that ye may eat flesh, and drink blood. Ye shall eat the flesh of the mighty, and drink the blood of the princes of the earth, of rams, of lambs, and of goats, of bullocks, all of them fatlings of Bashan. And ye shall eat fat till ye be full, and drink blood till ye be drunken, of My sacrifice which I have sacrificed for you. Thus ye shall be filled at My table with horses and chariots, with mighty men, and with all men of war, saith the Lord God. And I will set My glory among the heathen, and all the heathen shall see My judgment that I have executed, and My hand that I have laid upon them. So the house of Israel shall know that I am the Lord their God from that day and forward.

(39:23-29) And the heathen shall know that the house of Israel went into captivity for their iniquity: because they trespassed against Me, therefore hid I my face from them, and gave them into the hand of their enemies; so fell they all by the sword. According to their uncleanness and according to their transgressions have I done unto them, and hid My face from them. Therefore thus saith the Lord God; Now will I bring again the captivity of Jacob, and have mercy upon the whole house of Israel, and will be jealous for My holy name; after that they have borne their shame, and all their trespasses whereby they have trespassed against Me, when they dwelt safely in their land, and none made them afraid. When I have brought them again from the people, and gathered them out of their enemies' lands, and am sanctified in them in the sight of many nations; then shall they know that I am the Lord their God, which caused them to be led into captivity among the heathen: but I have gathered them unto their

own land, and have left none of them any more there. Neither will I hide My face any more from them: for I have poured out My spirit upon the house of Israel, saith the Lord God.

[48] Whilst Daniel's prophecies must obviously rate primary place, with respect to Old Testament scriptures concerning the last days; Ezekiel, a prophet of the captivity of Judah, also received revelations of considerable importance.

Tragically, in recent years, Ezekiel's prophecy has been used in attempts to find scriptural support for evidence of Unidentified Flying Objects (UFO's or Flying Saucers). Such enthusiasts glibly cite Ezekiel's experiences (chapters 1 and 10) as his record of encounters with, or visitations by, aliens from outer space. Even a casual glance at the scriptures quoted, should suffice to show to anyone that Ezekiel's experiences were genuine revelations from God (with resultant prophetic ministry to the nation Israel,) and bear no comparison with the pathetic nonsense purported to have come from space visitors. Further, a comparison with John's experience on Patmos (Revelation 1and 4) confirms and supports the view that Ezekiel's experiences were divinely ordained.

Ezekiel's prophecy merits far more attention than can be devoted to it in these considerations and in so many other respects a study of his prophecy would be immensely profitable. The following notes are offered as a very brief and basic guide to the prophecy as a whole, but the intention is to draw particular notice to those portions related to the events of the last days.

BACKGROUND to Ezekiel's Prophecy

[49] To appreciate the prophecy of Ezekiel, it should be seen in the light of the history of the nation Israel. Briefly, the twelve tribes of Israel settled in the Promised Land, but were only truly united as one nation for a relatively short period under King David and on his death, the kingdom passed to his son Solomon. Unfortunately, Solomon's excesses and extravagances assisted in dividing the nation again and when Solomon died, ten tribes refused to accept the iron rule that his son Rehoboam foolishly intended to impose upon them (BC 976, 1 Kings 12.) The ten tribes split from the rule of Judah (only the tribe of Benjamin remaining loyal) and the ten were collectively called Israel and appointed their own succession of kings in Israel (or Samaria.) Astonishingly, this was divinely instigated and approved; the two nations (Israel and Judah) were individually blessed, when their worship conformed to the covenant that God had established with them and He sent prophets to both nations. [Beginners reading the Old Testament find it confusing, because they fail to understand this national division. It becomes easier to understand when the kings and prophets *of Judah* are recognised and distinguished from the kings and prophets *of Israel*.]

Israel under Jeroboam went into idolatry and immediately forsook the Law and under the rule of a continuous succession of ungodly kings, sank further into idolatry. This lasted about two hundred and fifty years and finally, as a result of God's judgment for their idolatry, (about which they were repeatedly warned by the prophets of those times,) the nation Israel was taken captive into Assyria (728 BC) and they were never to be scripturally mentioned again. However, during the times of Israel's flagrant and excessive idolatry there was a continual exodus of those sickened with idolatry, from all the ten tribes, who migrated to Judah, where a nucleus always worshipped the LORD. Judah never refused these Israelites entry to the tribal territories of Judah and Benjamin. In fact some of the more righteous kings in Judah in times of blessing, invited any remaining from Israel to join in their worship; so that when eventually, the nation Judah was taken into captivity to Babylon for idolatry; there were Israelites among them (undoubtedly representing all the ten tribes.) The twelve tribes might not be recognisable even to the Jews themselves, but it is certain the LORD knows and recognises all the surviving tribes of Israel, whom He has promised that He will eventually re-establish, reunite and restore.

[50] Judah, as a nation in its own right, continued for about a century and a quarter, (until BC 606) but during this time was subjected to domination either by Egypt or by Babylon. Since Jerusalem is geographically situated roughly halfway between the Nile and the Euphrates, the city became an ideal pawn, over which the successive rulers of Egypt or Babylon could contend, by claiming its inclusion within their respective empires. The original nations, of what eventually became the Persian Empire, were the Assyrians and the Chaldeans. The Persians were conquered by the Greeks and Alexander's colossal empire was divided after his death, *to the four winds.* It was with the Northern Empire (Syria, ruled by Seleucid Kings) that the Southern Empire (Egypt, ruled by the Ptolemys) was continually having territorial disputes, with Jerusalem being the main target for occupation during such conflicts because of its central position.

King Josiah of Judah, who supported the Babylonians, lost his life at Megiddo (BC 609) when he attempted to prevent Pharaoh Necho going to assist the Assyrians in their fight against Babylon. In his fury over his defeat, on their way back to Egypt, Pharaoh Necho led his army into Jerusalem and imposed a tribute on the city as punishment for the support that King Josiah had given the Babylonians. On Josiah's death in battle, his son Jehoahaz had been given the crown in Judah, but Pharaoh Necho replaced Jehoahaz (or Shallum,) by his brother Eliakim, whom Pharaoh renamed Jehoiakim (see 2 Kings 23:29-35, 1 Chronicles 3:15 & 2 Chron 36:3,4.) Later in the battle of Carchemish (BC 605) Nebuchadnezzar defeated Pharaoh Necho.

Nebuchadnezzar came to Jerusalem, in command of his armies to reclaim the city for Babylon. The siege was brief and Jehoiakim was captured, but he was given his throne and freedom again in return for pledging his allegiance to Nebuchadnezzar. This gesture was possibly in recognition of Josiah's earlier support against Egypt. Nebuchadnezzar withdrew and in his magnanimity took only a few token captives of the seed royal of Judah (including Daniel and his friends,) and some of the vessels of gold from the temple in Jerusalem, which were placed in the house of Nebuchadnezzar's gods in Babylon (whence Belshazzar later obtained them). This commenced the Servitude to Babylon (BC 605.) But then Nebuchadnezzar had to return immediately to Babylon because of the death of his father (Nabopalassar the military genius who founded the Babylonian Empire,) to establish his claim to the throne.

Foolishly within about three years Jehoiakim rebelled against the rule of Babylon; but it was five more years before Nebuchadnezzar could return from other battles to repay this rebellion. He returned with vengeance (2 Kings 24:10-20) Jehoiakim was slain during the siege and Jehoiachin was made king BC 598. (Jehoiakim see Jeremiah 22:18, 19 & 36:29, 30.) Nebuchadnezzar took all except the very poorest of people captive to Babylon (including Ezekiel, and Mordecai and Esther) with Jehoiachin, who had only ruled for three months and ten days and Nebuchadnezzar's army ransacked the city Jerusalem. This commenced The Captivity (BC 597.) It was the prophet Jeremiah, who had been trying with little success to warn these successive kings in Jerusalem of their folly, in not accepting the judgments of God that were to be imposed upon them by the Babylonians. Finally it was the king Zedekiah, who foolishly rebelled against Nebuchadnezzar in spite of Jeremiah's warnings and advice. For breaking his vow to serve Nebuchadnezzar, Zedekiah was made to witness the death of his own sons, then he was blinded and taken to Babylon (which he never saw of course, as Ezekiel had prophesied Ezekiel 12:13, compare Jeremiah 32:4, 34:3,) and he was slain there. This commenced the Desolations (BC 589, the destruction of Jerusalem and removal of captives were completed by 587 and lasted seventy years. Appendix 1 page 146.)

[51] Ezekiel was taken captive with Jehoiachin or Jeconiah (see Ezekiel 1:1 and compare 33:21 *"Our captivity"* and 40:1) and he seems to have been known to *One that escaped out of Jerusalem*, who sought him out. Nevertheless Ezekiel's ministry was to Israel and also to those of Judah in captivity with him (compare Ezekiel 2:2, 3:5 &17 to Israel and 8:1 to Judah.) Jeconiah King of Judah had been himself captive in Babylon for five years with Ezekiel, when Ezekiel's ministry commenced and the prospect for the nation was very poor. As a priest, Ezekiel would have felt the reproach of his nation even more keenly. These were the chosen people of God, yet in their captivity, Israel could offer Him no sacrifices, no offerings. The golden vessels from the temple in Jerusalem were now displayed in a house of idols in Babylon. [Nobody would have escaped from Jerusalem, and crossed the northern Arabian desert (Kedar) to Babylon on his own; he escaped the slaughter in Jerusalem and was taken captive to Babylon with others (effectively, he escaped with his life by being taken captive.)]

[52] Nebuchadnezzar had appointed Zedekiah to rule in Jerusalem, but in his rebellion, against Jeremiah's counsel, Zedekiah lasted only eleven years in office and was eventually taken captive blinded into Babylon, where he was slain as Ezekiel had prophesied (see 2 Kings 25.) It was whilst Ezekiel was among the captives of Israel, by the river Chebar, that he was given the revelations of what was to happen to Judah and Jerusalem and what he was to tell the captives of Judah and Israel.

[53] From the summary of Ezekiel's prophecy (following) it will be seen that broadly speaking the prophecy is concerned with the judgments of God on Israel and Judah for their idolatry (chapters 1 to 35) but, in His mercy, He promised the eventual restoration of the land of Israel (chapter 36) and the revival of the twelve tribes united again as one nation (chapter 37). This is clearly last day prophecy, but one feature of Ezekiel's prophecy with respect to the restored nation Israel is the malice toward Israel of Gog and Magog (chapters 38 and 39,) and God's subsequent judgments on them for their manifest hatred of His people.

The Gog and Magog conflict is definitely last days, Gog is described as *"The chief prince of Meshech and Tubal"* (38:2, 3) and this is considered to be a symbolic, or figurative, name for the nations to the far north and north east of Israel. These nations, with Magog, are the descendants of Japheth (Genesis 10:2) and in Hebrew "the chief prince" is the "head or leader of Rosh, or Ro'sh", which possibly means Russia in modern terms. Gog (either as an individual or representing several nations in a symbolic sense) is responsible for inciting Magog and other nations, to make war on Israel. This tremendous combined force appears to be the climax of the attempts made to utterly destroy Israel in the last days. It is God's Personal intervention, which delivers the nation Israel from these combined forces, altogether a most formidable host against which the nation would stand no chance.

[54] The venom of Gog toward Israel echoes that seen previously, in "the little horn" (of Daniel's Dream and Daniel's Vision) and it is inspired by Satan. The nations involved in conflict against Israel under Gog's influence are Magog, Persia, Ethiopia (Cush), Libya, Gomer and Togarmah (see Ezekiel 38:5, 6 &15) with of course Ro'sh as previously noted. This combination of forces descends from the north to attack Israel (Ezekiel 39:2, see Figure 6) and it is evidently last days (Ezekiel 38:8-13). Special attention here might be drawn to the absolute astonishment displayed by Sheba and Dedan (Arab nations) and the *"merchants of Tarshish"* (having possibly some association with the ten kingdom confederation, since *"merchants"* suggests a trade interest or involvement, which is the feature of the alliance of the ten). Notice that these nations only express their misgivings about the onslaught as a question to Gog (Ezekiel 38:13) but no stronger protest is made. In the light of the overwhelming forces displayed by the Gog assemblage this is perfectly understandable. The scene is frightening, but it is given a completely new dimension by two wonderful scriptures (Ezekiel 38:4) *"And I will turn thee back and put hooks into thy jaws and I will bring thee forth*

and all thine army, horses and horsemen, all of them ...." and (Ezekiel 38:16) *"And thou shalt come up against My people of Israel, as a cloud to cover the land; it shall be in the latter days, and I will bring thee against My land that the heathen may know Me, when I shall be sanctified in thee, O Gog, before their eyes."* These words reveal the fact, that these totally overwhelming odds against the nation Israel; such massive forces, which stun other nations into making lame, verbal protests, are ordained of God Himself. His purpose in allowing such a terrifying event to happen is that He might sanctify Himself in battle on behalf of His nation Israel and thereby bring His judgments on these nations that have incurred His wrath. The really catastrophic consequences of His judgments were revealed (Ezekiel 38:14-23 and 39:1-22) and the resulting slaughter will be terrible in extreme.

[55] Ezekiel's prophecy closes with the revelations given to him of the measurements of the temple of God, which will be set up and also, the instructions for the ordinances of the priests and the division of the land to the Levites and the other tribes of Israel. Ezekiel saw in his visions the restoration of the Temple, The City of Jerusalem and the Land.

A point with respect to Ezekiel's prophecy is that the final onslaught of Satan himself against Jerusalem, after the Millenium reign of the LORD, involves Gog and Magog (See Revelation 20:7-9 [199].) Presumably, or possibly, at that time, Satan himself takes the role of Gog and inspiring the hatred of the nation Magog and any other nations that will join them, Satan himself attempts this last assault, in a terminal desperate effort to overthrow the Kingdom of Christ. The judgment and the total annihilation of this assemblage are from God Himself.

EZEKIEL SUMMARY OF CONTENTS

Chapters	Content
1 – 3	Ezekiel's vision and commission to prophesy
4 - 7	Types given to show judgments of Israel & Jerusalem
8 - 9	Idolatry of Jerusalem and consequent judgment
10	Glory of God taken from His temple, back to His throne
11 – 13	Deceit of princes of Judah, captivity and blindness of Zedekiah prophesied, false prophets and prophetesses rebuked.
14 - 17	Exhortation to repentance. Rejection of Jerusalem
18	God reveals His equity in judgment
19	Lament for the princes of Israel
20	The rebellions of Israel
21 - 22	Prophecy against Jerusalem and Ammonites
23 - 24	Judgment of Samaria and Jerusalem
25	Judgment of Ammonites, Moabites, Edomites and Philistines
26 - 28	Judgment and fall of Tyrus
29 - 30	Judgment of Egypt
31	Greatness and fall of Assyria
32	Lament for fall of Egypt
33	The justice and ways of God revealed
34	Judgments of shepherds of Israel. Promise of

	ultimate restoration under "My servant David"
35	Judgment of Seir
36	Promise of restoration of land of Israel
37	In resurrection of dry bones is revealed the revival of Israel (united with Judah) as a nation
38 - 39	Judgment of God against Gog and Magog for their malice and war against Israel
40 - 43	Measurements of the temple revealed and the return of God's glory to His house
44 - 46	Ordinances of priests given. Division of land for Levites
47 - 48	The issue of waters from the house of the Lord. Division of the land of Israel to the twelve tribes.

Chapter 7: HAGGAI & ZECHARIAH

[57] The captivity of Israel and Judah, as a result of their idolatry, eventually had to end as prophesied and the scriptural time, which marked the commencement of their restoration, was the day on which the foundation of the temple in Jerusalem was laid (see Appendix 1.) The surprising thing is that whilst the decree to rebuild Jerusalem and the temple was given by command of a Persian King (Cyrus - Ezra 1:1-4,) and an attempt was made to obey it, the foundation of the temple itself was not laid (Ezra 3:3-6.) What was accomplished (Ezra 3:8-13) was not a fulfilment of the prophecy, neither would it have satisfied the command of Cyrus. The reason for such failure was merely pathetic local opposition to those attempting to build in Jerusalem. That such petty efforts could alter the direct order of a Persian King was truly amazing and the only conclusion possible is that the work was frustrated for some divine purpose. It has been proved that the actual time of taken for the fulfilment of the prophecy (concerning the Seventy Weeks - see Daniel's Supplications, Chapter 4 and Appendix 1) exactly corresponds to the scriptural times and dates involved and this extends in every respect even to the date of the cross.

Accepting therefore, that the frustration of the early workers was in accord with the divine will, it must follow that later attempts to finish the work would need some encouragement and inspiration, to provoke the discouraged people of Israel to resume their work to restore the temple and Jerusalem. Scripturally the accounts, of what was involved in commencing the work of restoration, are recorded in Ezra and Nehemiah. The prophets Haggai and Zechariah were particularly inspired in their prophetic ministries to those Jews, who had returned from the captivity to do the work and who had been previously prevented. These two prophets rekindled the people's zeal to work and accomplish the declared will of God to His timetable (Ezra 4:23-5:2).

[58] Haggai

Haggai's prophecy concerns itself particularly with the rebuilding of the temple and is of great value since it provides the exact date historically on which the foundation was laid; but it has no evident last day applications and therefore its closer examination is beyond the scope of these considerations.

Haggai 2:10-19 *In the four and twentieth day of the ninth month, in the second year of Darius, came the word of the LORD by Haggai the prophet, saying, 'Thus saith the LORD of hosts; Ask now the priests concerning the law, saying, If one bear holy flesh in the skirt of his garment, and with his skirt do touch bread, or pottage, or wine, or oil, or any meat, shall it be holy?' And the priests answered and said, 'No'. Then said Haggai, 'If one that is unclean by a dead body touch any of these, shall it be unclean?' And the priests answered and said, 'It shall be unclean.' Then answered Haggai, and said, 'So is this people, and so is this nation before Me, saith the LORD; and so is every work of their hands; and that which they offer there is unclean. And now, I pray you, consider from this day and upward, from before a stone was laid upon a stone in the temple of the LORD: since those days were, when one came to an heap of twenty measures, there were but ten: when one came to the pressfat for to draw out fifty vessels out of the press, there were but twenty. I smote you with blasting and with mildew and with hail in all the labours of your hands; yet ye turned not to Me, saith the LORD. Consider now from this day and upward,* **from the four and twentieth day of the ninth month, even from the day that the foundation of the LORD's temple was laid,** *consider it. Is the seed yet in the barn? Yea, as yet the vine,* *and the fig tree, and the pomegranate, and the olive tree, hath not brought forth: from this day will I bless you.'*

[59] Zechariah

Zechariah's prophecy is also concerned with the time of the restoration work and the fulfilment of certain aspects of his prophecy is admittedly now a matter of history. But his prophecy extends well beyond the restoration of Jerusalem after the Babylonian captivity and in fact, reaches to the LORD's earthly ministry and beyond, even to His triumphant return in the last days. For this reason it is examined briefly here (a summary of the whole prophecy is given later [63]).

Attention might be drawn initially to references that evidently apply to the LORD's experience. (9:9). *Rejoice greatly, O daughter of Zion; shout, O daughter of Jerusalem: behold, thy King cometh unto thee: He is just, and having salvation; lowly, and riding upon an ass, and upon a colt the foal of an ass.* (11:12) *And I said unto them, If ye think good, give me my price; and if not, forbear. So they weighed for my price thirty pieces of silver.* There are some prophecies, which are not yet fulfilled (e.g.12:10) *And I will pour upon the house of David, and upon the inhabitants of Jerusalem, the spirit of grace and of supplications: and they shall look upon me whom they have pierced, and they shall mourn for him, as one mourneth for his only son, and shall be in bitterness for him, as one that is in bitterness for his firstborn.*

[60] Mention must also be made of the mysterious *IDOL SHEPHERD*.

(11:17) *Woe to the idol shepherd that leaveth the flock! The sword shall be upon his arm, and upon his right eye: his arm shall be clean dried up, and his right eye shall be utterly darkened.* The *idol shepherd* is a character in total contrast to the LORD, The Good

Shepherd. From his name, this character demands the idolatrous worship of his flock and (in the context of the prophecy) deserts them. Severe as his judgment appears, it is not absolutely final and the idol shepherd goes on living with his very distinctive wounds. The fulfilment of this prophecy, as a last day eventuality and applying to the beast himself, will be an outstanding vindication of scriptural truth.

[61] Some of Zechariah's prophecy is very difficult to understand and possible applications are suggested in these considerations. However it is quite likely, that certain aspects of this prophecy will make no real sense, until their actual fulfilment in Israel's experience of the last days. (In this respect, for example compare Genesis 49.)

In such cases all that might be admitted is that at least we recognise and acknowledge that the prophecies have last day significance and it would be foolish to attempt bizarre or wild speculation in a vain effort to explain everything. As the LORD Himself showed His disciples (Acts 1:7,) there are limits to the extent of our knowledge of the divine plan. Odd verses are obviously very significant but difficult to apply with certainty; for example Zechariah 13:8 *And it shall come to pass (that) in all the land, saith the LORD, two parts therein shall be cut off (and) die; but the third shall be left therein.* This verse is in the context of *Awake, O sword, against my shepherd* (compare also 11:8). We have to accept that such prophecies will be very meaningful and relevant (especially to the Jews) at the time of their ultimate fulfilment.

[62] The concluding chapter of Zechariah is evidently last days from its opening words:

(14:1-3) *Behold, the day of the LORD cometh, and thy spoil shall be divided in the midst of thee. For I will gather all nations against Jerusalem to battle; and the city shall be taken, and the houses rifled,* and the women ravished; and half of the city shall go forth into captivity, and the residue of the people shall not be cut off from the city. Then shall the LORD go forth, and fight against those nations, as when He fought in the day of battle.

(14:4-11) And His feet shall stand in that day upon the mount of Olives, which is before Jerusalem on the east, and the mount of Olives shall cleave in the midst thereof toward the east and toward the west, and there shall be a very great valley; and half of the mountain shall remove toward the north, and half of it toward the south. And ye shall flee to the valley of the mountains; for the valley of the mountains shall reach unto Azal: yea, ye shall flee, like as ye fled from before the earthquake in the days of Uzziah king of Judah: and the LORD my God shall come, and all the saints with Thee. And it shall come to pass in that day, that the light shall not be clear, nor dark: but it shall be one day which shall be known to the LORD, not day, nor night: but it shall come to pass, that at evening time it shall be light. And it shall be in that day, that living waters shall go out from Jerusalem; half of them toward the former sea, and half of them toward the hinder sea: in summer and in winter shall it be. And the LORD shall be king over all the earth: in that day shall there be one Lord, and His name one. All the land shall be turned as a plain from Geba to Rimmon south of Jerusalem: and it shall be lifted up, and inhabited in her place, from Benjamin's gate unto the place of the first gate, unto the corner gate, and from the tower of Hananeel unto the king's winepresses. And men shall dwell in it, and there shall be no more utter destruction; but Jerusalem shall be safely inhabited.

(14:12-15) And this shall be the plague wherewith the LORD will smite all the people that have fought against Jerusalem; Their flesh shall consume away while they stand upon their feet, and their eyes shall consume away in their holes, and their tongue shall consume away in their mouth. And it shall come to pass in that day, that a great tumult from the LORD shall be among them; and they shall lay hold every one on the hand of his neighbour, and his hand shall rise up against the hand of his neighbour. And Judah also shall fight at Jerusalem;

and the wealth of all the heathen round about shall be gathered together, gold, and silver, and apparel, in great abundance. And so shall be the plague of the horse, of the mule, of the camel, and of the ass, and of all the beasts that shall be in these tents, as this plague.

The consumption of the flesh of these enemies, *while they stand on their feet, and their eyes shall consume away in their holes and their tongue shall consume away in their mouth* horrors such as this, point to something like an atomic heat blast, totally awesome in its devastating effect.

(14:16-19) *And it shall come to pass, that every one that is left of all the nations which came against Jerusalem shall even go up from year to year to worship the King, the LORD of hosts, and to keep the feast of tabernacles. And it shall be, that whoso will not come up of all the families of the earth unto Jerusalem to worship the King, the LORD of hosts, even upon them shall be no rain. And if the family of Egypt go not up, and come not, that have no rain; there shall be the plague, wherewith the Lord will smite the heathen that come not up to keep the feast of tabernacles. This shall be the punishment of Egypt, and the punishment of all nations that come not up to keep the feast of tabernacles.*

(14:20, 21) *In that day shall there be upon the bells of the horses, HOLINESS UNTO THE LORD; and the pots in the LORD's house shall be like the bowls before the altar. Yea, every pot in Jerusalem and in Judah shall be holiness unto the LORD of hosts: and all they that sacrifice shall come and take of them, and seethe therein: and in that day there shall be no more the Canaanite in the house of the LORD of hosts.*

[63] ZECHARIAH SUMMARY OF CONTENTS

Chapters	Contents
1: 1-6	Exhortation to return to the Lord for blessing
1: 7-11	Date of vision. Vision of horses
1: 12-17	Words of comfort and hope for Jerusalem and Judah
1 : 18-21	Four horns and four carpenters, signifying the end of gentile oppression
2: 1-5	God's care for Jerusalem revealed
2: 6-9	Redemption of Zion i.e. the godly in Israel
2: 10-13	In restoration of Zion and Lord's dwelling with them, His blessing extends to other nations
3: 1-10	Joshua as High Priest of Israel (how can anyone read the church into this?) is cleansed of unrighteousness in the presence of the Lord; he is commissioned to walk with men of God and given the promise of THE BRANCH
4: 1-14	The success of Zerubbabel assured. The two anointed ones (compare Revelation 11: 3-12 [151][153])
5: 5-11	Vision of ephah (a measure equivalent to about 7.5 gallons) closed with lead cover, which Is taken by two winged women to Shinar *"to build it an house .... it shall be established .... and set there upon her own base."* Typically this represents the removal of idolatry from Israel to establish it in Shinar, the province of Babylon in which the tower of Babel, the foundation of idolatry, was built. In the last days idolatry is brought to its fulness and finally judged in its place of origin (see Revelation 17, 18 [184][190]).

	The beast himself represents and personifies the ultimate in idolatrous worship.
6: 1-8	Vision of four chariots (compare Revelation 6:2-8 [130][133])
6: 9-15	Explaining THE BRANCH (above) and it is Joshua the High Priest in Jerusalem at the time of Zechariah's prophecy. [The Branch of Isaiah's prophecy (Is 11:1) does refer to the LORD, but this does not warrant drawing the same conclusion in Zechariah's prophecy, which leads to confusion, Zechariah has revealed who The Branch is.]
7: 1-14	The LORD's answer to those who enquire concerning fasting
8: 1-22	Promises of the restoration of Jerusalem
9: 9-11	Blessing of Zion. A famous prophecy fulfilled by the LORD as He entered Jerusalem on an ass
9: 12-17	Blessing promised on Israel
10: 1-12	Exhortation to seek the LORD not idols. Restoration
10: 13-17	Judgment. Breaking bond of Judah and Israel and shepherds
11: 1-17	Slaughter of the sheep. The Idol Shepherd (see Ezekiel 34)
12: 1-14	Judgment of Jerusalem
13: 1-9	Judgment, cutting off idols and false prophets. Promise of deliverance to one third of inhabitants
14: 1-3	The Day of The LORD. Destruction of nations gathered together against Jerusalem

14: 4-11	LORD's coming to Mount Olives (the consequences of this are worth considering with suitable map.) (Compare 14:8 with Ezekiel 47:1-12)
14: 12-15	Destruction of nations in more detail
14: 16-19	Nations warned in last days to turn to LORD or face judgment
14: 20, 21	All the vessels of the LORD in Jerusalem shall be holy.

Chapter 8: NEW TESTAMENT TEACHINGS

[64] The Old Testament considerations have shown that the last days' prophecies concern the nation Israel and reveal the terrible persecution of that nation as a direct result of the antagonism of the beast. This is the tribulation from which their Messiah, the LORD Jesus Christ, on His return delivers the nation, when He comes to establish His kingdom (see Chapter 17.)

The Church was a complete mystery to the Old Testament prophets (although it was prophesied clearly that gentiles would be blessed see Genesis 12:3, 18:18 etc) and the Church remained totally hidden in the plan of God, until it was revealed by Paul. If this were not true, it would mean that Israel had had no choice, but were destined to reject the LORD when He came, because it would have been previously revealed (and therefore ordained) that God had a place for the Church. The Jewish choice was entirely free and they could have accepted the LORD Himself. This would not have cancelled the Old Testament prophecies concerning the last days; it would have brought their fulfilment to fruition almost immediately after the LORD's death on the cross. (Scripturally *the Church* means those believers considered to be members of the Body of the LORD Jesus Christ and the *True Church* must be distinguished from any nominal Christian church, or religious orders.) It is highly likely that every Christian denomination contains members of His Church!

The Jewish rejection of the LORD was inspired by their spiritual leaders at that time; but in the foreknowledge of God, the Jewish rejection of His Son justifiably enabled Him to offer salvation to the gentiles for that indeterminate period of His grace known as *the times of the gentiles*. For this period, blindness in part has happened to Israel as a nation and this is the teaching of Paul's epistle to Rome (see especially Romans 11). Paul as the apostle to the gentiles could claim total authority for his teachings.

This dispensation, this time of the gentiles, *will come to an end*. Not abruptly, this never happens with the dispensations of God, there is an overlapping, a transitional period as one dispensation ends and the next begins. This will become apparent as the scriptures are considered, but the point is made that the testimony or witness to GOD (now given to His Church,) will be given back to the Jewish nation in the last days.

The New Testament teachings on the last days are excellent, which would be expected *from* the apostle John (The Revelation), *from* the apostles Paul and Peter, and most especially *from* the LORD Jesus Christ Himself. So many believers fail to appreciate what is involved, because the Church is blatantly inserted (in chapter headings or titles across the pages of the Bible) when the scriptural references are so plainly referring to Israel or Judah, with no regard for the Old Testament foundational prophecies and no consideration for the unique position that the nation Israel holds in the will of God. Even more astonishing, is their ignoring the truth that the Church was never mentioned in the Old Testament (in which the concerns are the nations; Israel and Judah.)

[65] The definite Jewish involvement in the last days is accepted and these New Testament prophecies are considered with no attempt to include the Church to suit any school of thought. The Church does have a part and place in the plan of God, as will be shown, but it will surprise many to learn that the teachings of The LORD Himself do not clearly include the Church in the last day eventualities, quite simply because the Church is not involved in most of them.

Some of the doctrines taught in the past have been too patriotic or too prejudiced in their basic conceptions to accept the simple truth revealed in the New Testament. In some doctrines, attempts to scripturally prove a favourite idea or theme, the wildest applications have been made of prophecies, with no regard at all for the Old Testament foundation. Even today, these doctrines of men colour a great deal of thought on the last days; as a consequence of which, many believers fear the very idea of the LORD's coming, when for the Church, the New Testament teachings are quite plain in confirming that His coming for the Church is a matter for great rejoicing.

[66] In their New Testament order, the teachings of the LORD Himself, of the apostle Paul and of the apostle John (The Revelation) are to be considered in turn. In general terms however, it might be remarked concerning each of these:

The Teachings of the LORD Jesus Christ Himself

The LORD's discourses on the last days are found in the gospels, Matthew, Mark and Luke, these are distinguished from John's gospel which presents the Divine Son of God. John's gospel contains no teachings on the last days, but John was given The Revelation. (The LORD's Own teachings are found in Matthew 23:1-25:46, Mark 13:1-37, Luke 17:20-37 and 21:5-38.) The various accounts of the LORD's teachings show (1) He discussed these things with His disciples on several occasions (the two accounts in Luke prove this.) (2) Records of the same discourse (e.g. Mark 13 and Luke 21) give different views, which broaden or enlarge the whole picture, in the same way that several witnesses to an incident can enable experts to reconstruct the whole affair with greater accuracy. Why are the various scriptures speaking of the same thing inevitably branded - contradictory? In truth they are always complementary.

The Teachings of the Apostle Paul

These are found mainly in his epistles to Thessalonians and Timothy and are superb in their content and expression as will be seen.

The Revelation of the Apostle John

The Revelation given to John eclipses even Daniel's prophecy and it should be seen as a wonderful evidence of the love the LORD had for John, the disciple who loved the LORD and listened to His every word. There was no need for John to write anything in his gospel about the last days; it was all included in The Revelation. It is noted however, that nobody can look at John on Patmos and imagine that the true Church is exempt from suffering tribulation even martyrdom at times, for the LORD Jesus Christ. (A truth also made evident in the experiences of Paul and others.) But to teach that the true Church will go through the agonies of the great tribulation of the Jewish nation (which is their judgment as a nation, for their rejection of the Messiah, the Christ,) when the Church has by its very existence proved its acceptance of Him is not in accord with the teachings of the New Testament.

But let us proceed to examine these teachings and prove these truths scripturally

The LORD's Teachings in MATTHEW

[67] (23:1-12) *Then spake Jesus to the multitude, and to His disciples, saying, "The scribes and the Pharisees sit in Moses' seat: all therefore whatsoever they bid you observe, that observe and do; but do not ye after their works: for they say, and do not. For they bind heavy burdens and grievous to be borne, and lay them on men's shoulders; but they themselves will not move them with one of their fingers. But all their works they do for to be seen of men: they make broad their phylacteries, and enlarge the borders of their garments, and love the uppermost rooms at feasts, and the chief seats in the synagogues, and greetings in the markets, and to be called of men, 'Rabbi, Rabbi.' But be not ye called Rabbi: for one is your Master, even Christ; and all ye are brethren. And call no man your father upon the earth: for one*

is your Father, Which is in heaven. Neither be ye called masters: for one is your Master, even Christ. But he that is greatest among you shall be your servant. And whosoever shall exalt himself shall be abased; and he that shall humble himself shall be exalted.

(23:13-33) But woe unto you, scribes and Pharisees, hypocrites! For ye shut up the kingdom of heaven against men: for ye neither go in yourselves, neither suffer ye them that are entering to go in. Woe unto you, scribes and Pharisees, hypocrites! For ye compass sea and land to make one proselyte, and when he is made, ye make him twofold more the child of hell than yourselves. Woe unto you, ye blind guides, which say, 'Whosoever shall swear by the temple, it is nothing; but whosoever shall swear by the gold of the temple, he is a debtor!' Ye fools and blind: for whether is greater, the gold, or the temple that sanctifieth the gold? And, 'Whosoever shall swear by the altar, it is nothing; but whosoever sweareth by the gift that is upon it, he is guilty.' Ye fools and blind: for whether is greater, the gift, or the altar that sanctifieth the gift? Whosoever therefore shall swear by the altar, sweareth by it, and by all things thereon. And whoso shall swear by the temple, sweareth by it, and by Him that dwelleth therein. And he that shall swear by heaven, sweareth by the throne of God, and by Him that sitteth thereon. Woe unto you, scribes and Pharisees, hypocrites! For ye pay tithe of mint and anise and cummin, and have omitted the weightier matters of the law, judgment, mercy, and faith: these ought ye to have done, and not to leave the other undone. Ye blind guides, which strain at a gnat, and swallow a camel. Woe unto you, scribes and Pharisees, hypocrites! For ye make clean the outside of the cup and of the platter, but within they are full of extortion and excess. Thou blind Pharisee, cleanse first that which is within the cup and platter, that the outside of them may be clean also. Woe unto you, scribes and Pharisees, hypocrites! For ye are like unto whited sepulchres, which indeed appear beautiful outward, but are within full of dead men's bones, and of all uncleanness. Even so ye also outwardly appear righteous unto men, but within ye are full of hypocrisy and iniquity. Woe unto you, scribes and Pharisees, hypocrites! Because ye build the tombs of the prophets, and garnish the sepulchres of the righteous, and say, 'If we had been in the days of our fathers, we would not have been partakers with them in the blood of the prophets.' Wherefore ye be witnesses unto yourselves, that ye are the children of them which killed the prophets. Fill ye up then the measure of your fathers. Ye serpents, ye generation of vipers, how can ye escape the damnation of hell?

(23:34-39) Wherefore, behold, I send unto you prophets, and wise men, and scribes: and some of them ye shall kill and crucify; and some of them shall ye scourge in your synagogues, and persecute them from city to city: that upon you may come all the righteous blood shed upon the earth, from the blood of righteous Abel unto the blood of Zacharias son of Barachias, whom ye slew between the temple and the altar. Verily I say unto you, All these things shall come upon this generation. O Jerusalem, Jerusalem, thou that killest the prophets, and stonest them which are sent unto thee, how often would I have gathered thy children together, even as a hen gathereth her chickens under her wings, and ye would not! Behold your house is left unto you desolate. For I say unto you, Ye shall not see Me henceforth, till ye shall say, 'Blessed is he that cometh in the name of the LORD.'"

(23) The LORD's outright castigation of the scribes and Pharisees shows that He was under no illusions Himself, regarding the effect of their doctrines and influence on His people. In the woes, that He pronounced, He was warning, not only the scribes and Pharisees, but that generation of the devastating consequences of their rejection of Him.

[68] (24:1, 2) *And Jesus went out, and departed from the temple: and His disciples came to Him for to shew Him the buildings of the temple. And Jesus said unto them,* "See ye not all these things? Verily I say unto you, There shall not be left here one stone upon another, that shall not be thrown down."

Turning His back on the temple (24:1) the LORD departed, a most solemn occasion. His disciples, perhaps in an attempt to persuade Him not to leave the temple and all it represented to their nation, sought to impress Him with the glory of the place, the magnificence of the building itself and the impressive, colossal stones. The LORD's reply to this (24:2) was prophetic and He extended the desolation of the people as a nation, to the temple itself, its utter destruction was a certainty and His prophecy was fulfilled to the letter, not one stone was left upon another!

(24:3-28) *And as He sat upon the mount of Olives, the disciples came unto Him privately, saying, "Tell us, when shall these things be? And what shall be the sign of Thy coming, and of the end of the world?" And Jesus answered and said unto them, "Take heed that no man deceive you. For many shall come in My name, saying, 'I am Christ'; and shall deceive many. And ye shall hear of wars and rumours of wars: see that ye be not troubled: for all these things must come to pass, but the end is not yet. For nation shall rise against nation, and kingdom against kingdom: and there shall be famines, and pestilences, and earthquakes, in divers places. All these are the beginning of sorrows. Then shall they deliver you up to be afflicted, and shall kill you and ye shall be hated of all nations for My name's sake. And then shall many be offended, and shall betray one another, and shall hate one another. And many false prophets shall rise, and shall deceive many. And because iniquity shall abound, the love of many shall wax cold. But he that shall endure unto the end, the same shall be saved. And this gospel of the kingdom shall be preached in all the world for a witness unto all nations; and then shall the end come. When ye therefore shall see the abomination of desolation, spoken of by Daniel the prophet, stand in the holy place,(whoso readeth, let him understand:) then let them which be in Judea flee into the mountains: let him which is on the housetop not come down to take any thing out of his house: neither let him which is in the field return back to take his clothes. And woe unto them that are with child, and to them that give suck in those days! But pray ye that your flight be not in the winter, neither on the sabbath day: for then shall be great tribulation, such as was not since the beginning of the world to this time, no, nor ever shall be. And except those days should be shortened, there should no flesh be saved: but for the elect's sake those days shall be shortened. Then if any man shall say unto you, 'Lo, here is Christ, or there'; believe it not. For there shall arise false Christs, and false prophets, and shall shew great signs and wonders; insomuch that, if it were possible, they shall deceive the very elect. Behold, I have told you before. Wherefore if they shall say unto you, 'Behold, He is in the desert'; go not forth: 'Behold, He is in the secret chambers'; believe it not. For as the lightning cometh out of the east, and shineth even unto the west; so shall also the coming of the Son of man be. For wheresoever the carcase is, there will the eagles be gathered together.*

In private, on the Mount of Olives, the disciples approached the LORD to ask Him about these things;

note their two part question: (24:3) *When shall these things be?*

What shall be the sign of Thy coming, and of the end of the world?

Regarding the first part of their question, this must refer in context, to the destruction of the temple; but the LORD had already spoken of this as a future event and He expanded no further, for it was not relevant to the other question posed.

The disciples had asked the LORD for THE sign (singular) of the LORD's coming and of the end of the world; in this context consider His reply (24:4, 5 *And Jesus answered... ...deceive many*) A clear warning concerning false Christs! This reference to the imposters of Christ (The Messiah) has relevance to the Jews of the last days. The true Church has already accepted Him and these last day deceivers would have no effect on anyone knowing the LORD in the way that His true Church does. The purpose of these impostors is to deceive the Jews, who will be desperately looking for Messiah to come and establish His kingdom on earth.[25]

24: 6 Wars and rumours of wars (how futile the LORD's teachings make the efforts of those seeking peace, there will be no peace on earth until He rules).

24: 7 Conflict of nations and kingdoms, famines, pestilences and earthquakes in different places.

24: 8 "*All of these* (i.e. all these things together) *are the beginning of sorrows*" (pangs/travail as the agonies of childbearing, in His choice of words, the LORD has revealed that all these things, like the pangs of birth, shall increase in frequency and in intensity as the time approaches.)

24: 9 Persecution of all nations *for My name's sake.* The only name mentioned in context is CHRIST, which in the light of the appearances of the false Christs now has international significance in the last days. All nations are involved against His nation. Nations have not so far combined together to persecute the Church in this way, for believing on The LORD Jesus Christ.

This international antagonism towards the Jews is for their acceptance of their Messiah and their rejection of the one universally accepted at that time i.e. the beast, who is seeking to establish himself as god.

---

[25] As already noted, (paragraph [64]) the transition from one dispensation to another is never abrupt but overlapping and the appearance of False Christs must be seen in this light. Primarily the False Christs are intended to deceive Israel, as the nation is being re-established as His witnesses on earth. But even now it is evident in current events that False Christs are leading Christians astray with horrendous consequences in some cases. Astonishingly it seems that relatively affluent people are deceived and attracted by what appears to be enlightened teaching, they throw their all into discipleship for these "Messiah" figures, totally ignoring the scriptural truths about the LORD's return. Scripturally the LORD's return is not a simple, single event. His return for His church totally removes His followers from the earth; and His return for His earthly people Israel, necessarily involves several appearances/events. BUT when He comes, He will be unmistakable and nobody will have any doubts about His authenticity, such will be the Glory that surrounds Him. Any and every earthly figure claiming to be The Christ can be safely ignored – the power and the glory will be evident to all involved whenever He comes or appears (see also paragraph [233 & 234] and Chapter 17.)

24: 10 Offence, betrayal and hatred (this is among the Jews).

24: 11 False prophets deceive many (are these to deceive the church, who have accepted Him by faith?).

24: 12 Iniquity abounding causes many to lose their love for Christ (compare this with the little horn prevailing against the saints, Daniel 7: 24-28 [23].)

24: 13 The endurance necessary to obtain salvation in those days.

24: 14 The Kingdom Gospel (not the Gospel of Grace as preached to the gentiles) as preached by John the Baptist and the Lord Himself, to be preached again worldwide to herald the establishment of His kingdom (of what value is this ministry to His church, which as His body occupies a better, heavenly place with Him?) [The scriptural Gospels are explained in Appendix 5.]

24: 15 *The abomination of desolation* seen standing in the holy place. This can only have significance to the Jews since it applies to Jerusalem.

24: 16-20 *Then let them which be in Judea flee....* etc. a strong warning, but obviously applicable to Jews *in Judea* at the time of these eventualities.

24: 21, 22 *Great tribulation* - in fact, the greatest. Nothing has ever been seen like this before and nothing like it shall ever be seen again. Such words, in the light of the horrific, historical facts already known of the sufferings of the Jews, are terrible to contemplate. It is no wonder that the time is shortened for the elect's sake (the Jews again, see following.)

24: 23-28 Attempts to persuade the elect that their Messiah (confirming the elect are the Jews) has appeared, are to be ignored. The emphasis is that the elect are not to go looking for Him (the Christ) for He will come for them. (The true Church is not looking for The Christ, the Church has accepted Him.)

(24:29-35) *Immediately after the tribulation of those days shall the sun be darkened, and the moon shall not give her light, and the stars shall fall from heaven, and the powers of the heavens shall be shaken: and then shall appear the sign of the Son of man in heaven: and then shall all the tribes of the earth mourn, and they shall see the Son of man coming in the clouds of heaven with power and great glory. And He shall send His angels with a great sound of a trumpet, and they shall gather together His elect from the four winds, from one end of heaven to the other. Now learn a parable of the fig tree; When his branch is yet tender, and putteth forth leaves, ye know that summer is nigh: so likewise ye, when ye shall see all these things, know that it is near, even at the doors. Verily I say unto you, This generation shall not pass, till all these things be fulfilled. Heaven and earth shall pass away, but My words shall not pass away.*

24:29 Darkness and heavenly catastrophes. The *stars shall fall from heaven* this has always been ridiculed scientifically, as too preposterous to be taken literally. But now, man-made satellites fit the picture perfectly, which shows the accuracy of the LORD's prophecies. The consternation that the destruction of the satellites would cause can be imagined - the immediate loss of worldwide

communication facilities and especially the loss of vital strategic data would create panic. There is far more involved in the LORD's words however and the fulfilment of this prophecy is well beyond our imaginations.

24:30 The *sign* of the Son of man appears in heaven, all the earth shall mourn. The disciples' request for *the sign* of the LORD's coming has been answered. *The sign* appears at His coming in the heavens - and it is, *His coming in the clouds.* This was also the sign given to His disciples, by the angels, as they watched Him ascend. Acts1:9-11 *And when He had spoken these things, while they beheld, He was taken up; and a cloud received Him out of their sight. And while they looked stedfastly toward heaven as He went up, behold, two men stood by them in white apparel; which also said, "Ye men of Galilee, why stand* ye gazing up into heaven? This same Jesus, Which is taken up from you into heaven, SHALL SO COME IN LIKE MANNER AS YE HAVE SEEN HIM GO INTO HEAVEN."

24: 31 The angels are sent to gather His elect from the four corners of the earth, whence they have

been scattered in the awful persecution at the time. (The Tribulation has finished for the Jews at this point, but the world now faces the wrath of the Lamb of God. See Revelation 14: 14-20 [175].)

24: 32, 33 Parable of the fig tree (Israel in typology.)

24: 34, 35 *This generation shall not pass till all these things be fulfilled....* etc. This text is taken by some to mean that particular age group contemporary with the LORD. But the word used implies a "line of descent" or "line of generations" such as the line of Israel. Since the LORD is replying to a question on the last days, this seems a more sensible interpretation of the word i.e. that the line of Israel, or the Jewish nation, which shall not pass away until all these things are fulfilled (compare Daniel 7:18 &27 and Malachi 3:6.)

(24:36-51) *But of that day and hour knoweth no man, no, not the angels of heaven, but My Father only.* (These words of the LORD make every date offered for the end of the world total nonsense.) *But as the days of Noe were, so shall also the coming of the Son of man be. For as in the days that were before the flood they were eating and drinking, marrying and giving in marriage, until the day that Noe entered into the ark, and knew not until the flood came, and took them all away; so shall also the coming of the Son of man be. Then shall two be in the field; the one shall be taken, and the other left. Two women shall be grinding at the mill; the one shall be taken, and the other left. Watch therefore: for ye know not what hour your Lord doth come. But know this, that if the goodman of the house had known in what watch the thief would come, he would have watched, and would not have suffered his house to be broken up. Therefore be ye also ready: for in such an hour as ye think not the Son of man cometh. Who then is a faithful and wise servant, whom his lord hath made ruler over his household, to give them meat in due season? Blessed is that servant, whom his lord when he cometh shall find so doing. Verily I say unto you, that he shall make him ruler over all his goods. But and if that evil servant shall say in his heart, 'My lord delayeth his coming'; and shall begin to smite his fellowservants, and to eat and drink with the drunken; the lord of that servant shall come in a day when he looketh not for him, and in an hour that he is not aware of, and shall cut him asunder, and appoint him his portion with the hypocrites: there shall be weeping and gnashing of teeth.*

24:36-51 The LORD revealed the general oblivion of the world to the impending judgments of God (compare Daniel 12:10 *None of the wicked shall understand.*) The LORD exhorts the Jews, who still believe, to watch continually for His coming in the last days. This is very important, as evidenced and emphasised by His following teachings. A lesson on the remorse of those, who fail to watch for Him. (This theme of watchfulness carries on into His parable teachings on the ten virgins and the talents, which are examined next.)

[69] (25:1-13) *Then shall the kingdom of heaven be likened unto ten virgins, which took their lamps, and went forth to meet the bridegroom. And five of them were wise, and five were foolish. They that were foolish took their lamps, and took no oil with them: but the wise took oil in their vessels with their lamps. Whilst the bridegroom tarried, they all slumbered and slept. And at midnight there was a cry made, 'Behold, the bridegroom cometh; go ye out to meet him.' Then all those virgins arose, and trimmed their lamps. And the foolish said unto the wise, 'Give us of your oil; for our lamps are gone out.' But the wise answered, saying, 'Not so, lest there be not enough for us and you: but go ye rather to them that sell, and buy for yourselves.' And while they went to buy, the bridegroom came; and they that were ready went in with him to the marriage: and the door was shut.*

Afterward came also the other virgins, saying, 'Lord, Lord, open to us.' But he answered and said, 'Verily I say unto you, I know you not.' Watch therefore, for ye know neither the day nor the hour wherein the Son of man cometh. 25: 1-13 The parable of the ten virgins. This involves two separate issues: firstly, the custom in the East is to "go to meet" honoured guests or visitors and escort them to their destination. [Scripture affords many examples of this: Genesis14:17, Numbers 22:36, Judges 11:34, 1 Samuel 18:6 & 25:20, 2 Samuel 10:5, 2 Kings 2:15, John 12:13, Acts 28:15.] Secondly, when the bridegroom comes, always on the night of the wedding, in procession to receive his bride and take her to his home; the rites of hospitality demand that her friends (the virgins) and relations go out to meet him, to conduct him to her house. By ancient regulation however, no one is allowed to go out at night without carrying a light, in the case of women a small oil lamp, the men carry torches (fire brands.) Nobody without a light, or coming late, would ever be admitted to the celebrations in the bride's house after the welcoming procession, no excuses are accepted. Who do the virgins represent? Only the friends of the bride, therefore they cannot be His body, (the Church,) or the Jews, (His bride.) At the time this parable will apply, in the last days, it is suggested therefore that the virgins are the proselytes, converts to Judaism, or more broadly, friends of the bride, those who support the Jews in those awful times. The oil, in respect of the illumination they have, or the anointing, could be applied to the Holy Spirit, Whose comfort and power will be desperately needed in those times. It should be emphasised that the LORD's promise of the Holy Spirit was to the Jews primarily (John 14:16-18, 26) and Peter confirmed this on the day of Pentecost (Acts 2:39.) To suggest that the Holy Spirit is removed from the earth, when the Church is raptured, is absurd. This idea stems from attempts to insert The Holy Spirit quite unnecessarily and wrongly, into Paul's teachings (see [96-101] 2 Thessalonians 2.)

(25:14-30) *For the kingdom of heaven is as a man travelling into a far country, who called his own servants, and delivered unto them his goods. And unto one he gave five talents, and to another two, and to another one; to every man according to his several ability; and straightway took his journey. Then he that had received the five talents went and traded with the same, and made them other five talents. And likewise he that had received two, he also gained other two. But he that had received one went and digged in the earth, and hid his lord's money. After a long time the lord of those servants cometh, and reckoneth with them. And so he that had received five talents came and brought other five talents, saying, 'Lord, thou deliveredst unto me five talents: behold, I have gained beside them five talents more.' His lord said unto him, 'Well done, thou good and faithful servant; thou hast been faithful over a few things, I will make thee ruler over many things: enter thou into the joy of thy lord'. He also that had received two talents came and said, 'Lord, thou deliveredst unto me two talents: behold, I have gained two other talents beside them.' His lord said unto him, 'Well done, good and faithful servant; thou hast been faithful over a few things, I will make thee ruler over many things: enter thou into the joy of thy lord.' Then he which had received the one talent came and said, 'Lord, I knew thee that thou art an hard man, reaping where thou hast not sown, and gathering where thou hast not strawed: and I was afraid, and went and hid thy talent in the earth: lo, there thou hast that is thine.' His lord answered and said unto him, 'Thou wicked and slothful servant, thou knewest that I reap where I sowed not, and gather where I have not strawed: thou oughtest therefore to have put my money to the exchangers, and then at my coming I should have received mine own with usury. Take therefore the talent from him, and give it unto him which hath ten talents. For unto every one that hath shall be given, and he shall have abundance; but from him that hath not shall be taken away even that which he hath.*

And cast ye the unprofitable servant into outer darkness: there shall be weeping and gnashing of teeth'

25:14-30 The parable of the talents, which underlines the lessons iven in the parable of the virgins. During His absence and when He comes, the LORD expects faithfulness. (Teachings that imply we should use our fleshly *talents* in the LORD's service are plain sickening; the talent was a weight measure, equivalent to about eighty pounds.) The LORD wants faith in terms of good stewardship not fleshly abilities and the parable is intended for the Jews in the last days.

(25:31-46) *When the Son of man shall come in His glory, and all the holy angels with Him, then shall He sit upon the throne of His glory: and before Him shall be gathered all nations: and He shall separate them one from another, as a shepherd divideth his sheep from the goats: And He shall set the sheep on his right hand, but the goats on the left. Then shall the King say unto them on His right hand, 'Come, ye blessed of My Father, inherit the kingdom prepared for you from the foundation of the world: for I was an hungred, and ye gave Me meat: I was thirsty, and ye gave Me drink: I was a stranger, and ye took Me in: naked, and ye clothed Me: I was sick, and ye visited Me: I was in prison and ye came unto Me.' Then shall the righteous answer Him, saying, 'LORD, when saw we Thee an hungred, and fed Thee? Or thirsty, and gave Thee drink? When saw we Thee a stranger, and took Thee in? Or naked, and clothed Thee? Or when saw we Thee sick, or in prison, and came unto Thee?' And the King shall answer and say unto them, 'Verily I say unto you, Inasmuch as ye have done it unto one of the least of these My brethren, ye have done it unto Me.' Then shall He say also unto them on the left hand, 'Depart from Me, ye cursed, into everlasting fire, prepared for the devil and his angels: for I was an hungred, and ye gave Me no meat: I was thirsty, and ye gave Me no drink: I was a stranger, and ye took Me not in: naked, and ye clothed Me not: sick, and in prison, and ye visited Me not.' Then shall they also answer Him, saying, 'LORD, when saw we Thee an hungred, or athirst, or a stranger, or naked, or sick, or in prison, and did not minister unto Thee?' Then shall He answer them, saying, 'Verily I say unto you, Inasmuch as ye did it not to one of the least of these, ye did it not to Me'. And these shall go away into everlasting punishment: but the righteous into life eternal."*

25: 31- 46 The final judgment, when the sheep (the Jews) and the goats (Greeks, or more broadly the gentiles, for this nation was considered typical of all gentile nations and to any Jew, the Greeks represented the world in general terms) are separated and judged. The inheritance for the faithful is a kingdom *prepared for you from the foundation of the world* (25:34) an eternal place of blessing, planned of God before creation.

[70] Before leaving Matthew's account of the LORD's teachings, it must be appreciated that these are brief comments and a much broader view of the scriptures should be taken, to fully grasp the depth of the LORD's teachings concerning the last days.

For example *The days of Noah* (Matthew 24:37) should truly be considered in the light of the activities of all Noah's contemporaries (as revealed in Genesis 4:16-26,) for Cain's descendants continued until the Flood and the account of Noah (Genesis 6-9,) describes only part of the picture. The inventions and developments noted in the scriptures, tent dwellings, cattle, harp and organ, artifacts in brass and iron - and the various professions represented in them - will be revived in the last days. The spiritual wickedness and the violence of that generation, which so grieved God and moved Him to wipe them out with the flood, will also feature prominently in the last days. A superficial glance at scriptures is not enough to discover how much it truly contains and exploring such obvious leads as "*The days of Noah*" will lead to a much more enlightened view of what to expect.

For example, Genesis 4:20-22 *And Adah bare Jabal: he was the father of such as dwell in tents, and of such as have cattle. And his brother's name was Jubal: he was the father of all such as handle the harp and organ. And Zillah, she also bare Tubal-cain, an instructer in brass and iron:*

Everything mentioned can be expected to be evident in the last days to the same extremes as in the booming populations of Noah's times.

Tent dwellers need not be considered merely in respect of recognised wandering nomadic cultures, (Bedouin, Mongolian, and Lapplanders etc) or even other recognised groups. In the last days this will apply much more broadly to include those living in self-erected shelters, the vast shanty towns on the outskirts of large cities from South America to India, and to the increasing street populations now a recognised feature of Western culture cities. Who can deny or ignore the accuracy of the LORD's words in revealing such evidences, or signs, to an even greater extreme for us to identify the last days?

[71]

The musical explosion, probably dating from the sixties, when popular music became so prominent, ably assisted by transistor radios and superb technology for recording and distributing records, tapes and discs, is yet another sign. It is amazing that nobody challenges the paradox that the musical presenters, the disc jockeys and the artists themselves use true love as the main theme - but collectively represent an astonishing range of broken marriages and completely unscriptural behaviour. Likewise the violence that is tolerated in sport reveals man's total inadequacy to cope with his situation. If a man cannot control his violence in sporting activities, which are supposed to encourage healthy, safe competition, how can he be expected to control his violence in other circumstances? Yet Christians are lampooned and derided as hypocrites.

How many appreciate that keeping cattle means the destruction of forests or jungle for grazing land? Ecologically this is disastrous but it is another scriptural sign of the last days. (Genesis 4:16-26) The descendants of Cain were tent dwellers, cattlemen, inventors of music, metal artificers etc and these are evidently characteristics from the days of Noah, that can be expected to be strongly revived in the last days, on the LORD's Own teachings and authority. Massive migrations of populations of different languages will also be evident in the last days with the problems of accommodation and integration that these would cause. (See also [78].) But Noah's times extended well after the Flood and for example, the dispersion of peoples of different languages at the building of the tower of Babel is yet another sign.

Chapter 9: The LORD's Teachings in MARK and LUKE

[72] MARK

(13:1-8) *And as He went out of the temple, one of His disciples saith unto Him, 'Master, see what manner of stones and what buildings are here!' And Jesus answering said unto him, "Seest thou these great buildings? There shall not be left one stone upon another that shall not be thrown down." And as He sat upon the mount of Olives, over against the temple, Peter and James and John and Andrew asked Him privately, 'Tell us, when shall these things be And what shall be the sign when all these things shall be fulfilled?' And Jesus answering them began to say, "Take heed lest any man deceive you: for many shall come in My name, saying, 'I am Christ'; and shall deceive many. And when ye shall hear of wars and rumours of wars, be ye not troubled: for such things must needs be; but the end shall not be yet. For nation shall rise against nation, and kingdom against kingdom: and there shall be earthquakes in divers places, and there shall be famines and troubles: these are the beginnings of sorrows.*

(13:9-13) *But take heed to yourselves: for they shall deliver you up to councils; and in the synagogues ye shall be beaten: and ye shall be brought before rulers and kings for My sake, for a testimony against them. And the gospel must first be published among all nations. But when they shall lead you, and deliver you up, take no thought beforehand what ye shall speak, neither do ye premeditate: but whatsoever shall be given you in that hour, that speak ye: for it is not ye that speak, but the Holy Ghost. Now the brother shall betray the brother to death, and the father the son; and children shall rise up against their parents, and shall cause them to be put to death. And ye* shall be hated of all men for My name's sake: but he that shall endure unto the end, the same shall be saved.

(13:14-23) *But when ye shall see the abomination of desolation, spoken of by Daniel the prophet, standing where it ought not, (let him that readeth understand,) then let them that be in Judea flee to the mountains: and let him that is on the housetop not go down into the house, neither enter therein, to take any thing out of his house: and let him that is in the field not turn back again for to take up his garment. But woe to them that are with child, and to them that give suck in those days! And pray ye that your flight be not in the winter. For in those days shall be affliction, such as was not from the beginning of the creation which God created unto this time, neither shall be. And except that the Lord had shortened those days, no flesh should be saved: but for the elect's sake, whom He hath chosen, He hath shortened the days. And then if any man shall say to you, 'Lo, here is Christ; or Lo, He is there'; believe him not: for false Christs and false prophets shall rise, and shall shew signs and wonders, to seduce, if it were possible, even the elect. But take ye heed: behold, I have foretold you all things.*

(13:24-31) *But in those days, after that tribulation, the sun shall be darkened, and the moon shall not give her light, and the stars of heaven shall fall, and the powers that are in heaven shall be shaken. And then shall they see the Son of man coming in the clouds with great power and glory. And then shall He send His angels, and shall gather together His elect from the four winds, from the uttermost part of the earth to the uttermost part of heaven. Now learn a parable of the fig tree; When her branch is yet tender, and putteth forth leaves, ye know that summer is near: so ye in like manner, when ye shall see these things come to pass, know that it is nigh, even at the doors. Verily I say unto you, that this generation shall not pass, till all these things be done. Heaven and earth shall pass away: but My words shall not pass away.*

(13:32-37) *But of that day and that hour knoweth no man, no, not the angels which are in heaven, neither the Son, but the Father.* (The repetition of this truth makes it absolutely inviolate Mathew 26:36.) *Take ye heed, watch and pray: for ye know not when the time is. For the Son of man is as a man taking a far journey, who left his house, and gave authority to his servants, and to every man his work, and commanded the porter to watch. Watch ye therefore: for ye know not when the master of the house cometh, at even, or at midnight, or at the cockcrowing, or in the morning: lest coming suddenly he find you sleeping. And what I say unto you I say unto all, Watch."*

[73] The account of the LORD's teachings in Mark is very similar to that in Matthew. The LORD's leaving the temple, the disciples' coming to Him and their commenting on the stones of the building, to which the LORD replied that not one stone would be left upon another. Then again, on the Mount of Olives, the disciples (and those involved on this occasion were named by Mark, as Peter, James, John and Andrew) came to the LORD with their different questions (13:4.)

When shall these things be? (i.e. the destruction of the temple)

What shall be the sign when all these things shall be fulfilled?

Mark showed that these disciples knew that certain things had to be fulfilled, before the signs of His coming and the end of the world. These disciples wanted to know THE sign that would indicate to them that everything had been fulfilled.

The LORD's reply in Mark's account followed a similar pattern:

13: 5, 6   False Christ's deceiving many

13: 7, 8   Wars, rumours of wars[26] earthquakes, famines,

---

[26] Notice, the LORD warned them not to be troubled spiritually about this *"for such things must needs be."* People are troubled spiritually and it gets them nowhere, when they start

	troubles - the beginning of sorrows (travail).
13: 9-13	Hatred to the Jews (note v9 *synagogues*) and the terrible treachery among them.
13: 14-23	The awful tribulation of the elect, the Jews (note especially v14 Daniel's ministry was for the Jews and Judea can only mean the Jewish inhabitants).
13: 24	The sun darkened, the moon not giving her light, *after that tribulation.*
13: 25	The heavenly signs (compare Matthew 24: 29.)
13: 26	*THEN shall they see the Son of Man coming.* So that in the context of Mark's account, *the* sign (*when all these things shall be fulfilled*) marking the end of the tribulation is in the LORD's words, *"The sun shall be darkened, and the moon shall not give her light, and the stars of heaven shall fall, and the powers that are in heaven shall be shaken."*
13: 27	His angels are sent to gather His elect (see also [175] Revelation 14: 14-20.)
13: 28-37	Closing exhortations to pay attention to these things as soon as they begin to happen and to be faithful stewards prepared for the LORD's coming at any time.

[74] From Mark's account, the emphasis was on THE sign which denoted the end of the tribulation, a most fitting point to underline in the gospel of the faithful servant. From the LORD's teachings, THE

---

blaming God for wars, etc. This was just the sort of attitude that the LORD was warning His disciples against. Such events are part of the worldly pattern and these things are bound to happen, but none of these things will affect God's plan.

sign, which marked the end of the tribulation, was *"The sun shall be darkened, and the moon shall not give her light."* The darkness of the world at this time indicates the dawning of the light for the nation Israel.

[75] LUKE

(17:20-37) *And when He was demanded of the Pharisees, when the kingdom of God should come, He answered them and said, "The kingdom of God cometh not with observation: neither shall they say, 'Lo, here! or lo there! for, behold, the kingdom of God is within you." And He said to the disciples, "The days will come, when ye shall desire to see one of the days of the Son of man, and ye shall not see it. And they shall say to you, 'See here; or see there'; go not after them, nor follow them. For as the lightning, that lighteneth out of the one part under heaven, shineth unto the other part under heaven; so shall also the Son of man be in His day. But first must He suffer many things, and be rejected of this generation. And as it was in the days of Noe, so shall it be also in the days of the Son of man. They did eat, they drank, they married wives, they were given in marriage, until the day that Noe entered into the ark, and the flood came, and destroyed them all. Likewise also as it was in the days of Lot, they did eat, they drank, they bought, they sold, they planted, they builded; but the same day that Lot went out of Sodom it rained fire and brimstone from heaven, and destroyed them all. Even thus shall it be in the day when the Son of man is revealed. In that day, he which shall be upon the housetop, and his stuff in the house, let him not come down to take it away: and he that is in the field, let him likewise not return back. Remember Lot's wife. Whosoever shall seek to save his life shall lose it; and whosoever shall lose his life shall preserve it. I tell you, in that night there shall be two men in one bed; the one shall be taken, and the other shall be left. Two women shall be grinding together; the one shall be taken, and the other left. Two men shall be in the field; the one shall be taken, and the other left."* And they answered *and said unto Him, 'Where LORD?' And He said unto them, "Wheresoever the body is, thither will the eagles be gathered together."*

[76] Luke contains two accounts of the LORD's last day teachings and the first is especially interesting because the LORD was replying initially to the Pharisees, who had demanded to know when the Kingdom of God should come. In their arrogance, they demanded an answer of Him, concerning a truth not revealed to man, not even to angels (see Matthew 24:36 and Acts 1:7.) But the LORD was more than equal to them, His reply was superb.

17:20 *He answered them* (the Pharisees, not His disciples) *and said 'The kingdom of God cometh not with observation.'* The Greek word for *observation* is PARATERESIS and it is always used in a bad sense; it means keeping a special eye on something, in a sinister, or superstitious or hostile way.

The previous New Testament uses of the word all convey this sense most convincingly and, although it is a digression, these examples merit close attention for the LORD was revealing the unacceptable attitude, how *not to look*, or the wrong spiritual outlook, for the last days.

Mark 3:2 *And they watched Him, whether He would heal him on the Sabbath day; that they might accuse Him.*

Luke 6:7 *And the scribes and the Pharisees watched Him, whether He would heal on the Sabbath day.*

Luke 14:1 *As He went into the house of one of the chief Pharisees to eat bread on the Sabbath day, that they watched Him.*

Luke 17:20 The LORD's use of the word *observation* (as above).

Luke 20:20 *And they watched Him, and sent forth spies. Which should feign themselves just men, that they might take hold of His words, so that they might deliver Him unto the power and authority of the governor.*

Acts 9:24 *But their laying await was known of Saul. And they watched the gates day and night to kill him.*

Galatians 4:10 *Ye observe* (= watch for) *days, and months, and times, and years.* This was Paul's rebuke to the Galatians for their observing or regarding times in such a superstitious or religious way, in their experience. (Believers would do well to note this for the lesson it contains.) These various examples convey the meaning of the LORD's words perfectly.

Returning to the LORD's experience with the Pharisees, He had in His reply turned the tables beautifully on these Pharisees, who continually watched Him so malevolently. In effect the LORD had told them that the way they looked at everything (with suspicion and malice,) they would never see the Kingdom of God when it came! It must be appreciated that the LORD was not speaking to worldly people. He was addressing SPIRITUAL leaders, men who had perfected their outward act of holiness, piety and humility for pure show. For inwardly they were full of malice, hatred, venom, envy toward anyone, who expressed anything like a real love for God, or for His people. Their eyes were keen to seek evil, to find fault in Him and consequently they would never see Him as the One, Who could have brought the kingdom of God to that generation. But the LORD's reply contained more:

17: 21 *Neither shall they say, 'Lo here!' or, 'Lo there!' for behold, the kingdom of God is within you.* The LORD told them also, that they should not listen to any guidance from others, to "Look here!" or "Look there!" He taught that the Kingdom of God was within (literally "among") them at that time. The LORD was trying to tell them, that His presence in their midst put the kingdom of God within their grasp. His presence, as the King of Israel, would have made the place a kingdom, if only they had accepted Him in their hearts as their king. But there was no real desire to recognise Him, because He did not conform to their idea of a spiritual man and certainly not to their conception of the Messiah and King. This rejection was prophesied (Isaiah 53:1-3) so the LORD could, and did, accept it, but the Pharisees in their blindness were full of hostility, bitterness, hatred, malice and darkness. They would never see the Kingdom of God, for in their blindness they could not see the King Himself.

[77] The LORD had dealt with the Pharisees. *And He said unto the disciples....* and for His disciples the LORD had very different words. This was still in the context of the question the Pharisees had demanded of Him, but the change in tone was evident.

17:22 *And He said unto the disciples, 'The days will come when ye shall desire to see one of the days of the Son of man, and ye shall not see it.'* The LORD was telling His disciples, that the time would come when they would long to have another opportunity to talk to Him, as they did then, but the chance would never come. Note this!

The LORD was addressing Jews who believed in Him and His remarks must apply to Jews, who seek Him when He is no longer around, what a lesson for His people in the last days. Listen to His advice:

17:23 *And they shall say to you, 'See here!' or 'See there!' go not after them, nor follow them.* The LORD was telling His disciples, in His absence, not to listen to anyone else. His words *"Go not after them"* (i.e. to listen to them) *"Nor follow them"* as guides, or Messiahs (for many will come pretending to be Him, or claiming to be The Christ). These words are not to be treated lightly, or dismissed at a glance, if His people are to survive in those terrible times they must look to Him (or in His absence, to His Word,) and nobody else, this is a vital truth. Note especially, how the LORD continued:

17:24 *For as the lightning, that lighteneth out of the one part under heaven, shineth unto the other part under heaven; so shall also the Son of man be in His day.* In context of His remarks, in which the LORD was speaking of His return to establish the kingdom of God (and this was still a possibility within the lifetime of His disciples.) The LORD warned them not to be persuaded to look to anyone else; then He revealed that His coming would be like the lightning itself. His coming would be an unmistakable event, manifest across the heavens, a phenomenal, dazzling spectacle, well beyond man's puny powers to imitate or counterfeit. (Compare Acts 1:9-11 *This same Jesus, which is taken up from you into heaven, shall so come in like manner as ye have seen Him go into heaven.* His coming will be in a cloud - a fantastic sight, totally unmistakable - yet it will be *this same Jesus*!) This is THE SIGN of The Son of Man (Matthew 24:30) - not an enormous cross suspended in space or anything like that (such imaginations suit Hollywood.) Later, at His farcical trial (Matthew 26:62-65,) the high priest was incensed that the LORD made no reply to the false witnesses and said, "*I adjure thee by the living God, that thou tell us whether thou be The Christ, The Son of God*". The LORD's reply was brilliant – *"Thou hast said:"* (this is a synonym, for an emphatic "Yes!" or a strong affirmative; we have the same expression in English, "You said it!" This means, "Yes! You have it right exactly!") The high priest would have accepted the LORD's answer as an emphatic, positive reply. *"Nevertheless I say unto you, hereafter shall ye see the Son of man sitting on the right hand of power, and coming in the clouds of heaven."* This does not contradict what the LORD had told the Pharisees that they would not see the Kingdom of God coming. The LORD knew that His affirmative reply to the priest would mean His certain death, yet He did not hesitate to emphatically confirm He was the Christ (*"Thou hast said"*.) But with His characteristic perception, the LORD had included in His reply, words which will enable His people eventually to realise that their hope is in Him and to encourage them to look for *this same Jesus*. The LORD's reply was superb, in effect He was saying "Yes! I am The Christ of God (and you will crucify Me) *nevertheless, I say unto you, hereafter* (as a nation, as My people) *shall ye see the Son of man sitting on the right hand of power, and coming in the clouds of heaven.*"

This was not stretching things too far, simply because this is what will happen and the LORD's reply covered it beautifully.

[78] Returning to our considerations however, in His reply to His disciples the LORD had revealed that His coming will be a phenomenal, heavenly spectacle; the disciples were to have no fear of missing Him, that event will be unmistakable. But before that day comes, there are many things to happen. The LORD revealed some as He continued.

17:26 *But first must He suffer many things, and be rejected of this generation.*

The LORD's rejection by His people would come first; the LORD presented this as a fact, not an obstacle about their believing in Him. His rejection by many was to Him a necessary part of His experience, it had been prophesied. Then the LORD gave two scriptural examples of things that would happen in the last days –

17:26, 27 *And as it was in the days of Noe, so shall it be also in the days of the Son of man. They did eat, they drank, they married wives, they were given in marriage, until the day that Noe entered into the ark, and the flood came, and destroyed them all.* (See [8].)

17:28, 29 *Likewise also as it was in the days of Lot; they did eat, they drank, they bought, they sold, they planted, they builded; but the same day that Lot went out of Sodom it rained fire and brimstone from heaven, and destroyed them all.*

The LORD used the days of Noah and the days of Lot to illustrate His teachings (the other gospels make no mention of Lot in this context) and these are familiar Old Testament scriptures. (See [71] page 52.) If they are examined carefully, the signs and the evil characteristics are there: the violence and spiritual wickedness of Noah's times [the defiance of that generation is revealed in the words of Eliphaz the Temanite, Job 22:15-18, and the defiant, open homosexuality of Sodom.] Comments on these characteristics would be expected, but the LORD pointed to *eating and drinking* in both cases; along with other perfectly normal, everyday pursuits - marriage, (notice especially the absence of any reference to marrying wives in the case of Sodom,) buying, selling, planting, building - the usual, daily activities. In His choice of words, the LORD was drawing attention to the fact, that in spite of the vile behaviour of those generations, the people continued in their everyday life (eating, drinking etc.) not bothered about the deterioration in moral standards, quite indifferent to the depths of sin into which their contemporaries were sinking and choosing to mind their own business - as long as they could continue eating, drinking etc. Their attitude condoned the wickedness, they exempted themselves from blame, accepted no responsibility for what was plainly happening around them. None of them sought God for mercy, to entreat Him to turn the evil away, nobody made any sacrifices to Him, nobody fasted in earnest concern, and nobody cared as long as they could eat and drink. Those generations perished for such a complacent attitude and this was the point that the LORD was making; this is the same spirit, the same attitude that will prevail in the last days. (It is evident already!)

[79] There is however another important lesson from the LORD's teachings. Speaking of His coming as the Son of man, the LORD had made it clear, that this would be as unmistakable as lightning, but as unexpected as the Flood, or the destruction of Sodom. But notice especially that in referring to the deliverance of Noah, the LORD said, *"UNTIL the day that Noe entered into the ark, and the flood came, and destroyed them all."* In respect of Lot, the LORD said, *"the SAME DAY that Lot went out of Sodom it rained fire and brimstone"* In Noah's case the LORD was speaking of time in a general sense, because the Flood did not come the same day that Noah entered into the ark. But in Lot's case, the Lord was speaking of a specific time the *SAME day*; and it is in these two ways i.e. general and specific, that we must regard that time, for He plainly declared, (17:30,) *Even thus shall it be in the day when the Son of man is revealed.* It is in reference to that same day, when He shall be revealed, that the LORD gave His warnings, as He continued - and firstly, He was regarding that day in its general sense - as a period of time (for the Jews.)

17: 31-33 In that day, he which shall be upon the housetop, and his stuff in the house, let him not come down to take it away: and he that is in the field, let him likewise not return back. Remember Lot's wife. Whosoever shall seek to save his life shall lose it; and whosoever shall lose his life shall preserve it.

The custom was that in a real, genuine emergency (and only then) anyone, who really had to move fast, could take advantage of the flat roofs and run the length of the street on the housetops avoiding any crowds to hinder him in the street. [This was called *The Road of the Roofs* by the Rabbis, (see Dr A Edersheim's *Sketches of Jewish Social Life in the days of Christ,* Chapter 6 p93.)] The LORD's words convey that sense of life-saving emergency in those terrible days - flee for your life, do not worry about anything else, just go! Survival means real speed, the slightest delay in those days will be fatal. The LORD's example of Lot's wife[27] is a scriptural warning for anyone, who imagines that even a backward glance is permissible, it is no laughing matter.

[80] The lesson is that it is better to lose everything in terms of worldly possessions, if one values one's own life - this is excellent survival technique in real extremity. But there is more:

17: 34-36 I tell you, in that night there shall be two men in one bed; the one shall be taken, and the other left. Two women shall be grinding together; the one shall be taken and the other left. Two men shall be in the field; the one shall be taken and the other left.

---

[27] Why the fact Lot's wife was turned into a pillar of salt, should be considered amusing is another example of the contradictory attitudes of this world. This truth is treated with a smirk, as if she became a glorious salt cellar; the woman was petrified on the spot by a blast of volcanic gas and ash! Examples of this can be seen in the ruins of Pompeii and these are not laughed at. If she had obeyed the instructions, and kept going, she would have avoided such a death. The LORD was giving a terrifying example of the consequences of disobedience – His words have a devastating way of being right, it is absolute folly to treat them flippantly.

Such examples cover the night (in bed) the morning (grinding) and the evening (the field) and the common factor in each case is that *one shall be taken and the other left*. This suggests a selection, as if from betrayal - otherwise *BOTH would be taken* (if it were a matter of killing or destruction.) In those times nobody can be trusted, one must be on guard and trust nobody, the wise thing is to look after oneself, get away from it all. This is the lesson for that time in a general sense.

But in the context of the LORD's remarks (and it was the LORD Who had drawn attention to time firstly in a general sense and secondly, in a specific sense,) following His words, the *same day that Lot went out of Sodom* i.e. a specific time, the LORD continued, *"even thus shall it be in the day when the Son of man is revealed."* The disciples were fascinated and they wanted to know one thing: *And they answered and said unto Him, "Where LORD?"* The disciples would know that in reference to Lot, the LORD was warning them of sudden destruction, they would know "When", because He was speaking of the day *when the Son of man is revealed;* so they asked the question they wanted answered, *"Where LORD?"* And His reply, which must be seen in reference to a specific time i.e. the day of His coming, was: *"Wheresoever the body is, thither will the eagles be gathered together."* (Compare Revelation 19:17, 18 & 21.) The unmistakable lesson referring to this specific time is that it happens *WHEN* He comes as The Word of God, *WHERE* the eagles are gathered. The body (or carcase,) typifies "the dead" and the gathering of the vultures (eagles do not eat carrion, but vultures are similar in flight,) or carrion birds is by divine command, to clear up the corpses after the terrible slaughter on that specific day - and this particular event has been prophesied (Ezekiel 39:4, 17-22, [47] & Revelation 19:17 [194].) This is the same day to which the LORD Himself referred, a specific day when He comes (to His people, the Jews.) The body (the word means a carcass or carcase) means something slain and this agrees with His warnings about saving one's life. The eagles (or vultures) are the same carrion birds as mentioned in Job (39:27-30) *"Where the slain are there is she"*. The body, or those about to be slain, is Jerusalem when compassed with armies (Luke 21:20 [86].)

The LORD's teachings to His disciples extended well beyond His reply to the malevolent Pharisees. He had taught His disciples of His rejection (engineered by the Pharisees later) and He warned His disciples not to listen to others, pointing especially to spiritual leaders like the Pharisees. They were teachers of no value, whose spirituality was outward show, dressing up in elaborate religious garments, but whose true concept of spiritual truth was nil. In the last days it will be the teachings of the LORD, His wonderful words, which will save lives especially among His Own people Israel, for the Jews will be the main target for the awful tribulation.

[81] The emphasis in these considerations is obviously on the last day fulfilment of prophecies, but it is not denied that the same scriptures have had meanings for and applications to some events, which have already passed into history. The ultimate rejection of the LORD in its most final act, the cross, did not, as many believe, result in the immediate rejection of the Jewish nation by God and the prompt formation of the gentile church on the day of Pentecost. The transition was far more gradual than that and it took a generation (the period of the Acts of the Apostles) to realise. His disciples and others waiting in Jerusalem on the day of Pentecost were Jews or proselytes (Jewish converts,) the latter being the fruits of the fervent, evangelical spirit in the Jews. (The LORD Himself had acknowledged this both for its zeal and also for its spiritual ineffectiveness Matthew 23:15.) Peter's discourse on the outpouring (Acts 2:14-36,) was addressed throughout to his own nation and he applied the fulfilment of Joel's prophecy to Israel (the term "sons and daughters" could include proselytes.) This powerful witness of Peter's (enabled by the Holy Spirit) was the beginning of a ministry to the Jewish nation (the gentiles involved being very much in a minority) which continued throughout Acts. (See Appendix 5, particularly The Gospel of GOD.)

[82] This fully accords with the LORD's Own ministry, which was to

Israel (Matthew 15:24,) although He recognised that there were others *"Which are not of this fold"* (John 10:16.) In view of Peter's obvious hesitation, when the LORD offered him a ministry to these other sheep, it is clear he did not relish the thought of the gentiles being given such a chance (John 21:15-17.) Later Peter was given a special vision (Acts 10) to enable him to minister to Cornelius and in spite of this he found it very difficult (compare Acts 10:28 and v34-36.) The other apostles in Jerusalem contended with Peter for his ministering to the gentiles (Acts 11) and even though Peter gave account for this, none of the apostles took the ministering to the gentiles any further, but remained in Jerusalem. Paul stated quite categorically, that Peter ministered to the circumcision (Galatians 2:7,) which proves this conclusively. Concerning Paul, scripturally it is quite true that the LORD's ultimate intention, to use him to reach the gentiles, was manifest (to Ananias) at the time of his conversion (Acts 9:15,) but throughout the period of the Acts of the Apostles, Paul preached to the Jew first. The exceptions to this, in Antioch of Pisidia (Acts 13:14-52) and in Corinth (Acts 18:1-6) were because of particularly heavy local opposition. But in each case (Compare Acts 14:1 and Acts 18:7 and v19) Paul resumed his ministry to the Jews first, as soon as the opportunity came. It was not in fact, until the end of the period covered by Acts (see Acts 28:25-28,) that Paul, in Rome, pronounced the solemn truth, that the gospel ministry was now open to the gentiles, *And they will hear it.*

[83] It is probably at this same time, when in Rome, that Paul was enabled to add his postscript to his epistle to Rome (Romans 16:25-27.) This was concerning *the revelation of the mystery, which was kept secret since the world began, but now is made manifest, and by the scriptures of the prophets, according to the commandment of the everlasting God, made known to all nations for the obedience of faith.* Paul realised that the way was now open for all nations to partake of God's wonderful grace (please note it involves *the obedience of faith*, this is what the grace is for, obedient faith). But Paul had not been allowed to reveal this, when he actually wrote the epistle to Rome earlier, because at that time, the ministry was still

being offered to the Jew first.

[84] Returning to the LORD's Own teachings on the last days, these were given on the assumption that the Jews could (and should) accept Him (the LORD never deprived them of that option.) Had the Jews accepted Him, He could have fulfilled the scriptures (obviously the Romans would have crucified Him as the King of the Jews, for this would have challenged Caesar's authority.) The Jews having accepted Him as their king would have been empowered by the Holy Spirit to be His witnesses and they would have entered into the tribulation at that time. In their rejection of Him that particular generation lost their land and Jerusalem was utterly destroyed, as the LORD prophesied. Even acknowledging that some of His prophecies applied to the destruction of the temple and Jerusalem at that time; this does not negate their further application in the last days. (Other scriptures too, were written when that awful judgment was imminent and certainly have some applications to those terrible events - compare for example Hebrews 12:25-29, 1 John 2:8 and Revelation 1:1.) It is suggested therefore, that even as history tends to repeat itself, these prophecies will see their ultimate and final fulfilment in the terrible events of the tribulation.

[85] These remarks have been a digression, to explain that the scriptures being considered are not dogmatically claimed to have no other application than to the last days. On the contrary, the other possible fulfilments are readily acknowledged and recognised as further evidence of the inspiration of scriptures. Some historical applications are tenuous; others are plainly hare-brained (these might perhaps be equated with some equally wild prophetic applications that have been made.) However it must be said that some scholars have produced serious and interesting possible historical fulfilments, which but for their efforts would have escaped recognition.

In this spirit therefore, the LORD's teachings are considered concerning the last days and to resume: His teachings in the later chapter of Luke are examined.

[86] (Luke 21:5-24) *And as some spake of the temple, how it was adorned with goodly stones and gifts, He said, "As for these things which ye behold, the days will come, in the which there shall not be left one stone upon another, that shall not be thrown down." And they asked Him, saying, 'Master, but when shall these things be? And what sign will there be when these things shall come to pass?' And He said, "Take heed that ye be not deceived: for many shall come in My name, saying, 'I am Christ'; and the time draweth near: go ye not therefore after them. But when ye shall hear of wars and commotions, be not terrified: for these things must first come to pass; but the end is not by and by." Then said He unto them, "Nation shall rise against nation, and kingdom against kingdom: and great earthquakes shall be in divers places, and famines, and pestilences; and fearful sights and great signs shall there be from heaven. But before all these, they shall lay their hands on you, and persecute you, delivering you up to the synagogues, and into prisons, being brought before kings and rulers for My name's sake. And it shall turn to you for a testimony. Settle it therefore in your hearts, not to meditate before what ye shall answer: for I will give you a mouth and wisdom, which all your adversaries shall not be able to gainsay nor resist. And ye shall be betrayed both by parents, and brethren, and kinsfolks, and friends; and some of you shall they cause to be put to death. And ye shall be hated of all men for My name's sake. But there shall not an hair of your head perish. In your patience possess ye your souls. And when ye shall see Jerusalem compassed with armies, then know that the desolation thereof is nigh. Then let them which are in Judea flee to the mountains; and let them which are in the midst of it depart out; and let not them that are in the countries enter thereinto. For these be the days of vengeance, that all things which are written may be fulfilled. But woe unto them that are with child, and to them that give suck, in those days! for there shall be great distress in the land, and wrath upon this people. And they shall fall by the edge of the sword, and shall be led away captive into all nations: and Jerusalem* shall be trodden down of the Gentiles, until the times of the Gentiles be fulfilled.

(21:25-33) *And there shall be signs in the sun, and in the moon, and in the stars; and upon the earth distress of nations, with perplexity; the sea and the waves roaring; men's hearts failing them for fear, and for looking after those things which are coming on the earth: for the powers of heaven shall be shaken. And then shall they see the Son of man coming in a cloud with power and great glory. And when these things begin to come to pass, then look up, and lift up your heads; for your redemption draweth nigh." And He spake to them a parable; "Behold the fig tree, and all the trees; when they now shoot forth, ye see and know of your own selves that summer is now nigh at hand. So likewise ye, when ye see these things come to pass, know ye that the kingdom of God is nigh at hand. Verily I say unto you, This generation shall not pass away, till all be fulfilled. Heaven and earth shall pass away: but My words shall not pass away.*

(21:34-36) *And take heed to yourselves, lest at any time your hearts be overcharged with surfeiting,* (sickness caused by gluttony,) *and drunkenness, and cares of this life, and so that day come upon you unawares. For as a snare shall it come on all them that dwell on the face of the whole earth. Watch ye therefore, and pray always, that ye may be accounted worthy to escape all these things that shall come to pass, and to stand before the Son of man."*

[87] The second account in Luke reveals that the whole discourse took place in the temple (not outside as in Matthew and Mark,) this is no contradiction, it is perfectly possible. The LORD's comments were inspired by the remarks of some, who were most impressed with the elaborate adornments and large stones used in the structure of the temple. The Lord took the opportunity to remind them that the object of their admiration, the temple itself, was temporal.

(Luke) 21:6 *As for these things which ye behold, the days will come, in the which there shall not be left one stone upon another, that shall not be thrown down.* This provoked them,

21:7 *And they asked Him, saying, "Master, but when shall these things be? And what sign will there be when these things shall come to pass?"*

Note their questions: WHEN SHALL THESE THINGS BE?

WHAT SIGN WILL THERE BE WHEN THESE THINGS SHALL COME TO PASS?

And consider the LORD's reply -

21:8 *And He said, "Take heed that ye be not deceived: for many shall come in My name, saying, 'I am Christ;' and the time draweth near: go ye not after them."*

The warning was about being deceived by these false Christs and there will be many of them. This warning should not be esteemed lightly, at the time this applies it will be serious; there will be many and these will deceive many, because they will have the ability to do so, they will not be obvious charlatans in every case, but clever, deceptive and unscrupulous - their appearance is an indication that THE time draweth near.

The remarkable consistency of the three gospel accounts on this particular sign is evidence of its importance. The appearance of many false Christs is the most significant sign, the FIRST real sign in fact, to the Jewish nation that the last days are come. The point might be made too, that the appearance of the antichrists during the lifetime of the apostles (1 John 2:18 and 4:3) was further evidence that the situation at that time was potentially capable of fulfilling last day prophecy. The false Christs and the antichrists are kindred spirits and scripturally each is an evident sign of the last days.

21:9 *But when ye shall hear of wars and commotions, be not terrified:*

for these things must first come to pass; but the end is not by and by.

These things must FIRST come to pass, but the end is not *by and by* (i.e. not immediately, or not yet; compare Matthew 24:6 and Mark 13:7).

21:10 *Nation shall rise against nation, kingdom against kingdom.*

21:11 *Earthquakes, famines, pestilences, fearful sights, great signs from heaven.*

21:12 *But before all these,* (The events of verses 9-11) *they shall lay hands on you, and persecute you.*

The PERSECUTION of the Jews, which commences *before all these things,* is the start of a long travail for that nation, which culminates in the TRIBULATION.

[88] There is a very significant difference between Luke's account and those of Matthew and Mark (which refer to these events as *"the beginning of sorrows"* i.e. travail.) Luke associates the persecution of the Jews with events BEFORE the tribulation and also with the appearances of false Christs.

As noted above, this was fulfilled to some extent during the lifetime of the apostles and therefore, Luke's account can justifiably be related to the destruction of the temple (AD 70) and the persecution of the Jews at that time. This is quite valid, since it does not diminish from or contradict the last day application of the accounts in Matthew or Mark and allows for the scripture in Luke to apply in both cases.

[89] 21:12-24 *But before all these, they shall lay their hands on you.... ...until the times of the Gentiles be fulfilled.* His teachings can therefore be considered quite justifiably, in the light of the awful events and happenings associated with the siege of Jerusalem and the destruction of the temple. But as explained, to confine these verses to history and consider them completely fulfilled would be an unnecessary restriction, possibly resulting in missing their last days fulfilment and the solemn warnings contained therein for the tribulation yet to come. Once again it will apply in the last days.

21:13 *And it shall turn to you for a testimony* i.e. to the Jewish nation in the last days and the following will apply with just as much force,

21:22 *For these be the days of vengeance, that all things which are written may be fulfilled.*

The destruction of the temple and Jerusalem finished the Jewish experience and commenced the times of the gentiles with such literal vengeance (this was prophesied by the LORD Himself Luke 19:41-44.) But there evidently remains a future destruction of Jerusalem to take place in the last days (compare Zechariah 12 and 14.) Jerusalem, it might be noted, is still trodden down of the Gentiles, inasmuch as the Jews have not yet fully reinstated their sacrifices and offerings.

21:23, 24 *But woe unto them that are with child, and to them that give suck in those days! For there shall be a great distress in the land, and wrath upon this people. And they shall fall by the edge of the sword, and shall be led away captive into all nations: and Jerusalem shall be trodden down of the Gentiles, until the times of the Gentiles be fulfilled.*

Luke's account continued, in accord with Matthew and Mark, as follows :

21:25 Heavenly signs, distress of nations, even the sea is disturbed.

21:26 Men dying of sheer terror. Heavenly powers shaken.

21:27 THEN shall they (the world) see the Son of man coming. That unmistakable event, (compare Luke 17:24 and Revelation 14:14-20.)

21:28 An exhortation. When these things begin to come to pass *then look up, and lift up your heads!*

This will not be the time for the real Jew to be ashamed; his redemption, his Redeemer, is at hand. Nobody will ever despise that nation again.

21:29-31 The parable of the fig tree springing forth, a sign of the emergence of Israel as a nation in the last days. This points to the imminent establishment of the kingdom of God on earth for ever and ever.

21:32, 33 The certainty of this prophecy.

21:34-36 Warnings about being unprepared for that day. Notice the whole world is caught unprepared. (Compare [70] the parables of Matthew 25.)

[90] Throughout Luke's account the main concern is the nation Israel in the last days, but his record is especially valuable since it allows the sequence of the last days events to be followed properly. Thus, *before all these things* the persecution of the Jews commences, then the signs as follows:

1   False Christs - the time draweth near (21:8)

2   Wars and commotions - these must FIRST come to pass (21:9)

3   Nation against nation, kingdom against kingdom (21:10)

4   Earthquakes, famines, pestilences, sights, signs (21:11)

5   Tribulation of Israel (21:12-24)

6   Heavenly catastrophes (21:25,26)

7   World sees Son of man coming (17:27)

The most dramatic points to note as definite signs are:

I   The appearance of the many false Christs, which commences the signs to the nation Israel

II   The wars and commotions are the first events of the last days

III   The persecution of the nation Israel *"For My name's sake"* this is international

(21:12) *But before all these, they shall lay their hands on you, and persecute you, delivering you up to the synagogues, and into prisons, being brought before kings and rulers for My sake.* And occurs when (21:13) *It shall turn to you* (the Jews) *for a testimony.*

Because, at this time, the true Church has gone!

[Acts 2:17-21: Peter's discourse on the day of Pentecost, contains a valuable reference to the lasts days (quoting Joel's prophecy,) see footnote 28 next page.]

[91] Before leaving the LORD's teachings in the gospel accounts, it is useful to compare them together in their basic contents.

Comparison of Gospel accounts of the LORD's last day teachings

Matthew 24	Mark 13	Luke 21
5 Many false Christs	6 Many false Christs	8 Many false Christs
6 Wars and rumours	7 Wars and rumours	9 Wars and rumours
7 Nation v Nation Kingdom v Kingdom	8 Nation v Nation Kingdom v Kingdom	10, 11 Nation v Nation Kingdom v Kingdom
Famines, Pestilences, Earthquakes	Earthquakes, Famine, Troubles	Earthquakes, Famines, Pestilences
9-28 Tribulation of the Jews	9-23 Tribulation of the Jews	12-24 Tribulation of the Jews
29 Heavenly Catastrophes[28]	24 Heavenly Catastrophes	25 Heavenly Catastrophes and sea disturbed
29 Coming of the Son of man	29 Coming of the Son of man	29 Coming of the Son of man

Before all these things - the persecution of the Jews

Many false Christs - the indication that the time draweth near.

Wars and rumours - these "*First cometh to pass*" and are the prelude,

---

[28] In Acts 2:17-21 the Apostle Peter gives an inspired rendition of Joel's prophecy 3:27-31, which concerns the events of the last days; and mentions the heavenly signs; specifically the moon's turning to blood and the sun to darkness. Note Peter's words: v20, *The Sun shall be turned into darkness and the moon into blood, before that great and notable day of the LORD come.* These are clearly the penultimate signs of the LORD's actually coming, to deliver and rule His earthly people, His bride, Israel.

to the real events of the last days.

Nations, Kingdoms, - these events are the beginning of sorrows, travail (compare *Famines etc* Romans 8:19-23 and also four horsemen of Revelation).

Tribulation of Jews - this is world-wide and is *"For My name's sake"*. At this time the testimony turns to the Jews.

Heavenly catastrophes – these are the most awesome and spectacular signs preceding His coming.

The consistency in the details of the events described is evident, but these considerations have established that the differences in the accounts are to be found in the various signs given in answer to the disciples' questions:

When shall these things be?	Their question in reference to the destruction of the Temple, which the LORD did not explain.
What shall be the sign of Thy coming, and of the end of the world?	His coming in the clouds (Matthew 24:30 [69]).
What shall be the sign when all these things shall be fulfilled?	The sun shall be darkened etc (Mark 13:26 [73])
What sign will there be when these things shall come to pass?	The persecution of Israel, previous to the tribulation (Luke 21:12 [87]).

Chapter 10: Paul's teachings in THESSALONIANS & TIMOTHY

[92] 1 THESSALONIANS

It is essential to distinguish between the ministry of the LORD Jesus Christ Himself (to His people Israel) and the ministry of the apostle Paul to the emerging church. In its initial conception, for a generation in fact, the Church was mainly formed from Jewish and proselyte converts and Paul's epistles reflect this. However when Paul eventually acknowledged that the Gospel of Grace was open for the gentiles, his prison epistles (Ephesians, Philippians and Colossians) marked this change. But nowhere did Paul amend or rescind the last day teachings, which occur in his earlier epistles (confirming they are of particular interest to the Jewish nation, converted or unconverted to Christianity.) These considerations therefore regard Paul's teachings as applicable to the true Church in the last days (a view shared by the earliest Church fathers.) But it should be recognised that the Jewish converts during Paul's early ministry could have expected (and did) an immediate fulfilment of these teachings. This would have happened, if the nation had repented and accepted the ministry of the apostles' preaching the Gospel of God, for the duration of *The Acts* (See Appendix 5.)

The scriptural order of Paul's last day teachings corresponds to their chronological order, which helps in their examination.

[93] 1 Thessalonians 4 and 5

To this church, Paul wrote first regarding the LORD's coming for His

Own and note the qualification (i.e. belief in the resurrection,) which distinguished the true Church.

(4:13-17) *But I would not have you to be ignorant, brethren, concerning them which are asleep, that ye sorrow not, even as others which have no hope. For if we* (i.e. the Church) *believe that Jesus died and rose again even so them also which sleep in Jesus will God bring with Him. For this we say unto you by the Word of the LORD, that we which are alive and remain unto the coming of the LORD shall not prevent them which are asleep, for the LORD Himself shall descend from heaven with a shout, with the voice of the Archangel, and with the trump of God: and the dead in Christ shall rise first: then we which are alive and remain shall be caught up together with them in the clouds, to meet the LORD in the air: so shall we ever be with the LORD.*[29]

The purpose behind Paul's writing this (4:13) was to comfort them that they should not sorrow about those that "sleep" (i.e. those who had died in the LORD.) Speaking of the *"times and seasons,"* Paul recognised the knowledge that the Thessalonians possessed already from his own teachings, concerning the *day of the LORD*. This must be distinguished from the LORD's coming, as above, for those in His church who are alive when He comes and those who are already

---

[29] Compare 1 Cor 15:50-58. *Now this I say, brethren, that flesh and blood cannot inherit the kingdom of God; neither doth corruption inherit incorruption. Behold, I shew you a mystery; We shall not all sleep, but we shall all be changed, in a moment, in the twinkling of an eye, at the last trump: for the trumpet shall sound, and the dead shall be raised incorruptible, and we shall be changed. For this corruptible must put on incorruption, and this mortal must put on immortality. So when this corruptible shall have put on incorruption, and this mortal shall have put on immortality, then shall be brought to pass the saying that is written, Death is swallowed up in victory. O death, where is thy sting? O grave, where is thy victory? The sting of death is sin; and the strength of sin is the law. But thanks be to God, which giveth us the victory through our LORD Jesus Christ. Therefore, my beloved brethren, be ye steadfast, unmoveable, always abounding in the work of the LORD, forasmuch as ye know that your labour is not in vain in the LORD.*

asleep (who have died,) who rise first; so that all meet together with Him in the air. This is the glorious rapture of believers that occurs when the LORD comes for His Church, this event is called *the day of Christ*.

Paul had already said (4:13)*"I would not have you ignorant brethren"* concerning those that sleep, so he explained firstly, about the LORD's coming for them that are His (i.e. His Church, which is raptured) and then, Paul continued (in the light of the *"times and seasons"*) to talk about the *day of the LORD* coming *as a thief in the night* (5:2). Paul's remarks about the *"times and seasons"* were an allusion to the observations being made at the time that current events were pointing to the LORD's coming. However Paul was far more aware of what was involved and he showed that the LORD's coming was not imminent in his second epistle.

[94] But let us examine what else Paul wrote in more detail.

5:1-4 *But of the times and the seasons brethren, ye have no need that I write unto you. For yourselves know perfectly that the day of the LORD so cometh as a thief in the night. For when they shall say, 'Peace and safety:' then sudden destruction cometh upon them, as travail upon a woman with child; and they shall not escape. But ye, brethren, are not in darkness, that that day should overtake you as a thief.*

Paul had distinguished between the Church (brethren) and *they* or *them* (in its context undoubtedly the unbelieving Israel, but in broader view the unbelieving world generally.) This distinction was further emphasised in Paul's following words -

5:5-8 *Ye are all the children of light, and the children of the day; we are not of the night, nor of darkness. Therefore let us not sleep, as do others; but let us watch and be sober. For they that sleep sleep in the night; and they that be drunken are drunken in the night. But let us, who are of the day, be sober, putting on the breastplate of faith and love; and for an helmet, the hope of salvation.*

Paul's teachings were wonderful assurance for the true Church concerning God's provision for their safety.

5:9-11 *For God hath not appointed us to wrath* (i.e. the tribulation, covering the events of THE DAY OF THE LORD, as will be seen) *but to obtain salvation by our LORD Jesus Christ, Who died for us, that whether we wake or sleep we should live together with Him, wherefore comfort yourselves together, and edify one another even as also ye do.*

Paul's whole point was that God *hath not appointed us to wrath* and this merits strong emphasis, because many Christians live in abject fear of the LORD's coming (for His Church) quite unnecessarily. This is the result of appallingly bad teaching, which fails to differentiate between the LORD's coming for His Church, this is called *the day of Christ* (or the rapture) and the *day of the LORD* which is His day (His time) of judgment on the world. There is no need at all for such fear, the believer is at peace with God in Christ and there is no condemnation for such. Throughout these verses Paul had stressed the differences between the Church (brethren,) and the unbelievers (them,) the *day of the LORD* comes upon THEM unawares, not His Church.

[95] Paul has shown that the LORD's coming for His Church is a wonderful deliverance, which comes before the *day of the Lord*. Also Paul has adequately covered those, who have died (bodily) before that event, those who rise first, and those, who are alive when He comes, who are caught up with them to be with Him forever. This miraculous event (*the rapture* as it is sometimes called, although this is not a scriptural term,) happens *in the twinkling of an eye* and the world will probably be so wrapped up with the terrible events which coincide, that they will fail to appreciate what has happened. Some

catastrophic eventuality (quite possibly a nuclear attack, or even a phenomenal natural disaster) will cover this whole eventuality. When the world is confidently claiming "Peace and safety," the terrible destruction will come (the true Church disappears,) and the day of the LORD comes like a thief. Not on the true Church, which is anxiously looking forward for their deliverance (for this is what it is,) from the tribulation. Those, who survive this sudden destruction, must face the awesome judgments of God, for rejecting His Son, from which the LORD has delivered His Church (those who believe on Him.) This rapture is the true hope of a believer that he or she might be alive, when the LORD comes for His Church.

[96] Having in this first epistle to Thessalonica clarified the position of the true Church (including those, who are already asleep in the LORD,) with respect to the LORD's coming for them. Also having revealed the sudden destruction that comes upon the world as the judgments of God are poured out; in his second epistle to the Thessalonians, Paul explained the indications (or signs,) that these things are about to take place.

2 THESSALONIANS (1:3-12) *We are bound to thank God always for you, brethren, as it is meet, because that your faith groweth exceedingly, and the charity of every one of you all toward each other aboundeth; so that we ourselves glory in you in the churches of God for your patience and faith in all your persecutions and tribulations that ye endure: which is a manifest token of the righteous judgment of God, that we may be counted worthy of the kingdom of God, for which ye also suffer: seeing it is a righteous thing with God to recompense tribulation to them that trouble you; and to you who are troubled rest with us, when the LORD Jesus shall be revealed from heaven with His mighty angels, in flaming fire taking vengeance on them that know not God, and that obey not the gospel of our LORD Jesus Christ: who shall be punished with everlasting destruction from the presence of the LORD, and from the glory of His power; when He*

shall come to be glorified in His saints, and to be admired in all them that believe (because our testimony among you was believed) in that day. Wherefore also we pray always for you, that our God would count you worthy of this calling, and fulfil all the good pleasure of His goodness, and the work of faith with power: that the name of our LORD Jesus Christ may be glorified in you, and ye in Him, according to the grace of our God and the LORD Jesus Christ.

[97] Paul's evident sympathy for the Thessalonians (for the persecutions and tribulations that they were enduring at the time he wrote to them) did not move him to pray for any deliverance for them. Rather his prayers were directed to the LORD to enable them to go through the experience worthily. Because Paul had made it clear that they were suffering these things for the kingdom of God and he had revealed the tribulation, which would be poured out on these troublesome people, who knew not God, who obeyed not the gospel of our LORD Jesus Christ, who would be punished. The recompense to those, who troubled the Church, (which opposition in the main came from the Jewish faction, who followed Paul around trying to undermine and destroy his work) was tribulation, which was coming in any case, for their rejection of the LORD. But for those, who were being so persecuted and troubled, the promise was *"Rest with us"* i.e. with Paul and the others who had believed. So whilst the LORD poured His vengeance out on the enemies of His Church, (and for those contemporary with Paul, some of them probably saw this in the destruction of Jerusalem and the persecution of the Jews that followed,) His Church enjoyed the rest and peace that the LORD had given them. (There would have been very few Christians in Jerusalem at the time that it was under siege; for the Church had been scattered through their continual persecution by the Jews and the original believers would have died, or as they said *fallen asleep in Him.*)

[98] Paul next drew attention to things, which he had told them during his ministry to that church and unfortunately, in the translation of this the meaning has become obscured and needs explanation.

2:1-5 *Now we beseech you, brethren, by the coming of our LORD Jesus Christ, and by our gathering together unto Him* (these remarks are to be considered **in the light of** that gathering together, the rapture of the Church mentioned in his previous epistle) *that ye be not soon shaken in mind, or be troubled, neither by spirit, nor by word, nor by letter, as from us, as that the day of Christ* (more correctly, "*the day of the LORD*" but unfortunately the A.V. translators inserted "Christ" here,) *is at hand. Let no man deceive you by any means: for that day shall not come, except there come a falling away first, and that man of sin be revealed, the son of perdition; who opposeth and exalteth himself above all that is called God, or that is worshipped; so that he as God sitteth in the temple of God, shewing himself that he is God. Remember ye not, that when I was yet with you, I told you these things?*

Addressing himself to his brethren in the church in Thessalonica, Paul exhorted them *by the coming of our LORD Jesus Christ, and by our gathering together unto Him* i.e. in the light of the rapture or the gathering together of the Church.[30]

[99] So that being confident of their part in that glorious rapture, Paul exhorted them *that ye be not soon shaken in mind* (i.e. troubled by any thoughts) *or be troubled, neither by spirit* (i.e. the spiritual gifts being misused or abused to introduce such error) *nor by letter, as from us,* (i.e. by letters or epistles claiming to have been written by Paul or the apostles,) *as that the day of the LORD* (this is the correct term, as in original texts, but the translators inexplicably put

---

[30] If Paul had included the term, but he did not in this epistle, this would be correctly called THE DAY OF CHRIST compare Philippians 1:10, 2:16. The Day of Christ is the day when He comes for His Church, the day of the rapture itself, and it is a day of rejoicing for the Church. It is a completely different *day* from the Day of the Lord, which is the time of His judgment and wrath.

"Christ" here, which denotes another day entirely) *is at hand.* This *day of the LORD* (which was what Paul actually wrote,) is a time of judgment, which commences with the coming of the LORD for the Jews in the last day deliverance. The Day of the LORD originates in Old Testament prophecy (Isaiah 2:12 etc.) and the term occurs twenty times in scriptures; it is also found in terms of wrath or vengeance and it occurs four times in the New Testament.

Paul appreciated that the *day of the Lord* [he was speaking to the Thessalonians in terms of events that would occur *after* their being gathered together to Him, i.e. it was understood that what Paul was describing happened AFTER the rapture] would not come before two definite events: first, the falling away and the second, the revelation of the man of sin. Paul has insisted that they were not to be shaken, or troubled, or disturbed, or persuaded in effect, in any way at all (by thoughts, spiritual gifts, preaching or epistles) that the *day of the LORD* would come before these two events. The meaning of falling away was self-evident; it meant a turning away from God. (This could have applied to the church to whom Paul wrote and also to the Jews; it can also be applied to the Church and Jews in the last days.) The churches today still expect revival before the LORD comes, Paul taught beyond any shadow of doubt that there would be a falling away, not any increase. The other certain eventuality before the day of the LORD commenced was the revelation of the man of sin.

[100] Concerning the *man of sin,* whose revelation is one of the two signs, Paul wrote of *"the son of perdition* (or doom) *who opposeth and exalteth himself above all that is called God, or that is worshipped; so that he as God sitteth in the temple of God, shewing himself that he is God.*

This is the verse that so many misinterpret or misunderstand. At the time Paul wrote, *the temple in Jerusalem* did exist; but it must be remembered that in the three gospel accounts the LORD's last day teachings commenced with the destruction of that temple. There is

no scripture at all that indicates this temple will be rebuilt before the LORD's coming. From this verse in Thessalonians, some infer that because *the son of perdition ... .as God sitteth in the temple of God,* that the temple has to be rebuilt in Jerusalem. As already noted, this brings problems, because the temple site is occupied by the Muslim shrine, The Dome of The Rock. In the past commentators have endeavoured to explain how this shrine might be removed, suggesting earthquakes, holy wars, etc. for they all acknowledge that its removal is a considerable obstacle to overcome.

But, in the context of Paul's remarks, the man of sin sets himself up as God (i.e. just as if he were God himself) and *sitteth in the temple of God.* So that, whatever the man of sin ("as God") chose to call "*the temple of God*" it would be just that. He could if necessary use the Dome of The Rock itself, as *his* temple of God; or anything else for that matter. The point being that the temple (of the Jews) does not have to be rebuilt in Jerusalem to fulfil this prophecy in the last days.

Paul then exhorted the Church, in the light of their rapture, not to be persuaded that the *day of the LORD* would come before the falling away and the revelation of the man of sin. This is in perfect harmony with the LORD's Own teachings, for He spoke of the persecution of the Jews at the start of their tribulation (see Luke 21:12, 13,) *when it shall turn to you for a testimony*; because the true Church will have gone, gathered to be with Him. The timing of this event must be very close to the beginning of the seventieth week, when the times of the gentiles will have finished and the beast will be about to *confirm the covenant*, which marks the commencement of that final week and his *confirmation of the covenant* is scripturally the deed that positively identifies him.

[101] Paul continued, and a verse occurs, which is difficult to understand because of the translation.

2:6, 7 *And now ye know what withholdeth* (= holds fast) *that he might be revealed in his time. For the mystery of iniquity doth already work: only he who now letteth* (= holds fast) *will let until he be taken out of the way.*

This is a difficult verse for translators and it has led to further errors, when interpreters have tried to apply a literal meaning, neglecting (or not realising) that the Greek contains two figures of speech an ELLIPSIS and also an IDIOM. To explain these:

An ELLIPSIS - this means that the writer has left a "gap" or a "deliberate omission", by excluding words from a clause or sentence. This draws more attention to the previous use of the words, or puts emphasis on the more important clause. In this case, the translators have supplied the words "*will let*" (quite correctly) to convey the sense in their translation. But this is insufficient in this instance, because, whilst it does correctly emphasise the verb "*letteth*" in the previous clause, it neglects the fact that the Greek verb KATECHO is a transitive verb. It requires an object, to which it can apply (or an accusative case.)

Other uses of the word in the New Testament illustrate this:

Matthew 21:38	*Let us **seize** on his inheritance*
Luke 4:42	*.... and **stayed** him, that he should not depart.*
Romans 1:18	*Who **hold** the truth in unrighteousness*
1 Thessalonians 5:21	***Hold fast** that which is good*
2 Thessalonians 2:6	*Now ye know what **withholdeth** that he might be*
2 Thessalonians 2:7	*he who now **letteth*** (no object, because of ellipsis in text of epistle) ***will let*** (supplied correctly by translators, to try and convey

	the sense, but they omitted an object) *until he be taken out of the way*
Hebrews 10:23	Let us **hold fast** the profession of our faith

The verb KATECHO means TO HAVE(something) or HOLD FAST (on to something) or TO HOLD FIRMLY (something) as conveyed in the above examples. Quite clearly, the provision by the translators of "*will let*" was a step in the right direction, but this does not reveal the full meaning of what Paul was trying to emphasise by using an ellipsis.

An IDIOM is basically a peculiar way of saying things, or a common manner of speaking, attributable to a specific class of people or nation. The idiom in this verse is *out of the way*, which is a recognised Greek term, which always implied definite action by the person himself, or by others, to remove somebody (or something) as a deliberate act. The term is found elsewhere and these other uses confirm this quite clearly:

Matthew 13:49	*sever the wicked **from among** the just* (the Greek idiom "out of the way" has been used here and it conveys the sense of removal by force, the wicked being taken forcibly from the just).
Acts 23:10	(Paul) *to take him **by force from among** them* (the Greek "out of the way")
Colossians 2:14	refers to the handwriting of ordinances which Christ "***took it out of the way***" (as translated).

Now, having discussed the figures of speech the ellipsis and the idiom ("out of the way") used in this verse; it has to be considered to try and grasp its meaning a little more accurately.

It might now be written:

For the mystery of iniquity doth already work: only he who now holds fast (onto something) *will hold fast* (onto something) *until he be removed by force.*

For the full meaning to become quite clear, the accusative case, the objects of the verbs, the "somethings" must be supplied and it is not sufficient to repeat just the verb (as in the translation in the King James Authorised Version.)

Further, any attempts to provide the meaning (by providing the objects) must be done within the context of what Paul was writing and he was talking about the revelation of the man of sin. With respect to this revelation of the man of sin (and having reminded the Thessalonians that he had told them all about these things, when he was with them 2:5) Paul continued:

2:6 *And now ye know what withholdeth that he might be revealed in his time. For the mystery of iniquity doth already work: only he who now letteth will let until he be taken out of the way.*

Re-writing this fully, in the light of the above explanation: it is suggested it might read thus:

And now ye know what withholdeth that he might be revealed in his time. For the mystery of iniquity doth already work: only he who now holds fast (onto that mystery of iniquity or lawlessness) *will hold fast* (onto that mystery of iniquity or lawlessness) *until he be removed by force.*

This suggests that he who *holds fast onto the mystery of iniquity* is Satan himself and his involvement, with the ultimate manifestation (revelation) of the man of sin, is a scriptural truth. In his place now, in the heavenly realms, Satan exercises his control over the powers of darkness. When Satan is cast down (as in Revelation 12) i.e. when he is *removed by force,* or *taken out of the way,* and knowing that his time is limited, Satan will set up his final masterpiece, the man of sin, whose revelation means that the day of the LORD is at hand. But there is a further revelation of *that Wicked* (= lawless one) who is only revealed after Satan has been removed by force (from his present heavenly status/position.)

This is the very point that Paul was trying to make in his epistle to the Thessalonians.

This teaching is not in accord with the usual attempts to explain this verse; it is sometimes claimed that *"he who now letteth"* refers to the Holy Spirit, Who is supposed to be restraining iniquity until He is removed with the Church in the rapture (or some such modified version of this idea). But this concept, or interpretation, is not supported by any other scripture and is out of context with what Paul wrote. (2:8-10) *And then shall that wicked* (= the lawless one) *be revealed whom the LORD will consume with the spirit of His mouth, and shall destroy with the brightness of His coming: even him whose coming is after the working of Satan with all power and signs and lying wonders, and with all deceivableness of unrighteousness in them that perish; because they received not the love of the truth, that they might be saved.*

The revelation of the lawless one is within the Church (to whom Paul was writing). It has no relevance to lawlessness or lawless ones in the world, which are nothing new. The surprise in this is that such a one could exert so much influence or power in the Church; but this *is after the working of Satan with all power, signs, lying wonders, deceivableness*. These verses are usually applied to the *"man of sin"* (v3). But the fact is that there are *two* characters referred to, *the man of sin revealed* (v1) and (v8) *that Wicked* (= the lawless one,) in the Church, who has to be *the false prophet*. (See also [163] & [182].) The man of sin will not be lawless, his confirming the covenant established his agreement that the Jews should have a legal right to make their offerings; and in due course the man of sin will impose his own tyrannical rule, with very strict laws that will offend all.

[102] In conclusion, it might also be recalled that Paul's epistle was written to counter the false teachings extant at that time, that the *Day of the LORD was at hand* and Paul exhorted that **they be not shaken in mind** (thoughts), *Spirit* (prophecy or gifts of the Spirit), *nor by word* (preaching), *or letter* (epistle), that such a thing was true. The inclusion of "the Spirit" (in Paul's list of the various means by which such a doctrine or persuasion might be introduced,) suggests that some of the false teachers at that time were attempting to use the ministry of **the gifts of the Spirit** in an unscrupulous manner to introduce this lie.

Most appropriately therefore in his epistle to Timothy, Paul wrote to warn of the false doctrines introduced by evil spirits in the last days; which are our next consideration.

1 TIMOTHY

[103] Paul's epistles to Timothy contained various exhortations and useful guidance for the young minister, but his teachings on the last days were quite clear.

1 Timothy 4:1-3 *"Now the Spirit speaketh expressly, that in the latter times some shall depart from the faith, giving heed to seducing spirits and doctrines of devils* (= demons) *speaking lies in hypocrisy: having their conscience seared with a hot iron: forbidding to marry, and commanding to abstain from meats, which God hath created to be received with thanksgiving of them which believe and know the truth."*

From Paul's epistles *the ministry of the Holy Spirit through His gifts* was fully accepted in the early church and the Holy Spirit would have been quite aware of the truth that the LORD's return was not in the immediate future (as many believed at that time.) However, it was probably the outpouring of the Holy Spirit on the day of Pentecost, which helped convince Satan and his hosts that the last days were close at hand and they must have used every device and doctrine that they could muster, to oppose the early Church. This opposition backfired with a vengeance, for it was as a consequence of the savage efforts to destroy the Church that the gospels and the epistles were written and their real value was also recognised and acknowledged fairly quickly. The true epistles and gospels in circulation were challenged by many spurious and pathetic attempts to copy or imitate them; but this merely revealed to the early church elders the importance of their establishing what was acceptable as inspired and worthy of inclusion in holy writ.

The New Testament also covers every doctrine and means used to oppose the Truth and to distract believers from the life of faith (obedience) that the Gospel of Grace brought to believing gentiles. The early Church not only survived all these attacks, in fact it thrived under the opposition. Undoubtedly (from Paul's writings to Timothy,) the Holy Spirit played no small part, in ministering through His gifts, the truths and exhortations necessary to counter the false doctrines that were being circulated to try and cause havoc and unbelief.

[104] Paul pointed to the fact that the Holy Spirit had spoken about *seducing spirits* and the same Holy Spirit also inspired Paul, as he penned the words or dictated them, to note what their evil doctrines involved. Since these doctrines are *scripturally* a feature of the last days, they merit attention and provide further evidence of the accuracy of scriptures.

In the last days it will be these same doctrines and devices of demons that will be employed to try and destroy the faith of some. The doctrines are listed, but the observation is made that these teachings will be a most definite feature of the opposition that the Church can expect to be manifested in the last days. With such plain warnings, it seems quite obvious that the answer to such opposition must lie in seeking to establish a true foundation in the Truth, the Word of God. Yet modern trends in the established church seem to advertise the continual folly of men, who rather than holding steadfastly to the truth so frequently abandon it for nonsensical substitutes in an effort to attract people. A church that seeks to please worldly people with worldly methods is inevitably going to become a worldly minded church and of no value spiritually. Paul's comment shows how much he valued the guidance and ministry of the Holy Spirit in the Church. It has to be said, that "Pentecostal" churches, which for fear of false prophecy, suppress the prophetic ministry available for the church, are depriving themselves of a powerful tool or ministry with which to combat erroneous teaching (see 1 Corinthians 11:19.) The false doctrines revealed in the New Testament are not confined to those listed in Timothy (which are included,) neither is the list given considered to be exhaustive, it is merely a foundation on which others may build.

[105] THE DOCTRINES OF DEMONS OR FALSE DOCTRINES.

1. *Reintroduction of The Law* (Ref. Acts 15, Romans, Galatians) Notice especially (Galatians 1:8) *"but though we, or an angel from heaven, preach any other gospel unto you than that ye have received, let him be accursed.'* This is how such doctrines are ministered, from the pulpit, by preaching. (Compare 2 Corinthians 11:14, 15.)

2. *Carnality, Fornication, Idolatry* (1 Corinthians Revelation 2:20) These three are generally associated and are dealt with in Paul's first letter to Corinth.

   Carnality (1 Corinthians 3) is having respect to the things of men and the world. Revelation gives examples of the three together and notice, fornication is taught as a doctrine.

3. *Denial of The Resurrection* (1 Corinthians 15, 2 Timothy 2) Mentioned in all the gospel records, the resurrection is a basic tenet of true believers, to deny it is to deny the power of God.

4. *Righteousness by Works* (Ephesians 2:9)

   This doctrine cancels faith (as belief) in the perfect sacrifice of the LORD Jesus Christ and is an attempt to establish man's own righteousness through his own works; it is totally unacceptable to God.

5. *Philosophy, Traditions, Fables* (Colossians 2:4, 8 16-18 2 Tim 4:4)

   Note the fleshly appeal in these *"enticing words and vain deceit"*. The real danger in such things is the absence of anything of real spiritual value. (Caught up in the fleshly attractions, enticing words, vanity, clever arguments, flattery etc they fail to see that there is nothing of the truth therein.)

6. *Meat, Drink, Holy Days, Marrying* (Rom 14 Col 2:16 and 1 Tim 4:3)

    It is especially noteworthy (Romans 14:2) that the vegetarian is the weakest one; spiritually speaking (this is scriptural fact.) But the choice whether or not to eat meat of course is with the individual (Romans 14:6.) Meat was given to man after The Flood (Genesis 9:3, 4) which suggests that the previously vegetarian diet had disadvantages in spiritual terms. Demons evidently favour a vegetarian diet in their followers, but in their extreme doctrines, they demand blood sacrifices and eventually, this can extend to human sacrifices.

7. *The day of Christ is at hand* (2 Thess 2:1, 2)

    The frequent "*dates when the Lord will come*" are all demonically inspired, but few appreciate the fact. When many people are persuaded to wait in vain for such an event, it adds to the confusion of men and discredits the coming of the LORD in the eyes of many. There have been times historically, when this doctrine has caused national panic. But the LORD's Own words are plain enough and a true believer should not entertain such doctrines (see Matt 24:36, Mark 13:32.)

8. *Denial of The Father and The Son* (1 John 2:22)

    This is one of the doctrines of the antichrists.

9. *Denial that Christ has come in the flesh* (1 John 4:1-3 2 John 7)

Another doctrine of the antichrists.

10. *False Apostles, Teachers, and Prophets* (2 Corinthians 11:13, 2 Peter 2)

The basic sign of these (2 Pet 2:3) is their *covetousness* and consistently in the New Testament, *money, greed, covetousness* and such motives *invariably* indicate these false ministers. In spite of such plain teachings against them, they still thrive and exploit many gullible believers. (Compare Acts 20:28-33 and 1Thessalonians 2:3-7 & 11 for the contrast found in the Apostle Paul.)

[106] 2 TIMOTHY

In Paul's second epistle to Timothy, he warned the young minister of what to expect in the last days in more general terms.

2 Timothy 3:1-5 *"This know also, that in the last days perilous* (difficult or dangerous) *times shall come, for men shall be lovers of their own selves, covetous, boasters, proud, blasphemers, disobedient to parents, unthankful, unholy, without natural affection, trucebreakers, false accusers, incontinent* (without self control), *fierce, despisers of those that are good, traitors, heady* (rash), *highminded, lovers of pleasures more than lovers of God, having a form of godliness, but denying the power thereof: from such turn away."*

The whole context of Paul's comments revealed mankind's becoming the very opposite of what God wanted in the last days (a further reflection of the days of Noah,) and for true believers the promises were contempt and persecution from these men (3:3,) *despisers of those that are good.* Also (2 Timothy 3:12) *Yea, and all that will live godly in Christ Jesus shall suffer persecution.* Believers fail to recognise that this is one of the "promises" of GOD, it will surely happen. In the light of this Paul exhorted Timothy to continue to preach the Word, even when men turned from the truth to fables (4:2, 4) *Preach the word; be instant in season, out of season; reprove, rebuke, exhort with all longsuffering and doctrine. For the time will come when they will not endure sound doctrine; but after their own lusts shall they heap to themselves teachers, having itching ears; and they shall turn away (their) ears from the truth, and shall be turned unto fables.* Yet again this is a last day characteristic, a revival of the fables (folklore,) (in which so much occult material is introduced,) which commenced in Noah's times (Genesis 6:1-4.) However quaint, charming, entertaining, interesting or appealing these tales might appear to be, realistically they are lies, fantasies, total fiction, they can do nothing for the eternal state of man, and spiritually they are totally valueless. It is truly incredible how such blatant rubbish can appeal at all to professing believers, but the tragedy is that in so many cases it does. Paul's teachings to Timothy were not that the last days were coming upon the Church, but Paul was revealing the characteristics of the opposition in the last days, so that the Church could recognise that the last days were reflected in the events of those early times. Of course Paul's teachings will be the means of enabling believers to confidently recognise these same signs manifested in the last days.

[It deserves mention that Cinematography and now Television have provided further means of presenting the occult, witchcraft, fables, folklore, horror, and science fiction in fabulous colour and with incredibly realistic effects (nowadays, sometimes invented by and enhanced with computers.) People (adults) actually cry at the death of a cartoon animal in Disney films, and horror films are so common place and have reached such an extreme that even children are hardly shocked by the most depraved and bloodthirsty scenes. Science fiction or fantasy films effortlessly depict journeys through space and project people into environments that are in truth totally impossible for human habitation and in real terms well beyond man's reach. It is all swallowed whole, and yet the truths of scripture are neglected, or even worse, mocked.

Hell is not the place to reflect how effortlessly one was robbed spiritually.]

Chapter 11: THE REVELATION
(Introduction & the Seven Churches.)

[107] *Introduction.* The Revelation is <u>a prophecy</u> (1:3) this applies to the whole of the book and these considerations are made with this fundamental truth as their basis. The different schools of prophetic interpretation have been adequately represented by their adherents in their own writings and their ideas might be acknowledged as interesting and alternative points of view. But dogmatism in any form tends to be too restrictive and for example, rigidly confining a declared prophecy to a past historical event and claiming therein its complete fulfilment, contradicts the declared purpose of prophecy and restricts belief to boundaries set by the opinions of men.

The views taken are based on the foundations already established from the scriptures. There is no suggestion that these considerations exhaust, or fully explain, the possible fulfilments of this wonderful Prophecy. The purpose is to try and understand these writings in the light of the scriptures examined and to enable believers to comprehend something of the wonderful blessings to be found in this remarkable book. The only caution is to recognise that Interpretations and understanding must be scripturally based; believers should not be too tempted to project world events or circumstances into the various revelations given, in a frantic and vain effort to explain every verse.

Prophetic scripture is divinely inspired, it has to be absolutely true and in its ultimate fulfilment it will satisfy even its most critical students. There is no requirement or necessity to force meanings and applications into trivial or insignificant (or even catastrophic) events. In their fulfilment these prophecies will glorify God.

It might be as well to emphasise, that in recognising the immediate application of some of the writings of The Revelation to the imminent judgment on Israel at the time it was written, this Prophecy, even in these same particulars, could apply yet again in its last days' fulfilment. The Roman reaction to the rebellion of the Jews led ultimately to the siege and destruction of Jerusalem, AD 70, and subsequently, the scattering or dispersion of that nation. This had been prophesied by the LORD Himself (see Matthew 24:2 and compare Luke 23:27-31.)

The Revelation applies primarily to the impending judgments of the last days, the final tribulation of the nation Israel and reveals also the wrath poured out on other nations, for rejecting Christ and/or persecuting His chosen people. This *excludes* the true Church, which will have been raptured before these events take place. The reasons for this view are explained as the study proceeds and it is hoped that others will acknowledge that this brings a refreshing light to much of the mystery, which shrouds The Revelation. The true title of the book is found in its opening words, but the idea that it was given to *"John the divine"* is not substantiated (whoever he was supposed to be.) The early Church fathers accepted that the Revelation was given to the beloved disciple, the apostle John.

[108] (1:1-3) *"The Revelation of Jesus Christ, which God gave unto Him, to show unto His servants things which must shortly come to pass; and He sent and signified it by His angel unto His servant John: who bare record of the Word of God, and of the testimony of Jesus Christ, and of all things that he saw. Blessed is he that readeth, and they that hear the words of this prophecy, and keep those things which are written therein: for the time is at hand."*

These wonderful opening words reveal that the Revelation was given to the LORD Jesus Christ by GOD, it is HIS Revelation therefore and the purpose of this gift was for Him, *to shew unto His servant's things which must shortly come to pass*. The term *servant(s)* was commonly used in the Old Testament in reference to Israel, it appears fourteen times in Revelation (contrast this with *sons* the term used for His believers in the Church and compare Romans 8:14-17 Galatians 4:1-7 and 1 John 3:1.)

The LORD sent and signified (= made known) the Revelation by His angel to His servant John, who in turn wrote the words he heard and the visions he saw, these comprise the Prophecy as written. Quite uniquely to The Revelation there is a blessing included to *he that readeth* (singular) *and they that hear* (plural) the *words of this prophecy*. The blessing is confined to *the words of this prophecy*, but for individuals who read, or those who hear, the words of The Revelation this blessing is given. The condition is that they *keep those things which are written therein,* so that the blessing is in their retention of, or holding onto, the truths of the Revelation.

[109] (1:4-6) *"John to the seven churches which are in Asia, Grace be unto you, and peace, from Him Which is, and Which was, and Which is to come; and from the seven Spirits which are before His throne; and from Jesus Christ, Who is the faithful witness, and the first begotten of the dead, and the prince of the kings of the earth. Unto Him that loved us, and washed us from our sins in His Own blood, and hath made us kings and priests unto God and His Father; to Him be glory and dominion for ever and ever. Amen."*

John addressed himself to the seven churches, which were in Asia; the Greek word translated "churches" is ecclesia and refers to those summoned, or called together. Originally it applied to citizens summoned by a herald to hear about affairs of state. The Septuagint (or the LXX as it is sometimes written,) used the same Greek word "ecclesia" and also their Hebrew word "synagogue" (transliterated directly into the Greek,) almost as synonymous terms. The LXX favoured the word synagogue, when a particular existing body or society was called together and ecclesia, when all (including proselytes, strangers and outsiders) were invited or called together.

Synagogues became more associated with Jewish worship after the formation of the early church and the early Christians themselves dropped the use of the word synagogue, in favour of ecclesia, because it included outsiders. Nevertheless, the very early churches were known as synagogues and the term can quite legitimately be applied to assemblies of exclusively Jewish believers in Christ; and also to strictly Jewish believers (those not believing in Christ.) It will be apparent that this Jewish application is strongly supported in the whole context of The Revelation.

These seven churches were in Asia, which was outside Palestine the main area for the early churches and there are no historical records or any clues regarding the existence of any of these seven assemblies in any existing manuscripts or writings. (The church at Ephesus, to which Paul addressed his epistle, was not the church mentioned in The Revelation as will be shown.) But even granting the existence of these churches, or synagogues (of believing Jews,) at that time (and there is nothing unreasonable in this;) the Revelation was intended particularly for these specific churches (synagogues). This does not restrict or confine the Prophecy to those particular times and it does have future, last days' applications and fulfilments. Such fulfilments would not necessarily apply to assemblies in exactly the same areas, (although this is a definite possibility,) but most certainly these epistles could apply to any assemblies in similar spiritual conditions as these churches in The Revelation.

John's opening words to these churches *grace be unto you, and peace from Him Which is and Which was, and Which is to come* (the word "Which" should be translated "Who" in such cases throughout the Revelation.) This description of Him would be instantly recognisable to any Jew as the meaning of His Hebrew name, *Jehovah;* even if the Jew was not able to speak Hebrew, or even if he were a Greek-speaking convert to Judaism this would be the case. So there can be no doubt that John's opening greeting to these churches was expressed in words plainly directed at Jewish believers. It must be understood, that we are looking at former Jews, or proselytes, who have gone on to believe in the LORD Jesus Christ, i.e. Christian-Jews, like John and the other apostles.

[110] It is of the utmost significance therefore, that John's next words are (1:7) *Behold, He cometh with clouds; and every eye shall see Him, and they also which pierced Him: and all kindreds of the earth shall wail because of Him. Even so, Amen.*

The coming described would be familiar to Jews especially, compare (Daniel 7:13) *"behold, one like the Son of man came with the clouds of heaven,"* (Zechariah 12:10) *"and they shall look upon Me Whom they have pierced,"* and the LORD's Own teachings to His disciples, which have already been shown to be totally Jewish in their application (see Matthew 24:30 [69].) Consider also the words of the angels (Acts 1:9-11 also with Matthew 24:30 [69]) addressed to *ye men of Galilee* (i.e. Jews) this coming of the LORD *with clouds* is for His people, the Jews, not for His Church. (1:8) *"I am Alpha and Omega, the Beginning and the Ending,"* saith the LORD, *"Which is, and Which was, and Which is to come, The Almighty."*

This whole verse conveys GOD's absolute power and control in the dazzling light of His faithfulness to His promises to His people. The LORD is Jehovah Elohim, the LORD GOD, which means the Covenant Keeping, Faithful LORD, Eternal, Immortal, Invisible, Immutable, Who was, Who is and Who is to come, The Creator. It is a powerful combination of titles, which is even further emphasised in the text by the addition of Who is and Who was and Who Is to come, The Almighty (Pantokrator) which expresses GOD's infinite power over all His creation (in the Revelation this word occurs nine times: 1:8, 4:8, 11:17, 15:3 16:7, 14 19:6, 15 & 21:22 and once only in 2 Corinthians 6:18.) This verse bears direct comparison with the lessons that Nebuchadnezzar learned as a result of his time of madness (Daniel 4 [6]), when Nebuchadnezzar acknowledged Who ruled in heaven and on earth (see also Daniel 7:18, 27 [10]). Such comparisons reveal the wonderful harmony of the scriptures, and confirm their truth.

[111] (1:9) *"I John, who also am your brother, and companion in tribulation, and in the kingdom and patience of Jesus Christ, was in the isle that is called Patmos, for the Word of God, and for the testimony of Jesus Christ."*

Patmos was considered to be the Roman equivalent of Devil's Island or Alcatraz, an island of confinement, a punishment prison, and a place for real troublemakers. Whatever means or reasons were used to put John, their *companion in tribulation*, on Patmos, these were not revealed; John made nothing of it, he merely said that he was there, *"for the Word of God, and (for) the testimony of Jesus (Christ)."* [*(for)* and *(Christ)* - these words not found in original texts.]

(1:10) *I was in the Spirit on the Lord's day, and heard behind me a great voice, as of a trumpet,* Another source of error occurs in the English translation, which leads many to believe that this refers to Sunday, (i.e. "the LORD's day" in English terms.) But the Greek is *he kuriake hemera*, which means *"the day of the Lord"* (see also 1 Thessalonians 5:2 2 Thessalonians 2:2 & 2 Peter 3:10.) Failing to appreciate this is the cause of many not understanding The Revelation from John's opening remarks. John found himself in the Spirit on *the day of the Lord*, i.e. he was enabled spiritually to see what was involved in that future day (or time) of judgment.

The LORD's teachings in the gospels relate to the events involved at the time that He comes again i.e. the day of the LORD, and The Revelation describes these events prophetically in more detail. This verse further establishes the whole of The Revelation as a Prophecy (see 1:3) pointing so clearly to the last days and the involvement of the nation Israel in what will happen. It should also be added that a trumpet in Old Testament scriptures was sounded as a call to battle or a rallying call for the LORD's people.

[112] THE SEVEN CHURCHES

(1:11) *Saying, "I am Alpha and Omega, the First and the Last: and what thou seest, write in a book, and send it unto the seven churches which are in Asia; unto Ephesus, and unto Smyrna, and unto Pergamos, and unto Thyatira, and unto Sardis, and unto Philadelphia, and unto Laodicea."*

The instruction to John was to write what he saw and send it to the seven churches in Asia. These ecclesia were named Ephesus, Smyrna, Pergamos, Thyatira, Sardis, Philadelphia and Laodicea; but were kept distinctly separate, although equally important, by the repeated use of the word "and" in each case. (The Seven Churches in Asia are shown in Figure 7; note their location in respect of the Isle of Patmos. Other New Testament churches are included for interest.) Each of the seven churches was precious to the LORD, He was concerned for and addressed, each church by name; more importantly, what He said applied to every member of each church, as will be seen.

[113] (1:12-20) *And I turned to see the voice that spake with me. And being turned I saw seven golden candlesticks; and in the midst of the seven candlesticks one like unto the Son of man, clothed with a garment down to the foot, and girt about the paps with a golden girdle. His head and His hairs were white like wool, as white as snow; and His eyes were as a flame of fire; and His feet like unto fine brass, as if they burned in a furnace; and His voice as the sound of many waters. And He had in His right hand seven stars: and out of His mouth went a sharp two-edged sword: and His countenance was as the sun shineth in his strength. And when I saw Him, I fell at His feet as dead. And He laid His right hand upon me, saying unto me, "Fear not; I am the First and the Last: I am He that liveth, and was dead; and, behold, I am alive for evermore, Amen; and have the keys of hell and of death. Write the things which thou hast seen, and the things which are, and the things which shall be hereafter; the mystery of the seven stars which thou sawest in My right hand, and the seven golden candlesticks. The seven stars are the angels of the seven*

churches: and the seven candlesticks which thou sawest are the seven churches."

The title *"The Son of man"* (with the definite article) always refers to The Christ; without the definite article, it refers to men of God (see Footnote 41 [232].) It is a familiar Old Testament title but it is never associated with the Church of the LORD Jesus Christ. Believers in His Church, His Body, are referred to as sons of God, never as sons of men.

The other expression *"angels of the seven churches"* is not found anywhere else in the New Testament in reference to ministers in churches. But it was used in Jewish synagogue terminology. The Ruler of the synagogue (Greek Archisunagogos) was responsible for its affairs, finances, repairs, regulating services etc in an overall sense. But the Head of the synagogue (Sheliach Tzibbur,) whose duties included praying, preaching and appointing the readers, was also known as The Angel, or Minister. This is the term used and it always applied to Jewish assemblies, never to churches involving gentiles. John's words were addressed to believing Jews, the angel or minister, in these seven churches.

[114] EPHESUS

(2:1-7) Unto the angel of the church of Ephesus write, These things saith He that holdeth the seven stars in His right hand, Who walketh in the midst of the seven golden candlesticks; I know thy works, and thy labour, and thy patience, and how thou canst not bear them which are evil: and thou hast tried them which say they are apostles, and are not, and hast found them liars: and hast borne, and hast patience, and for My name's sake hast laboured, and hast not fainted. Nevertheless I have somewhat against thee, because thou hast left thy first love. Remember therefore from whence thou art fallen, and repent, and do the first works; or else I will come unto thee quickly, and will remove thy candlestick out of his place, except

thou repent. But this thou hast, that thou hatest the deeds of the Nicolaitanes, which I also hate. He that hath an ear, let him hear what the Spirit saith unto the churches; To him that overcometh will I give to eat of the tree of life, which is in the midst of the paradise of God.

The first point to note is that works were taken into account in this church (in contrast Ephesians 2:8, 9 reads: *For by grace are ye saved through faith; and that not of yourselves: it is the gift of God: not of works lest any man should boast.*) It is is not a contradiction, it is a dispensational difference. The Ephesians to whom Paul addressed his epistle, were blessed *with all spiritual blessings in heavenly places in Christ* (Ephesians 1:3) in GOD's grace. But such grace does not apply in the day of the LORD, when the terms of the Jewish covenant are re-established under the Law. When this was written by John, it was directed to an assembly of Jews at the end of their dispensation (which is now in abeyance,) as the transition to the times of the gentiles was taking place. Concerning this synagogue, the LORD in His role as Judge was looking at everything and at Ephesus those, who believed in Him as the Christ, were given credit where due. His criticism came for their leaving *thy first love* and to understand what this would mean to a real Jew, requires reference to their law (see Deuteronomy 7:6-11.) There was clear warning for them to repent. The deeds of the Nicolaitanes hated by the saints at Ephesus and the LORD Himself are not actually described. There is no historical record of the Nicolaitanes and many suggestions have been advanced for what might be involved, (see Pergamos [116]) but the scripture offers no explanation. Finally, note the expression *"he that hath an ear"*: these words were exclusively the LORD's and He was exhorting the saints to pay attention to what the Spirit was saying to them in these synagogues. The use of these words always means that special attention should be given to what is being said and this is an individual responsibility. In this instance, the words that followed were *"to him that overcometh will I give to eat of the tree of life, which is in the midst of the paradise of God."* Such words will carry considerable weight in their last day application and their meaning for the Jews at that time will be far beyond anything that gentiles can appreciate in this present dispensation of grace.

[115] SMYRNA

(2:8-11) *"And unto the angel of the church in Smyrna write; These things saith the First and the Last, Which was dead and is alive; I know thy works, and tribulation, and poverty, (but thou art rich) and I know the blasphemy of them which say they are Jews, and are not, but are the synagogue of Satan. Fear none of those things which thou shalt suffer: behold, the devil shall cast some of you into prison, that ye may be tried; and ye shall have tribulation ten days: be thou faithful unto death, and I will give thee a crown of life. He that hath an ear, let him hear what the Spirit saith unto the churches, He that overcometh shall not be hurt of the second death."*

Attention is drawn to the words *"the blasphemy of them which say they are Jews and are not, but are the synagogue of Satan"*, applying this to members of the Church of the LORD Jesus Christ is most difficult. But in the Jewish context, these words afford striking confirmation of the view taken and present far less difficulty in application. In the last days, in such an assembly, there will be blasphemers, who outwardly claim to be Jews (compare the LORD's Own warnings about betrayal at this time, Matthew 24:10-12.) The implication was that these blasphemers were seeking to destroy the very nation, the Jews, to whom they claimed allegiance; in reality they were of the synagogue of Satan, they were deceitful and murderous in their intentions (compare John 8:33-57.) In Smyrna they succeed in destroying their brethren, hence the exhortation to be faithful unto death (compare also Revelation 20:4-6.)

[116] PERGAMOS

(2:12-17) *"And to the angel of the church in Pergamos write; These things saith He which hath the sharp sword with two edges; I know thy works, and where thou dwellest, even where Satan's seat is: and thou holdest fast My name, and hast not denied My faith, even in those days wherein Antipas was My faithful martyr, who was slain among you, where Satan dwelleth. But I have a few things against thee, because thou hast there them that hold the doctrine of Balaam, who taught Balac to cast a stumblingblock before the children of Israel, to eat things sacrificed unto idols, and to commit fornication. So hast thou also them that hold the doctrine of the Nicolaitanes, which thing I hate. Repent; or else I will come unto thee quickly, and will fight against them with the sword of My mouth. He that hath an ear, let him hear what the Spirit saith unto the churches; To him that overcometh will I give to eat of the hidden manna, and will give him a white stone, and in the stone a new name written, which no man knoweth saving he that receiveth it."*

A striking characteristic of Pergamos is that it is also the situation or location of Satan's seat (or throne, compare Revelation 13:2 & 16:10.) [Previously Satan's throne was in Tyre or Tyrus, see Ezekiel 28: (v1-10 applies to *the prince of Tyrus*, who was a man, Ithabolus II; but *the King of Tyrus* v11-19, was Satan.)] The reference to Antipas (which means "all against") must also have prophetic applications and his death seems to be a part of a trial imposed on the saints at Pergamos at that time, but they still held fast. (Herod Antipas being the ruler who beheaded John the baptist and who ridiculed the LORD. The name is not found elsewhere and there are no further details about the martyr Antipas. See Luke 3:19, 20 & 23:11.) The reference to Balaam is significant, because there will be many in the last days who will compromise their spiritual experience for money and who, like Balaam, will cause the betrayal and downfall of many in Israel.

In Pergamos it was the DOCTRINE [compare with the DEEDS in Ephesus (2:6)] of the Nicolaitanes that attracted the LORD's hatred. The fact that neither the deeds nor the doctrines are scripturally described, could point to the true definition of what these deeds and doctrines involve. In other words deeds and doctrines for which there are no scriptural supports are hated by the LORD. In the last days this could mean the introduction of completely new (but unscriptural) ideas; but, it could apply also to customs, traditions and the like, introduced with no scriptural authority. Things which have been allowed to come in and nullify the effect of the Word of God (compare Mark 7:1-13.) For the overcomers in Pergamos, the manna was hidden (i.e. laid up in store,) and the white stone can have a variety of meanings. Probably, the most appropriate is the "hospitality tally stone". This was the suggested name given to a stone that was broken and divided between the parties concerned (usually, it involved families, with relatives living in different towns or countries,) their names were inscribed on the pieces, which were kept carefully and safely. When any of the participants travelled, they could claim the hospitality agreed together, when they produced the matching piece of stone. It provided a convenient and foolproof method of ensuring family care and protection, in times when travelling and hospitality could be hazardous. In the white stone, the LORD was telling the saints at Pergamos that He was offering them a completely foolproof, individual invitation to partake of His hospitality and riches.

In closing these brief considerations on Pergamos, as *the seat of Satan* its situation is in the area taken by Lysimachus (one of Alexander the Great's Generals,) and Pergamos could have tremendous significance in the last days because of its association with the career or appearance of the beast. (See [43] and also Figure 4 with note.)

[117] THYATIRA

(2:18-29) *"And unto the angel of the church in Thyatira write; These things saith the Son of God, Who hath His eyes like unto a flame of fire, and His feet are like fine brass; I know thy works, and charity, and service, and faith, and thy patience, and thy works; and the last to be more than the first. Notwithstanding I have a few things against* thee, because thou sufferest that woman Jezebel, which calleth herself a prophetess, to teach and to seduce My servants to commit fornication, and to eat things sacrificed unto idols. And I gave her space to repent of her fornication; and she repented not. Behold, I will cast her into a bed, and them that commit adultery with her into great tribulation, except they repent of their deeds. And I will kill her children with death; and all the churches shall know that I am He which searcheth the reins and hearts: and I will give unto every one of you according to your works. But unto you I say, and unto the rest in Thyatira, as many as have not this doctrine, and which have not known the depths of Satan, as they speak; I will put upon you none other burden. But that which ye have already hold fast till I come. And he that overcometh, and keepeth My works unto the end, to him will I give power over nations: and he shall rule them with a rod of iron; as the vessels of a potter shall they be broken to shivers: even as I received of My Father. And I will give him the morning star. He that hath an ear, let him hear what the Spirit saith unto the churches."

Notice especially the LORD's words, *"I know thy works... ...and thy works; and the last (works) to be more than the first (works)."* The last works to which the LORD referred, were those for which He said, *"I will give unto every one of you according to your works"*. These were the burdens laid on these believers through the doctrines of Jezebel, because the LORD Himself would not add to these burdens upon them. But He expected them to do *the first (works),* which they knew were from Him, because their experience had been established originally in such obedience and His exhortation to them concluded with His promises *"to him that overcometh, and keepeth MY works unto the end."* Unmistakably, in this address there are allusions to high authority. The wife of King Ahab, Jezebel was the Old Testament character, who led Israel into idolatry. Notice too, the rewards for the overcomer in this place also relate to authority, power over nations and he shall rule them with a rod of iron, the morning star – all of which would convey a sense of ruling authority to a Jew (see Numbers 24:15-19.)

[118] SARDIS

(3:1-6) *And unto the angel of the church in Sardis write; These things saith He that hath the seven Spirits of God, and the seven stars; I know thy works, that thou hast a name that thou livest, and art dead. Be watchful, and strengthen the things which remain, that are ready to die: for I have not found thy works perfect before God. Remember therefore how thou hast received and heard, and hold fast, and repent. If therefore thou shalt not watch, I will come on thee as a thief, and thou shalt not know what hour I will come upon thee. Thou hast a few names even in Sardis which have not defiled their garments; and they shall walk with Me in white: for they are worthy. He that overcometh, the same shall be clothed in white raiment; and I will not blot out his name out of the book of life, but I will confess his name before My Father, and before His angels. He that hath an ear, let him hear what the Spirit saith unto the churches.*

Nowhere else does the LORD (or Paul for that matter,) ever imply that He would come to His Church as a thief. Paul in fact taught to the contrary concerning the Church (1 Thessalonians 5:4 [94]). But this does reflect the LORD's teachings to the Jews, His people, in which they were repeatedly warned to be prepared for His coming as unexpectedly as a thief (see Matthew 24:42-44 [69] and compare Revelation 16:15 [182]). Note that Sardis had a reputation, *a name that thou livest,* it was considered alive, lively, full of life; in reality it was dead. Fleshly enthusiasm, noise, music, singing, clapping, dancing etc are scripturally no indications of spiritual life.

[119] PHILADELPHIA

(3:7-13) *And to the angel of the church in Philadelphia write; These things saith He that is holy, He that is true, He that hath the key of David, He that openeth, and no man shutteth; and shutteth, and no man openeth; I know thy works: behold, I have set before thee an open door, and no man can shut it: for thou hast a little strength, and hast kept My word, and hast not denied My name. Behold, I will make them of the synagogue of Satan, which say they are Jews, and are not, but do lie; behold, I will make them to come and worship before thy feet, and to know that I have loved thee. Because thou hast kept the word of My patience, I also will keep thee from the hour of temptation, which shall come upon all the world, to try them that dwell upon the earth. Behold, I come quickly: hold that fast which thou hast, that no man take thy crown. Him that overcometh will I make a pillar in the temple of My God, and he shall go no more out: and I will write upon him the name of My God, and the name of the city of My God, which is New Jerusalem, which cometh down out of heaven from My God: and I will write upon him My new name. He that hath an ear, let him hear what the Spirit saith unto the churches.*

The key of David (compare Isaiah 22:22,) also has Jewish significance and also the words, *"Behold, I will make them of the synagogue of Satan, which say they are Jews, and are not, but do lie; behold, I will make them to come and worship before thy feet, and to know that I have loved thee."* This has a familiar ring (compare with Smyrna above,) impostors, false apostles, again seeking to betray the true Jews. The consequences of this were that these same impostors would be made to worship before the believing Jews, which suggest strongly that their efforts were to force the Jews to worship something particularly obnoxious, or wrong. To attempt to apply these verses to the true Church leads to real difficulties; but for the Jews, such things are evidently possible in the last days. In fact the introduction of idolatry by force is one of the means used to try and destroy the nation spiritually, since it would negate their covenant relationship with the LORD. (Note: *Them that dwell upon the earth,* or earth-dwellers, in Revelation this expression occurs seven times 3:10, 6:10, 11:10, 13:8, 14, 14:6, 17:8 compare Philippians 3:19, 20.)

[120] LAODICEA

(3:14-22) *And unto the angel of the church of the Laodiceans write; These things saith the Amen, the faithful and true Witness, the beginning of the creation of God; I know thy works, that thou art neither cold nor hot: I would thou wert cold or hot. So then because thou art lukewarm, and neither cold nor hot, I will spue thee out of My mouth. Because thou sayest, I am rich, and increased with goods, and have need of nothing; and knowest not that thou art wretched, and miserable, and poor, and blind, and naked: I counsel thee to buy of Me gold tried in the fire, that thou mayest be rich; and white raiment, that thou mayest be clothed, and that the shame of thy nakedness do not appear; and anoint thine eyes with eyesalve, that thou mayest see. As many as I love, I rebuke and chasten: be zealous therefore, and repent. Behold, I stand at the door, and knock: if any man hear My voice, and open the door, I will come in to him, and will sup with him, and he with Me. To him that overcometh will I grant to sit with Me in My throne, even as I also overcame, and am set down with My Father in His throne. He that hath an ear let him hear what the Spirit saith unto the churches.*

"The Amen" is a title transliterated from the Hebrew word, its meaning as a title is "Truth" (see Isaiah 65:16.) It must be said, that the true Church of the present dispensation of grace has to buy nothing. Everything is freely given to us by God in Christ (compare Romans 8:32 Philippians 4:19 etc) but this was not the case for Laodicea, who was counselled to buy gold that had been proved in the fire. More importantly however, the description of the LORD's standing at the door and knocking, referred to the customary call to a wedding feast (compare Luke 12:36-38.) It is a gross blunder, a mark of a novice in scriptural understanding, to use this text to preach that the LORD is appealing to sinners to let Him into their hearts. (The Amen and the Beginning of the creation of GOD are divine titles of the LORD associated with the creation of GOD; which the LORD Himself distinguished; see Mark 13:19.)

[121]

In this examination of the seven churches, emphasis has been placed on the distinctly Jewish application; but it has been shown also that these scriptures primarily apply to the last days' Jewish experience. Whilst the sites of these assemblies (or their towns) can be located geographically (even modern tourist atlases show them,) these churches remain remarkably obscure historically. They may have been a particular group of interest to John the apostle, especially during his confinement on Patmos, which might have occurred because of his involvement with them. Concerning John, the LORD Himself (see John 21:22) suggested to Peter that He had plans for John, relating to His coming (which could have happened within John's lifetime, had the Jews accepted the ministry of the apostles.) Perhaps The Revelation given to His servant John was in part a compensation for the immense disappointment John must have felt, when he realised that Israel was not going to accept, what was being offered to them in the Gospel of God.

That these writings or letters may have applied to the churches or assemblies in the named places is neither disputed nor challenged. These exhortations cannot be dismissed as totally fulfilled with such vague ideas of what was involved. To deny or neglect a future last days' fulfilment would be culpable neglect and the view is maintained that the whole of The Revelation has a vital significance and application to the nation Israel in the last days.

[122]

One final point to note, before leaving these churches; the revelation of the LORD Himself, as described by John (1:12-20), is repeated in its features and its order, in the writings addressed to the churches. It can be seen (1:11) that His instruction to John was that *"What thou seest, write in a book, AND SEND IT UNTO THE SEVEN CHURCHES etc"* and together with the fact, that the features of His description are spread over the seven churches, this strengthens the view that, each individual member of all of the churches was able to *"hear what the Spirit saith unto the churches"*. Further, it means that nobody was exempt from any of the LORD's exhortations and warnings. But it is in the particular details from the description of the LORD, that He must be viewed in each of the churches. For example to Ephesus He is described (2:1) as *He that holdeth the seven stars in His right hand, Who walketh in the midst of the seven golden candlesticks.* To Smyrna He is *the First and the Last, Which was dead, and is alive.* These particulars are significant and should be considered in each case, but their further study is beyond the scope of these considerations.

Chapter 12: The Revelation (Heavenly Vision & The Seven Seals)

[123] (4:1-11) *After this I looked, and, behold, a door was opened in heaven: and the first voice which I heard was as it were of a trumpet talking with me; which said, "Come up hither, and I will shew thee things which must be hereafter." And immediately I was in the Spirit: and behold, a throne was set in heaven, and One sat on the throne. And He that sat was to look upon like a jasper and a sardine stone: and there was a rainbow round about the throne, in sight like unto an emerald. And round about the throne were four and twenty seats: and upon the seats I saw four and twenty elders sitting, clothed in white raiment; and they had on their heads crowns of gold. And out of the throne proceeded lightnings and thunderings and voices: and there were seven lamps of fire burning before the throne, which are the seven Spirits of God. And before the throne there was a sea of glass like unto crystal: and in the midst of the throne, and round about the throne, were four beasts full of eyes before and behind. And the first beast was like a lion, and the second beast like a calf, and the third beast had a face as a man, and the fourth beast was like a flying eagle. And the four beasts had each of them six wings about him; and they were full of eyes within: and they rest not day and night, saying, "Holy, holy, holy, Lord God Almighty, Which was, and is, and is to come." And when those beasts give glory and honour and thanks to Him that sat on the throne, Who liveth for ever and ever, the four and twenty elders fall down before Him that sat on the throne, and worship Him that liveth for ever and ever, and cast their crowns before the throne, saying, "Thou art worthy, O Lord, to receive glory and honour and power: for Thou hast created all things, and for Thy pleasure they are and were created."*

John's account of his heavenly experience is very remarkable, so concise, yet full of detail and undeniably inspired. Anyone, who doubts this, should read some of the pathetic attempts made to counterfeit or copy this revelation. John's words ring true throughout; his words are so wonderfully adequate that nothing needs to be added. This passage contains such a wealth of information on the throne of God that it merits some consideration in its own right.

[124]

John was called up to this experience and immediately in the Spirit he saw the throne of God (compare Paul's experience 2 Corinthians 12.) The elders around the throne are heavenly beings. There is no hint of any earthly associations for them and their places and position are part of some divine order, their crowns of gold are evidence of their highly exalted position (compare Revelation 14:3 [170]). The seven Spirits of God will be considered later in terms of their association with the Lamb (5:6). The "beasts" are in fact "creatures" (the Greek word here is ZOA singular, or ZOON plural) and from the description given these are the cherubim. (Compare Ezekiel 1:5-14 and 10:20; also note Revelation 5:8, 11 [125] which confirm they are not angels.) The cherubim are truly wonderful created beings, i.e. creatures, not beasts, this is an unfortunate translation in the AV since scripturally the term beast signifies a lack of godliness or godly awareness, (in its ultimate extreme in The Beast himself,) and this is not a characteristic of the cherubim. The cherubim have very strong divine associations and it might be observed:

= The cherubim are always associated with God's throne

= They are never worshipped, but offer worship

= They represent creation and life to the Creator (see

Genesis 3:24)

= Their number is FOUR which relates to created earth

= They symbolise the heads of four created animal orders (lion as king of wild animals, ox as king of domestic animals, eagle as king of birds, man with dominion over animals.)

= They proclaim God's holiness and power over His creation.

The response of the elders to the praise of the cherubim is a wonderful description of heavenly worship. It can be seen that the purpose of (GOD's) creation was and is to bring pleasure to God. Ultimately this objective will be accomplished to His eternal glory and He will be totally vindicated for His wisdom in creating everything, in spite of all that has opposed His divine will.

[125] (5:1-14) *And I saw in the right hand of Him that sat on the throne a book written within and on the backside, sealed with seven seals. And I saw a strong angel proclaiming with a loud voice, "Who is worthy to open the book, and to loose the seals thereof?" And no man in heaven, nor in earth, neither under the earth, was able to open the book, neither to look thereon. And I wept much, because no man was found worthy to open and to read the book, neither to look thereon. And one of the elders saith unto me, "Weep not: behold, the Lion of the tribe of Juda, the Root of David, hath prevailed to open the book, and to loose the seven seals thereof." And I beheld, and, lo, in the midst of the throne and of the four beasts, and in the midst of the elders, stood a Lamb as it had been slain, having seven horns and seven eyes, which are the seven Spirits of God sent forth into all the earth. And He came and took the book out of the right hand of Him*

that sat upon the throne. And when He had taken the book, the four beasts and four and twenty elders fell down before the Lamb, having every one of them harps, and golden vials full of odours, which are the prayers of saints. And they sung a new song, saying, "Thou art worthy to take the book, and to open the seals thereof: for Thou wast slain, and hast redeemed us to God by Thy blood out of every kindred, and tongue, and people, and nation; and hast made us unto our God kings and priests: and we shall reign on the earth." And I beheld, and I heard the voice of many angels round about the throne and the beasts and the elders: and the number of them was ten thousand times ten thousand, and thousands of thousands; saying with a loud voice, "Worthy is the Lamb that was slain to receive power, and riches, and wisdom, and strength, and honour, and glory, and blessing." And every creature which is in heaven, and on the earth, and under the earth, and such as are in the sea, and all that are in them, heard I saying, "Blessing, and honour, and glory, and power, be unto Him that sitteth upon the throne, and unto the Lamb for ever and ever." And the four beasts said, "Amen." And the four and twenty elders fell down and worshipped Him that liveth for ever and ever.

[126] Another wonderful heavenly revelation, but tragically its contents have been distorted by artistic extremes in vain attempts to portray its symbolism. But, considering what is written, John described a book (a scroll, the writing on both sides,) sealed with seven seals. The Angel's challenge was *"Who is worthy to open the book, and to loose the seals thereof?"* This brought the truth that *"No man in heaven, earth or under the earth was able to open the book, neither to look thereon."* John's reaction to this, his weeping, shows firstly, that he was capable of displaying fleshly emotions in the heavenly experiences given to him and secondly, expressed his real concern. John appreciated that the scroll contained a revelation of special significance and immense value to mankind. The search for anyone worthy to open the book was worldwide, it was not confined to the nation Israel and it included men, who had lived previously, now in heaven or under the earth i.e. in the grave. An elder told John not to weep and revealed to him, He, Who had been found worthy, *"the Lion of the tribe of Juda, the root of David* (distinctly Jewish) *hath prevailed* (had the physical strength and the mental power) *to open the book, and to loose the seals thereof."*

John's next words are wonderful, *"And I beheld, and, lo, in the midst of the throne and of the four beasts, and in the midst of the elders, stood a Lamb as it had been slain, having seven horns and seven eyes, which are the seven Spirits of God sent forth into all the earth."* This description has sadly inspired some of the most grotesque illustrations of a seven horned and seven eyed lamb and these ridiculous concepts have been accepted and even published. Such artists have only proved their total inability to help anyone draw the right conclusions and their nightmare efforts have added nothing to anyone's spiritual understanding. The LORD Jesus Christ Himself has likewise been depicted with a sword blade extending from His mouth, in equally idiotic portrayals (of 1:16.) These words are a graphic description of the effects of the words He speaks, of His authority as The Word of God, not a literal fact.

[127] To return to John's description however, considering the seven Spirits of God (see also 4:5) these have been described as *seven lamps of fire burning before the throne* and therefore are akin to the seven candlesticks (or lamps, of 1:12.) The seven Spirits (1:4 & 3:1) are a feature of God's throne and from these seven Spirits was ministered grace to their earthly counterparts (1:4) i.e. the seven lamps or seven churches. These seven Spirits are associated in the sense of GOD's power, knowledge, control and authority over them and their number, seven, is divine.

[128] The Lamb (5:6) *as it had been slain* bearing the marks of the sacrificial death that it had suffered. Its *having seven horns and seven* *eyes* was explained *which are the seven Spirits of God sent forth into all the earth.* The horns and eyes are not described in the Lamb's head, the horns and eyes, from the very context of the description, depict the same seven Spirits of God. It is suggested, from the use of the word "eyes" that these seven Spirits are the Watchers, the Holy Ones, whose decree and demand resulted in Nebuchadnezzar's madness. (See Daniel 4, note especially v13, 14 which show that the Watcher and the Holy One are the same being, and also v17 & 23.) The Lamb is revealed in this verse as having been sacrificed and having the same authority as the One on the throne, i.e. GOD Himself, by virtue of the Lamb's control and power over the seven Spirits of God. Obviously anyone, who imagines a woolly sheep with seven horns and seven eyes, has missed the whole point. Compare the testimony of John the baptist also to the Lamb of God on earth. John the baptist saw no sheep, he saw Jesus of Nazareth as a man[31].

In his experience the Apostle John saw the Lamb as it had been slain in heavenly places, he saw the risen LORD Jesus Christ, with the marks of His sacrificial death still evident in His wounds, but the

---

[31] There is no end to such absurdities and because (for example,) painters have included little dogs trailing around after the LORD in some of their works, there are actually those who assume this to be true and exalt pets to a ludicrous level (in spite of the fact dogs are rarely kept as pets in the Middle East, except perhaps as puppies for children.) A famous painting in a Manchester Museum depicts a group of fawning women showing a baby to a man in advanced middle age, and this is supposed to represent their showing the child Christ to John the Baptist! Another picture (also in Manchester,) was referred to by Cunningham Geikie D.D. in his book The Holy Land and the Bible (1887) in his description of the southern edge of the Dead Sea. *The range of salt hills at the south, known as Jebel Usdum, is no less fitting boundary of the Sea of death. Holman Hunt resided here for several days in 1854, and has given us in his terrible picture of* "the Scapegoat" *an embodiment of the landscape of that portion of the Dead Sea at sunset – a vision of the most appalling desolation.* The painting depicts a terrified bleating animal in the wilderness, with a rainbow in the far distance. Whilst the artist's ability is not questioned (he was a founder member of the Pre-Raphaelite School,) he totally missed the lesson of the scapegoat. The scapegoat was intended to be set free in the wilderness and a goat is admirably adapted to survive in desert conditions, for (as Dr Geikie confirmed,) they live wild in this same area. The liberated scapegoat demonstrated that the national guilt of sin had been taken away; the scapegoat (which would never be seen again,) thereby typifying the truth that after the atonement, the people of Israel were free from the guilt of sin for another year. In the LORD's times the Jews themselves missed the real lesson of the scapegoat, the unfortunate animal (ordained to be set free) was merely cast off the nearest cliff to its death.

divine authority of GOD Himself was also evidently His by right. The title or name of The Lamb is used to emphasise the LORD Jesus Christ's absolute submission, His obedience (which is what real faith is all about, doing what God says, obeying Him,) in His commitment to the revealed will of God. This of course stands in The Revelation in vivid contrast to the absolute, blasphemous rebellion of the beast, who is described later. The Lamb, the LORD Jesus Christ in His heavenly status, took the book (5:7-14) and this act inspired His worship by all in heaven. This worship above everything else revealed His true status in heavenly places that He could be worshipped and glorified at the throne of God; (because John was in the Spirit not in the flesh, this does not contradict John 1:18.) The worthiness of the Lamb had been established in His obedience, His sacrifice, the cross. The power of the Lamb (revealed in His control and authority over the seven Spirits of God,) was as great as God's Own power; He was therefore able to read the book. His physical strength and spiritual power had been totally proved. When the Lamb took the book or scroll, out of the *right hand of Him that sat upon the throne,* the heavenly worship in response testified in every respect to the worthiness of the Lamb. The Lamb could open the seals and as the seals were broken, the scroll was opened to reveal what was contained in the scroll. The tremendous and wonderful revelations following are the revealed will of God given to the Lamb Who was worthy (compare Revelation 1:1.) John himself was not permitted to see or copy anything from the scroll as it was unsealed, but from what John described of what he saw, when the seals were broken, some indication is given of what was involved or written in the scroll.

[129]

The key to understanding the opening of the seals is found in the LORD's Own teachings and to assist in making this comparison, each seal is considered in turn and compared with the gospel accounts and other relevant scriptures. The events of the seven seals (and subsequently, the seven trumpets and seven vials,) so graphically and wonderfully described in the Revelation, should not be allowed to cloud the LORD's Own teachings. He taught emphatically, that things would be *as in the days of Noah* and *as in the days of Sodom* and these truths must apply; the events described in The Revelation are additional details, further revelations, to His Own teachings.

[130] THE FIRST SEAL

(6:1,2) *And I saw when the Lamb opened one of the seals, and I heard, as it were the noise of thunder, one of the four beasts saying, "Come and see." And I saw, and behold, a white horse: and he that sat on him had a bow; and a crown was given unto him: and he went forth conquering, and to conquer.*

It is amazing that some commentators in the past have been so willing to put the LORD Himself on one of the four horses and their favourite choice is usually the white horse (presumably from comparison with Revelation 19:11 [194], although that is a totally different revelation.) In the context here, as the Lamb, The LORD Jesus Christ is opening these seven seals and there is no reason to suppose that He is one of the four riders. From the gospel accounts of His teachings, the commencement of the events of the last days was consistently shown to be the appearances of many false Christs. The rider on the white horse is therefore taken to typify this; the successful preaching of the doctrines of the false Christs, for this rider conquers. A quick comparison of the gospel verses confirms this: Matthew 24:25 *For many shall come in My name, saying, 'I am Christ' and shall deceive many.* Mark 13:6 *For many shall come in My name saying, 'I am Christ'; and shall deceive many.* Luke 21:8 *And He said, "Take heed that ye be not deceived: for many shall come in My name, saying, 'I am Christ', and the time draweth near: go ye not therefore after them."*

[131] THE SECOND SEAL

(6:3, 4) *And when He had opened the second seal, I heard the second beast say, "Come and see." And there went out another horse that was red: and power was given to him that sat thereon to take peace from the earth, and that they should kill one another, and there was given unto him a great sword.*

This rider on the red horse takes peace from the earth and this is by heavenly decree, as the second seal is opened. Prophecy as clear as this makes mankind's efforts for peace pretty futile. At this time the earthly way may be by political negotiation, treaties and such means, but, when this seal is opened, war and killing are ordained. Compare the LORD's teachings again in the order given in the gospel accounts: Matthew 24:6 *And ye shall hear of wars and rumours of wars* Mark 13:7 *And when ye shall hear of wars and rumours of wars, be ye not troubled: for such things must needs be; but the end shall not be yet.* Luke 21:9 *But when ye shall hear of wars and commotions, be not terrified: for these things must first come to pass; but the end is not by and by.*

Significantly, concerning the rider on the red horse, the *"power was given unto him to take peace from the earth, and that they should kill one another."* Effectively this means the withdrawal of the proclamation of the heavenly hosts made at the birth of the LORD Jesus Christ (Luke 23:14) *peace on earth and goodwill to men.* Having rejected the grace of GOD ministered and manifest through His Son, mankind faces the spiritual and fleshly conflicts on earth as various powers and authorities in high places seek to take control (of nations) by force.

The seals are evidently in step with His teachings, but of course, the efforts of men to make peace will continue as Paul also taught (1 Thessalonians 5:3). *For when they shall say, "Peace and safety"; then sudden destruction cometh upon them, as travail upon a woman with child; and they shall not escape.* The sobering truth from Paul's teachings is that at this particular time, when they are convinced that they have succeeded in achieving peace, in their smug satisfaction they are destroyed, because the circumstances and inspiration for war have not changed. A world that crucified the Prince of Peace cannot expect to enjoy peace, until He is re-established in His rightful place. The LORD consistently encouraged His people not to be troubled by these eventualities, which are part of the scenario of the last days; the Jews were not to allow such things to distract them in their efforts to seek and serve Him.

[132] THE THIRD SEAL

(6:5, 6) *And when He had opened the third seal, I heard the third beast say, "Come and see." And I beheld, and lo, a black horse; and he that sat on him had a pair of balances in his hand. And I heard a voice in the midst of the four beasts say, "A measure of wheat for a penny, and three measures of barley for a penny; and see thou hurt not the oil and the wine."*

A penny was a day's wages for a working man and the measure of wheat (equivalent to about a pint and a half dry measure) would yield a cup or so of flour. Barley was normally considered cattle food and only the poorest people used it to make bread, unless wheat was very scarce. Note the restraint *and see thou hurt not the oil and the wine.* This command protects the fruit of the OLIVE and the fruit of the VINE, (compare Romans 11:13-25 and John 15.) These are the very basic necessities of life (and both trees typify Israel.) The LORD's Own teachings are in total harmony, Matthew 24:7 *And there shall be famines, and pestilences,* Mark 13:8 *And there shall be famines and troubles,* Luke 21:11 *And famines and pestilences.* Famines and various plagues (pestilences) inevitably follow wars (the outcome of the second seal,) this third seal is in perfect accord with the LORD's words.

[133] THE FOURTH SEAL

(6:7, 8) *And when He had opened the fourth seal, I heard the voice of the fourth beast say, "Come and see." And I looked, and behold, a pale horse: and his name that sat on him was Death, and Hell followed with him. And power was given unto them over the fourth part of the earth, to kill with sword, and with hunger, and with death, and with the beasts of the earth.*

In figure, or type, "death" has already been anticipated in the *pestilences and troubles* of the third seal; because these in extreme cause death. Death's companion Hell, would be better rendered "The Grave," for in the majority of its scriptural occurrences the word sheol is so translated. The revelation is a terrible portrayal of Death and The Dead or The Grave and the extent of their combined killing power *over the fourth part of the earth* is a frightening proportion to contemplate. Again, the methods used: *"sword, hunger, death, and the beasts of the earth,"* provide ample scope for serious thought. The sword usually symbolises authority or rule, suggesting national or governmental powers are being abused to destroy people. Hunger, this has to be distinguished from famine (the third seal) which is caused by natural disasters such as drought, earthquakes, floods etc. Hunger implies no shortage of food, but access forbidden or denied, it might even be enforced, perhaps as a means of genocide. The beasts of the earth also offer an intriguing and frightening range of possibilities, from animal borne plagues or diseases, to the ravages of insects, even packs of formerly domestic dogs roaming in war torn or devastated areas and even the frightening prospect of germ warfare. These are all merely suggestions, but in view of the very high mortality rate, there is probably far more involved; the fulfilment of this seal will be most frightening and dramatic.

The LORD's Own teachings (in total harmony with these seals,) at this point were summarised: Matthew 24:8 *"All these are the beginning of sorrows"* (and "these" from the previous verses in Matthew, when added together, equate to the events of the first four seals.) The LORD continued however, Matthew 24:9 *"Then shall they deliver you up to be afflicted, and shall kill you: and ye shall be hated of all nations for My name's sake."* Could it be that the Jews are actually blamed for these previous disastrous events? This period therefore marks the beginning approximately, of the seventieth week, for at this time it is "they" i.e. the other nations, killing the Jews (not "him", the Beast,) the world hates the Jews generally for their testimony, which might have included references to the disasters happening everywhere as evidences of divine judgments (see Revelation 11 especially v10 [151 &152]).

[134] THE FIFTH SEAL

(6:9-11) *And when He had opened the fifth seal, I saw under the altar the souls of them that were slain for the Word of God, and for the testimony which they held: and they cried with a loud voice, saying, "How long, O Lord, Holy and True, dost Thou not judge and avenge our blood on them that dwell on the earth?" And white robes were given unto every one of them; and it was said unto them, that they should rest yet for a little season until their fellowservants also and their brethren, that should be killed as they were, should be fulfilled.*

The cry for vengeance is not the language of the Church of the LORD Jesus Christ, these also address Him as Lord (Despotees) i.e. Master, as of slaves or servants; not the LORD (Kurio) of the true believing church. The fifth seal appears to cover the events of the first half of the final, or seventieth, week; the *souls* of those slain and crying for vengeance, are His servants killed by other nations of the world in the persecution leading up to and including, that period. During this first half of the week, the beast himself observes the covenant that he has confirmed, but his treachery is manifested in the deaths of those *that should be killed as they were* , which will happen in the middle of the final week.

From Matthew (24:15-22) the middle of this week is marked by the placing of the abomination of desolation in the holy place. Whereas previously, the Jews have been persecuted worldwide, this changes everything and they are no longer safe even in their own land. Now their only chance is their fleeing into the wilderness, for the beast's intention is to destroy Israel *spiritually*, by demanding they worship him, or *physically*, by putting them to death. Consider the LORD's Own words of warning in these terms and recognise the turning point it brings to the Jewish experience, in their own land. *"When ye therefore shall see the abomination of desolation, spoken of by Daniel the prophet, stand in the holy place, (whoso readeth, let him understand;) then let them which be in Judea flee into the mountains: let him which is on the housetop not come down to take any thing out of his house: neither let him which is in the field return back to take his clothes, and woe unto them that are with child, and to them that give suck in those days! But pray ye that your flight be not in the winter, neither on the sabbath day: for then shall be great tribulation, such as was not since the beginning of the world to this time, no nor ever shall be. And except those days should be shortened, there should no flesh be saved: but for the elect's sake those days shall be shortened.*

This is a most terrible time to consider, but for the elect's sake, the Jewish people, mercifully the time is shortened to avoid their total obliteration.[32]

[135] THE SIXTH SEAL

(6:12-17) And I beheld when He had opened the sixth seal, and lo, there was a great earthquake; and the sun became black as sackcloth of hair, and the moon became as blood; and the stars of heaven fell unto the earth, even as a fig tree casteth her untimely figs, when she

---

[32] The mysterious period of two thousand and three hundred days, of Daniel 8:14, has application at this time; for it works out to 6 years and 140 days (using the lunar year of scripture, of 360 days, see also Appendix 2 and Appendix 3.)

is shaken of a mighty wind. And the heaven departed as a scroll when it is rolled together; and every mountain and island were moved out of their places. And the kings of the earth, and the great men, and the rich men, and the chief captains, and the mighty men, and every bondman, and every free man, hid themselves in the dens and in the rocks of the mountains; and said to the mountains and rocks, "Fall on us, and hide us from the face of Him that sitteth on the throne, and from the wrath of the Lamb: for the great day of His wrath is come; and who shall be able to stand."

The wrath of the Lamb, this is the DAY OF THE LORD, first mentioned by Isaiah (13:6) and last mentioned in The Revelation (1:10). This prophecy has been ridiculed in the past, since the idea of stars (the heavenly suns) falling to earth was too preposterous for scientifically minded man to take seriously. But as already shown in terms of the LORD's Own teachings, which are in perfect accord with The Revelation, in the modern idiom, satellites could literally fulfil this prophecy quite adequately (or even asteroids.) The removal of the satellites would cause immediate panic, for the great powers would no longer be able to monitor each others' military forces and their communications would be drastically disrupted. Finding satisfactory historical fulfilment for this prophecy has also been a considerable problem for that particular school of interpretation, but it is so obviously in agreement with the LORD's Own superb teachings on the last days that further comment is unnecessary, His words speak adequately. Matthew 24:29 *"Immediately after the tribulation of those days shall the sun be darkened, and the moon shall not give her light, and the stars shall fall from heaven, and the powers of the heavens shall be shaken."*

Mark 13:24, 25 *"But in those days, after that tribulation, the sun shall be darkened, and the moon shall not give her light, and the stars of heaven shall fall, and the powers that are in heaven shall be shaken."*

Luke 21:25,26 *"And there shall be signs in the sun, and in the moon, and in the stars; and upon the earth distress of nations, with perplexity; the sea and the waves roaring; men's hearts failing them for fear, and for looking after those things which are coming on the earth: for the powers of heaven shall be shaken."*

The Day of the LORD, *the great day of His wrath,* involves far more than the events described under the sixth seal, which seem to point more to its arrival than its total fulfilment. The seventh seal relates directly to this Day of the LORD, this same period. The details after the opening of the seventh seal cover the consequences of His wrath, and continue with the sounding of the seven trumpets and the pouring out of the seven vials. These will be considered in their turn, but returning to the sixth seal, note the question from mankind *"who shall be able to stand?"* What follows next is the divine answer to this question.

[The opening of the seals is discussed further Chapter 18 The Events of the Last Days page 131.]

[136]

(7:1-4) *And after these things I saw four angels standing on the four corners of the earth, holding the four winds of the earth, that the wind should not blow on the earth, nor on the sea, nor on any tree. And I saw another angel ascending from the east, having the seal of the living God: and he cried with a loud voice to the four angels, to whom it was given to hurt the earth and the sea, saying, "Hurt not the earth, neither the sea, nor the trees, till we have sealed the servants of our God in their foreheads." And I heard the number of them which were sealed: and there were sealed an hundred and forty and four thousand of all the tribes of the Children of Israel.*

The sealing of the servants of God, obviously delaying the action of the angels, tends to diminish the impact of their work. The consequences of no wind blowing on the earth would be devastating ecologically. There would be no circulation of air, no cloud movement, no global heat exchanges - the ultimate effects cannot be imagined. Quite possibly the scientific explanation for this phenomenon will be the *greenhouse effect*, or something like that.

The twelve tribes are named here (7:5-8) Juda, Reuben, Gad, Aser, Nepthalim, Manasses, Simeon, Levi, Issachar, Zabulon, Joseph and Benjamin. This list differs from those in Genesis (35 & 49) in which Dan has been replaced by Manasses. But in Ezekiel (48) it is revealed that ultimately Dan will be restored. There is no difficulty with this 144,000, they are clearly Jews of the twelve tribes, who are sealed, or protectively covered in some way, to go through the day of wrath. This partly answers the question posed earlier, *"Who shall be able to stand?"* But there is another standing multitude described.

[137]

(7:9-17) After this I beheld, and lo, a great multitude, which no man could number, of all nations, and kindreds, and people, and tongues, stood before the throne, and before the Lamb, clothed with white robes, and palms in their hands; and cried with a loud voice, saying, "Salvation to our God Which sitteth upon the throne, and unto the Lamb." And all the angels stood round about the throne, and about the elders and the four beasts, and fell before the throne on their faces, and worshipped God, saying, "Amen: Blessing, and glory, and wisdom, and thanksgiving, and honour, and power, and might, be unto our God for ever and ever. Amen." And one of the elders answered, saying unto me, "What are these which are arrayed in white robes? And whence came they?" And I said unto him, "Sir, thou knowest." And he said to me, "These are they which came out of great tribulation, and have washed their robes, and made them white in the blood of the Lamb. Therefore are they before the throne of God, and serve Him day and night in His temple: and He that sitteth on the throne shall dwell among them. They shall hunger no more, neither thirst any more; neither shall the sun light on them, nor any heat. For the Lamb which is in the midst of the throne shall feed them, and shall lead them unto living fountains of waters: and God

shall wipe away all tears from their eyes."

This multitude are those *which came out of great tribulation,* so they cannot be the Church, which is not involved in the tribulation; and neither does the Church have to wash their robes (compare 1 Corinthians 6:11.) This multitude is comprised of the peoples of all nations, distinguishing them from the Jews, who are covered in the 144,000 from the twelve tribes previously mentioned, but by virtue of their deliverance from tribulation, they have suffered with or for the Jews. Notice especially the assurances that these are given that they shall hunger no more, neither thirst, nor suffer exposure to heat, or sun; this must give some indication of what they have endured. In the last days the salvation of the Jews is *for their works,* for this is a different dispensation (the Jews are not under Grace at that time when works would count for nothing; as is now the case for the true Church.) (See Appendix 5.)

[138] This completes the answer to the question *"Who shall be able to stand?"* in the great day of His wrath. It will be the 144,000 of the Jewish tribes sealed to go through the tribulation and this countless multitude, that no man could number, who have proved their true calibre as human beings. The nations, kindreds and peoples displaying the calibre to support the LORD's people in those awful days, are those for whom God has an eternal place.

It must be appreciated, that whilst the Church has already gone in its glorious rapture, the testimony has again fallen to the Jewish nation who, with their characteristic zeal, have gone and preached to the whole world; no doubt fired and inspired by the ministry of the two witnesses (Revelation 11 [151 – 153]).

This heavenly multitude is the fruit of the Jewish nation's ministry in the last days. These are proselytes, and Jewish sympathisers, who with the Jews at that time look forward to and long for, the establishment of the Kingdom of God on earth, when justice, honesty and peace can be restored to mankind forever (see also Revelation 14:1-5 and 19:5-10 [170] [192]).

[139] THE SEVENTH SEAL

(8:1) *And when He had opened the seventh seal, there was silence in heaven about the space of half an hour.*

The silence is compelling, especially after the voices of the four beasts following the opening of the first four seals and the events following the opening of the fifth and sixth. The seventh seal marks the end of the sequence of events of the seals and John next describes the details concerning the sounding of the seven trumpets. It is suggested that the seven trumpets are not in succession after the seven seals, but coincident and that the seven trumpets are associated with the seven seals, the case for this is strengthened when the trumpets are examined.

Chapter 13: The Revelation (The Seven Trumpets)

[140]

(8:2) *And I saw the seven angels which stood before God; and to them were given seven trumpets.*

The events following the sounding of these seven trumpets are stages in the outpouring of the wrath of the Lamb and complement the events of the seven seals; but before the trumpets are sounded there is an offering made.

(8:3-6) *And another angel came and stood at the altar, having a golden censer; and there was given unto him much incense, that he should offer it with the prayers of all saints upon the golden altar which was before the throne. And the smoke of the incense, which came with the prayers of the saints, ascended up before God out of the angel's hand. And the angel took the censer, and filled it with fire of the altar, and cast it into the earth: and there were voices, and thunderings, and lightnings, and an earthquake. And the seven angels which had the seven trumpets prepared themselves to sound.*

It might be recalled, that the opening of the Fifth Seal (6:9-11 [134]) enabled John to see the souls of those slain for the Word of God under the altar and he heard their cry for judgment and vengeance. This angel's offering of the incense with the prayers of all saints reveals that God accepted those prayers. The soundings of the seven trumpets herald a succession of events and there is a remarkable similarity between the events of the seven trumpets and the events of the seven seals already described.

[141] THE FIRST TRUMPET

(8:7) *The first angel sounded, and there followed hail and fire mingled with blood, and they were cast upon the earth: and the third part of trees was burnt up, and all green grass was burnt up.*

The destruction of vegetation described need not be literally fulfilled in the fiery consumption of trees and grass exclusively, the mixture of hail, fire and blood, suggests a variety of causes - the elements, man and natural means, possibly. This is a reasonable assumption, because there is no evidence of panic or mass hysteria or concern because of manifestly divine judgment; there are very likely logical, earthly, or scientific explanations for this loss; but, undeniably, it has been prophesied!

[142] THE SECOND TRUMPET

(8:8, 9) *The second angel sounded, and as it were a great mountain burning with fire was cast into the sea: and the third part of the sea became blood; and the third part of the creatures which were in the sea, and had life, died; and the third part of the ships were destroyed.*

Again, this is not necessarily a total, immediate, spectacular destruction; it could be fulfilled over a period of years. Such a dramatic loss in a short time would provoke a reaction, but there is nothing in the verses to suggest this happens. The world goes on just the same, oblivious to the fulfilments of the prophecies of God.

[143] THE THIRD TRUMPET

(8:10, 11) *And the third angel sounded, and there fell a great star from heaven, burning as it were a lamp, and it fell upon the third part of the rivers, and upon the fountains of waters; and the name of the star is called Wormwood: and the third part of the waters became Wormwood; and many men died of the waters, because they were made bitter.*

The loss of life *many men died* reaches considerable proportions, but there is an explanation; the many men died *of the waters, BECAUSE they were made bitter.* This is understandable, it is a question of contamination, or pollution, of fresh waters and in the usual way, it would be played down politically and economically, with no compensation made and survivors probably being encouraged to consider themselves lucky to escape.

[144] THE FOURTH TRUMPET

(8:12) *And the fourth angel sounded, and the third part of the sun was smitten, and the third part of the moon, and the third part of the stars; so as the third part of them was darkened, and the day shone not for a third part of it, and the night likewise.*

The consequences of this need to be examined, for example, how would such a reduction in hours of daylight affect crops and harvests? This would also cool our planet over a period of time. What will be the long term effects of this loss of light and heat?

The first four trumpets have all had earthly consequences and these in the context of The Revelation result from the outpouring of the wrath of the Lamb. Yet there is no indication within the text that the world reacts in any dramatic or concerted way to any of the events described. As noted, there appears to be earthly or natural or scientific explanations for these calamities (pollution, natural disasters, volcanic dust, earthquakes etc.) The Revelation is a prophecy, which has to be believed to appreciate its purposes and benefits; and this takes faith. Faith is what the natural man lacks and a real believer should not expect mankind to accept, (what he might recognise spiritually as obvious,) the consequences of divine judgment. But this lack of response was itself prophesied, (Daniel 12:10 *none of the wicked shall understand,*) which confirms that God's judgments and purposes are not contingent upon the reactions of man for their execution or fulfilment. The next verse expresses the heavenly reaction in the realisation of what is about to follow.

[145] THE THREE WOES

(8:13) *And I beheld, and heard an angel flying through the midst of heaven, saying with a loud voice, "Woe, woe, woe, to the inhabiters of the earth by reason of the other voices of the trumpet of the three angels, which are yet to sound!"*

In the texts the word "angel" is AETOS, (which means "eagle" and as such it is translated Revelation 4:7, 12:14, Matthew 24:28, Luke 17:37). But the proclamation made concerns three "woes," which are associated with the final three trumpets.

The other references to these woes are:

(9:12) *One woe is past and behold there are two woes more hereafter*

(11:14) *The second woe is past; and behold the third woe cometh quickly*

These three woes will be considered separately in their turn, but it is noted that these woes are the laments of the flying eagles over the release of the forces of hell: (first) the locusts from the pit, (second) the four angels bound in the Euphrates and (third) the descent of Satan to earth; (compare the power, delegated to each of these forces.) The woes appear to commence in the final week, when Satan is cast down. Initially the horrors are to men, but in the final stages the suffering is to the inhabiters of the earth and the sea. The three woes and the last three trumpets are unmistakably associated (and occur after the fourth trumpet i.e. the darkening of the sun.) The eagle *flying through the midst of heaven* is not in heaven itself, but in that intermediate, mysterious heaven, the domain of the heavenly spiritual forces, which control the world. (The heavenly forces, which opposed the errand of the heavenly messenger sent to Daniel - see Daniel 10:12-21 [39]). There is a break in John's account before the third woe is described, but to continue these considerations, let us proceed to consider the fifth trumpet and the first of the woes in more detail.

[146] THE FIFTH TRUMPET and THE FIRST WOE

(9:1-12) *And the fifth angel sounded, and I saw a star fall from heaven unto the earth: and to him was given the key of the bottomless pit. And he opened the bottomless pit; and there arose a smoke out of the pit, as the smoke of a great furnace; and the sun and the air were darkened by reason of the smoke of the pit. And there came out of the smoke locusts upon the earth: and unto them was given power, as the scorpions of the earth have power. And it was commanded them that they should not hurt the grass of the earth, neither any green thing, neither any tree; but only those men which have not the seal of God in their foreheads. And to them it was given that they should not kill them, but that they should be tormented five months: and their torment was as the torment of a scorpion, when he striketh a man. And in those days shall men seek death, and shall not find it; and shall desire to die, and death shall flee from them. And the shapes of the locusts were like unto horses prepared unto battle; and on their heads were as it were crowns like gold, and their faces were as the faces of men. And they had hair as the hair of women, and their teeth were as the teeth of lions. And they had breastplates, as it were breastplates of iron; and the sound of their wings was as the sound of chariots of many horses running to battle. And they had tails like unto scorpions, and there were stings in their tails: and their power was to hurt men five months. And they had a king over them, which is the angel of the bottomless pit, whose name in the Hebrew tongue is Abaddon, but in the Greek tongue hath his name Apollyon. One woe is past; and behold, there come two woes more hereafter.*

These are not natural locusts because they have a king over them (compare Proverbs 30:27) and they inflict pain. The release of these terrible locusts is surely cause for great lamentation. Their sole purpose is to torment men, who desire death to release them from the agonies of their attack. The Hebrew word (arbeh) means "swarmer", which conveys the multitudes of these insects, they are described (Joel 1:4) in the four stages of the development of the locust. Locusts in flight also emit an ominous, characteristic sound and this is mentioned *the sound of their wings*, which will be a terrifying note, inspiring fear of the terrible destruction they cause (like the sound of wasps, or hornets can do in view of their painful stings, on a much smaller scale.) *Abaddon* (= destruction, see Job 18:14 *the king of terrors*, also *destruction* 26:6, 28:22, 31:12 Psalm 88:11 Proverbs 15:11, 27:20.) *Apollyon* (= destroyer) a truly frightening ruler of the place of endless destruction; he is not Satan, who has a separate role to play.

[147] THE SIXTH TRUMPET and THE SECOND WOE

(9:13-21) *And the sixth angel sounded, and I heard a voice from the four horns of the golden altar which is before God, saying to the sixth angel which had the trumpet, "Loose the four angels which are bound in the great river Euphrates." And the four angels were loosed, which were prepared for an hour, and a day, and a month, and a year, for to slay the third part of men. And the number of the army of the horsemen were two hundred thousand thousand: and I heard the number of them. And thus I saw the horses in the vision, and them that sat on them having breastplates of fire, and of jacinth, and brimstone: and the heads of the horses were as the heads of lions; and out of their mouths issued fire and smoke and brimstone. By these three was the third part of men killed, by the fire, and by the smoke, and by the brimstone, which issued out of their mouths. For their power is in their mouth, and in their tails; for their tails were like unto serpents, and had heads, and with them they do hurt. And the rest of the men which were not killed by these plagues yet repented not of the works of their hands, that they should not worship devils and idols of gold, and silver, and brass, and stone, and of wood, which neither can see, nor hear, nor walk: neither repented they of their murders, nor of their sorceries, nor of their fornication, nor of their thefts.*

The sixth trumpet heralds the release of the four angels from the river Euphrates, notice the precise timing - the exact hour, day, month and year are known and until this time, these angels are bound. The purpose of their release is to slay the third part of men and this frightening army of horsemen is the method used. The slaughter commences on their release, confirming that the forces involved are spiritual and men stand no chance. This is divine judgment on idolatry, the fruits of spiritual wickedness, but there is no repentance, astonishingly they do not change their minds about their worship. The end of this woe is particularly noted in scripture [154].

There is a digression next, as John describes a succession of things revealed to him, before he wrote of the sounding of the seventh trumpet.

[148] (10:1-4) *And I saw another mighty angel come down from heaven, clothed with a cloud; and a rainbow was upon his head, and his face was as it were the sun, and his feet as pillars of fire: and he had in his hand a little book open: and he set his right foot upon the sea, and his left foot on the earth, and he cried with a loud voice, as when a lion roareth: and when he had cried, seven thunders uttered* *their voices. And when the seven thunders had uttered their voices, I was about to write: and I heard a voice from heaven saying unto me, "Seal up those things which the seven thunders uttered, and write them not."*

A vivid picture, yet the words that the mighty angel cried, and the voices of the seven thunders in reply, were not recorded; John was forbidden to write them. Speculation is pointless; there are some heavenly utterances, which are not for the ears of mortal man. That John was permitted to hear them in his spiritual experience, confirmed that these utterances relate in some way to the Revelation at this point, but the secrets were not to be revealed.

[149] (10:5-7) *And the angel which I saw stand upon the sea and upon the earth lifted up his hand to heaven, and sware by Him that liveth for ever and ever, Who created heaven, and the things that therein are, and the earth, and the things that therein are, and the seas, and the things which are therein, that there should be time no longer: but in the days of the voice of the seventh angel, when he shall begin to sound, the mystery of God should be finished, as He hath declared to His servants the prophets.*

The oath of the angel does not indicate the complete end of time; this is obvious, because other eventualities (e.g. most notably, the Millennium,) are time related. But as far as the gentiles are concerned and also with respect to the Jews, time is finished ie the completion of the final week, or the seventieth week of prophecy, *The End* has come. The end means the end of gentile domination in Jerusalem, and over Israel particularly. The kingdoms of the world were all temporal, the Kingdom of God is eternal and in its establishment, time becomes meaningless, events now relate to the day of the LORD (see Daniel 2:44 [2] & 12:6,7 [42].)

[150] (10:8-11) *And the voice which I heard from heaven spake unto* me again, and said, "Go and take the little book which is open in the hand of the angel which standeth upon the sea and upon the earth." And I went unto the angel, and said unto him, "Give me the little book." And he said unto me, "Take it, and eat it up; and it shall make thy belly bitter, but it shall be in thy mouth sweet as honey." And I took the little book out of the angel's hand, and ate it up; and it was in my mouth sweet as honey: and as soon as I had eaten it, my belly was bitter. And he said unto me, "Thou must prophesy again before many peoples, and nations, and tongues, and kings."

The commission given to John is difficult to understand, but since the next revelation given to John concerns the two witnesses. It is suggested (but this is pure speculation,) that had the Jewish nation repented at that time, this prophetic ministry might have applied to John personally. However, its eventual fulfilment in the last days is something for which the Jewish nation will have to wait, but this prophetic ministry must be associated with the re-establishment of the Jewish witness.

[151] (11:1-13) *And there was given me a reed like unto a rod: and the angel stood, saying, "Rise and measure the temple of God, and the altar, and them that worship therein. But the court which is without the temple leave out, and measure it not; for it is given unto the gentiles: and the holy city shall they tread under foot forty and two months*. And I will give power unto My witnesses, and they shall prophesy a thousand two hundred and threescore days*, clothed in sackcloth". These are the two olive trees, and the two candlesticks standing before the God of the earth, and if any man will hurt them, fire proceedeth out of their mouth, and devoureth their enemies: and if any man will hurt them, he must in this manner be killed. These have power to shut heaven, that it rain not in the days of their prophecy: and have power over waters to turn them to blood, and to smite the earth with all plagues, as often as they will, and when they shall have finished their testimony, the beast that ascendeth out of* *the bottomless pit shall make war against them, and shall overcome them, and kill them. And their dead bodies shall lie in the street of the great city, which spiritually is called Sodom and Egypt, where also our Lord was crucified. And they of the people and kindreds and tongues and nations shall see their dead bodies three days and an half, and shall not suffer their dead bodies to be put in graves. And they that dwell upon the earth shall rejoice over them, and make merry, and shall send gifts one to another; because these two prophets tormented them that dwelt on the earth. And after three days and an half, the spirit of life from God entered into them, and they stood upon their feet; and great fear fell upon them which saw them. And they heard a great voice from heaven saying unto them, "Come up hither." And they ascended up to heaven in a cloud; and their enemies beheld them. And the same hour was there a great earthquake, and the tenth part of the city fell, and in the earthquake were slain of men seven thousand: and the remnant were affrighted, and gave glory to the God of heaven.*

[*(iv) *forty and two months* *(vi) *a thousand two hundred and threescore days* are two more of the unique references linking Daniel and Revelation. Appendix 3.]

[152] This passage contains so much: John given a reed to measure the temple and the altar, and the holy city given to the gentiles for forty and two months (three and a half years in lunar months.) For a thousand two hundred and threescore days (also three and a half years in lunar months) power is given to the two witnesses; their power bears direct comparison with that displayed in the experiences of Moses and Elijah (see also Malachi 4:4-6.)

It is in his war against these two witnesses, that the Beast is first mentioned in The Revelation (he is considered in more detail later,) but notice the description of him: *the beast that ascendeth out of the bottomless pit.* The word *resurrection* is never used in scripture in application to the Beast, although no doubt this is what he will claim for himself. This is the first feature of the beast to which attention is drawn in Revelation; and the second is his war with the two witnesses, whom he overcomes. This is no small feat in the light of the power that these two witnesses display, but his success has already been qualified scripturally with the words *and when they shall have finished their testimony.* The apparent victory of the Beast has not diminished their ministry and it is by divine permission that he (apparently) overcomes them, when their testimony is finished. People on earth will not see the success of the Beast in this light of course and they will rejoice in the Beast's triumphing over the witnesses, who have testified to them for three and a half years. Their bodies are left on display, whilst they celebrate. Then in the height of their rejoicing and exchanging gifts, celebrating the beast's victory, suddenly the witnesses are seen to stand on their feet and in response to a heavenly command they ascend to heaven. The consternation and fear this inspires can hardly be imagined and within an hour an earthquake devastates the city *where also our Lord was crucified* (which has to be Jerusalem.)

[153] THE TWO WITNESSES

The early church fathers considered these scriptures would be fulfilled in the last days[33], and believed or accepted that *the two witnesses* (of Revelation 11:3-12) would be Moses and Elijah, because firstly these two prophets had scripturally displayed the power given to the two witnesses in the last days (v6). Secondly Moses and Elijah appeared together at the LORD's transfiguration, so it was clearly assumed they might be the two witnesses of Revelation.

---

[33] This is confirmed by the fact that John the Baptist was most definitely associated with the LORD's ministry, and from the time the LORD ministered the last days commenced (Hebrews 1:1) although, because the Jews failed to repent, the Kingdom is in abeyance.

The early fathers considered that because the two witnesses could *call down fire* that they had to be Moses and Elijah although this is not quite accurate, *fire proceedeth out of their mouth,* is not the same as calling down fire from heaven, which was what Elijah did (2 Kings 1:10 and 12); but it has to be conceded that smiting the earth with plagues was apparently part of Moses' experience. Moses did not exactly call down fire (see Exodus 9:23, 24) *And Moses stretched forth his rod toward heaven: and the LORD sent thunder and hail, and the fire ran along upon the ground; and the LORD rained hail upon the land of Egypt. So there was hail, and fire mingled with the hail, very grievous, such as there was none like it in all the land of Egypt since it became a nation.*)

The other problem with including Moses as one of the two witnesses is that he died (Deuteronomy 34:5 & 7 this is repeated,) his death is undeniable. Further the fact that Satan wanted the dead body of Moses (Jude v9) does not mean that the LORD necessarily intended to send Moses again in the last days. [A valid suggestion for *Satan's use* of the body of Moses, is that Satan would have made it an object of worship for the Jews; which would have been a fatal mistake for Israel.] However if Moses were to be killed again by the beast as one of the two witnesses, this would mean that Moses had died twice, and this is not allowed scripturally. *It is appointed unto man once to die*[34]*, and after this the judgment* Hebrews 9:27 (The *second death*[35] does not mean that anyone partakes of dying twice in the worldly sense.)

If Moses and Elijah were the two witnesses (as some of the early fathers believed) it would mean that Elijah who did not die, (he was

---

[34] Those raised from the dead by Elijah, Elishah and the LORD are clearly restored to life in the same body; they would still die again eventually; these are miraculous exceptions to the divine appointment for man for divine reasons.

[35] Revelation 20:14 *And death and hell were cast into the lake of fire. This is the second death.* Scripturally *the second death* refers to the ultimate judgment of the wicked, who are resurrected to be judged according to their works before GOD by the LORD Jesus Christ; and if no righteousness is found in them, they are cast forever into the lake of fire.

caught up to heaven in the chariot of the LORD,) would be partnered by Moses who did die. This presents considerable difficulties.

The only other scriptural character who did not die was Enoch, who was translated (Genesis 5:24) *And Enoch walked with GOD; and he was not; for GOD took him.* Paul very kindly provided the essential further details on this, note his words (Hebrews 11:5) *By faith Enoch was translated THAT HE SHOULD NOT SEE DEATH; and was not found, because GOD had translated him: for before his translation he had this testimony, that he pleased GOD.* GOD revealed through Paul that He translated Enoch *that he should not see death,* (in his lifetime,) so he could possibly be one of the two witnesses, who the beast kills.

Then again, if John the Baptist was evidently a type of Elijah (and he could have been Elijah if the people had accepted John as such,) this makes it a pretty shaky case for assuming one of the witnesses has to be Elijah (simply because he called down fire from heaven, and was caught up to heaven as witnessed by Elisha.) However, quite clearly the LORD's speaking to Israel *commenced* the last days (Hebrews 1:1). John the Baptist's ministry could have been (on the LORD's authority) the fulfilment of Malachi's prophecy that the LORD would send Elijah. This was evident also from the angel Gabriel's words to Zacharias, Luke 1:17 *"And he* (John) *shall go before Him* (the LORD) *in the spirit and power of Elias (= Elijah) and turn the hearts of the fathers to the children, and the disobedient to the wisdom of the just; to make ready a people prepared for the LORD."*

The two witnesses of the last days must necessarily have phenomenal spiritual calibre as the LORD's fearless witnesses against the Beast (who is permitted to overcome them.) This must have been typified (to some extent) in the combined witness of John and the LORD. Because had the Jews accepted John the Baptist as Elijah, he could well have been one of the two witnesses (although they had not been revealed at that time of course,) and the LORD Himself could have been the other witness. So the question remains – who are the two, whom the Beast overcomes and kills[36]?

The two witnesses are not Moses and Elijah, for the reasons stated above and the two witnesses are not named (scripturally), the truth is that sometimes GOD does not reveal everything in advance and He has chosen to hide these two witnesses, until they are manifested at the right time. But it cannot be stated with absolute certainty, who the two witnesses are; however scripturally Elijah's successor was Elisha. [It has already been shown; [44] that Daniel is a scriptural possibility.]

[154] (11:14) *The second woe is past; and behold, the third woe cometh quickly.*

This verse relates to the sixth trumpet [147], because it states plainly the second woe is past and also declares that the third woe cometh quickly. But this involved the release of the angels in the River Euphrates. The Euphrates has always been the natural barrier that prevents invasion from the Far East into the Middle East (for oil) and even Europe (for their wealth.)

John next describes the seventh trumpet and the third woe.

[155] THE SEVENTH TRUMPET & THE THIRD WOE

(11:15-19) *And the seventh angel sounded; and there were great voices in heaven, saying, "The kingdoms of this world are become the*

---

[36] The death of the two witnesses occurs in the middle of the final week, after their three and a half years testimony; but scripturally a period 1040 days occurs in the middle of the week, separating its two halves. This would not count in Israel's time, i.e. as part of the week itself, since it is a period of idolatry, when the abomination of desolation is set up in Jerusalem. [See also Appendices 2 & 3.]

Kingdoms of our Lord, and of His Christ; and He shall reign for ever and ever." And the four and twenty elders, which sat before God on their seats, fell upon their faces, and worshipped God, saying, "We give Thee thanks, O Lord God Almighty, Which art, and wast, and art to come; because Thou hast taken to Thee Thy great power, and hast reigned. And the nations were angry, and Thy wrath is come, and the time of the dead, that they should be judged, and that Thou shouldest give reward unto Thy servants the prophets, and to the saints, and them that fear Thy name, small and great; and shouldest destroy them which destroy the earth." And the temple of God was opened in heaven, and there was seen in His temple the ark of His testament: and there were lightnings, and voices, and thunderings, and an earthquake, and great hail.

Concerning the seventh trumpet it has already been stated, (10:7) *But in the days of the voice of the seventh angel, when he shall begin to sound, the mystery of God should be finished, as He hath declared to His servants the prophets.* This was considered to refer to the end of the previously prophesied dispensations (the end of the seventieth week of the Jewish prophecy of seventy weeks and the end of the times of grace for the gentiles,) and to focus attention on the fact that time in scriptural terms now relates to the day of the LORD. In John's account as the seventh trumpet is sounded, the great voices in heaven proclaim the establishment of the kingdoms of the LORD and of His Christ and the elders in their praises reveal that it is time to reward *Thy servants the prophets.* There is nothing that would rate higher as a reward to any prophet, than his or her being enabled to see the literal fulfilment, in its ultimate divine sense, of the prophecies that he or she ministered. What follows next is astonishing, even in The Revelation.

Chapter 14: The Revelation (The Woman, Dragon, Beast, False Prophet)

[156] (12:1-17) *And there appeared a great wonder in heaven; a woman clothed with the sun, and the moon under her feet, and upon her head a crown of twelve stars: and she being with child cried, travailing in birth, and pained to be delivered. And there appeared another wonder in heaven; and behold a great red dragon, having seven heads and ten horns, and seven crowns upon his heads. And his tail drew the third part of the stars of heaven, and did cast them to the earth: and the dragon stood before the woman which was ready to be delivered, for to devour her child as soon as it was born. And she brought forth a man child, who was to rule all nations with a rod of iron: and her child was caught up unto God, and to His throne. And the woman fled into the wilderness, where she hath a place prepared of God, that they should feed her there a thousand two hundred and threescore days. And there was war in heaven: Michael and his angels fought against the dragon; and the dragon fought and his angels, and prevailed not; neither was their place found any more in heaven. And the great dragon was cast out, that old serpent, called the Devil, and Satan, which deceiveth the whole world: he was cast out into the earth, and his angels were cast out with him. And I heard a loud voice saying in heaven, "Now is come salvation, and strength, and the kingdom of our God, and the power of His Christ: for the Accuser of our brethren is cast down, which accused them before our God day and night*. And they overcame him by the blood of the Lamb, and by the word of their testimony; and they loved not their lives unto the death. Therefore rejoice, ye heavens, and ye that dwell in them. Woe to the inhabiters of the earth and of the sea! For the devil is come down unto you, having great wrath, because he*

knoweth that he hath but a short time." And when the dragon saw that he was cast unto the earth, he persecuted the woman which brought forth the man child. And to the woman were given two wings of a great eagle, that she might fly into the wilderness, into her place, where she is nourished for a time, and times, and half a time, from the face of the serpent. And the serpent cast out of his mouth water as a flood after the woman, that he might cause her to be carried away of the flood. And the earth helped the woman, and the earth opened her mouth, and swallowed up the flood which the dragon cast out of his mouth. And the dragon was wroth with the woman, and went to make war with the remnant of her seed, which keep the commandments of God, and have the testimony of Jesus Christ.

[*It is worth noting that v10, *And I heard a loud voice saying in heaven, "Now is come salvation, and strength, and the kingdom of our God, and the power of His Christ: for the accuser of our brethren is cast down, which accused them before our God day and night"* is the central verse of the Revelation. This might be also the voice that broke *the silence in heaven about a space of half an hour.* (8:1)]

[157] This portion of John's writing probably contains the key to understanding the whole of the Revelation; but it is difficult and it would be impossible without The LORD's Own teachings. The woman has to be the nation Israel, (compare Genesis 37:9-11) very few commentators if any seriously contest this. Again, the dragon, the serpent, the devil, Satan himself presents no problem; he is quite clearly identified in these titles; which utterly contradict the ridiculous, horned figures that adorned early bibles illustrating this portion. At the time of this prophecy's fulfilment, Satan's power is revealed in the control he exercises; seven heads, ten horns and seven crowns upon the heads. The ten horns could represent an alliance of nations controlled by him (probably the ten kingdom alliance that he gives to the Beast,) and the seven heads and seven crowns might represent completely different groups or combinations of power nationally or even spiritually. Satan controls all these and they are his in their worship (whatever they profess to worship, it makes no difference, as the god of this world Satan controls them.) The dragon's tail drew the third part of the stars of heaven (representing heavenly beings, powers or authorities,) which were cast to the earth. The clear implication is that there are heavenly hosts following the dragon, who are cast down with him and they have no further heavenly place, status, control, authority. (Compare Daniel 10:12-14 [39&40] and Ephesians 6:11,12.) [Note: (Luke 10:17-20) The LORD's response, when the seventy returned to Him rejoicing, *"LORD, even the devils are subject unto us through Thy name"*, brought His teaching. *"I beheld Satan as lightning fall from heaven. Behold, I give unto you power to tread on serpents and scorpions, and over all the power of the enemy: and nothing shall be any means hurt you."* This was most significant, because it showed that the LORD had seen Satan's casting down, with his hosts, which was why He had invested His disciples with power over demons, for they had been cast down and on earth they were being used to oppose the establishment of the kingdom. But in the Jewish rejection of the Gospel of GOD preached for the period of the Acts of the Apostles, by the apostles, or *them that heard Him,* Satan reinstated himself in heavenly places and John's vision reveals Satan's ultimate and final casting down.]

[158] The problems in interpreting this prophecy arise with the man child, who has to be The LORD Jesus Christ and, whilst this might be obvious to some, critics of this, take the view that there are no other scriptures to support the fact that the woman's child was caught up to God and to His throne. The LORD's ascension (as described Acts 1,) presents no such picture, but even if it were stretched, to apply to this man- child's deliverance, this only presents further problems. For this prophecy in The Revelation is then being applied to a past event, a glaring anomaly that is found nowhere else in scripture. [See footnote 5 page 16.]

The solution is simple, the man-child has to be the Body of The Lord Jesus Christ, His True Church and His body's being caught up to God and His throne is a future (not a past) event, as will be seen.

[159] The woman flees after the deliverance of her man-child, into the wilderness *where she hath a place prepared of God.* The most likely location for one such wilderness refuge is the abandoned city of Petra (scripturally called Selah or Joktheel - see 2 Kings 14:7 and Isaiah 16:1-5 Note the exhortation for Moab to provide shelter for the outcasts.) Formerly a thriving city in Idumea, on what was then a main caravan route, Petra was carved out of the solid rock over many centuries by its former inhabitants. Whilst some of it has dilapidated, there are still numerous habitable shelters in the deserted ruins. Petra was never conquered. Since its access was so difficult down a very narrow gorge, its defence was a far easier task than attacking the place. Petra was simply abandoned, when an alternative caravan route was discovered, which provided the necessary watering places for the beasts and travellers and which ran more or less parallel with the eastern coast of the Mediterranean. Most good encyclopaedias give details and photographs of this fascinating place Petra, and its suitability as a last day refuge for the nation Israel will be readily appreciated. But there are without doubt many other caves and suitable hiding places in the wilderness of Judea.

[160] The war in heaven between Michael and his angels and the dragon and his angels cannot be imagined: but in the context of the prophecy, they do fight. The outcome is defeat for the dragon and his hosts and they are cast down to earth. Michael is the Archangel appointed to defend the nation Israel (see Daniel 10:13, 20, 21 [39] & 12:1 [42]). Michael's involvement and his victory probably accounts for the survival of the woman and her being enabled to flee to the wilderness. The heavenly defeat of Satan and his casting down to earth are the causes of his terrible fury and wrath toward Israel.

When Satan is cast down (12:10, and as noted above this is the central verse of the Revelation,) the proclamation of victory is immediately followed by the heavenly lament, *"Woe!"* (The Third Woe 12:12 [155].) This Woe is expressed on behalf of the inhabiters of the earth and the sea, who now become the target of Satan's wrath. His immediate reaction is to attempt to destroy the woman with a flood (compare Daniel 9:26 [33]) but this proves unsuccessful, because the earth overcomes this naturally. [It is interesting that the earth itself is scripturally credited for its action, this confirms that the whole earth is a wonderful harmonious, extremely complex, network of ecosystems ordained by God to maintain His creation.] If Satan deserves any admiration, it has to be for his determination and in his rage he turns to make war with the remnant, the faithful few left of that nation Israel (12:17 compare also Romans 9:7, 8 & 29.) For this war, Satan employs a new tactic - The Beast.

[161] THE BEAST

(13:1-10) *And I stood upon the sand of the sea, and saw a beast rise up out of the sea, having seven heads and ten horns, and upon his horns ten crowns, and upon his heads the name of blasphemy. And the beast which I saw was like unto a leopard, and his feet were as the feet of a bear, and his mouth as the mouth of a lion; and the dragon gave him his power, and his seat, and great authority. And I saw one of his heads as it were wounded to death; and his deadly wound was healed: and all the world wondered after the beast. And they worshipped the dragon which gave power unto the beast: and they worshipped the beast, saying, "Who is like unto the beast?" and "Who is able to make war with him?" And there was given unto him a mouth speaking great things and blasphemies; and power was given unto him to continue forty and two months. And he opened his mouth in blasphemy against God, to blaspheme His name, and His tabernacle, and them that dwell in heaven. And it was given unto him to make war with the saints and to overcome them; and power was given him over all kindreds, and tongues, and nations. And all that dwell upon the earth shall worship him, whose names are not written in the book of life of the Lamb slain from the foundation of the world. If any man have an ear, let him hear. He that leadeth into captivity shall go into captivity: and he that killeth with the sword must be killed with the sword. Here is the patience and the faith of the saints.*

At this time the description of the Beast in Revelation is most appropriate. Satan has failed in his personal attempt to destroy the nation Israel, which has been scattered and some at least have fled to the wilderness. (The LORD's Own teachings recommended such action at this particular time, see Matthew 24:16-20.) The times appointed for the refuge of the woman in the wilderness and, for the Beast to continue in the power of Satan are the same (12:6, 14 and 13:5.) Satan has empowered this character and established him, for Satan's main objective is the total destruction of Israel. The means, by which the Beast will attempt to accomplish this, is idolatry: either Israel worships the Beast and his image, (thereby forsaking God and nullifying His covenant,) or they are slain. The nation Israel is to be destroyed spiritually, or physically, but ruthlessly and totally; for this would prevent the establishment of the Kingdom of God (which will end Satan's dominion on earth, and that is what Satan wishes to prevent at all costs.)

[162] The ultimate dictator, the Beast, has the power at his disposal to make the destruction of Israel possible (confirmed beyond doubt by the fact *these days are shortened*) and he uses this power with desperate savagery. John's description reveals so much, the Beast had *one of his heads as it were wounded to death; and his deadly wound was healed*. He has already been described as (11:7) *the beast that ascendeth out of the bottomless pit,* so that previously the Beast has been slain and brought back to life. In his restoration and reinstatement he has also made a deal of some sort with Satan (compare Daniel 11:38, 39 [42]) and he displays this extraordinary

power given to him, in his furious rage toward Israel. The Beast overcomes the two witnesses, who until that time had spectacularly destroyed their opponents; but the Beast himself appears apparently indestructible having survived death and overcome the two witnesses. The world stands in awe, visibly and totally impressed. The blasphemy of a man so empowered and inspired by Satan cannot be imagined; it will be frightening in its intensity and extremity. (It was this blasphemy, which so impressed Daniel - see Daniel 7:8, 11 [17] [19]). The Beast will far exceed all known boundaries in this respect and his blasphemy will have an utterly demoralising effect on people generally, who will not only be totally sickened by it, but will find it impossible to believe in a God, Who can tolerate (apparently) such vile extremes of evil spoken against Him.

Other factors worthy of notice, in the light of other scriptures, are that the beast rises up having seven heads, ten horns and ten crowns; (compare with the dragon, *seven heads and ten horns, and seven crowns* - Revelation 12:3 [156].) Except for the crowns the description is the same, for the dragon gives his power to the Beast. (The difference in the crowns will be explained in the fulfilment of the prophecy and it could mean a simple re-adjustment of minor or smaller kingdoms, which the Beast creates or takes over in his own strength as political expedients.) The dragon also gives the Beast his power, his seat (Pergamos, compare Revelation 2:13 [116]) and great authority. What this means in addition to the horns, heads and crowns is difficult to determine, but it is certainly a most formidable combination of power and authority to find in such an evil man.

The Beast becomes a most daunting, ruthless, fearsome character and as an opponent to Israel, he appears to be able to manipulate men at his whim, so few resist him. The world at this time will learn some sobering lessons in terms of the destruction, death and suffering that such a man can inflict and this is enabled basically because the world rejected GOD's appointed ruler, His Own Son. The nations, who supported the beast's meteoric rise, will pay bitterly for supporting the beast against Israel.

Anyone would imagine that one person like the Beast would be quite enough. Yet John reveals a truth as frightening as it is hideous, there is *another beast*, another character, The False Prophet; and he is fully revealed only in The Revelation. Whilst the Beast is the man Satan uses to try and destroy Israel; the other beast, the False Prophet is the man, whom Satan inspires to deceive the world into accepting the Beast. The whole concept is insidious, more especially because it is dramatically successful, but only for a limited time.

[163] THE FALSE PROPHET

(13:11-18) *And I beheld another beast coming up out of the earth; and he had two horns like a lamb, and he spake as a dragon. And he exerciseth all the power of the first beast before him, and causeth the earth and them that dwell therein to worship the first beast, whose deadly wound was healed. And he doeth great wonders, so that he maketh fire come down from heaven on the earth in the sight of men, and deceiveth them that dwell on the earth by the means of those miracles which he had power to do in the sight of the beast; saying to them that dwell on the earth, that they should make an image to the beast, which had the wound by a sword, and did live. And he had power to give life unto the image of the beast, that the image of the beast should both speak, and cause that as many as would not worship the image of the beast should be killed. And he causeth all, both small and great, rich and poor, free and bond, to receive a mark in their right hand or in their foreheads: that no man might buy or sell, save he that had the mark, or the name of the beast, or the number of his name. Here is wisdom. Let him that hath understanding count the number of the beast: for it is the number of a man; and his number is six hundred threescore and six.*

Another beast this character (later called the False Prophet [182]) is the ultimate "wolf in sheep's clothing" (see Matthew 7:15.) This beast is not exactly described like a lamb, but *he had two horns like a lamb*. This cannot be dismissed lightly; the two horns suggest a duality of power, associated with a lamb (or sheep,) which scripturally points to Jews or Christians, or both. Such a character (who is manifestly or outwardly *spiritual* because he is the false *prophet*) could display Christian beliefs outwardly, which have a very strong Jewish foundation. This beast is ominous and every bit as dangerous as his predecessor the Beast himself. He speaks as a dragon, inspired by Satan himself. This is totally in accord with Paul's teachings on the Lawless One in his letter to Thessalonians [101]. Accepting for the moment that the false prophet is the ultimate wolf in sheep's clothing, let us examine this possibility scripturally.

[164] In commissioning His disciples (Matthew 10:16-23 & Luke 21:12) the LORD sent them out among wolves, which at the time were the Roman authorities (the association of Rome in its very foundation with the wolf fable is well known.) The LORD warned them of the opposition they would face and He even spoke of their persecution. *"But when they persecute you in this city, flee ye into another: for verily I say unto you, ye shall not have gone over the cities of Israel, till the Son of man be come."* This just cannot be coincidence!

The possibility that the false prophet (the ultimate wolf) is a Roman exists and further, the ten kingdom confederation of the last days arises within the boundaries of the Roman empire, but not necessarily, though possibly, under the influence of Rome (Daniel 7:23-28 [23].) It would clearly be to the False Prophet's advantage to have Roman associations therefore. The ten kingdom confederation is mainly an economic alliance, the False Prophet organises not only the worship of the Beast, but he initiates the use of the brand or mark that the Beast's followers must adopt and exhibit openly, to trade. (See [168]) The Beast (whose capitol is Babylon,) will (through the false prophet) considerably enlarge his economic empire (powers), and of course, the price to pay is worshipping the beast and his image (which the false prophet has encouraged and enabled the Beast to set up, in Jerusalem.)

[165] From the LORD's teachings, the wolves amongst whom He sent His disciples were the Romans, the ruling authority over many nations at that time. Throughout their Empire the Romans maintained very careful control of any semblance of religious or political organisation, which might be the possible cause of any insurrection or challenge to Caesar. But from The LORD's words this same commission to His people extends *till the Son of man be come.* This must apply in the last days and therefore everything that He said to His disciples will have significance and fulfilment at that time.

[166] The Beast himself first appears among the ten kingdom confederation and the False Prophet having Roman associations, (since as shown above he establishes the worship of the Beast by imposing the brand or mark for the purposes of trading,) provides the link between the two characters within the confederation of ten. The LORD's teachings to His disciples have reinforced this view.[37] The two horns like a lamb have already been suggested as representing an outwardly Christian belief with strong Jewish foundations and this presents a formidable doctrinal basis to present to Jews, to authenticate the Beast's claims for worship. This could be the religious power exerted and it would of course, if it were presented in the first half of the final week after the covenant had been confirmed, bring the False Prophet and the Beast into direct conflict with the two witnesses. The False Prophet *spake like a dragon* i.e. as the god of this world, the arch deceiver himself and *he exerciseth all the power of the first beast before him.* These are no mean accomplishments and his spiritual influence will be phenomenal. The

---

[37] In Nebuchadnezzar's Image, the ten toes were seen as a confederation in the Roman Empire, iron, then the iron and clay combination of the legs and feet. The ten kingdoms need not themselves be Roman, but would be within the boundaries of the old Roman Empire.

False Prophet would not be able to persuade the true Church to worship the Beast, (for it will have been removed,) but the remaining, nominal or religious church(es) would probably be united under his control anyway.

[167] It is the False Prophet, who deceives the world into making an image of the beast and this is undoubtedly *the abomination that maketh desolate*. He makes the image speak and it can cause the death of those that will not worship it. The LORD Himself referred to this *abomination of desolation spoken of by Daniel the prophet standing where it ought not* (Mark 13:14 and from Matthew 24:15, this means standing *in the holy place,*) this is a frightening way to introduce idolatry to Israel.

The Babylonian captivity and the loss of their land had effectively cured Israel of its idolatry (but sadly, it had not cured their unbelief or disobedience.) In the last days this attempt, to force idolatry upon the nation, is a satanically inspired effort to rob the nation forever of its favoured place in the sight of God and to prevent the establishment of the Kingdom of God on earth.

Images that weep and bleed, or that make noises and even speak, are not new; such claims are as old as idolatry itself and ventriloquism was originally invented as an art of idolatrous priests (any good reference library will furnish particulars.) An image that can kill is new! Whether the False Prophet accomplishes this with trickery, or (as seems likely) with spiritual power, it makes no difference; it is just as spiritually intimidating.

[168] The False Prophet also introduces the system whereby nobody might trade unless he had the mark, or the name, or the number of the name. The famous 666, this number has been the cause of tremendous interest and speculation throughout history and it features strongly in many occult writings. Various scholars have detected this number in the names of several dictators (lists have been compiled by some,) and even emblems (the Nazi swastika was one,) are claimed to have been derived from 666[38]. Surprisingly, nobody seems to show much interest in the mark of the beast, whatever it is, or the name of the beast, which are equally potent signs in the worship and trade organised by the False Prophet. It should be recognised by anyone considering the number of the beast, that it is specifically stated it *is the number of a MAN*, its association with anything else is premature or of no significance. Scripturally the number has to apply to a man, who has links with a ten kingdom confederation (and it will be a necessity to trade,) outside of this it has no scriptural relevance.

[169] NOTE; It might be remarked that there is a school of thought which attempts to present Judas Iscariot as the False Prophet, let us examine this:

The suggestion is based partly on the fact that the *lamb with two horns* scripturally points to Israel (a sheep being the national animal emblem or type for that nation,) and partly also on the use of the term *son of perdition*. This term was used firstly by the LORD (John 17:12) in clear reference to Judas Iscariot. The same expression appears in Paul's writings (2 Thessalonians 2:3 [98]) in obvious application to the Beast, the man of sin. The Beast himself is most certainly not a Jew (as will be seen later,) but there are those who attempt to argue that Paul used this term to imply the Beast was Judas Iscariot. This is their basic argument and on this they build their flimsy doctrine, the exact purpose of which is vague.

In the context of what Paul actually wrote, theirs is a difficult assumption to accept; because Paul wrote of the man of sin as the

---

[38] Just one example: if the alphabet is numbered from A = 100 to Z = 125, then the name H (107) I (108) T (119) L (111) E (104) R (117) totals 666. Whilst quite justifiably, Hitler might be regarded as *a type* of the Beast, he was clearly not born in the right place or at the right time to be any more than that, (nevertheless, let us not forget that under his rule six million Jews died!)

son of perdition and separately of the Wicked (or Lawless One [101]) the False Prophet associated with the Beast. Their view maintained therefore is that Paul meant the Beast in his reference to the son of perdition and nobody else. The possibility that Judas Iscariot could be the False Prophet is rejected, for the following reasons.

1. Scripture plainly teaches that the body of Judas rotted to pieces (Acts 1:18) and whilst Satan might be able to restore life to a corpse, there is nothing scripturally to substantiate any claim that Satan could remake a body. The Beast for example is restored to life, but evidently bears the marks of his death. The fact that Satan required the body of Moses (Jude 9) shows that he could not make a copy of it. [Because Satan possibly intended to make the body of Moses an object of worship for the children of Israel, he was denied any right or claim to it.]

2. The word "perdition" (the Greek word means ruination or loss, in a spiritual sense; hence it is applied to eternal damnation or eternal doom.) In the New Testament the word is applied to others besides Judas and the Beast (see Philippians 1:28, 1 Timothy 6:9 and Hebrews 10:39.) There is no justification therefore for claiming it applies exclusively to Judas.

3. The use of the title "son of perdition" for Judas (by the LORD,) and for the Beast (by Paul,) associates them rather in their willingness to allow Satan to use them for monetary gain in their worldly lives (compare Daniel 11:38) than in any other sense. There is not sufficient warrant for the suggestion that the use of the term was to imply it was the same person in each case.

4. Judas Iscariot as the arch traitor of history would be the worst possible choice as a witness, or prophet, in view of his monumental treachery. To suggest (as some do) that it might be Judas and that he would have to be anonymous in this role, is too absurd to pursue.

5. No scripture at all indicates a resurrection, or rising from the

dead for Judas Iscariot. The appearance of the False Prophet *coming up out of the earth* (13:11) in John's words, shows merely that his appearing is the same as any other man (in the sense of Genesis 3:19 - *dust thou art, and unto dust shalt thou return.*) The False Prophet is born like any other man.

From these considerations the suggestion that Judas Iscariot is the False Prophet of the last days is totally rejected.

Chapter 15: The Revelation (The Seven Vials & The Whore of Babylon)

[170] *(14:1-5) And I looked, and lo, a Lamb stood on the Mount Sion, and with Him an hundred forty and four thousand, having His Father's name written in their foreheads. And I heard a voice from heaven, as the voice of many waters, and as the voice of a great thunder: and I heard the voice of harpers harping with their harps: and they sung as it were a new song before the throne, and before the four beasts, and the elders: and no man could learn that song but the hundred and forty and four thousand, which were redeemed from the earth. These are they which were not defiled with women; for they are virgins. These are they which follow the Lamb whithersoever He goeth. These were redeemed from among men, being the firstfruits unto God and to the Lamb. And in their mouth was found no guile: for they are without fault before the throne of God.*

The previous 144,000 (Revelation 7:4-17 [136]) were a completely different group. They were from the twelve tribes of Israel. They were sealed in their foreheads to protect them, for they were on earth to go through the tribulation (the events involved in the outpouring of the wrath of the Lamb,) and for them their heavenly place was assured. This 144,000 are redeemed from the earth, from among men (not Israel,) and are virgins. (There can be no quibble or argument for it is explained *these are they which were not defiled with women.*) They are guileless, they follow the Lamb and they are the firstfruits to God and to the Lamb.

But who are they? Not Israel, (the previous 144,000 covered that,) and not the Church (which has gone before the main events described in the Revelation have taken place.)

With the previous 144,000 there was also the multitude, *which no man could number, of all nations, and kindreds, and people, and tongues.* One of the elders described them to John *"These are they which came out of great tribulation, and have washed their robes ...etc"* (7:14). So that a multitude of all nations (apart from those sealed of Israel,) come out of the tribulation; the people who refused to worship the beast and who would die rather than submit. It is therefore suggested that this 144,000 on Mount Sion with the Lamb, are the firstfruits, (the male virgins, who qualify in these respects,) from among that multitude of all nations that no man could number. This would mean that before those throne in heaven would be the 144,000 of the twelve tribes of Israel and on earth, on Mount Sion with the Lamb, would be 144,000 redeemed from among men, who endured or survived the tribulation. This 144,000 have displayed the calibre, the qualities, the self-sacrifice and the faith to join the ranks of those with the Lamb. These are the first fruits in the last days of the Jewish ministry to all nations, the proselytes converted to God, when the Jewish witness is restored (see Luke 21:13 and compare Matthew 24:14 & Mark 13:10.) In those dreadful times the Jews will take their obedience to the LORD's commands seriously (e.g. fulfilling Matthew 28:19, 20 and Mark 16:15,16. Compare Matthew 23:29.)

[171] (14:6, 7) *And I saw another angel fly in the midst of heaven, having the everlasting gospel to preach unto them that dwell on the earth, and to every nation, and kindred, and tongue, and people, saying with a loud voice, "Fear God, and give glory to Him; for the hour of His judgment is come: and worship Him that made heaven, and earth, and the sea, and the fountains of waters."*

This is the Everlasting Gospel (gospel = good news) proclaimed since the fall in Eden and preached originally by Enoch and Noah. There are five gospels in scripture and these should be distinguished (see Appendix 5,) but the Everlasting Gospel is the worldwide gospel (to every nation, kindred, tongue and people,) proclaimed when the LORD has established His kingdom on earth.

[172] (14:8) *And there followed another angel, saying, "Babylon is fallen, is fallen, that great city, because she made all nations drink of the wine of the wrath of her fornication."*

This proclamation declares quite plainly the fall of Babylon (what this actually involves is revealed later Revelation 17, 18 [184 – 191]).

[173] (14:9-12) *And the third angel followed them,* (the previous angels) *saying with a loud voice, "If any man worship the beast and his image, and receive his mark in his forehead, or in his hand, the same shall drink of the wine of the wrath of God, which is poured out without mixture into the cup of His indignation: and he shall be tormented with fire and brimstone in the presence of the holy angels, and in the presence of the Lamb: and the smoke of their torment ascendeth up for ever and ever: and they have no rest day nor night, who worship the beast and his image, and whosoever receiveth the mark of his name. Here is the patience of the saints: here are they that keep the commandments of God, and the faith of Jesus."*

This is plain enough, it applies to those who worship the beast and his image and who have received his mark or his name in the forehead or hand; it cannot apply to the Church, which has gone! The saints are *they that keep the commandments of God, and the faith of Jesus* in those times i.e. Jews and their converts.

[174] (14:13) *And I heard a voice from heaven saying unto me, "Write blessed are the dead which die in the LORD from henceforth: Yea, saith the Spirit, That they may rest from their labours; and their works do follow them."*

The true Church sleeps in the LORD (1 Corinthians 15:18, 20 etc) but these die (compare also Revelation 2:10) and their works follow them (again, compare Revelation 2:2, 26 3:8 etc.) The scriptures are absolutely consistent in their teachings, when they are examined properly.

[175] (14:14-20) *And I looked, and behold a white cloud, and upon the cloud One sat like unto The Son of man, having on His head a golden crown, and in His hand a sharp sickle. And another angel came out of the temple, crying with a loud voice to Him that sat on the cloud, "Thrust in Thy sickle and reap: for the time is come for Thee to reap; for the harvest of the earth is ripe!" And He that sat on the cloud thrust in His sickle on the earth; and the earth was reaped, and another angel came out of the temple which is in heaven, he also having a sharp sickle, and another angel came out from the altar, which had power over fire; and cried with a loud cry to him that had the sharp sickle, saying, "Thrust in thy sharp sickle, and gather the clusters of the vine of the earth; for her grapes are fully ripe!" And the angel thrust in his sickle into the earth, and gathered the vine of the earth, and cast it into the great winepress of the wrath of God. And the winepress was trodden without the city, and blood came out of the winepress, even unto the horse bridles, by the space of a thousand and six hundred furlongs.*[39]

This is a difficult passage; in its context it follows the proclamation of the fall of Babylon and the judgment of those who worship the beast. It therefore applies to the final reaping of The Son of man, when He removes all those who worshipped idols, separating them for the wrath of God, as He comes to establish the Kingdom (Matthew 24:24-31 Mark 13:27 Luke 17:20-37, 21:27 & Acts 1:9-11.) His coming

---

[39] The furlong (= stadius, which was about 220 yards) is an accurate translation, and the distance involved is approximately two hundred miles, which was the length of Palestine or Israel during the LORD's times.

as The Son of man in the clouds results in His gathering His elect for Himself. The wrath of the Lamb has been vented, the wrath of God follows, but the Lamb gathers His elect to leave the wicked to face that wrath. His elect are His chosen people Israel.

[In the Revelation (14:18-20) The *harvest of the earth* and the *vine of the earth* are reaped by the Son of man; as the context shows this is a time of severe judgment (compare Deuteronomy 32:32, 33 and Matthew 13:24-30.) This event is followed by heavenly worship and rejoicing (Revelation 15:1-5); but when the temple in heaven is opened (15:5-8) worship is no longer possible until the seven vials were poured out and fulfilled.]

[176] THE SEVEN VIALS

(15:1-8) *And I saw another sign in heaven, great and marvellous, seven angels having the seven last plagues; for in them is filled up the wrath of God. And I saw as it were a sea of glass mingled with fire: and them that had gotten the victory over the beast, and over his image, and over his mark, and over the number of his name, stand on the sea of glass, having the harps of God. And they sing the song of Moses the servant of God, and the song of the Lamb, saying, "Great and marvellous are Thy works, Lord God Almighty; just and true are Thy ways, Thou King of saints. Who shall not fear Thee, O Lord, and glorify Thy name? For Thou only art holy: for all nations shall come and worship before Thee; for Thy judgments are made manifest". And after that I looked, and, behold, the temple of the tabernacle of the testimony in heaven was opened: and the seven angels came out of the temple, having the seven plagues, clothed in pure and white linen, and having their breasts girded with golden girdles. And one of the four beasts gave unto the seven angels seven golden vials full of the wrath of God, Who liveth for ever and ever. And the temple was filled with smoke from the glory of God, and from His power; and no man was able to enter into the temple, till the seven plagues of the seven angels were fulfilled.*

First there is the rejoicing of those who had the victory over the beast and his image, his mark and the number of his name (i.e. every aspect of his worship and the trading involved with those signs.) This confirms that even in the awful extremities of those times, there are those faithful people, who prevail and do not succumb to these impositions and their rewards are eternal. Then come the seven angels having the seven last plagues *and in them is filled up the wrath of God*. Such words make it totally incredible that anyone can have the audacity to attempt to relegate these plagues to historical events. The world has never experienced the wrath of GOD in these terms. In these vials (the Greek word used refers to a bowl or basin wider in diameter than it is deep,) *is filled up the wrath of GOD,* this cannot be lightly esteemed, or dismissed; divine judgments merit the utmost respect and serious consideration, these are inflicted in GOD's justice and might!

[177] THE FIRST VIAL

(16:1, 2) *And I heard a great voice out of the temple saying to the seven angels, "Go your ways, and pour out the vials of the wrath of God upon the earth". And the first went, and poured out his vial upon the earth; and there fell a noisome and grievous sore upon the men which had the mark of the beast, and upon them which worshipped his image.*

This is the judgment of The Eternal GOD (about which men were warned 14:9-12 [173]) being poured out, there is no time limit to this noisome and grievous sore. But notice that the beginning of the outpouring of the wrath of GOD is on the kingdom of the Beast, GOD's wrath commences on the kingdom that Satan seeks to establish to oppose the Kingdom of GOD.

[178] THE SECOND VIAL

(16:3) *And the second angel poured out his vial upon the sea; and it became as the blood of a dead man: and every living soul died in the sea.*

This is awesome to contemplate, every living soul in the sea dies, this completes the judgment that commenced in the wrath of the Lamb, with the sounding of the second trumpet (8:9 [142]) From Genesis (2:7) *And the LORD God formed man of the dust of the ground, and breathed into his nostrils the breath of life; AND MAN BECAME A LIVING SOUL.* Scripturally *a living soul* must breathe air; therefore, this second vial kills whales, dolphins, seals (pinnipeds), penguins; not necessarily everything such as fish and flying seabirds, but this is only a suggestion, a complete wipe out of all sea life is possible (compare Revelation 21:1 [201] *"and there was no more sea".*)

[179] THE THIRD VIAL

(16:4-7) *And the third angel poured out his vial upon the rivers and fountains of waters; and they became blood, and I heard the angel of the waters say, "Thou art righteous, O Lord, Which art, and wast, and shalt be, because Thou hast judged thus. For they have shed the blood of saints and prophets, and Thou hast given them blood to drink; for they are worthy." And I heard another out of the altar say, "Even so, Lord God Almighty, true and righteous are Thy judgments."*

This again extends or completes the judgment commenced in the third trumpet on fresh waters (8:10, 11 [143]). This vial must make the fresh waters completely undrinkable. Countries that rely for their water supplies from rivers, which originate in and pass through other countries, might be denied their water, because of the shortages of fresh water. This deprivation of fresh water supplies could precipitate wars quite easily, water is a vital necessity for life.

[180] THE FOURTH VIAL

(16:8, 9) *And the fourth angel poured out his vial upon the sun; and power was given unto him to scorch men with fire. And men were scorched with great heat, and blasphemed the name of God, which hath power over these plagues: and they repented not to give Him glory.*

(Compare with the fourth trumpet 8:12 [144]) This is a terrible judgment; such heat from the sun would make life unbearable, particularly with a shortage of water. Their blasphemy is totally ineffective (it always is,) for whatever man says about GOD does not affect Him in the slightest.

Blasphemers are defying or challenging GOD to destroy them (with some searing heavenly blast, or lightning etc), GOD is never provoked to react to such pathetic people; to destroy them He needs only to deny them their next breath! When, or if, that happens, they will bitterly regret the breath they wasted so foolishly blaspheming Him.

[181] THE FIFTH VIAL

(16:10,11) *And the fifth angel poured out his vial upon the seat of the beast; and his kingdom was full of darkness; and they gnawed their tongues for pain, and blasphemed the God of heaven because of their pains and their sores, and repented not of their deeds.*

The fifth trumpet (9:1-11 [146]) had brought the judgment of the release of the locusts from the pit upon mankind, the fifth vial is directed at the kingdom of the beast. Notice that in spite of their agonising pains, they blasphemed (again,) and repented not!

[182] THE SIXTH VIAL

(16:12-16) *And the sixth angel poured out his vial upon the great river Euphrates and the water thereof was dried up, that the way of the kings of the east might be prepared. And I saw three unclean spirits like frogs come out of the mouth of the dragon, and out of the mouth of the beast, and out of the mouth of the false prophet. For they are the spirits of devils, working miracles, which go forth unto the kings of the earth and of the whole world, to gather them to the battle of that great day of God Almighty. Behold, I come as a thief. Blessed is he that watcheth, and keepeth his garments, lest he walk naked, and they see his shame. And He gathered them together into a place called in the Hebrew tongue Armageddon.*[40]

This is the first time the False Prophet is so named (previously he was *another beast*, [163].) It is time to examine the False Prophet in more detail. The LORD Himself said (John 5:43), *"I am come in My Father's name, and ye receive Me not. If another shall come in his own name, HIM ye will receive."* From Paul's second epistle to Thessalonians (2:8 [101]) it was shown that the Wicked (= the lawless one) was a different character from the beast, and that he appeared in the church, it is suggested therefore that this character is *another that shall come in his own name.* John also wrote in his epistle (1 John 2:18) *Little children, it is the last time: and as ye have heard that Antichrist shall come, even now are there many antichrists; whereby we know that it is the last time. They went out from us, but they were not of us; for if they had been of us, they would no doubt have continued with us: but they went out, that they might be made manifest that were not all of us.* The Antichrist must come (this is most definitely last days, *the last time* mentioned twice,) and the antichrists are those, who have forsaken the church, the backsliders or apostates. But the Antichrist himself, in the context of John's words, must be expected in the Church (not His body, the true Church, which has already been raptured; this refers to the Church of

---

[40] The association in the New Testament of the thief, with watching and keeping one's garments, refers to the Roman method of keeping sentries or watchmen awake on duty. The duty officer on his rounds at night would approach stealthily like a thief, and he was permitted to set fire to the garments of any sentry or watchman he found sleeping. The culprit was not relieved of his duty, which he had to complete with his burns and what rags he had left and THEN, on his march back to the barracks after duty, his folly and shame were made public. [94][118][219]. For ARMAGEDDON see Appendix 6.

the Antichrist, a religion:) and for this reason it is claimed here that the (ultimate) Antichrist and the False Prophet are the same person.

[183] THE SEVENTH VIAL

(16:17-21) *And the seventh angel poured out his vial into the air; and there came a great voice out of the temple of heaven, from the throne, saying, "It is done!" And there were voices, and thunders, and lightnings; and there was a great earthquake, such as was not since men were upon the earth, so mighty an earthquake, and so great. And the great city was divided into three parts, and the cities of the nations fell: and great Babylon came in remembrance before God, to give unto her the cup of the wine of the fierceness of His wrath. And every island fled away, and the mountains were not found. And there fell upon men a great hail out of heaven, every stone about the weight of a talent: and men blasphemed God because of the plague of the hail; for the plague thereof was exceeding great.* [Compare *the great hail* here with Job 38:22, 23.]

The seventh vial results in a spectacular series of frightening eventualities: *thunders and lightnings* (note the plural nouns, no limit to their numbers, awesome) *and a great earthquake,* worldwide in its effects, destroying *the cities of the nations.* Followed by hail (*every stone about the weight of a talent* = eighty pounds; this would mean hail over a foot in diameter) this is quite possible, but thankfully extremely rare.

In the manifestation of a suitably fitting conclusion (the seventh vial) to the outpouring of Divine wrath *there came a great voice out of the temple of heaven, from the throne, saying, "It is done!"*

Very little further comment is necessary on the seven vials, but a comparison of the events of the seven trumpets with the events of the seven vials is most revealing; for it shows the accord and unity between the wrath of the Lamb and the wrath of God (See [245]-[251]).

[184] THE JUDGMENT OF THE GREAT WHORE

(17:1-18) *And there came one of the seven angels which had the seven vials, and talked with me, saying unto me, "Come hither; and I will shew unto thee the judgment of the great whore that sitteth upon many waters: with whom the kings of the earth have committed fornication, and the inhabitants of the earth have been drunk with the wine of her fornication." So he carried me away in the Spirit into the wilderness: and I saw a woman sit upon a scarlet coloured beast, full of names of blasphemy, having seven heads and ten horns. And the woman was arrayed in purple and scarlet colour, and decked with gold and precious stones and pearls, having a golden cup in her hand full of abominations and filthiness of her fornication: and upon her forehead was a name written, MYSTERY, BABYLON THE GREAT, THE MOTHER OF HARLOTS AND ABOMINATIONS OF THE EARTH. And I saw the woman drunken with the blood of the saints, and with the blood of the martyrs of Jesus: and when I saw her, I wondered with great admiration. And the angel said unto me, "Wherefore didst thou marvel? I will tell thee the mystery of the woman, and of the beast that carrieth her, which hath the seven heads and ten horns. The beast that thou sawest was, and is not; and shall ascend out of the bottomless pit, and go into perdition: and they that dwell on the earth shall wonder, whose names were not written in the book of life from the foundation of the world, when they behold the beast that was, and is not, and yet is. And here is the mind which hath wisdom. The seven heads are seven mountains, on which the woman sitteth, and there are seven kings: five are fallen, and one is, and the other is not yet come; and when he cometh, he must continue a short space. And the beast that was, and is not, even he is the eighth, and is of the seven, and goeth into perdition. And the ten horns which thou sawest are ten kings which have received no kingdom as yet; but receive power as kings one hour with the beast. These have one mind, and shall give their power and strength unto the beast. These shall make war with the Lamb, and the Lamb shall overcome them: for He is LORD of lords, and KING of kings: and they that are with Him are called, and chosen, and faithful." And he saith unto me, "The waters which thou sawest, where the whore sitteth, are peoples, and multitudes, and nations, and tongues. And the ten horns which thou sawest upon the beast, these shall hate the whore, and shall make her desolate and naked, and shall eat her flesh, and burn her with fire. For God hath put in their hearts to fulfil His will, and to agree, and give their kingdom to the beast, until the words of God shall be fulfilled. And the woman which thou sawest is that great city, which reigneth over the kings of the earth.*

Notice *one of the seven angels which had the seven vials* was appointed to *shew unto thee the judgment of the great whore*. It seems reasonable to suggest that this was probably the fifth angel, whose vial was poured out on the kingdom of the beast (Babylon). (See also 21:9 page 137.)

[185]

This chapter is one of the most spectacular and illuminating portions of the Revelation and it has inspired much thought and again many artistic attempts to portray its events. Yet in spite of the explanation given, there are many, who totally misapply what is recorded. The whore is Babylon, her name is written on her forehead (and the following chapter gives the details of the fall of Babylon.) Notice too, the beast carries the whore, yet the favourite interpretation of this passage for centuries has been that the beast is the pope and the whore is the Roman Catholic Church. But the pope does not carry the Roman Catholic Church, neither does the world wonder at the pope. Babylon cannot be considered a church, it is quite plainly stated, she is *that great city* and scripturally from its inception Babylon has been noted for its rebellion against God. In the last days Babylon will become again a great city. In its restored glory and splendour it will become powerful and rich, a major centre of commerce and trade, it may be the intended commercial and religious capital of Satan's kingdom. Babylon will be totally and finally destroyed in God's wrath and judgment.

[186] THE EIGHT KINGS

Consider now the description of the beast (17:8-11) and note the particular emphasis in this passage, the repetition: *the beast thou sawest was, and is not.....the beast that was, and is not, and yet is.....the beast that was, and is not, even he is the eighth.* Further, special attention was drawn to this (17:9) *and here is the mind which hath wisdom, the seven heads are seven mountains on which the woman sitteth* - what is the particular point to which the wise were directed?

Notice the angel continued *"And"*, what follows therefore merits equal attention or emphasis. His next words were, *"and there are seven kings: five are fallen, and one is, and the other is not yet come and when he cometh he must continue a short space. And the beast that was, and is not, even he is the eighth and is of the seven, and goeth into perdition."*

These eight kings are most interesting (it should be realised that they have nothing to do with the ten kings of 17:12,) because the beast (*who was and is not and yet is* etc as emphasised in the context,) comes into this succession of eight kings as *the seventh* and *as the EIGHTH* king. This agrees perfectly with the fact that the beast is not one of the ten kings (kingdoms). He arises from outside somewhere and comes into the confederation of ten, to take over three initially and then subsequently he rules the whole confederation. This is a totally different sequence or succession.

The succession depicted is:

FIVE (*who are fallen*) plus ONE (*who is*) plus ONE (*who cometh*) plus ONE (*the eighth*)

This must afford a most useful clue to the national identity of the beast himself, *even he is the eighth, and is of the seven.* Note it is the whole succession that counts. Seeking historical answers to this (which is obviously the usual method to adopt for any succession of kings,) has proved a challenging task for many scholars and the various lists of kings' names proposed are interesting.

But the solution requires answers to all of the following questions:

= Who are the FIVE fallen? (Before The Revelation)

= Who is the ONE that is?

= Who is the ONE to come?

= Who is the EIGHTH? (The beast himself.)

Those worthies, who have earnestly sought for historical answers, have neglected the truth, *that the best interpreter of scripture is scripture.* In the context of this revelation to John (which is all about the judgment of Babylon,) the scriptures offer an explanation, which is far more acceptable and in fact much more adequate, than any historical solution offered. Because *scripturally*, there are FIVE fallen kings of Babylon, there is ONE who is king of Babylon, there is ONE who cometh to be king of Babylon and he is the EIGHTH king of Babylon.

The explanation of these scriptural truths is as follows:

1-5   The FIVE fallen kings of Babylon are: 1 Nebuchadnezzar* king of Babylon (2 Kings 24:1 Daniel etc); 2 Belshazzar King of Babylon (Daniel 7:1); 3 Evil Merodach king of Babylon (2 Kings 25:27); 4 Cyrus king of Babylon (Ezra 5:13); and 5 Artaxerxes king of Babylon (Nehemiah 13:6).

6   The ONE who is king of Babylon, is Satan himself (Isaiah 14:4-23).

7   The ONE NOT YET COME will be the beast himself, who dies in battle.

8   The EIGHTH king of Babylon is the beast restored after his death. (He is of the seven, in that he was the seventh of the succession and also he is the Eighth.)

[*In Daniel the king is called *Nebuchadnezzar*, in Jeremiah he is called *Nebuchadnezzar* and *Nebuchadrezzar*, and in Ezekiel he is called *Nebuchadrezzar*, but it is the same king.]

From this succession it must be concluded that scripturally the Beast of the last days comes from Babylon (the nation, modern day Iraq,) not necessarily the city itself and he rules as king of Babylon. This is in perfect harmony with the prophecy of Jeremiah (see Footnote 14 [34],) that at the end of the seventy years the LORD would judge Babylon and its king. Further, this explains (13:1-10 [161]) *"the beast.... having seven heads.....and I saw one of his heads as it were wounded to death; and his deadly wound was healed"*. Scripturally, it is as the seventh scriptural king of Babylon, that the beast is mortally wounded and his wound healed.

[187]

The angel next explains to John the ten horns (17:12-14) and his opening remark makes any historical application (previous to The Revelation, or the last days,) impossible: *"the ten horns which thou sawest are ten kings, WHICH HAVE RECEIVED NO KINGDOM AS YET."* And the angel continues to explain that these ten kings *"receive power as kings one hour with the beast."* This has to be entirely last days for their involvement is with the beast and yet, there are those, who persist in attempted to explain these ten horns historically. It is quite plainly stated that *the ten horns, are ten kings which have received no kingdom as yet.* (This makes a total mockery of historical efforts to interpret these kingdoms.) For this can only mean that they have never ruled previously, these kingdoms have never been recognised before[41]. The hour* seems a remarkably brief period to

---

[41] In spite of this clear assertion that these *are ten kings, WHICH HAVE RECEIVED NO KINGDOM AS YET*; there have been numerous suggestions made. Sir Robert Anderson made the shrewd;; observation : "There is presumption against finding in past times a partial accomplishment of such a prophecy, but the fact that twenty-eight different lists, including sixty-five 'kingdoms', have been put forward in the controversy, is a proof how

take literally, especially in application to a confederation of ten kingdoms. It would seem that when these ten are completely unified and properly organised with the beast as their overall head and in control for this one hour, then suddenly in the judgment on Babylon, it is all destroyed. This possibility cannot be ignored. But it could of course take months, even years, to fully organise such an alliance and in the catastrophic events of the judgment of Babylon, it could all be wiped out in an hour. In its fulfilment this one hour should be quite special; certainly the time of the triumphing of the ten nations, in their apparent success under the Beast's leadership, is very short-lived. (As a twelfth part of a day, and taking the day as a year, *the hour* might be interpreted as one month.)

Their single-mindedness and dedication in their service and allegiance to the Beast is absolute for this period, *"these have one mind, and shall give their power and strength unto the beast."* (7:13.) But the terrible consequences of their loyalty can be seen in the folly into which the Beast leads them (17:14) *"these shall make war with the Lamb, and the Lamb shall overcome them: for He is LORD of lords, and KING of kings."* However successful their confederation has been economically and militarily, (and realistically, the combined efforts of ten nations could be capable of producing dramatic results,) their conflict with the Lamb is totally disastrous. The Beast in fact probably leads them himself in conflict against Israel, because he is not in Babylon when it is destroyed. The angel actually says that the Lamb shall overcome them, so that the ten nations continue, they are not totally destroyed, but reserved for His impending judgments.

[188]

Finally, (17:15) the angel gives John details concerning the whore, *"the waters which thou sawest, where the whore sitteth are people*

---

worthless is the evidence of any such fulfilment." [*The Coming Prince* Chapter 3, page 40, footnote 2.]

and multitudes, and nations, and tongues." The waters were only mentioned in the angel's opening words to John (17:1,) but are included in the final portion of the angel's explanation of these things. As a feature of the whore's influence, this reveals that her power is worldwide and obviously the world has totally supported the last days' development and prosperity of Babylon.

[189]

(17:16, 17) *"And the ten horns which thou sawest upon the beast, these shall hate the whore, and shall make her desolate and naked, and shall eat her flesh, and burn her with fire. For God hath put in their hearts to fulfil His will, and to agree, and give their kingdom to the beast, until the words of God shall be fulfilled."*

Another amazing fact is brought to light that whilst the ten kingdoms and their alliance has been engineered and they give their loyalty and total support to the beast, eventually they detest and hate the place of his authority and rule. Notice their ability to agree together is inspired of GOD; He is in absolute control all the time and permits this co-operation among these nations to fulfil His will. It is not, as men might imagine in their vanity, the result of their political skills and liberality and diplomacy and business acumen; their apparent success has all been ordained in the will of God to destroy them (for the one thing they will have in common is their consuming hatred for Jews.) The woman, the whore is finally positively identified as THAT GREAT CITY and her name is BABYLON and John next describes the judgment of God on that city.

[190] THE JUDGMENT OF BABYLON

(18:1-24) *And after these things I saw another angel come down from heaven, having great power; and the earth was lightened with his glory. And he cried mightily with a strong voice, saying, "Babylon the great is fallen, is fallen, and is become the habitation of devils, and the hold of every foul spirit, and a cage of every unclean and hateful bird. For all nations have drunk of the wine of the wrath of her fornication, and the kings of the earth have committed fornication with her, and the merchants of the earth are waxed rich through the abundance of her delicacies." And I heard another voice from heaven, saying, "Come out of her My people, that ye be not partakers of her sins, and that ye receive not of her plagues. For her sins have reached unto heaven, and God hath remembered her iniquities. Reward her even as she rewarded you, and double unto her double according to her works: in the cup which she hath filled fill to her double. How much she hath glorified herself, and lived deliciously, so much torment and sorrow give her: for she saith in her heart, 'I sit a queen, and am no widow, and shall see no sorrow'. Therefore shall her plagues come in one day, death, and mourning, and famine; and she shall be utterly burned with fire: for strong is the LORD GOD Who judgeth her. And the kings of the earth, who have committed fornication and lived deliciously with her, shall bewail her, and lament for her, when they shall see the smoke of her burning, standing afar off for the fear of her torment, saying, 'Alas, alas, that great city Babylon, that mighty city! for in one hour is thy judgment come.' And the merchants of the earth shall weep and mourn over her; for no man buyeth their merchandise any more: The merchandise of gold, and silver, and precious stones, and of pearls, and fine linen, and purple, and silk, and scarlet, and all thyine wood, and all manner vessels of ivory, and all manner vessels of most precious wood, and of brass, and iron, and marble, and cinnamon, and odours, and ointments, and frankincense, and wine, and oil, and fine flour, and wheat, and beasts, and sheep, and horses, and chariots, and slaves, and souls of men. And the fruits that thy soul lusted after are departed from thee, and all things which were dainty and goodly are departed from thee, and thou shall find them no more at all. The merchants of these things, which were made rich by her, shall stand afar off for the fear of her torment, weeping and wailing, and saying 'Alas, alas, that great city, that was clothed in fine linen, and purple and scarlet, and decked with gold, and precious stones, and pearls!' For in one hour so great riches is come to nought. And every shipmaster, and all the company in ships, and sailors, and as many as trade by sea, stood afar off, and cried when they saw the smoke of her burning, saying, 'What city is like unto this great city!' And they cast dust on their heads, and cried, weeping and wailing, saying, 'Alas, alas, that great city, wherein were made rich all that had ships in the sea by reason of her costliness!' for in one hour is she made desolate. Rejoice over her, thou heaven, and ye holy apostles and prophets; for God hath avenged you on her." And a mighty angel took up a stone like a great millstone, and cast it into the seas, saying, "Thus with violence shall that great city Babylon be thrown down, and shall be found no more at all!" And the voice of harpers, and musicians, and of pipers, and trumpeters, shall be heard no more at all in thee; and no craftsman, of whatsoever craft he be, shall be found any more in thee; and the sound of a millstone shall be heard no more at all in thee; and the light of a candle shall shine no more at all in thee; and the voice of the bridegroom and of the bride shall be heard no more at all in thee: for thy merchants were the great men of the earth; for by thy sorceries were all nations deceived. And in her was found the blood of prophets, and of saints, and of all that were slain upon the earth.*

[191]

The lengthy description of the judgment of Babylon is quite straightforward and full of detail; notice especially the repetition (v10, 17 & 19) *in one hour is thy judgment come. In one hour so great riches is come to nought. In one hour is she made desolate.* This emphasises the point made earlier (17:12 [187]) about the ten kings who *receive power as kings one hour with the beast* and confirms that when their confederation reaches its ultimate goal, their moment of success and triumph, then in one hour it is all destroyed. Notice also the *kings of the earth ... shall bewail her; the merchants of the earth shall mourn over her; the merchants of these things shall stand afar off for fear of her torment; every shipmaster, the company in ships, and sailors stood afar off and cried.* All these categories have been mortified and affected by the downfall of Babylon. The *merchants of these things* are possibly the traders within the city itself, who must flee before the destruction commences, revealing that they may have had some warning in advance.

Chapter 16: The Revelation (Marriage, Millenium, New Jerusalem)

[192] THE MARRIAGE OF THE LAMB

(19:1-10) *After these things I heard a great voice of much people in heaven, saying, "Alleluia; Salvation, and glory, and honour, and power, unto the LORD our God: for true and righteous are His judgments: for He hath judged the great whore, which did corrupt the earth with her fornication, and hath avenged the blood of His servants at her hand." And again they said, "Alleluia." And her smoke rose up for ever and ever. And the four and twenty elders and the four beasts fell down and worshipped God that sat on the throne, saying, "Amen; Alleluia!" And a voice came out of the throne, saying, "Praise our God, all ye His servants, and ye that fear Him, both small and great." And I heard as it were the voice of a great multitude, and as the voice of many waters, and as the voice of mighty thunderings, saying, "Alleluia: for the LORD God omnipotent reigneth. Let us be glad and rejoice, and give honour to Him: for the marriage of the Lamb is come, and His wife hath made herself ready." And to her was granted that she should be arrayed in fine linen, clean and white: for the fine linen is the righteousness of saints. And he saith unto me, "Write, Blessed are they which are called unto the marriage supper of the Lamb." And he saith unto me, "These are the true sayings of God." And I fell at his feet to worship him. And he said to me, "See thou do it not: I am thy fellowservant, and of thy brethren that have the testimony of Jesus: worship God: for the testimony of Jesus is the spirit of prophecy."*

[193]

Whilst the world mourns for the devastating judgment of Babylon; and whilst God is glorified in heavenly places and for the revelation of His omnipotence in such judgments; then comes the announcement of the marriage of the Lamb, concluding, *"Blessed are they which are called unto the marriage supper of the Lamb."* There is the additional assurance, *"These are the true sayings of God."* In the light of the awesome judgments being outpoured, such an assurance is truly inspired, revealing not only the wonderful control that God has over all, but also the delightful prospect of the marriage of the Lamb and *His wife hath made herself ready*. His wife is Israel, His people. His wife, His bride, and cannot be considered to be His Church, for the following reasons:

1. To fulfil the law, Jesus Christ could not marry outside Israel.

2. The bride is mentioned in the New Testament by John the baptist (John 3:29) who was the last of the Old Testament prophets and his ministry was to Israel. John had no knowledge of, or ministry to, the (gentile) Church. The Revelation has been shown to apply consistently to the Jewish nation of the last days and again, in respect of the bride, this is true (compare 21:2, 9 [201] & 22:17 [205]).

3. Reference to Romans (7:4) should be made in the light of Paul's opening words (7:1) *"I speak unto them that know the law."* Paul's writings were addressed to the Jews in Rome, he was trying to make a point to them, and he does not say that the Church is the bride of the Lamb at all, and the term "bride of Christ" is not found in scripture

4. In Ephesians (5:28-33) Paul does not refer to the Church as the bride of the Lamb, but as His BODY, which has to be masculine (this further supports Ephesians 1:22, 23.)

5. Old Testament references, notably in Isaiah and Hosea, refer to the Jewish nation as the betrothed of the LORD and nowhere in scripture does the LORD ever alter or deny this relationship.

6. The true (mainly gentile) Church is always referred to in masculine terms His body, sons, etc.

7. The Church has a distinctly heavenly calling and status and marriage is not a heavenly occupation according to the LORD's Own teachings (Matthew 22:29 etc). Marriage has strictly earthly associations, which is where Israel is promised to be blessed of God, in the establishment of His kingdom on earth.

8. Paul's remarks (2 Corinthians 11), which yet again make no reference whatsoever to the bride, should be considered in their context (see v1) *"would God ye could bear with me a little in my folly,"* Paul acknowledged that his illustration here was foolish, unless seen in its proper perspective.

To persist in the dogma, that the Bride is the Church of Christ, is to diminish the Church's true heavenly status as His body and to ignore the plain teaching of scripture. It also makes tremendous difficulties for anyone attempting to understand the events of the last days, because it means attempting to insert the Church in the scriptural place belonging to Israel.

[194] JUDGMENT OF THE BEAST & THE FALSE PROPHET

(19:11-21) *And I saw heaven opened, and behold a white horse; and He that sat upon him was called Faithful and True, and in righteousness He doth judge and make war. His eyes were as a flame of fire, and on His head were many crowns; and He had a name written, that no man knew, but He Himself. And He was clothed with a vesture dipped in blood: and His name is called The Word of God. And the armies which were in heaven followed Him upon white horses, clothed in fine linen, white and clean. And out of His mouth goeth a sharp sword, that with it He should smite the nations: and He shall rule them with a rod of iron: and He treadeth the winepress of the fierceness and wrath of Almighty God. And He hath on His vesture and on His thigh a name written, KING OF KINGS AND LORD OF LORDS. And I saw an angel standing in the sun; and he cried with a loud voice, saying to all the fowls that fly in the midst of heaven, "Come and gather yourselves together unto the supper of the great God; that ye may eat the flesh of kings, and the flesh of captains, and the flesh of mighty men, both free and bond, both small and great." And I saw the beast, and the kings of the earth, and their armies, gathered together to make war against Him that sat on the horse, and against His army. And the beast was taken, and with him the false prophet that wrought miracles before him, with which he deceived them that had received the mark of the beast, and them that worshipped his image. These both were cast alive into a lake of fire burning with brimstone. And the remnant were slain with the sword of Him that sat upon the horse, which sword proceeded out of His mouth: and all the fowls were filled with their flesh.*

[195]

No longer described as the Lamb, His names are Faithful and True, and *a name written, that no man knew*, and The Word of GOD, and KING OF KINGS AND LORD OF LORDS, under these titles He makes war. As The Word of God, His word is powerful in extreme *that with it He should smite nations, and the remnant were slain with the sword ...which proceedeth out of His mouth*. The beast has led the armies of the kings of the earth to destroy Jerusalem and Israel. But the LORD's coming is to deliver His people, His bride, and He destroys their armies - the beast and the false prophet being cast alive into the lake of fire. It is to this slaughter that the fowl of the air are called to feast themselves on the dead. The intended carcase was to be Israel, but the LORD has overcome their enemies and the carrion birds feed on their carcasses. (Associating the scriptures and revealing that the event happens, when the LORD comes as The Word of God, see Ezekiel 39:1-7 & Matthew 24:28.)

[196] THE MILLENNIUM

(20:1-10) *And I saw an angel come down from heaven, having the key of the bottomless pit and a great chain in his hand. And he laid hold on the dragon, that old serpent, which is the Devil, and Satan, and bound him a thousand years, and cast him into the bottomless pit, and shut him up, and set a seal upon him, that he should deceive the nations no more, till the thousand years should be fulfilled: and after that he must be loosed a little season. And I saw thrones, and they sat upon them, and judgment was given unto them: and I saw the souls of them that were beheaded for the witness of Jesus, and for the Word of God, and which had not worshipped the beast, neither his image, neither had received his mark upon their foreheads, or in their hands; and they lived and reigned with Christ a thousand years. But the rest of the dead lived not again until the thousand years were finished. This is the first resurrection. Blessed and holy is he that hath part in the first resurrection: on such the second death hath no power, but they shall be priests of God and of Christ, and shall reign with Him a thousand years. And when the thousand years are expired, Satan shall be loosed out of his prison, and shall go out to deceive the nations which are in the four quarters of the earth, Gog and Magog, to gather them together to battle: the number of whom is as the sand of the sea. And they went up on the breadth of the earth, and compassed the camp of the saints about, and the beloved city: and fire came down from God out of heaven, and devoured them. And the devil that deceived them was cast into the lake of fire and brimstone, where the beast and false prophet are, and shall be tormented day and night for ever and ever.*

[197]

Notice especially, *and I saw the souls of them that were beheaded for the witness of Jesus, and for the Word of God, and which had not worshipped the beast, neither his image, neither had received his mark upon their foreheads, or in their hands;* etc. These words confirm beyond doubt, that beheading is the punishment ruthlessly inflicted on those who will not worship the beast and his image. This shows the extremes of Satan in his efforts to destroy the Jews and the power exercised in those terrible times by the Beast and the False Prophet. In their destruction those souls, who died believing in GOD, are rewarded.

This is the time when the LORD rules all nations with a rod of iron (19:15 [194] and compare 12:5 [156],) during which Satan is bound for a thousand years (the term Millennium is not used in scriptures, but it is the word used to describe this scriptural period). The purpose for which Satan is imprisoned is given *that he should deceive the nations no more.* No matter how many might scoff at the suggestion, the truth is that Satan does inspire the hatred, mistrust and war between nations and he does so in his incessant efforts to frustrate the divine purposes of God.

[198]

Notice John wrote *"I saw thrones, and they sat upon them, and judgment was given unto them;"* this applies to the LORD and His Father primarily (see 3:21 [120], also compare Matthew 25:31 [67] and Daniel 7:9-11 [10]); but also to those appointed to sit with Them in judgment and these reign with Him for this same period. Those who died in refusing to accept the worship of the beast or his mark, take part in the first resurrection. These again are nothing to do with the Church, and these events concern the Jewish nation mainly, but also those who have accepted their witness and supported them, in the Jewish rejection of, and their opposition to, the worship of the

Beast. It should be appreciated that the terrible ferocity of the Beast to establish his worship by the Jews, fails in its purpose because of the faithful remnant, who refuse to submit to his demands; and the Beast is Satan's penultimate attempt to prevent the establishment of the Kingdom of heaven on earth. Their faithfulness and seeking their Messiah's help justifiably enables GOD to send His Son to bring about their victorious deliverance, but the opposition they face is fiercesome in extreme.

[199]

The release of Satan means the immediate resumption of his former activities, deceiving nations to follow him in the final assault on the saints (the Jews,) and the beloved city Jerusalem (compare [55]). In this battle they are totally destroyed by GOD Himself and the devil is cast into the lake of fire to join the beast and the false prophet. It reveals how capable Satan is at deceiving nations. Those, who attempt to invoke his powers for personal use, fail to appreciate the scriptural truth, which reveals that Satan's personal involvement with individuals is very rare. The Satanic power given to the Beast is quite unique.

[200] THE GREAT WHITE THRONE

(20:11-15) *And I saw a great white throne, and Him That sat on it, from Whose face the earth and the heaven fled away; and there was found no place for them. And I saw the dead, small and great, stand before God; and the books were opened: and another book was opened, which is the book of life: and the dead were judged out of those things which were written in the books, according to their works. And the sea gave up the dead which were in it; and death and hell delivered up the dead which were in them: and they were judged every man according to their works. And death and hell were cast into the lake of fire. This is the second death. And whosoever was not found written in the book of life was cast into the lake of fire.*

The great white throne set up for God to judge the world of mankind; earlier this was the throne that John had seen in heaven (4:2-6 [124].) It is necessary to distinguish between the judgment of saints in heaven, which is for rewards (see 2 Corinthians 5:6-11) and the judgment of mankind on earth, which is according to truth and every man is answerable for himself (see Romans 1:16-2:16 esp. 2:2.)

[201] THE NEW JERUSALEM, THE HOLY CITY, THE BRIDE

(21:1-27) *And I saw a new heaven and a new earth: for the first heaven and the first earth were passed away; and there was no more sea. And I John saw the holy city, New Jerusalem, coming down from God out of heaven, prepared as a bride adorned for her husband. And I heard a great voice out of heaven, saying, "Behold, the tabernacle of God is with men, and He will dwell with them, and they shall be His people, and God Himself shall be with them, and be their God. And God shall wipe away all tears from their eyes; and there shall be no more death, neither sorrow, nor crying, neither shall there be any more pain: for the former things are passed away." And He that sat upon the throne said, "Behold, I make all things new." And He said unto me, "It is done. I am Alpha and Omega, the beginning and the end, I will give unto him that is athirst of the fountain of the water of life freely. He that overcometh shall inherit all things; and I will be his God and he shall be My son. But the fearful, and unbelieving, and the abominable, and murderers, and whoremongers, and sorcerers, and idolaters, and all liars, shall have their part in the lake which burneth with fire and brimstone: which is the second death." And there came unto me one of the seven angels which had the seven vials full of the seven last plagues, and talked with me, saying, "Come hither, I will shew thee the bride, the Lamb's wife." And he carried me away in the spirit to a great and high mountain, and shewed me that great city, the holy Jerusalem, descending out of heaven from God. Having the glory of God: and her light was like unto a stone most precious, even like a jasper stone, clear as crystal; and had a wall great and high, and had twelve gates, and at the gates twelve angels, and names written thereon, which are the names of the twelve tribes of the children of Israel: on the east three gates; on the north three gates; on the south three gates; and on the west three gates. And the wall of the city had twelve foundations, and in them the names of the twelve apostles of the Lamb. And He that talked with me had a golden reed to measure the city, and the gates thereof, and the wall thereof. And the city lieth foursquare, and the length is as large as the breadth: and he measured the city with the reed, twelve thousand furlongs. The length and the breadth and the height of it are equal.*

And he measured the wall thereof, an hundred and forty and four cubits, according to the measure of a man, that is, of the angel. And the building of the wall of it was of jasper: and the city was pure gold, like unto clear glass. And the foundations of the wall of the city were garnished with all manner of precious stones. The first foundation was jasper; the second, sapphire; the third, a chalcedony; the fourth, an emerald; the fifth, sardonyx; the sixth, sardius; the seventh, chrysolite; the eighth, beryl; the ninth, a topaz; the tenth, a chrysoprasus; the eleventh, a jacinth; the twelfth, an amethyst. And the twelve gates were twelve pearls; every gate was of one pearl: and the street of the city was pure gold, as it were transparent glass. And I saw no temple therein; for the Lord God Almighty and the Lamb are the temple of it. And the city had no need of the sun, neither of the moon, to shine in it: for the glory of God did lighten it, and the Lamb is the light thereof. And the nations of them which are saved shall walk in the light of it: and the kings of the earth do bring their glory and honour into it. And the gates of it shall not be shut at all by day: for there shall be no night there. And they shall bring the glory and honour of the nations into it. And there shall in no wise enter into it any thing that defileth, neither whatsoever worketh abomination, or maketh a lie: but they which are written in the Lamb's book of life.

Note again 21:9 *one of the seven angels which had the seven vials full of the seven last plagues, talked with me saying, 'Come hither, I will shew thee the bride, the Lamb's wife.'*

(Compare 17:1 page 128) This might well be the *same* angel (because John did not write *another.*) To show John the judgment of *the great whore* the angel took him into the wilderness; but to show John *the bride, the Lamb's wife,* the angel took John to a great and high mountain and showed him the holy Jerusalem descending out of heaven from GOD.

[202]

This is the final consummation and therefore especially significant to believing Jews. This is their absolute vindication, in the fulfilment of GOD's promises, the Bride, the nation Israel in the New Jerusalem, is established in her glorious earthly place and in her relationship with the Lamb as His bride. A brief comparison can be made between the Whore of Babylon (the antithesis of The Bride,) and the New Jerusalem:

THE WHORE, BABYLON	THE BRIDE, THE NEW JERUSALEM
Founded by Nimrod,	No foundation, prepared, planned and built by God,
Entirely man made,	Built on promises of God,
In every respect vile,	In every respect clean and holy,
Built in defiance of God,	Built in the will of God,
Destroyed forever.	Established forever.

[203]

(22:1-5) *And he shewed me a pure river of water of life, clear as crystal, proceeding out of the throne of GOD and of the Lamb. In the midst of the street of it, and on either side of the river, was there the tree of life, which bare twelve manner of fruits, and yielded her fruit every month: and the leaves of the tree were for the healing of the nations. And there shall be no more curse: but the throne of GOD and of the Lamb shall be in it: and His servants shall serve Him: and they shall see His face; and His name shall be in their foreheads. And there shall be no night there; and they need no candle, neither light of the sun; for the LORD GOD giveth them light: and they shall reign for ever and ever.*

These verses complete the description of the New Jerusalem.

[204]

(22:6, 7) *And he said unto me, "These sayings are faithful and true: and the LORD GOD of the holy prophets sent His angel to shew unto His servants the things which must shortly be done. Behold, I come quickly: blessed is he that keepeth the sayings of the prophecy of this book."*

The assurance of the LORD's coming quickly (note especially the repetition of this v12 & v20.)

[205]

(22:8, 9) *And I John saw these things, and heard them. And when I had heard and seen, I fell down to worship before the feet of the angel which shewed me these things. Then saith he unto me, "See thou do it not: for I am thy fellowservant, and of thy brethren the prophets, and of them which keep the sayings of this book: worship GOD."*

The angel rejects John's worship, notice his command to John, "Worship GOD."

[206]

(22:10-21) *And He saith unto me, "Seal not the sayings of the prophecy of this book: for the time is at hand. He that is unjust, let him be unjust still: and he which is filthy, let him be filthy still: and he that is righteous, let him be righteous still: and he that is holy, let him be holy still. And, behold, I come quickly; and My reward is with Me to give every man according as his work shall be. I am Alpha and Omega, the beginning and the end, the First and the Last. Blessed are they that do His commandments, that they may have right to the tree of life, and may enter in through the gates into the city. For without are dogs, and sorcerers, and whoremongers, and murderers, and idolaters, and whosoever loveth and maketh a lie. I Jesus have sent Mine angel to testify unto you these things in the churches. I am the Root and Offspring of David. And the bright and morning Star." And the Spirit and the bride say, 'Come.' And let him that heareth say, 'Come.' And let him that is athirst come. And whosoever will, let him take the water of life freely. For I testify unto every man that heareth the words of the prophecy of this book, If any man shall add unto these things, GOD shall add unto him the plagues that are written in this book: and if any man shall take away from the words of the book of this prophecy, GOD shall take away his part out of the book of life, and out of the holy city, and from the things which are written in this book. He which testifieth these things saith, "Surely I come quickly." Even so, come LORD Jesus. The grace of our LORD Jesus Christ be with you all. Amen.*

Notice the balance in the LORD's titles given in conclusion, with those given at the beginning of the Revelation (compare 1:8). There are six categories excluded from the heavenly city:

dogs, sorcerers, whoremongers, murderers, idolaters, liars. These deserve further examination:

Dogs	the Greek word is kuon, which means dog or hound (the Hebrew word is keleb, which means to yelp or attack, a dog, it is also a euphemism for a male prostitute.) But the scriptural view of dogs is plain
	2 Peter 2:22 *the dog is turned to his own vomit again*, it is a very unclean animal.
Sorcerers	the Greek word is pharmakos (also 21:8) whence the English word, pharmacist and in its original meaning, it applied to those who dealt in drugs to control people and the lives of others. It might be added, that this is largely where the power of witchcraft lies. It has such obviously significant meanings in the light of modern drug trafficking and proves again the remarkable accuracy of prophecy.
Whoremongers	(Greek pornos,) those who sell themselves or others for sexual exploitation (compare 1 Corinthians 6:15-20.)
Murderers	(Greek phoneus) the word is always applied to those who commit intentional murder or homicide. God does not sanctify murder because of terrorist acts, or patriotic causes, or religious fanaticism, or personal revenge, or for any other reason or motive. Murderers are excluded.
Idolaters	this word is transliterated from the Greek (eidolatres) and it means "image servant" or as they prefer image worshippers! Idolaters love to be considered devout, humble, sincere etc. In reality, they are as much concerned with the "image" of themselves that they project, or present, in their worship; as they are with the object of their worship. These are also excluded,

	idolatry is a work of the flesh; an outward act, not a spiritual experience in the sight of God, for it totally ignores His will and His declared commands.
Liars	(compare 21:8, the Greek word is pseudes, which means untrue, deceitful, wicked, false,) in one word this describes the category plainly enough, but the description is expanded to *whosoever loveth and maketh a lie*, which expresses so beautifully the oily, slick, smart, clever attitude of the practised liar – for whom there is no place.

[207]

The LORD confirms (v16) that He sent His Angel that John might testify these things unto the churches, (notice especially the titles used in the verse - compare with 1:18 & 3:7) so that from its beginning to its end the Revelation is clearly addressed mainly to the Jews. The warnings (v18, 19) for those who would add anything to The Revelation, or for those who would take anything from The Revelation, are unique to the book (compare 1:3.) The inclusion of these warnings has undoubtedly preserved The Revelation as it is, a most wonderful prophecy; otherwise no doubt man would have added to or taken much from it. It is a most fitting prophecy with which to close the canon of scriptures and its teachings contain so much.

He which testifieth these things saith, "Surely I come quickly." Even so, come LORD Jesus. The grace of our LORD Jesus Christ be with you all. Amen.

The Revelation closes with the assurance of His coming and of His abiding grace.

Chapter 17: Summary

[208]

The assurances given to Daniel (7:18, 22 & 27 [4]) in his earlier experiences, (*that the saints of the MOST HIGH shall take the kingdom and possess the kingdom for ever,*) bore fruit in his life later. For when seeking understanding in prophecies (Daniel 9 [33]) Daniel displayed a heart seeking for GOD's will to be done, rather than mere knowledge. It is this same spirit, which the LORD Himself fostered in His instructions on praying to His Own disciples (Luke 11:2.) His example opens with the request, *Thy Kingdom come*. A heart that can truly pray for such things, knowing to some extent at least what is involved, must have previously sought for real understanding in such matters; otherwise it would be merely vain repetition of words.

[209]

The fulfilment of scriptural prophecies can be recognised to be in accord with a wonderful overall divine plan. This has been illustrated most notably in the timing of the LORD's birth and death, but the scriptural term *the last days* does not refer to a short time, it is a dispensation, which is actually divided by the times of the gentiles, that wonderful dispensation of grace to mankind. *The last days was* an expression as familiar to the Jewish nation, as it is to the Church today and it has the same meaning. The last days refers to the time of the LORD's coming as Messiah to deliver and to rule His nation Israel. Whatever school of thought they adhere to, practically all prophetic students agree on this one point, that the times in which we live now are immediately before the commencement of the last days.

[210]

The dispensations of scripture are a study in their own right, but whatever dispensations are considered, the transition from one dispensation to another has never been abrupt, it has always happened over a period. Regarding the last days, from its earliest mention (Genesis 49:1) it has always applied to the coming of Messiah to Israel. But His return is conditional on the Jewish acceptance of their Messiah in the person of the LORD Jesus Christ (Matthew 23:39 & Luke 13:34, 35.) This is confirmed scripturally from Peter's discourse (Acts 3.)

The dispensation of the last days commenced when GOD spoke to Israel through His Son (Hebrews 1:1, 2). GOD spoke through the LORD's personal ministry to the Jews (to whom that epistle was later addressed,) but whilst some accepted Him, the majority of that nation rejected Him. The rejection of the LORD Himself and then the rejection of the ministry of the apostles (during the period covered by the Acts of the Apostles, when the Gospel of God was ministered,) resulted not so much in the closing of the door of salvation for the Jewish nation; but in the opening of the door of salvation for all nations (gentiles). Paul recognised this (Acts 28:25-28) and revealed that the Gospel of Grace was offered to the gentiles; since which time, the last days are in abeyance and the "times of the gentiles" have come (Romans 11 and see Appendix 5). It deserves emphasis too, that Israel (as might be expected, in this dispensation of Grace,) is not totally cut off; for as Paul wrote, (Romans 11:25) *that blindness IN PART is happened to Israel, until the fulness of the gentiles be come in*. The blindness is *in part* not total, which means some Jews can be saved (and such conversions although not too common are not rare.) To their credit, such converted Jews bring a refreshing perspective to their scriptures, and a calibre of belief in the LORD that is conspicuously blessed.

[211]

The signs are however that these *times of the gentiles* are drawing to their close and the situation developing now reveals that the prophetic events of the last days are beginning to appear not as possibilities but realities. The transition dispensationally has begun and this fact has been recognised by bible students since the time that Israel was re-established in her own land.

[212]

The ultimate purpose of GOD's will is the establishment in Jerusalem of His kingdom on earth. From the earliest revelations given to Daniel it was made clear that there would be a succession of four world empires ruling over Jerusalem (Babylon, Persia, Greece and Rome) and these were to re-emerge in the last days as nations.

[213]

The appearance of the Beast will be recognised in his association with a ten kingdom confederation (of kingdoms, which have never previously existed,) and whilst this has to be within the boundaries of the Roman Empire, it does not necessarily initially have to be controlled by Rome, although in view of the involvement of the False Prophet this might be possible. In fact, although the Beast has mediocre influence at first, then representing three of the ten, he rises to assume control and authority over the whole alliance.

The unmistakable association of the ten nations within the Roman boundaries understandably leads many to jump to the obvious conclusion that the confederation of Rome (the Common Market, the E.E.C. or whatever it is called) is the most likely combination of nations to be taken over by the Beast in his rise to power. However, this is not evident in scriptures and an association of ten nations is described (Psalm 83:6-11,) which are all traditional enemies of the nation Israel and their express purpose is the extinction of that people *to cut them off from being a nation.* (It also speaks of seven enemies which the Lord had previously destroyed.) Commentators have never found such a confederation of ten in the past history of Israel, which is no surprise and leads to the other possibility that this has a prophetic, future fulfilment.

The tenfold association described (in Psalms) comprises: Edom, The Ishmaelites, Moab, The Hagarenes,[42] Gebal, Ammon, Amalek, The Philistines, Tyre, Assur (Assyria.) The important thing about the alliance is that it is mainly Arab nations and this makes it a much more likely prospect. However the real point is that the ten kingdom *confederation*, (bound by agreement or treaty,) over which the Beast takes total control, does not necessarily have to be Roman, or European. In fact scripturally it is far more likely to be Arab nations (although it is of course accepted that in financial and economic terms such a combination could have strong ties with the E.E.C. or other national combinations.) [See also Footnote 39 page 109.]

[214]

These events are only part of a very complex last days' scenario, depicted so wonderfully in the teachings of the LORD Jesus Christ and recorded in the three gospel accounts. The sequence from His teachings is clear: the appearances of many false Christs, means that the time (the end) draws near and reveals that there will be many claiming divine powers and rights as Messiahs.

The LORD's teachings are in perfect harmony with the events of the seven seals of the Revelation and in His prediction *"behold the fig*

---

[42] The Hagarenes – these are scripturally those descended from Hagar, who are Jetur, Nephish, and Nodab (1 Chronicles 5:10 & 19). From
1 Chronicles 1:31, the sons of Ishmael are Jetur, Nephish and Kedemah; Ishmael must have had Jetur and Nephish through his own mother Hagar. Nodar was another son of Hagar's but not by Ishmael; and Kedemah was a son of Ishmael, not through Hagar. The Hagarites or Hagarenes are descendants of Hagar through her sons Jetur & Nephish (their father being Ishmael,) and her son Nodab (father unknown.)

tree and all the trees" (Luke 21:9) He pointed to the last days' growth of nationalism. This means bloodshed (confirmed in the events of the seven seals,) and following the predicted false Messiahs, (who will continue to appear,) the first things the LORD spoke of were the wars, rumours of wars, conflicts of nations. These He described as the *beginning of sorrows* (travail,) which in its allusion to birth pangs, teaches that such earthly troubles will increase in frequency and intensity as the end approaches.

At some time during these events, the Church is raptured; the world is apparently preoccupied with incessant strife, wars, conflicts etc to such an extent that the world seems oblivious, or indifferent, to the removal of the Church. Perhaps in the wars and destruction of those days the loss of so many at one time is expected (or is it so few?) What seems certain, is that stupendous efforts are made to bring peace (perhaps after a particularly horrendous sequence of fighting and killing,) and this results in a treaty, or covenant, negotiated after much endeavour (evident from the manifest great satisfaction in its accomplishment.) This includes all the warring factions and of course especially Israel, the target at that time of so much hatred and violence. What the treaty involves is not clear, but Israel has to concede something in return for international recognition and the right to reinstate its true worship and sacrifice in Jerusalem. (Such dramatic changes would only be accomplished by considerable concessions from both sides.) There is one notable exception, the Beast, whose recognition occurs when he confirms the covenant and this precisely marks the commencement of the final week, the seventieth week of prophecy. The Beast and his people come and destroy the city and the sanctuary (Daniel 9:26 etc) his people could be his own nation (Babylon,) or possibly the people of the three nations among the ten that he initially represents. The jubilation at the acceptance of the peace treaty is prophesied as being very short-lived (1 Thessalonians 5:3 [94].)

[215]

As a nation Israel has been developing spiritually for some time and when these events occur, the witness of the Church and of the nation Israel could be contemporary, as the transition from one dispensation to another takes place. The Church is removed sometime before the middle of the final week, because Paul placed *our gathering together* before the day of the LORD, which commences immediately after the positive identification of the Beast in his confirmation of the covenant (2 Thessalonians 2 [98].)

Scripturally, the Beast is a most complex character; originating in Babylon (the country, now called Iraq,) not necessarily the city Babylon, although this is quite possible; his identification prophetically comes, when he appears among the ten kingdom confederation. His rise to power however, is accomplished by a mixture of flattery, deceit and skill. The Beast is undoubtedly involved in a whole series of disputes, conflicts, disagreements with other parties and other nations. Prophecy does not necessarily portray events in exact chronological order, so the descriptions of the various campaigns and battles involving the Beast (e.g. Daniel 11, which must have also last days' applications,) need to be considered, whilst allowing some latitude in the order of their actual fulfilment. It would be unwise to be dogmatic in applying such prophecies in advance, but in every case a satisfactory fulfilment will be accomplished manifestly to the Jews.

What is clear, is that in battle at sometime the Beast is mortally wounded and receives the distinctive injuries to his right eye and right arm. This experience marks the pivoting point of his career, for in death or the grave he makes an agreement with Satan, who raises him up as his instrument for the total destruction of the nation Israel.

In his new role, as the conqueror of death, the Beast is supported and strengthened by a most formidable ally, the False Prophet. He quickly capitalises on the Beast's apparent invincibility and persuades the world or worshippers of the Beast to make an image (probably of gold, like Nebuchadnezzar's) which can speak and even cause the death of those who will not worship it. In this triumphant role the Beast's victory over the two witnesses is his ultimate success in the eyes of the world, which has been embarrassed by the spiritual zeal that these two witnesses have inspired in Israel for at least the duration of the first half of the final week.

Their death commences the awesome persecution of the Jews by the Beast himself, known as the great tribulation; the period about which the LORD Himself warned His people with such solemn words, *"When ye see the abomination of desolation, spoken of by Daniel the prophet stand in the holy place .... then let them which be in Judea flee etc"* The holy place at this time is Jerusalem, not as some imagine, a Jewish temple that has to be built. The establishment in Jerusalem of this ghastly image of the Beast is a most clear sign and to those who will listen, it provides the warning for them to flee for their very lives. This period is the time of the most savage persecution of the Jewish people in their entire history (which makes it truly hideous in extreme,) and the strongest scriptural warnings are given to the Jews for this reason. A particular characteristic of the Beast that merits special attention is his terrible blasphemy. This is Satanic in its inspiration and it is to an extreme that beggars description, for it will offend many and literally destroy the faith of some. But it must be regarded in its scriptural perspective, for it is permitted for a strictly limited time.

[216]

The end of those terrible days for the Jews is marked by heavenly catastrophes (from the LORD's Own teachings,) and then comes the Son of man. This is not a straightforward sequence that takes place in one day. The LORD taught that the heavenly events are followed by *"the sign of the Son of man in heaven"* and also *"they shall see the Son of man coming in the clouds of heaven with power and great glory."* This is *the sign* which the Jews are looking for and every eye shall see Him. BUT, (and this is what many fail to appreciate,) the LORD does NOT actually come to effect the total deliverance of His people at this time. His appearance marks the end of their tribulation, which is not mentioned again; but He disappears and during this time the faithfulness of His people in His absence is proved. It is to this time of His absence (as the coming bridegroom) that the parable of the ten virgins and the parable of the talents apply (See [269]).

The coming of the LORD is not a single event; it is a little more complicated than that and in fact merits separate consideration.

Chapter 18: The LORD's COMINGS

[217]

The term "The Second Advent" has no scriptural warrant, it is an invention of man and like the expression, "His Second Coming", it tends to contribute to the general confusion and misunderstanding in the Church that the LORD's (second) coming is a single event, (broadly it is usually applied to the LORD's final appearance at the last great judgment.) Thus it became an event to contemplate with an impossible mixture of hope and fear, depending on which scriptures are being considered. The Second Advent was considered to embrace all the references to the LORD's coming again; which has contributed to the utter confusion that exists in churches (generally) concerning the LORD's comings. The reason being that ministers, commentators, could exclude or ignore what they chose and use whatever scriptures they selected to teach their particular favourite point of view. Once this term *the second advent* (or the second coming) is abandoned, and the scriptures are examined properly, the LORD's comings (for there are several) fall into their proper places and become coherent parts of the wonderful divine plan.

It is evident in the New Testament that the early converts to Christianity were taught that the LORD's coming again for His Church was an event that would be realised within their lifetime; this was their hope and it was incorporated in their customary daily greeting, "Maranatha".[43]

---

[43] Maranatha - Aramaic, meaning "Our Lord come", the word occurs just once in the New Testament

(1Corinthians 16:22) where it is associated with "Anathema", which means "bar, curse,

The early churches' daily communions (which later became weekly meetings,) were their method of worshipping Him and remembering Him *till He come* (see 1 Corinthians 11:26 and compare Acts 2:46.) Further, the New Testament closes with His promise, *"Behold, I come quickly"* (repeated three times, Revelation 22:7, 12 and 20) to which the apostle John responded *"Amen. Even so, come, LORD Jesus."* The LORD's coming for His Church is a scriptural truth, a promise accepted by believers from the beginnings of the early church.[44]

[219]

Within the lifetime of the apostles there were those that scoffed, *"Where is the promise of His coming?"* and the apostle Peter, who acknowledged this taunt, exhorted believers, *"Beloved, be not ignorant of this one thing, that one day is with the LORD as a thousand years, and a thousand years as one day. The LORD is not slack concerning His promise, as some men count slackness; but is longsuffering to usward, not willing that any should perish, but that all should come to repentance. But the day of the LORD will come as a thief in the night; in the which the heavens shall pass away with a great noise, and the elements shall melt with fervent heat, the earth also and the works that are therein shall be burned up."* (2 Peter 3:4 and 8-10 cf Psalm 50:3, Micah 1:4.)

---

accursed, excommunicated" (see also Acts 23:14, Romans 9:3, 1 Corinthians 12:3 & Galatians 1:8,9.) In using both words together, it is suggested that Paul was saying, "Let him be accursed, when our LORD comes." (Bullinger contends that the words are not connected at all, and should be treated separately.)

[44] Note: Those who appeal to Hebrews (9:28 *So Christ was once offered to bear the sins of many; and unto them that look for Him shall He appear THE SECOND TIME without sin unto salvation.*) as scriptural support for the use of the term His Second Advent, or His Second Coming, fail to appreciate the word rendered "appearing" cannot in this instance be used as a synonym for "coming". The word merely means "be seen" (see 1 Corinthians 15:5-8 where it occurs five times, and is translated as "seen";) and there is no definite article in the original text, which states "a second time". This truth relates to the priestly work of Christ, for all believers, and this is not a reference to His Coming in the context of the last days.

[220]

In considering the LORD's coming, the point has to be made that there are several Greek words associated with the coming of the LORD Jesus Christ (and it is no surprise, these same words are used in reference to the coming of the anti-christ.) The words used are:

Parousia (= coming,) *Epiphanea* (= appearing,) *Apokalupsis* (= revelation, manifestation.)

These different words are all used in reference to the several comings of the LORD, so that His comings cannot be distinguished readily, or identified easily, merely by the word used. It is much more important to recognise that there are scripturally several appearances or comings of the Lord and failing to recognise and distinguish between these is the cause of much confusion, about what is actually involved when He comes.

Any attempts to understand the events concerning the LORD's comings will be made much easier if the purposes of His comings are understood and to appreciate these future events it is necessary to understand the past.

[221]

GOD's purpose in His creation, particularly with respect to mankind, has not yet been realised. Adam was not deceived but the Woman believed Satan's lie that in disobedience to GOD's command, they would not die, but become gods themselves (Genesis 3:5 and 1 Timothy 2:13, 14). Cain murdered Abel in the mistaken idea that the LORD would have no alternative but to accept his offering. The succeeding generations of Adam and Eve became more evil and violent until the times of Noah, when the LORD brought an end to their wickedness with the Flood. At this time Enoch and Noah preached their warnings of impending judgment, but they were ignored (2 Peter 2:5 Jude 14.) After such a wonderful deliverance in the ark, it is difficult to imagine the revulsion with which Noah must have regarded Ham's sin against him and Noah's curse on Canaan the son of Ham was servitude (Genesis 9:18-27.) In Shem's line, some nine generations later, Abram appeared and this man and his descendants through Isaac and Jacob (Israel) were the people through whom GOD chose to bless mankind, and He will eventually accomplish His original purpose in creation and bring His blessing on mankind. It needs to be stressed that His blessing promised to Abraham extended to all mankind *"in thy seed shall ALL nations of the earth be blessed"* (Genesis 22:18.) It must follow therefore that this present Christian dispensation, this time of grace, cannot be the last period in GOD's dealings with mankind.

It was to this glorious prospect of the nation Israel, as His witnesses on earth, enjoying His blessing on them and the whole world, that the visions of the prophets were directed and they were given no concept whatsoever of the intervening "times of the gentiles".[45] The divine purpose was always that Israel would be His witnesses and *"Mine house shall be called a house of prayer for all people"* (Isaiah 43:10, 12 & 56:7.) His divine intention has never been fulfilled in Israel's history in the spirit in which it was intended. For example, during the LORD's times (and probably for over a century previously,) the Jews were an extremely evangelical nation, a fact the LORD Himself acknowledged (Matthew 23:15) making converts (or proselytes, as circumcised converts to Judaism are known,) throughout the Roman Empire. It was this zeal which accounted for the diversity of nations in Jerusalem at the Feast of Weeks, Pentecost (Acts 2:5 & 8-11.) But the Jews themselves treated gentiles, even their proselytes, with considerable disdain and contempt - for example, they had Roman authority to put any gentile to death on the spot if he or she ventured beyond the court of the gentiles in

---

[45] "Times of the gentiles" this is one of the terms or titles given to the present dispensation, the time of grace, when salvation is offered freely to all mankind, INCLUDING not excluding THE JEWS (for the blindness of the Jews is only in part, some are therefore saved.)

their temple.[46] Even in the early church, Peter was called to account by his contemporary apostles over his involvement with gentiles (Acts 11:1-18.)

[222]

It is a tragedy that the history of the "gentile" church manifests a similar attitude toward the Jews! Undoubtedly, the early Church suffered considerably for the first three centuries through their persecutions by the Jews; this continued even after the destruction of Jerusalem and the Jewish dispersion in the ruthless Roman reaction to their rebellion. It was only after Christianity became nationally accepted by the Romans, when wrongly believing that GOD had cast away His people, the church leaders subsequently encouraged Jewish persecution and this trend has prevailed in varying degrees and in different countries even to the present time. Their error was in assuming that whilst grace was freely given in the calling offered to the gentiles, it meant that the Jews were cut off totally and could be treated badly, because they had crucified the LORD.

The church leaders saw no divine judgments or restraints for their appalling behaviour in such persecutions of the Jews and neglected the truth that the wicked and unjust are called to account for their actions eventually and are reserved until the day of judgment (2 Peter 2:9.) Paul himself taught quite plainly (Romans 11:1,2) *"God hath not cast away His people which He foreknew"* and (11:25) *"for I would not, brethren, that ye be ignorant of this mystery, lest ye should be wise in your own conceits; THAT BLINDNESS IN PART is happened to Israel, until the fulness of the gentiles be come in."* The

---

[46] Contrast the Jewish attitude to their gentile converts or proselytes with the LORD's Own way, even with the enemies of His people. He smote the Philistines with emerods, when in their ignorance they touched the ark; but His judgements on Israel, who knew what was holy, and disobeyed His commands, were more severe and instantaneous (see I Samuel 6:19 – 21 and 2 Samuel 6:6-8).

Church, the Body of Christ, is not and never has been, exclusively gentile - it has always been offered to the Jews first and to gentiles as fellow heirs (Ephesians 3:6.)

The present situation, the day of grace, is spiritually abnormal, for the people of the covenant are cut off (not totally, the blindness is in part,) and this was not GOD's original intention, it resulted from the Jewish rejection of His Son as their Messiah. The *"times of the restitution of all things"* (as Peter was inspired to refer to them - Acts 3:19-26, esp. v21) refer to those times when the nation Israel will be restored to their rightful place as His witnesses to all nations and eventually the world will then enjoy the peace and blessing that God intended.

[223]

The mystery, about which Paul spoke in reference to this present time of the gentiles, (Romans 11:25ff) was not that the gentiles should be blessed (for this was revealed in His promise to Abraham *"in thy seed shall ALL nations of the earth be blessed".*) The mystery was in the time, the period, the dispensation, during which the fulness of the gentiles would be enabled to come in to His church, His body. When this is complete (and "when" is the mystery, for the dispensation is of indeterminate length,) there *shall come out of Sion the Deliverer* (Romans 11:26.) In its context this quite plainly refers to a coming of the LORD to reinstate, to their covenanted place in His will, His people Israel. *"To whom pertaineth the adoption, and the glory and the covenants and the giving of the law, and the service of God and the promises; whose are the fathers, and of whom as concerning the flesh Christ came, Who is over all, blessed for ever. Amen."* (Romans 9:4, 5 note especially the present tense, this divine purpose has never altered.)

It can be seen from these considerations therefore that there are two distinct events to recognise. First, the fulness of the gentiles being added to the Church, His Body, completing this time of grace and second, the reinstatement, or restitution, of His witnesses, His nation Israel on earth as His Bride. Eventually, of course, there is the marriage of the Lamb; but the manifestation of His Body (the true Church) and His Bride (the nation Israel,) necessarily depends in each case on the manifestations of the LORD Himself.

The LORD's comings may therefore be considered in this light (i) His coming for His Body, His Church (see [224] – [229]) and (ii) His comings for His Bride, His earthly people, Israel (see [230] – [234]).

(i)　　HIS COMING FOR HIS BODY, HIS CHURCH.

[224]

(1) 1 Corinthians 15:51, 52 (2) Philippians 3:20, 21 (3) 1 Thessalonians 4:13-18 (4) 2 Thessalonians 1:3-2 (5) Titus 2:11,13

[225]

The mystery of the duration of the period or dispensation, "the times of the gentiles", is not the only New Testament mystery and Paul points to another, in respect of the LORD's coming for His church (1) *"Behold I shew you a mystery, we shall not all sleep, but we shall all be changed, in a moment, in the twinkling of an eye, at the last trump: for the trumpet shall sound, and the dead shall be raised incorruptible, and we shall be changed."* Note the repetition for emphasis *we shall all be* changed and *we shall be changed*, and this wonderful transformation takes place *in a moment, in the twinkling of an eye,* the moment, when believers in Him, mortals on earth, are transformed, changed from mortality to immortality. This is when those who "sleep" (a lovely euphemism that the early church used for those who died in Christ, i.e. *believing in Christ*) will be raised from the dead, in incorruptible bodies. The early church regarded death as sleep (bodily) and to be absent from the body was to be present with the Lord. But Paul taught about the change that occurs in His Body of believers, when He comes for His Church (those that remain on earth,) and bringing with Him those believers who have previously died, or fallen asleep.

But there is another wonderful truth revealed, because Paul tells us WHEN this change takes place *at the last trump: for the trumpet shall sound.* Evidently, Paul had a revelation about this and his inspired choice of words leads to the obvious question, "What trumpet is the last?" (Could this be *the seventh trumpet*, the last of the seven? - see Revelation 8:1 [139], 9:13 [147] and especially 11:15-19 [155]).

From these scriptures, the Church is caught up to heavenly places, as Satan is cast down from heavenly places, at the sounding of the last trumpet - and this coincides with the opening of the temple of God in heaven. His heavenly body of believers can worship in His temple and as His heavenly priests their access is assured. The LORD's coming for His Church is a single event, which precedes His comings for Israel or His Bride.

[226]

In the next reference (2) Paul wrote *"For our conversation is in heaven; from whence also we look for the Saviour, the LORD Jesus Christ: Who shall change our vile body, that it may be fashioned like unto His glorious body, according to the working whereby He is able even to subdue all things unto Himself."* Paul's teaching leaves us no room to doubt that the LORD's coming for His church will *change our vile body that it may be fashioned like unto His glorious body.* In these two references from Paul's epistles, (concerning the LORD's coming for His Church, His Body,) all believers are taught to expect a transformation, a change. It was this possibility, this prospect, which so excited or thrilled the early converts. His coming was the hope of those alive and their resurrection from the dead through Him was the hope of those who slept - in each case, whether alive or dead, their bodies would be changed from corruptible to incorruptible, from mortal to immortal.

[227]

Paul's early epistles were written to mainly Jewish converts, who would have been familiar with the Old Testament and therefore they would have had a very sound foundation regarding the LORD's promises. In his first epistle to Thessalonica, Paul realised that he was writing also to gentile converts and at that time their leaders were being martyred. As usual in times of extreme opposition, the enemy lost no opportunity to add to the torment. The Thessalonian church was also subjected to false teachers' attempting to persuade these oppressed believers that their beloved leaders and elders, who had died for their LORD, had lost the wonderful hope of being resurrected to be with Him and them, when He came. This was the cause of their grief and extreme sadness over those who had died. For this reason Paul wrote (3) *"But I would not have you ignorant brethren, concerning them which are asleep, that ye sorrow not, even as others which have no hope. For if we believe that Jesus died and rose again, even so them also which sleep in Jesus will GOD bring with Him. For this we say unto you by the Word of the LORD, that we which are alive and remain unto the coming of the LORD shall not prevent them which are asleep. For the LORD Himself shall descend from heaven with a shout, with the voice of the archangel, and with the trump of GOD: and the dead in Christ shall rise first: then we which are alive and remain shall be caught up together with them in the clouds, to meet the LORD in the air; and so shall we ever be with the LORD. Wherefore comfort one another with these words."*

[228]

Paul's words confirm that *we who are living* are right to believe in that hope (i.e. that His coming is imminent,) and also Paul's teachings establish that those, who are alive when He comes, will have no advantage over those sleeping, who in fact rise first.

In his second epistle to Thessalonians Paul clearly distinguishes between the LORD's coming for His Church and His coming to execute vengeance (4) *"We are bound to thank GOD always for you, brethren, as it is meet, because that your faith groweth exceedingly, and the charity of every one of you all toward each other aboundeth: so that we ourselves glory in you in the churches of God for your patience and faith in all your persecutions and tribulations that ye endure: which is a manifest token of the righteous judgment of GOD, that ye may be counted worthy of the kingdom of God, for which ye also suffer: seeing it is a righteous thing with God to recompense tribulation to them that trouble you; and to you who are troubled rest with us, WHEN THE LORD JESUS SHALL BE REVEALED FROM HEAVEN WITH HIS MIGHTY ANGELS, IN FLAMING FIRE TAKING VENGEANCE ON THEM THAT KNOW NOT GOD, AND OBEY NOT THE GOSPEL OF OUR LORD JESUS CHRIST; WHO SHALL BE PUNISHED WITH EVERLASTING DESTRUCTION FROM THE PRESENCE OF THE LORD, AND FROM THE GLORY OF HIS POWER; WHEN HE SHALL COME TO BE GLORIFIED IN HIS SAINTS, AND TO BE ADMIRED IN ALL THAT BELIEVE (BECAUSE OUR TESTIMONY AMONG YOU WAS BELIEVED) IN THAT DAY. Wherefore also we pray always for you, that our GOD would count you worthy of this calling, and fulfil all the good pleasure of His goodness, and the work of faith with power: that the name of our LORD Jesus Christ may be glorified in you, and ye in Him, according to the grace of our GOD, and the LORD Jesus Christ. Now we beseech you, brethren, BY THE COMING OF OUR LORD JESUS CHRIST, AND BY OUR GATHERING TOGETHER UNTO HIM,* (NOTE THIS: what follows does not involve believers, who have already been gathered together unto Him!) *that ye be not soon shaken in mind, or be troubled, neither by spirit, nor by word, nor by letter as from us, as that the day of Christ* (correctly as in the original texts, this should read the *'day of the LORD'* being the time of His judgment and vengeance;) *is at hand*. (This was a further result of the erroneous teachings being introduced.) Their concerns in Thessalonica were not only that they had missed His coming for them, but that His vengeance was about to be outpoured and they would therefore have to endure the terrible tribulation, which was against the teachings that Paul had given them. *Let no man deceive you by any means: for that day shall not come, except there come a falling away first, and that man of sin be revealed, the son of perdition; who opposeth and exalteth himself above all that is called God, or that is worshipped; so that he as God sitteth in the temple of God, shewing himself that he is God. Remember ye not, that, when I was yet with you, I told you these things?* Central to Paul's comments is the truth, that he was telling them these things *by the coming of our LORD Jesus Christ and by our gathering together unto Him*. This was Paul's underlying assurance, that they were safe in view of the gathering together, the translation, of the Church. Paul warned them not to be persuaded by any man, or by any means, that the day of the LORD would involve them. Paul's writings to the Thessalonians are his only epistles which mention the 'day of the LORD' (regrettably translated 'Christ' in the Authorised Version,) or the day of vengeance. Paul's purpose in writing these lines was to combat the false teachers, who were attempting to deny, what he had already taught (*"Remember ye not, that, when I was yet with you, I told you these things?".*) But Paul also established in his first epistle to them, (1 Thessalonians 5:9) *"GOD hath not appointed us to wrath, but to obtain salvation by our LORD Jesus Christ, Who died for us, that, whether we wake or sleep, we should live together with Him"*. The context shows that Paul was referring to their deliverance from the tribulation that will come on His people Israel.[47] In the final reference (5) regarding the LORD's coming for His

---

[47] It is interesting, and worthy of notice, that in his first epistle to Thessalonians (5:1) Paul used exactly the same expression "*the times and seasons*" as Daniel (2:21) and also the LORD Himself (Acts 1:7).

Body, His Church, Paul speaks of *"the grace of GOD that bringeth salvation hath appeared to all men, teaching us that, denying ungodliness, and worldly lusts, we should live soberly, righteously, and godly, in this present world; looking for that blessed hope, and the glorious appearing of the great GOD and our Saviour Jesus Christ."* Nothing that Paul wrote casts the slightest doubt or shadow on that *glorious appearing of the great GOD and our LORD Jesus Christ.* The hope for the true Church, His Body, is as wonderful now as it was when it was first ministered - but why the delay, 2,000 years!

[229]

This is another mystery, this astonishing duration of time. There may be some truth in the suggestion that the LORD has not yet come, because the Church, like Israel, has not truly fulfilled its intended role. More significantly however, Paul wrote *"blindness in part is happened to Israel, UNTIL the fulness of the gentiles be come in"* (Romans 1:25.) This makes it plain that there is a completion, there is a fulness, a total, a limit, ordained for the Church, His Body. Their eventual number has to justify the sacrifice of GOD's Own Son and vindicate His faith and love for GOD His Father. This limit is settled in His divine will and wisdom and in His grace, time is therefore meaningless. The fulness of the Church and its removal when He comes are linked closely with the restoration of the testimony to Israel as His witnesses on earth. For their witness or testimony, on earth, in the light of the imminent establishment of the kingdom of Heaven, the nation Israel is targeted to suffer the awesome persecution and suffering that Satan imposes as he attempts to destroy them totally, through his agent, the man of sin, the beast. The LORD's coming for His Church, The Rapture, is a single event (it compares with Enoch's translation) and at His coming those who sleep and those who are alive are united with Him forever.

(ii) THE LORD'S COMING FOR HIS BRIDE, HIS EARTHLY PEOPLE, ISRAEL.

[230]

There are some extraordinary misconceptions and misunderstandings about the LORD's comings and frequently these reveal that no distinction is being made between the LORD's coming for His Church, His Body (a single event,) and His comings for His earthly people, His Bride, Israel. Even His coming as the LORD Jesus Christ, born in Bethlehem and ultimately crucified, is tainted with the idea that the LORD came to found a new religion. If this is accepted, it makes the Jewish religion (the only religion GOD has ever accepted,) obsolete and opens the way for persecuting them as heretics - this is partly what happened in the earlier centuries of the history of the church. Paul himself totally refutes this in his defence before Agrippa, when he had himself been charged with teaching a new religion, explaining, *"Having therefore obtained help of God, I continue unto this day, witnessing both to small and great, saying none other things than those which the prophets and Moses did say should come: that Christ should suffer, and that He should be the first that should rise from the dead, and should shew light unto the people, and to the Gentiles."* On Paul's authority, Christianity is truly an extension of the Jewish faith, (as obedience to the Law and the Prophets.) (*Not* it must be emphasised, of the Jewish *religion,* which resulted from their being taught the vain traditions of the Pharisees, so detested by the LORD.)

[231]

Some believe that the Millennium immediately follows the preaching of the Gospel of Grace, which is the message or ministry of this dispensation (see Appendix 5.) Others believe that the end of the world simply involves the LORD's coming to take His people to be with Him and then follows the total destruction of the sin-cursed earth with fire. Such ideas are an over-simplification of facts, gleaned from a superficial examination of scriptures.

The LORD Himself spoke of His coming as The Son of man throughout His ministry and He confirmed this again after His resurrection. His apostles taught about the hope of His coming for His Church and also spoke of His coming to execute vengeance and deliver His people; but it must be acknowledged and recognised that the LORD's Own ministry and His teachings were to Israel (see Matthew 15:24, Acts 3:25,26 & 13:46.)

[232]

In the LORD's Own teachings on His coming as "The Son of man", this title is never used in reference to His Church, it never appears in the epistles in reference to His coming (see Acts 7:56 and Hebrews 2:6) but it is used in The Revelation (1:13 & 14:14.)

Nobody in scripture ever addressed the LORD Himself using this title.[48]

---

[48] The New Testament references to The Son of man are: Matthew 8:20, 9:6 10:23 11:19 12:8, 32, 40 13:37, 41 16:13, 27, 28 17:9,12, 22 18:11 19:28 20:18, 28 24:27, 30, 37,44 25:13, 31 26:2, 24, 45, 64 Mark 2:28 8:31, 38 9:9,12, 31 10:33, 45 13:26, 34 14:21, 41, 62 Luke 3:38 5:24 6:5, 22 7:34 9:22, 26, 44, 56, 58 11:30 12:8, 10, 40 17:22, 24, 26, 30 18:8, 31 19:10 21:27, 36 22:22, 48, 69 24:7 John 1:51 3:13,14 5:27 6:27, 53, 62 8:28 12:34(twice) 13:31 Acts 7:56 Hebrews 2:6 Rev 1:13 14:14
The title, "*Son of man*", (without the definite article) is found in the Old Testament: Numbers 23:19 Job 25:6 35:8 Psalms 8:4 Isaiah 51:12 56:2 [Daniel 7:13 is the only Old Testament reference to *THE Son of man* (with definite article.)] (In Psalms 80:17 144:3 146:3 in Hebrew "son of Adam" referring to mortality of man.)
With the indefinite article "a", (or with no definite article "the",) the title "*son of man*" in reference to a prophet is found: Daniel 8:17 Jeremiah 49:18,33 50:40 51:43 Ezekiel 2:1, 3, 6, 8 3:1, 3, 4, 10, 17, 25 4:1, 16 5:1 6:2 7:2 8:5, 6, 8, 12, 15 11:2, 4, 15 12:2, 3, 9, 18, 22, 27 13:2, 17 14:3, 13 15:2 16:2 17:2 20:3, 4, 27, 46 21:2, 6, 9, 12, 14 21:19, 28 22:2, 18, 24 23:2, 36 24:2, 16, 25 25:2 26:2 27:2 28:2, 12, 21 29:2, 18 30:2, 21 31:2 32:2, 18 33:2, 7, 10, 12, 24, 30 34:2 35:2 36:1, 17 37:3, 9, 11, 16 38:2, 14 39:1, 17 40:4 43:7, 10, 18 47:6, Daniel 8:17.

[233]

For the duration of the period covered by the Acts of the Apostles (forty years approximately) the ministry of the Gospel of God (see Appendix 5) applied mainly to the Jews, but included gentiles (probably proselytes,) as for example, the house of Cornelius (Acts 10). The purpose of this ministry was to bring national repentance to the LORD's people, the Jews, for crucifying His Son. So that, in respect of His coming to restore the kingdom to Israel, the LORD Himself acknowledged that such decisions were His Father's to make (see Acts 1:1-11). It needs to be appreciated that "the day of the LORD" is an era (a time of wrath,) and the COMINGS (for there are more than one,) of the LORD for His people Israel are events within this era. Furthermore, these are totally separate from His coming for His Church, His Body.

[234]

The LORD's Own teachings on His coming as The Son of man are:

Matthew	*(1)* 13:36-43	*(5)* 24:1-46	*(8)* 25:31-46
Mark	*(2)* 8:38	*(6)* 13:1-37	
Luke	*(3)* 12:36-40	*(7)* 21:5-36	
	(4) 17:20-37		

The numerical order [*(1)* to *(8)*] given is chronological in respect of His ministry, His main teachings coming at the end of His time with His disciples.

(1) Matthew 13:36-43 Then Jesus sent the multitude away, and went into the house: and His disciples came unto Him, saying, "Declare unto us the parable of the tares of the field." He answered and said unto them, "He that soweth the good seed is the Son of man; the field

is the world; the good seed are the children of the kingdom; but the tares are the children of the wicked one; the enemy that soweth them is the devil; the harvest is the end of the world; and the reapers are the angels. As therefore the tares are gathered and burned in the fire; so shall it be in the end of this world. The Son of man shall send forth His angels, and they shall gather out of His kingdom all things that offend, and them which do iniquity; and shall cast them into a furnace of fire: there shall be wailing and gnashing of teeth. Then shall the righteous shine forth as the sun in the kingdom of their Father. Who hath ears to hear, let him hear".

(2) Mark 8:38 "Whosoever therefore shall be ashamed of Me and of My words in this adulterous and sinful generation; of him also shall the Son of man be ashamed, when He cometh in the glory of His Father with the holy angels.

(3) Luke 12:36-40 *And ye yourselves like unto men that wait for their lord, when he will return from the wedding; that when he cometh and knocketh, they may open unto him immediately, blessed are those servants, whom the lord when he cometh shall find watching: verily I say unto you, that he shall gird himself, and make them to sit down to meat, and will come forth and serve them. And if he shall come in the second watch, or come in the third watch, and find them so, blessed are those servants. And this know, that if the goodman of the house had known what hour the thief would come, he would have watched, and not have suffered his house to be broken through. Be ye therefore ready also: for the Son of man cometh at an hour when ye think not.*

(4) Luke 17:20-37 *And when He was demanded of the Pharisees, when the kingdom of God should come, He answered them and said,* "The kingdom of God cometh not with observation: neither shall they

say, 'Lo, here! or lo there! for, behold, the kingdom of God is within you." And He said to the disciples, "The days will come, when ye shall desire to see one of the days of the Son of man, and ye shall not see it. And they shall say to you, 'See here; or see there'; go not after them, nor follow them. For as the lightning, that lighteneth out of the one part under heaven, shineth unto the other part under heaven; so shall also the Son of man be in His day. But first must He suffer many things, and be rejected of this generation. And as it was in the days of Noe, so shall it be also in the days of the Son of man. They did eat, they drank, they married wives, they were given in marriage, until the day that Noe entered into the ark, and the flood came, and destroyed them all. Likewise also as it was in the days of Lot, they did eat, they drank, they bought, they sold, they planted, they builded; but the same day that Lot went out of Sodom it rained fire and brimstone from heaven, and destroyed them all. Even thus shall it be in the day when the Son of man is revealed. In that day, he which shall be upon the housetop, and his stuff in the house, let him not come down to take it away: and he that is in the field, let him likewise not return back. Remember Lot's wife. Whosoever shall seek to save his life shall lose it; and whosoever shall lose his life shall preserve it. I tell you, in that night there shall be two men in one bed; the one shall be taken, and the other shall be left. Two women shall be grinding together; the one shall be taken, and the other left. Two men shall be in the field; the one shall be taken, and the other left." And they answered and said unto Him, 'Where Lord?' And He said unto them, "Wheresoever the body is. thither will the eagles be gathered *together."*

(5) Matthew 24:1-46 [This is a considerable portion to repeat here and it may be found with comments in [68] and [69] (confirming the LORD was speaking of His coming as The Son of man.)]

(6) Mark 13:1-37 [Again a considerable portion to repeat here, it may

be found [72].]

(7) Luke 21:5-36 [This will be found [86].]

(8) Matthew 25:31-46 *When the Son of man shall come in His glory, and all the holy angels with Him, then shall He sit upon the throne of His glory: and before Him shall be gathered all nations: and He shall separate them one from another, as a shepherd divideth his sheep from the goats: And He shall set the sheep on his right hand, but the goats on the left. Then shall the King say unto them on His right hand, 'Come, ye blessed of My Father, inherit the kingdom prepared for you from the foundation of the world: for I was an hungred, and ye gave Me meat: I was thirsty, and ye gave Me drink: I was a stranger, and ye took Me in: naked, and ye clothed Me: I was sick, and ye visited Me: I was in prison and ye came unto Me.' Then shall the righteous answer Him, saying, 'LORD, when saw we Thee an hungred, and fed Thee? Or thirsty, and gave Thee drink? When saw we Thee a stranger, and took Thee in? Or naked, and clothed Thee? Or when saw we Thee sick, or in prison, and came unto Thee?' And the King shall answer and say unto them, 'Verily I say unto you, Inasmuch as ye have done it unto one of the least of these My brethren, ye have done it unto Me.' Then shall He say also unto them on the left hand, 'Depart from Me, ye cursed, into everlasting fire, prepared for the devil and his angels: for I was an hungred, and ye gave Me no meat: I was thirsty, and ye gave Me no drink: I was a stranger, and ye took Me not in: naked, and ye clothed Me not: sick, and in prison, and ye visited Me not.' Then shall they also answer Him, saying, 'LORD, when saw we Thee an hungred, or athirst, or a stranger, or naked, or sick, or in prison, and did not minister unto Thee?' Then shall He answer them, saying, 'Verily I say unto you, Inasmuch as ye did it not to one of the least of these, ye did it not to Me'. And these shall go away into everlasting punishment: but the righteous into life eternal."*

[235]

Nobody could seriously consider the LORD's teachings on His comings as the Son of man to Israel and conclude that He was speaking of a single eventuality. This is supported by The Revelation. (14:14) *And I looked, and behold a white cloud, and upon the cloud One sat like unto the Son of man, having on His head a golden crown, and in His hand a sharp sickle.* Compare this with (19:11) *And I saw heaven opened, and behold a white horse, and He that sat upon him was called Faithful and True, and in righteousness He doth judge and make war.*

These are different events and again from the Old Testament (Zechariah 14:1-4, [62]) comes the prophecy *"Behold, the day of the LORD cometh,.... for I will gather all nations against Jerusalem to battle....Then shall the LORD go forth, and fight against those nations, as when He fought in the day of battle. And His feet shall stand in that day upon the mount of Olives,.....and the mount of Olives shall cleave in the midst thereof toward the east and toward the west..."*

What happens? How do these comings of the LORD for Israel fit together?

The LORD's comings to Israel need to be considered in the context of the events of the last days.

Chapter 19: The Events of The Last Days

[236]

The Old Testament and New Testament prophecies have been examined and discussed, basically to establish what they contain in their contexts concerning the last days. The next task is to attempt to draw everything together: firstly, to show how wonderfully it all fits and secondly, to gain better understanding of what is involved. It would be possible to do this several ways, for example, our approach could be based on the LORD's Own wonderful teachings and everything could be examined in the context of His remarks. Alternatively, we could commence with Daniel's wonderful foundation teachings and extend from that. There are other alternatives also, but our approach is based on the truth concerning, *The Revelation of Jesus Christ, which God gave unto Him, TO SHEW UNTO HIS SERVANTS THINGS WHICH MUST SHORTLY COME TO PASS; and He sent and signified it by His angel unto His servant John.*

Our considerations are based on The Revelation. But Daniel's teachings are accepted of course, his basic foundation has been proven accurate and true and it is Daniel whom we have to thank for the revelation of the meaning of the seventy weeks. But our concern is not so much the historical past, as the prophetic future and especially *things which must shortly come to pass* which must be far more imminent now, than when John penned those words.

Likewise, we can regard the seven churches, or synagogues, as sufficiently considered for our purposes; although of course, in the very last times it is possible, and very likely, that these exhortations will be applicable to assemblies of Jewish believers, which have formed in the last days, and will no doubt prove invaluable in their ultimate fulfilment.

Our approach will follow the main themes of The Revelation, which are revealed in the consistent grouping of sevens; the *seven seals*, the *seven trumpets*, the *seven vials*.

[237] THE SEVEN SEALS

(Revelation 5:1) *And I saw in the right hand of Him that sat on the throne a book written within and on the backside, sealed with seven seals.*

The book or scroll was rolled up and sealed as it was rolled with a tape or cord threaded through and attached at each end of the roll, sealed with wax seals. Obviously, further seals could be added to seal off portions of the roll as it was rolled up. The person attempting to read the scroll could only read as far as the next seal, which he would have to break to continue. John was not allowed to read the scroll or book himself, but as each seal was broken, he was commanded to write what he saw and heard, as The Lamb, The LORD Himself, broke the seals.

The point however is that the seals applied to the scroll, the book and their opening covers all the eventualities and prophecies of The Revelation (this is evidently not the case with the seven trumpets and seven vials, which are much more closely associated with each other.)

[238]

Let us consider the seals (Revelation 6)

(v1, 2) *And I saw when the Lamb opened one of the seals, and I heard, as it were the noise of thunder, one of the four beasts saying, 'Come and see.' And I saw, and behold a white horse: and he that sat* on him had a bow; and a crown was given unto him: and he went forth conquering, and to conquer. (See [130])

(v3, 4) *And when He had opened the second seal, I heard the second beast say, 'Come and see,' And there went out another horse that was red: and power was given to him that sat thereon to take peace from the earth, and that they should kill one another: and there was given unto him a great sword.* (See [131])

(v5, 6) *And when He had opened the third seal, I heard the third beast say, 'Come and see.' And I beheld, and lo a black horse; and he that sat on him had a pair of balances in his hand. And I heard a voice in the midst of the four beasts say, 'A measure of wheat for a penny, and three measures of barley for a penny; and see thou hurt not the oil and the wine.'* (See [132])

(v7, 8) *And when He had opened the fourth seal, I heard the voice of the fourth beast say, 'Come and see.' And I looked, and behold a pale horse: and his name that sat on him was Death, and Hell followed with him. And power was given unto them over the fourth part of the earth, to kill with sword, and with hunger, and with death, and with the beasts of the earth.* (See [133])

[239]

The opening of the first four seals revealed *the Four Horsemen of the Apocalypse*, the inspiration for many paintings and book titles, even films; which have no relevance at all to the scriptural truth. It has already been pointed out (see [91]) that the events of the first four seals were in perfect harmony with the LORD's Own teachings on the last days. His teachings revealed: the coming of many false Christ's, as the first sign of all (the white horse) and then wars and rumours of wars, famines, pestilences and earthquakes (the red horse). In modern terms the consequences of the black horse could be considered to be raging inflation - prices becoming impossible. The final horse (pale, green, a healthy colour in plants, but in animals this is a sickly gangrenous green,) and the rider's name was Death, a scene of wholesale slaughter and death. But with respect to the things disclosed as the seals are opened revealing these four horsemen, who could argue that these signs are not already manifest? Whilst any or all of these things could be claimed to apply to some extent throughout history, their increase in the last decades is a matter of fact and they are still increasing in frequency and intensity, just like birth pangs. But the important thing about the seals is that everything revealed in the book is under GOD's control. The first seal, the white horse (which from the LORD's Own teachings has to be the appearances of the antichrists,) is the best example to illustrate this truth. The antichrists appear with increasing frequency and power, (until the appearance of the ultimate antichrist the False Prophet himself [101,163,182,194].) But their appearances and ministries will be merely evidences of GOD's control, they will be used to prove the calibre and faith of His people and ultimately His will prevails.

[240] Revelation 6

(V9-11) *And when He had opened the fifth seal, I saw under the altar the souls of them that were slain for the word of God, and for the testimony which they held: and they cried with a loud voice, saying, "How long, O Lord, holy and true, dost thou not judge and avenge our blood on them that dwell on the earth?" And white robes were given unto every one of them; and it was said unto them, that they should rest yet for a little season, until their fellowservants also and their brethren, that should be killed as they were, should be fulfilled.* (See [134])

The consequences of opening the fifth seal were very different from the previous seals, now there were martyrs, those *slain for the word of GOD, and for the testimony which they held*. Further, these were exhorted to rest until *their fellowservants also and their brethren, that should be killed as they were, should be fulfilled*. The martyrdoms were to continue, others were to be killed for the same reasons and this was permitted. Witnessing and testimony of this calibre belongs to the last days. This is in perfect harmony with the LORD's Own wonderful teachings and twice in the accounts this is mentioned before the setting up of the abomination of desolation. So these events occur before the commencement of the first half of the final week. It is also in total accord with this first half of the week, under the terms of the covenant made by the beast that the killings of the martyrs may have stopped. But in view of the fact that there are more *that should be killed as they were*, the persecution and killing will resume.

[241] Turning back to Matthew.

(Matthew 24:8-16) *All these are the beginning of sorrows.* (in reference to the events of the first four seals of Revelation 6)) *Then shall they deliver you up to be afflicted, and shall kill you: and ye shall be hated of all nations for My name's sake. And then shall many be offended, and shall betray one another, and shall hate one another. And many false prophets* (these must be distinguished from the false Christs of v4, 5) *shall rise, and shall deceive many. And because iniquity shall abound the love of many shall wax cold. But he that shall endure unto the end, the same shall be saved. And this gospel of the kingdom* (Appendix 5) *shall be preached in all the world for a witness unto all nations; and then shall the end come. When ye therefore shall see the abomination of desolation, spoken of by Daniel the prophet, stand in the holy place, (whoso readeth, let him understand:) then let them which be in Judea flee into the mountains:* (compare Mark 13:9-14 [69 & 72]).

The fifth seal unmistakably discloses events relating to the martyrdom of Jews. However, since the final week commences with the establishment of a covenant with this people (during which time their Jewish worship and sacrifice are accepted and permitted,) the martyrs must have died in persecutions, which occurred BEFORE the actual commencement of that week. The covenant is established as a considerable concession to the Jews by the beast and he maintains this agreement for the first half of the final week.

[242]

The fifth seal therefore covers the time of witnessing, the time of persecution BEFORE the commencement of the final week, then continues to cover the tribulation which happens during the last half of the final week itself. This can be asserted because the sixth seal applies to things after the tribulation, as follows:

(Revelation 6:12-17) *And I beheld when He had opened the sixth seal, and, lo, there was a great earthquake; and the sun became black as sackcloth of hair, and the moon became as blood; and the stars of heaven fell unto the earth, even as a fig tree casteth her untimely figs, when she is shaken of a mighty wind. And the heaven departed as a scroll when it is rolled together, and every mountain and island were moved out of their places. And the kings of the earth, and the great men, and the rich men, and the chief captains, and the mighty men, and every bondman, and every free man, hid themselves in the dens and in the rocks of the mountains; and said to the mountains* and rocks, *"Fall on us, and hide us from the face of Him that sitteth on the throne, and from the wrath of the Lamb: for the great day of His wrath is come; and who shall be able to stand?"* (See [135])

[243]

Compare the LORD's Own words (Matthew 24:29) *"Immediately after the tribulation of those days shall the sun be darkened, and the moon shall not give her light, and the stars shall fall from heaven, and the powers of the heavens shall be shaken."* (Mark 13:24, 25) *"But in those days, after that tribulation, the sun shall be darkened, and the moon shall not give her light, and the stars of heaven shall fall, and the powers that are in heaven shall be shaken."* (Luke 21:25, 26) *"And there shall be signs in the sun, and in the moon, and in the stars; and upon the earth distress of nations, with perplexity; the sea and the waves roaring; men's hearts failing them for fear, and for looking after those things which are coming on the earth: for the powers of heaven shall be shaken."* (See [69, 72 & 86])

This is the day of wrath spoken of by Isaiah (13:9, 10) and Joel (2:1-31); the frightening results of incurring the *wrath of the Lamb,* that astonishing contradiction in terms that adds even more to the revelation. Notice the sequence involving the Lamb: the *Lamb as it had been slain*, the *Lamb worthy to open the seals,* and now the WRATH of the LAMB (a contradiction in terms.) The kings, the great, the rich, the mighty and even the slaves instinctively know that this is the time to hide themselves. (The details of His wrath are revealed in the events of the seven trumpets, which confirm the view that the opening of the seven seals covers the eventualities of the seven trumpets and the seven vials.)

[244] Revelation

(8:1) *And when He had opened the seventh seal, there was silence in* heaven about the space of half an hour. (See [139])

There is a break in the narrative, as events are described concerning the wrath of the Lamb and it is difficult to decide, where the Revelation continues to describe what happens, when this silence ends. (Probably 13:10 *And I heard a loud voice in heaven,* the central verse of Revelation.) But another vivid contrast to the silence is to be found in John's description (16:1) *"And I heard a great voice out of the temple saying to the seven angels, "Go thy ways, and pour out the vials of the wrath of GOD upon the earth."*

The sixth seal (six is the number of man) covers the wrath of the Lamb, the *Son of man* and therefore it seems appropriate that the silence of the seventh seal (seven is the divine number) should apply to the wrath of God (outpoured in the seven vials.)

There is an immediate association therefore in the sixth and seventh seals, between the wrath of the Lamb and the wrath of GOD. In accordance with this (and recognising these have been already broadly examined in the context of The Revelation,) our purpose is to compare the seven trumpets (covering the wrath of the Lamb) and the seven vials (the fulness of the wrath of God.) The results are remarkable.

[245] THE FIRST TRUMPET AND THE FIRST VIAL

(8:7) *The first angel sounded, and there followed hail and fire mingled with blood, and they were cast upon the earth: and the third part of trees was burnt up, and all green grass was burnt up.* (See [141])

(16:2) *And the first went, and poured out his vial upon the earth; and there fell a noisome and grievous sore upon the men which had the mark of the beast, and upon them which worshipped his image.* (See [177])

In the wrath of the Lamb the earth is judged; and again in the wrath of God the earth as the habitation of those worshipping the beast is judged, with those worshipping the beast. It is not unreasonable to claim that in the destruction of the trees and grass already taking place that these events are already beginning to be manifested. Whilst the causes might be explained these days scientifically from pollution, toxic wastes, destruction of forests or jungles for cattle, or development etc the prophetic accuracy of scripture has to be admitted and in fact is confirmed further.

[246] THE SECOND TRUMPET AND THE SECOND VIAL

(8:8, 9) *And the second angel sounded, and as it were a great mountain burning with fire was cast into the sea: and the third part of the sea became blood; and the third part of the creatures which were in the sea, and had life, died; and the third part of the ships were destroyed.* (See [142])

(16:3) *And the second angel poured out his vial upon the sea; and it became as the blood of a dead man: and every living soul died in the sea.* (See [178])

The sea is judged firstly under the wrath of the Lamb and then totally under the fulness of the wrath of God. Only a fool could deny this has begun and whilst for some it might be hard admitting that the scriptures are correct, it has to be said that these things were prophesied with commendable brevity and accuracy. The prospect of every living thing in the sea dying is too awful to contemplate, but it is a certainty. His Church is delivered from such judgments, which are poured out by GOD on the world that has rejected and despised His Son as His followers.

[247] THE THIRD TRUMPET AND THE THIRD VIAL

(8:10,11) *And the third angel sounded, and there fell a great star from heaven, burning as it were a lamp, and it fell upon the third part of the rivers, and upon the fountains of waters; and the name of the star is called Wormwood: and the third part of the waters became wormwood; and many men died of the waters, because they were made bitter.* (See [143])

(16:4) *And the third angel poured out his vial upon the rivers and fountains of waters; and they became blood.* (See [179])

The judgments are on the sources of fresh waters. The star could of course be an asteroid, a colossal rock from outer space, which even in its brief passage through the atmosphere could have the effect of polluting or poisoning all fresh waters. The terrible loss of life, *many men died,* is because of the bitter waters. When the waters become blood the disaster cannot be imagined. As a necessity of life such water pollution or water shortage could cause wars. For example, where water sources originating in countries are extensively over-used for irrigation or industrial purposes and this deprives subsequent countries, which for centuries have relied on the flow. In dire shortages water becomes far more precious than oil for a country's survival. These judgments are truly terrifying.

[248] THE FOURTH TRUMPET AND THE FOURTH VIAL

(8:12) *And the fourth angel sounded, and the third part of the sun was smitten, and the third part of the moon, and the third part of the stars; so as the third part of them was darkened, and the day shone not for a third part of it, and the night likewise.* (See [144])

(16:8,9) *And the fourth angel poured out his vial upon the sun; and power was given unto him to scorch men with fire. And men were scorched with great heat, and blasphemed the name of GOD, Which hath power over these plagues: and they repented not to give Him glory.* (See [180])

These events have not been apparent so far and when they occur there may well be scientific explanations - volcanic or other dust in the atmosphere, destruction of the ozone layer etc. But such explanations can do nothing to discredit prophecies, which have been written for two thousand years.[49]

[249] THE FIFTH TRUMPET AND THE FIFTH VIAL

(9:1-3) *And the fifth angel sounded, and I saw a star fall from heaven unto the earth: and to him was given the key of the bottomless pit. And he opened the bottomless pit; and there arose a smoke out of the pit, as the smoke of a great furnace; and the sun and the air were darkened by reason of the smoke of the pit. And there came out of the smoke locusts upon the earth: and unto them was given power, as the scorpions of the earth have power.* (Etc to v12, see [146]).

(16:10, 11) *And the fifth angel poured out his vial upon the seat of the beast; and his kingdom was full of darkness; and they gnawed their tongues for pain, and blasphemed the GOD of heaven because of their pains and their sores, and repented not of their deeds.* (See [181]).

The blasphemy (evidenced also under the fourth vial,) is truly astonishing and their refusal to repent is included in the prophecy. Does this indicate their stubbornness or their fear of being seen to change their minds?

[250] THE SIXTH TRUMPET AND THE SIXTH VIAL

(9:13-15) *And the sixth angel sounded, and I heard a voice from the four horns of the golden altar which is before God, saying to the sixth*

---

[49] It should be noted that it is after the fourth trumpet that the three woes are pronounced (8:13) *"Woe, woe, woe, to the inhabiters of the earth by the reason of the other voices of the trumpet of the three angels, which are yet to sound!"*

angel which had the trumpet, "Loose the four angels which are bound in the great river Euphrates." And the four angels were loosed, which were prepared for an hour, and a day, and a month, and a year, for to slay the third part of men. (See [147])

(16:12-14) *And the sixth angel poured out his vial upon the great river Euphrates; and the water thereof was dried up, that the way of the kings of the east might be prepared. And I saw three unclean spirits like frogs come out of the mouth of the dragon, and out of the mouth of the beast, and out of the mouth of the false prophet. For they are the spirits of devils, working miracles, which go forth unto the kings of the earth and of the whole world, to gather them to the battle of the great day of GOD ALMIGHTY.* (See [182])

These are not contradictory but complementary judgments, in the first case the four angels are loosed at the sounding of the sixth trumpet and in the second case, the three unclean spirits are released to gather the kings of the earth to battle; but the great river Euphrates is the place on which the judgments are outpoured.

[251] THE SEVENTH TRUMPET AND THE SEVENTH VIAL

Note first: (10:7) *".... in the days of the voice of the seventh angel, when he shall begin to sound, the mystery of GOD should be finished, as He hath declared to His servants the prophets."*

(11:15) *And the seventh angel sounded; and there were great voices in heaven, saying, "The kingdoms of this world are become the kingdoms of our Lord, and of His Christ; and He shall reign for ever and ever."* (See [155])

(16:17-21) *And the seventh angel poured out his vial into the air; and there came a great voice out of the temple of heaven, from the throne, saying, "It is done." And there were voices, and thunders, and lightnings; and there was a great earthquake, such as was not since men were upon the earth, so mighty an earthquake, and so great.*

And the great city was divided into three parts, and the cities of the nations fell: and great Babylon came in remembrance before GOD, to give unto her the cup of the wine of the fierceness of His wrath. And every island fled away, and the mountains were not found. And there fell upon men a great hail out of heaven, every stone about the weight of a talent: and men blasphemed GOD because of the plague of the hail, for the plague thereof was exceeding great. (See [183])

Under the seventh trumpet	*The mystery of GOD should be finished.*
Under the seventh vial	*It is done.*

The combined judgments of the wrath of the Lamb followed by the fulness of the wrath of GOD are poured out upon:

1 The Earth 2 The Sea 3 The Rivers 4 The Sun 5 The Bottomless Pit and The Seat of the Beast 6 The Euphrates 7 Heaven, The Air.

The destruction of trees and the death of many sea creatures are already evident in our world to a scale approaching that indicated in the prophecies of the first and second trumpets and in spite of the efforts of an increasing number of concerned people, the trend continues. In the media, anxieties about freshwater sources in respect of increasing demand, decreasing availability and pollution have been expressed internationally. Conferences have been called already to discuss the water problems involved as a result of the demands of vast population increases, excessive irrigation, industrial demands, pollution and waste. Some experts even consider that ultimately freshwater supply (not oil) will be the main cause of conflict in the Middle East.

[252]

The point being made however is that in addition to the succession of events prophesied under the seven seals of the book (and some of these things are manifest already to some extent,) there are also evidences that the succession of judgments concerning the wrath of the Lamb has begun. Scripturally these can only be seen to continue until their ultimate and total fulfilment in the fullness of the wrath of God.

Whilst the seven trumpets and the seven vials cover these judgments more than adequately to identify what is involved; there are also other prophecies and events revealed in The Revelation. These are inserted in the book, just as they would be, if one were attempting to describe everything in conversation - one would have to digress, to explain other matters. So with the broad view of the sequence of the events of the seven seals and the evident association of the seven trumpets and seven vials in respect of the judgments outpoured, these other portions can be examined to build up the whole picture of what is involved.

[253] THE 144,000 OF THE TWELVE TRIBES OF ISRAEL

Between the opening of the sixth seal and the seventh seal is the account given by John of the sealing of the servants of God from the tribes of Israel (7:1-17) This has already been discussed and it needs only passing reference (See [136].)

[254] THE SEVEN THUNDERS

(10:1-11) *And I saw another mighty angel come down from heaven, clothed with a cloud: and a rainbow was upon his head, and his face was as it were the sun, and his feet as pillars of fire: and he had in his hand a little book open: and he set his right foot upon the sea, and his left foot on the earth. And cried with a loud voice, as when a lion roareth: and when he had cried seven thunders uttered their voices. And when the seven thunders had uttered their voices, I was about to write: and I heard a voice from heaven saying unto me, "Seal up those things which the seven thunders uttered, and write them not." And the angel which I saw stand upon the sea and upon the earth lifted up his hand to heaven, and sware by Him that liveth for ever and ever, Who created heaven, and the things that therein are, and the earth, and the things that therein are, and the sea, and the things which are therein, that there should be time no longer: but in the days of the voice of the seventh angel, when he shall begin to sound, the mystery of God should be finished, as He hath declared to His servants the prophets. And the voice which I heard from heaven spake unto me again, and said, "Go and take the little book which is open in the hand of the angel which standeth upon the sea and upon the earth." And I went unto the angel, and said unto him, "Give me the little book." And he said unto me, "Take it, and eat it up; and it shall make thy belly bitter, but it shall be in thy mouth sweet as honey." And I took the little book out of the angel's hand, and ate it up; and it was in my mouth sweet as honey: and as soon as I had eaten it, my belly was bitter. And he said unto me, "Thou must prophesy again before many peoples, and nations, and tongues, and kings."*

John did not write what the angel cried out, neither was John allowed to write what the seven thunders had uttered. It is pointless speculating on what might have been said, for the revelation has not been given. However it is this angel who swares by The Eternal God and Creator of All, *that there should be time no longer,* and this is explained as *the mystery of God should be finished, as He hath declared to His servants the prophets.* This cannot be the end of time in a literal sense, because for example, there are several references in what follows to intervals of time (*a thousand two hundred and threescore days; a time, and times, and half a time; forty and two months* etc) but it must mean THE END of time in respect of its prophetic fulfilment (specifically the times of the gentiles) especially the seventy weeks and this occurs in context with the sounding of the seventh trumpet (See [155].)

[255] THE TWO WITNESSES

(11:1-13) These have also been considered (see [151] – [153]).

[256] THE WOMAN AND THE DRAGON

(12:1-17) In previous considerations ([156] – [160]) it was established that the Woman was Israel, the dragon, Satan - and the man child, caught up to GOD and to His throne was the Body of The LORD Jesus Christ, His True Church. This can be explained as follows :

From the LORD's Own teachings, (Matthew 24:29-31) *"Immediately after the tribulation of those days shall the sun be darkened, and the moon shall not give her light, and the stars shall fall from heaven, and the powers of the heavens shall be shaken: and THEN shall appear THE SIGN OF THE SON OF MAN IN HEAVEN; and THEN shall all the tribes of the earth mourn, and they shall see THE SON OF MAN COMING in the clouds of heaven with power and great glory. And He shall send His angels with a great sound of a trumpet, and they shall gather together His elect from the four winds, from one end of heaven to the other."*

[257]

These are TWO separate events, *firstly*, immediately after the tribulation of those days, the darkening of the sun, the moon giving no light, the stars falling from heaven and the powers of heaven being shaken - this is referred to in the account of the Woman and the dragon, (12:4, 5) *and his tail drew the third part of the stars of heaven, and did cast them to the earth: and the dragon stood before the woman which was ready to be delivered, for to devour her child as soon as it was born. And she brought forth a man child, who was to rule all nations with a rod of iron: and her child was caught up unto God, and to His throne.* The appearance of *the sign of the Son of man in heaven* is the fulfilment of the promise of the angels (Acts 1:9-11) *And when He had spoken these things, while they beheld, HE WAS TAKEN UP; AND A CLOUD RECEIVED HIM OUT OF THEIR SIGHT. And while they looked stedfastly toward heaven as He went up, behold, two men stood by them in white apparel; which also said "Ye men of Galilee, why stand ye gazing up into heaven? this same Jesus, Which is taken up from you into heaven, SHALL SO COME IN LIKE MANNER AS YE HAVE SEEN HIM GO INTO HEAVEN."* This was the sign given to the apostles; His appearance in the clouds at the time of the heavenly signs (involving sun, moon etc) is the *first* indication of His coming *to rule all nations with a rod of iron* to take over the kingdoms of this world. Satan (the dragon) with his heavenly hosts makes a direct attack and the man child (His body,) is caught up to God and to His throne; whilst (12:7, 8 [156] & [160]) *there was war in heaven: Michael and his angels fought against the dragon, and the dragon fought and his angels, and prevailed not; neither was their place found any more in heaven.* This fulfils the third woe (12:12) *"Woe to the inhabiters of the earth and of the sea! For the devil is come down unto you, having great wrath, because he knoweth that he hath but a short time."* (See [155.] Compare [271])

[258]

The persecution, that has preceded these events, is nothing compared with the tribulation that follows and it is to the period of His total absence (from the time of His Body's being caught up to GOD and His throne, until He comes to deliver His people,) that the LORD's teachings about the wise and foolish virgins and the talents apply. His people are expected (having seen Him) to be faithful in His absence. This is in the face of the great wrath of the dragon, who seeks to destroy the woman and her seed *which keep the commandments of God, and have the testimony of Jesus Christ.* (12:17.)

[259]

The difficulty in considering these various things is finding the chronological order in which they can be placed. For example, in considering the two witnesses (11:7) *when they shall have finished their testimony, the beast that ascendeth out of the bottomless pit shall make war against them, and shall overcome them, and kill them.* (See [151] & [153]).

Then, (13:2, 3) *the beast which I saw was like unto a leopard, and his feet were as the feet of a beast, and his mouth as the mouth of a lion: and the dragon gave him his power, and his seat, and great authority. And I saw one of his heads as it were wounded to death; and his deadly wound was healed: and all the world wondered after the beast.* (See [161]). This is the same beast, at different stages in his experience and he evidently overcomes the two witnesses in the power he has been given by the dragon. The two witnesses testify for the first half of the final week and it is to the second half of that week that the extremes in the behaviour of the beast apply, the time of great tribulation.

[260]

(13:5-7) *And there was given unto him a mouth speaking great things and blasphemies; and power was given unto him to continue forty and two months. And he opened his mouth in blasphemy against God, to blaspheme His name, and His tabernacle, and them that dwell in heaven. And it was given unto him to make war with the saints, and to overcome them: and power was given him over all kindreds, and tongues, and nations.*

The beast's rise to power is consistently marked by evidences of his increasing wickedness and evil and this man has a long career.

[261] THE 144,000 REDEEMED FROM THE EARTH

(14:1-5 [170]) To be distinguished from the 144,000 redeemed from Israel.

[262] THE THREE FLYING ANGELS

These three angels with their proclamations are similar to, or perhaps a reflection of, the three woes; notice their individual messages:

The First Flying Angel (14:6, 7)

And I saw another angel fly in the midst of heaven, having the everlasting gospel to preach unto them that dwell on the earth, and to every nation, and kindred, and tongue, and people, saying with a loud voice, "Fear God, and give glory to Him; for the hour of His judgment is come: and worship Him that made heaven, and earth, and the sea, and the fountains of waters." (Everlasting Gospel - Appendix 5 and [171]).

The Second Flying Angel (14:8)

And there followed another angel, saying, "Babylon, is fallen, is fallen, that great city, because she made all nations drink of the wine of the wrath of her fornication." (See [172]).

The Third Flying Angel (14:9-12)

And the third angel followed them, saying with a loud voice, "If any man worship the beast and his image, and receive his mark in his forehead, or in his hand, the same shall drink of the wine of the wrath of GOD, which is poured out without mixture into the cup of His indignation; and he shall be tormented with fire and brimstone in the presence of the holy angels, and in the presence of the Lamb; and the smoke of their torment ascendeth up for ever and ever: and they have no rest day nor night, who worship the beast and his image, and whosoever receiveth the mark of his name. Here is the patience of the saints: here are they that keep the commandments of GOD, and the faith of Jesus. (See [173]).

These three angels are evidently associated (*the third angel followed them*):

> = the first angel brought the command to fear God, give glory to Him and worship Him
>
> = the second angel pronounced the fall of Babylon (the repetition means the fact is established -see Genesis 41:32)
>
> = the third angel brought the warning of the wrath of God for those who worship the beast, or his image, or receive his mark or the mark of his name.

These declarations are written in the Revelation that is sufficient; they are recorded and all can see and know when the time comes. There is a heavenly declaration recorded

(14:13) *And I heard a voice from heaven saying unto me, "Write, Blessed are the dead which die in the Lord from henceforth: Yea, saith the Spirit, that they may rest from their labours; and their works do follow them."* (See [174]).

The three flying angels are reflected or balanced by the angels from the temple in heaven.

[263] THE THREE ANGELS FROM THE TEMPLE

(14:14-20) *And I looked, and behold a white cloud, and upon the cloud One sat like unto the Son of man, having on His head a golden crown, and in His hand a sharp sickle. And another angel came out of the temple, crying with a loud voice to Him that sat on the cloud,*

"Thrust in Thy sickle and reap: for the time is come for Thee to reap; for the harvest of the earth is ripe." And He that sat on the cloud thrust in His sickle on the earth; and the earth was reaped.

And another angel came out of the temple which is in heaven, he also having a sharp sickle. And another angel came out from the altar, which had power over fire; and cried with a loud cry to him that had the sharp sickle, saying, "Thrust in thy sharp sickle, and gather the clusters of the vine of the earth; for her grapes are fully ripe." And the angel thrust in his sickle into the earth, and gathered the vine of the earth, and cast it into the great winepress of the wrath of God. And the winepress was trodden without the city, and blood came out of the winepress, even unto the horse bridles, by the space of a thousand and six hundred furlongs. (See [175]).

In the first instance we have the Son of man reaping the harvest of the earth (compare Matthew 13:24-30 & 36-43) then the angel reaps the vintage, the vine of the earth. {Compare the later description of the Lord (19:15 [194]) *out of His mouth goeth a sharp sword, that with it He should smite the nations: and He shall rule them with a rod of iron: and He treadeth the winepress of the fierceness and wrath of Almighty God.*} (Compare also Deuteronomy 32:32, 33 Isaiah 34:1-8 63:1-4 Joel 3:12-15 Zephaniah 3:8.)

[264] THE JUDGMENT OF BABYLON

(17, 18 [184] & [190]) The judgments are in accordance with the pronouncement of the second flying angel; there is no need for further comment. The judgment of Babylon does however come under the outpouring of the seventh vial (16:17 [183]) *And the seventh angel poured out his vial into the air; and there came a great voice out of the temple of heaven, from the throne, saying, "It is done."* (And 16:19) *And the great city was divided into three parts, and the cities of the nations fell: and great Babylon came in remembrance before God, to give unto her the cup of the wine of the fierceness of His wrath.*

Babylon is situated on the Euphrates, (The sixth angel with a trumpet, releases the four angels from the Euphrates (Revelation 9:14-21) which is dried up as a result of the sixth vial (Revelation 16:12). Having considered the events of the last days, to conclude this study His comings can be explained in this context; but it must be appreciated that the Church has no part in these considerations, His comings in the last days involve His earthly people, Israel, the Jews, His Bride.

Chapter 20: CONCLUSION The LORD's Comings for His People

[266]

(Revelation 1:7) *"Behold, He cometh with clouds; and every eye shall see Him, and they also which pierced Him: and all kindreds of the earth shall wail because of Him. Even so, Amen."*

This wonderful reminder in the opening of The Revelation has consistently been revealed as the sign of His coming (see Matthew 24:30 and Acts 1:9-11 [69]). In The Revelation, it is the first of His appearances mentioned to the Jews and it has to be their first sight of Him. Quite possibly, the description of the Lord given (Rev 1:13-18 [113] & [122]), which is repeated in certain particulars to some of the seven churches, will be especially significant or applicable to those last day assemblies in the actual sign of His coming.

But before His sign, His appearing in the clouds, He spoke of other signs (the events of the first four seals,) the appearances of false Christs, wars and rumours of wars, famines, hunger, death and earthquakes. These are all signs, marking the beginning of sorrows (travail, the agonies of childbearing,) and will be evident with increasing frequency and intensity as the time draws near.

The fifth seal covers the time of testimony for the Jews (the church having been taken previously of course,) and applies especially to the first half of the final, or seventieth week. The seventieth week is marked by three distinct phases:

= The Beginning - the week commences with the confirmation of a covenant between the Jews and the beast.

= The Middle - the first half of the week is terminated by the beast's violation of the covenant. He overcomes the two witnesses, who are resurrected and a great earthquake destroys a tenth of the city of Jerusalem. This marks the end of the second woe and the middle of the week.

[The beginning and middle of the seventieth week come under the events of the fifth and sixth seal.]

= The tribulation follows, and The End of the week occurs when the Jews are delivered out of the oppressions of the seventieth week (Daniel 9:24 [35]). (This deliverance is completed under the seventh seal.)

The sixth seal concerns events after the tribulation, this is the time of heavenly signs (Rev 6:12 [135]) the sun becomes black, the moon as blood and this is after the last of the signs given by the LORD takes place - the sign of His appearing in the clouds. The other signs were covered under the first four seals (above,) but as the Son of man it is appropriate that His appearing should come under the sixth seal (six being the number of man.) His coming in divine judgment is similarly found under the seventh seal (seven being the divine number.)

[267]

Concurrent to some extent at least with the events of the seven seals, are the events of the seven trumpets - the outpouring of the wrath of the Lamb; but it is noteworthy that after His sign, (His appearance in the clouds,) these events are manifestly more severe.

The three woes associated with the last three trumpets (Rev 8:13 [145]) have nothing to do with the wrath of God (the seven vials,) but are the laments of the flying angel over the release of the forces of hell to the earth. First the terrible locust-like creatures have power to torment (see [146],) then the four angels bound in the Euphrates have power to kill (see [147],) and finally, Satan himself is cast to earth as a result of his being cast out of heavenly places (see [156].) It is in the power given to him by Satan at this time, that the beast, restored after dying, overcomes the two witnesses and with the assistance of the False Prophet (similarly empowered [163],) the beast seeks to totally destroy the Jews demanding they worship his image or die.

[Note: The place of the man-child, His Body, His True Church, in the earth could be challenged by Satan at any time previous to the middle of the final week. The woe expressed about Satan's coming to earth must apply to the time he empowers the beast, after destroying the two witnesses.] But in heavenly places, (the man-child having been caught up to God and to His throne, whilst Michael and his angels cast Satan out,) the LORD's Body is perfected as all who believe in Him are united with Him. Whilst the events on earth continue to unfold, He will be glorified in those that believe and reward His brethren and sisters in His church as promised.

The end of the second woe is marked by an earthquake (Rev 8:13 [45] and 11:12-14 [154]) and this also occurs immediately after the two witnesses are called up to heaven. This confirms that the sixth seal and sixth trumpet are associated.

The third woe *the devil is come down* (Rev 12:12 [156]) is associated with the seventh trumpet (Rev 11:15 [155]) when the kingdoms of this world are proclaimed to be the kingdoms of our LORD and His Christ.

[268]

The wrath of GOD is revealed in the outpouring of the seven vials (Rev 16:1 [176] – [183]) and commences with the terrible sore on the worshippers of the beast's image. Then every living soul in the sea dies, from scripture (Genesis 2:7) it would appear this applies to those breathing air, i.e. mammals, seals, dolphins, whales; not necessarily fish, which "breathe" in water not air (Paul distinguished between these different kinds of flesh 1 Corinthians 15:39.) Fresh waters become as blood, scorching sun and then darkness on the kingdom of the beast follow as the wrath of GOD is outpoured. The release of the three unclean spirits from the mouths of the dragon, beast and false prophet follows and these gather the nations of the earth to the battle of Armageddon. The conclusion of His wrath is marked in the destruction of Babylon.

[269]

The awesome tribulation of the second half of the week, when the cruellest atrocities are inflicted on His people, are brought under control by His appearance - the *first* sign, His coming in the clouds, marking the end of the week {[234] (iv)(v)(vii) [75] [67] [86].} But, He disappears again and it is to this intervening time of waiting that the parables of the ten virgins and the talents apply. This is the time when the Bride and her companions, her supporters, are expected to wait for the coming of the Bridegroom, to be ready when He comes {(iii) [234].} The tribulation has ceased, but the persecution continues, as evidenced in the gathering of the nations to destroy Israel at Armageddon and the beast himself is at the head of this formidable array of forces. (See Figure 6. Note: the array of forces shown are compiled from the accounts in Daniel and elsewhere and could be seen in total combination, or any variation.)

[270]

The beast is not in Babylon when it is destroyed, but he and his armies are destroyed by the LORD's coming on a white horse with His armies (Rev 19:11 [194]) but when the LORD stands on the Mount of Olives (on a different occasion) it divides in a tremendous earthquake.

[271]

The coming of the Son of man in His glory is His final coming {(i)(ii)(vi)&(viii) [234], [67], [70] & [73].} This is the unmistakable *second* sign! (Compare [257]) The LORD's teachings followed the parables of the ten virgins and the talents (which covered His return as the Bridegroom,) and His opening words quite clearly established that these teachings relate to His ruling as The King. His enemies have been destroyed and He is claiming His divine right to rule. From His throne He rewards those who have done anything good, even to the least of His brethren and He curses those who did nothing. His Own words are more than adequate to describe this (and should be compared with Revelation 20:4-6 [196]). He also taught this in His parable of the tares (see Matthew 13:24-30 & 36-43.)

[272]

To conclude, the words of The King (Matthew 25:31-46):

"When the Son of man shall come in His glory, and all the holy angels with Him, then shall He sit upon the throne of His glory: and before Him shall be gathered all nations: and He shall separate them one from another, as a shepherd divideth his sheep from the goats: and He shall set the sheep on His right hand, but the goats on the left. Then shall the King say unto them on His right hand, 'Come, ye blessed of My Father, inherit the kingdom prepared for you from the foundation of the world: for I was an hungred, and ye gave Me meat: I was thirsty and ye gave Me drink: I was a stranger, and ye took Me in: naked and ye clothed Me: I was sick, and ye visited Me: I was in prison and ye came unto Me.' Then shall the righteous answer Him, saying, 'LORD, when saw we Thee an hungred, and fed Thee? Or thirsty, and gave Thee drink? When saw we Thee a stranger, and took

Thee in? Or naked, and clothed Thee? Or when saw we Thee sick, or in prison, and came unto Thee?' And the King shall answer and say unto them, 'Verily I say unto you, Inasmuch as ye have done it unto one of the least of these My brethren, ye have done it unto Me.' Then shall He say also unto them on the left hand, 'Depart from Me, ye cursed, into everlasting fire, prepared for the devil and his angels: for I was an hungred, and ye gave Me no meat: I was thirsty, and ye gave Me no drink: I was a stranger, and ye took Me not in: naked, and ye clothed Me not: sick, and in prison, and ye visited Me not.' Then shall they also answer Him, saying, 'LORD, when saw we Thee an hungred, or athirst, or a stranger, or naked, or sick, or in prison, and did not minister unto Thee?' Then shall He answer them saying, 'Verily I say unto you, Inasmuch as ye did it not to one of the least of these, ye did it not to Me.' And these shall go away into everlasting punishment: but the righteous into life eternal."

APPENDIX 1 The Babylonian Captivity Periods

THE SERVITUDE (70 Years)

Dates: From BC 605 (3rd year of Jehoiakim, 1st year of Nebuchadnezzar) To   BC 535 (Decree of Cyrus[50])

Scripture References: 2 Kings 24:1 Esther 2:5-7 Jeremiah 27:6, 8 & 1. Daniel 1:1, 2

Remarks: The Servitude resulted from the first invasion of Jerusalem by Nebuchadnezzar. Originally the LORD intended that Judah should remain in their land in servitude to Nebuchadnezzar. It was from this invasion that Daniel and his companions were taken captive to Babylon. After only 7 years, the Servitude was replaced by the Captivity..

Note: Although these different divine judgments are distinctly separate, (and overlap slightly,) the total period is usually referred to as The Captivity.

THE CAPTIVITY (70 Years)

Dates: From BC 598 (8th year of Nebuchadnezzar)   To   BC 536

Scripture References 2 Kings 24:10 Esther 2:5-7 Jeremiah 27:6, 17. 28:14. 29:10

Remarks Second invasion by Nebuchadnezzar when he took Jehoiachin into captivity with Ezekiel, and including Mordecai and Esther his niece. The message to those in captivity in Babylon was that the Lord would let them return to Jerusalem. (Ezekiel began to prophesy in Babylon, in the fifth year of the Captivity Period BC 594.) The *Captivity* commenced eight years after the *Servitude.* The

Captivity was stated to be for seventy years (Jeremiah 29:10-14) but lasted only 11 years and the Desolations were imposed.

THE DESOLATIONS (70 Years)

Dates: From BC 589 (17th year of Nebuchadnezzar) To BC 520 (2nd year of Darius Hystaspes)

Scripture References 2 Kings 25:1-17 Daniel 10:1 Jeremiah 25:8-11 & 32:1-5 Haggai 2:18

Remarks Third invasion by Nebuchadnezzar. Desolations prophesied. The Desolations ended with the laying of the foundations of the temple the second time (see Footnote 48 under Servitude.) [NOTE: The Seventy Years of the Servitude, or The Captivity or the Desolations have nothing to do with the Seventy Weeks of Daniel's Prophecy, (which commenced in (BC 445) 73 years after the Desolations ended.) But their consideration is essential for calculating and comprehending the dates for the commencement and end of the Seventy Weeks of Daniel. (See note The 70th Week below.) Note also: Daniel 10:1, the third year of Darius (BC 519) is the latest date mentioned in Daniel. Scripturally Daniel's Prophecy covers BC 605 to 519 = 86 years.

SUBSEQUENT EVENTS

BC 515 (Ezra 6:15) Temple dedicated (Seventy years interim period).

BC 445 (Nehemiah 1:2 2:5 6:15) Jerusalem restored and Daniel's 70 Weeks of years commence.

BC 397 Prophecy of Malachi completes Old Testament canon, ends first seven weeks (49 years) of Daniel's 70 Weeks, (leaving 62 weeks times 7 = 424 years.)

AD 32 Messiah cut off (The Cross) End of Daniel's 69th Week, leaving the final week.

Long before the final week commenced the *Times of the Gentiles* began. This is a period of indeterminate length, which commenced with Nebuchadnezzar's domination of Jerusalem (followed by the Persian, Greek and Roman Empires) and ends after the LORD comes for His Church, which will be followed by Daniel's 70th Week. (See following note on 70th Week.)

Endnote to Appendix 1.

To avoid the necessity of turning back continually to these notes, the particulars in this Appendix are repeated in context with the information in Appendix 7, *Daniel's Supplications and the Persian Kings.*

APPENDIX 2 The Lunar Year, The Seventy Year Period, Years of Servitude

THE LUNAR YEAR

The year involved in scripture is known as the Lunar Year, which simply involves twelve months of thirty days duration (i.e. 360 days.) This is the oldest known calendar year and would have been familiar to Abram and his contemporaries in Ur; the idea of having 360 degrees in a circle originated in this cycle of 360 days.

Scripturally it can be proved that the Lunar Year is involved simply by reference to The Flood. The first day of the flood is noted as the seventeenth day of the second month (Genesis 7:11) and the duration of the flood was 150 days, which ended on the seventeenth day of the seventh month (Genesis 8:3, 4). The only way five consecutive months can total 150 days, is if each month is thirty days duration, so the Lunar Year has to be used. (If the Jewish months are considered, it should be remembered that The Passover, when they came out of Egypt, changed the beginning of the Jewish Year from September to April, or Elul to Abib.)

THE SEVENTY YEAR PERIOD and YEARS OF SERVITUDE

The seventy weeks (i.e. 70 X 7 = 490 years) period has been proved to be a most significant period in Jewish history and several writers have noted the following examples (and others,):

Canaan to the Kingdom   Kingdom to Servitude*

490 years in each case   BC 1586-1096 (King Saul) -606 (Servitude)

With regard to the first period, Canaan to the Kingdom; an apparent scriptural contradiction was disproved and a remarkable truth revealed as follows;

(1 Kings 6:1) *And it came to pass in the four hundredth and eightieth year after the children of Israel were come out of the land of Egypt, in the fourth year of King Solomon's reign .....*

This scripture was compared with Paul's account of the same period (Acts 13:16-22) *Then Paul stood up, and beckoning with his hand said, "Men of Israel, and ye that fear God, give audience. The God of this people of Israel chose our fathers, and exalted the people when they dwelt as strangers in the land of Egypt, and with an high arm brought He them out of it. And about the time of forty years suffered He their manners in the wilderness. And when He had destroyed seven nations in the land of Chanaan, He divided their land to them by lot. And after that He gave unto them judges about the space of four hundred and fifty years, until Samuel the prophet. And afterward they desired a king: and God gave them Saul the son of Cis, a man of the tribe of Benjamin, by the space of forty years. And when He had removed him, He raised up unto them David to be their king; to whom also He gave testimony, and said, 'I have found David, the son of Jesse, a man after Mine Own heart, which shall fulfil all My will.'...."*

The figures given by Paul are: 40 years in the wilderness, 450 years under Judges, 40 years Saul - total 530 years. To this must be added, 40 years for David's reign and the first 3 years of Solomon's reign, which brings the total to 573 years. This is a discrepancy of 93 years, compared with the scripture in 1 Kings 6.

Credit must be given to somebody for discovering how to reconcile this difference (Sir Robert Anderson does mention how it is done, in his book *The Coming Prince,* but does not claim that he discovered this himself and it is mentioned by other writers;) which is by deducting from the time 450 years given for the period under the Judges in Israel, the years during which the Jews were in submission to other nations, as follows:

8 years under the king of Mesopotamia, 18 years under Moab, 20 years under Canaan, 7 years under Midian and 40 years under Philistines - a total of 93 years.

The significance of this is that the accuracy of the total in 1 Kings must have been accepted by the Jews themselves and they could only have accepted it in the same way, ie by allowing that the years of the servitude, captivity and desolation do not count, when Israel was out of the will of God. For Israel (or Judah) Daniel's seventy weeks commenced from the time the foundation of the Temple was laid after they had returned to Jerusalem.

Scripturally, it has been proved that there can be leaps or gaps in the timetable that God has ordained for His earthly people Israel. In their rejection at the cutting off of Messiah (at the end of the sixty-ninth week,) the "times of the gentiles" (recognised by Paul see Romans 1,) commenced and this period continues until the commencement of the final, seventieth week. This begins, from Gabriel's words to Daniel, when *the prince that shall come shall confirm the covenant with many for one week.* (Daniel 9:26, 27.)

*Note: Whilst The Servitude (to Babylon) was the original judgment imposed on Israel this was followed, (because of Judah's obstinacy in their idolatry,) by the Captivity and the Desolations. But the term Servitude can be applied in its broadest sense to the Gentile Domination of Jerusalem (or the land of Israel/Judah) from the time of Nebuchadnezzar to the present day. For in their rejection of the LORD Jesus Christ, the Jews brought upon themselves their rejection by GOD; when in His grace GOD offered salvation to the Gentiles. This dispensation *The Times of the Gentiles* will continue until the

Final Week (the last seven year period) of Daniel's prophecy commences; during which time the sceptre of world domination is restored to The King of Kings and LORD of Lords and His people on earth.

APPENDIX 3 The Final Week

(Daniel 9:24) *Seventy weeks are determined upon thy people and upon thy holy city, to finish the transgression, and to make an end of sins, and to make reconciliation for iniquity, and to bring in everlasting righteousness, and to seal up the vision and prophecy, and to anoint the most Holy.*

Concerning the Seventy Weeks (of years) of Daniel's Prophecy; the first seven weeks (49 years,) covered the completion of the Jewish Scriptures (by addition of Malachi's Prophecy). Then the sixty and two weeks (434 years), covered the so-called *silent years* (between the Old and New Testament,) when no prophet was heard in Judah, until John the Baptist and this period ended with the cutting off of Messiah (the Cross.)

For the fulfilment of the whole Prophecy, the 70th week (or final week) has yet to be completed.

It deserves particular emphasis from the outset of these considerations, that every detail and aspect of the Final Week has to be applied to the Jews in the last days.

The beginning of this final week is marked clearly enough, as also is the division of this final week; but in the context of Gabriel's remarks the end of the week is not as clearly defined: (9:27) *And he shall confirm the covenant with many for one week: and in the midst of the week he shall cause the sacrifice and the oblation to cease, and for the overspreading of abominations he shall make it desolate, even until the consummation, and that determined shall be poured upon the desolate.*

The final week (of seven years) commences when the Beast *shall confirm the covenant with many for one week:* the whole week of seven years, is therefore an established time recognised by the Beast, who is in control in Jerusalem. He rules as a gentile but permits their worship. However, *in the midst of the week he shall cause the sacrifice and the oblation to cease, and for the overspreading of abominations he shall make it desolate, even until the consummation, and that determined shall be poured upon the desolate.*

The middle of the week is clearly marked, when the Beast breaks the agreement; there is a period, an interval, in the middle of the week, which is therefore excluded as a fulfilment of the time (i.e. the final seven years) of the prophecy (this period's being out of the will of GOD, is valid and recognisable because the Jewish sacrifices and their worship have ceased.)

The second half of the final week will commence, when the sacrifices and worship resume.

The end of the seventieth week marks the end of Gentile domination of Jerusalem (or more broadly the Jewish nation); which commenced with Nebuchadnezzar and will end after the Beast is destroyed and then the sceptre of world domination passes to the LORD, (Who rules the world from the New Jerusalem.) Whilst the Jews do rule (politically) in Judah (or Israel) at the moment, their worship is prevented because the Temple site (the *only* acceptable place for the Jewish worship to be conducted,) is occupied by the Muslim Shrine, the Dome of the Rock. It would be a considerable concession for the Muslims to permit access to that site for the Jews to offer their sacrifices. This is effectively what will be accomplished by the Beast when he confirms the covenant.

As noted already (in the Introduction, and in the prophecies of Daniel and the Revelation) there are ten *unique references* which link, not only these prophecies; but reveal the actual times, or periods, into which this final week may be divided scripturally. These divisions are described in three distinct ways, as follows:

First of all there are seven *unique references* applying to the halves of the week:

A TIME, TIMES AND HALF (OR DIVIDING OF) A TIME (Two references in Daniel, One in Revelation)

(i) Daniel 7:25 *And he shall speak great words against the MOST HIGH, and shall wear out the saints of the MOST HIGH, and think to change times and laws: and they shall be given into his hand until a time and times and the dividing of time.*

(ii) Daniel 12:7 *And I heard the man clothed in linen, which was upon the waters of the river, when he held up his right hand and his left hand unto heaven, and sware by Him That liveth for ever that it shall be for a time, times, and an half; and when he shall have accomplished to scatter the power of the holy people, all these things shall be finished.*

(iii) Revelation 12:14 *And to the woman were given two wings of a great eagle, that she might fly into the wilderness into her place, where she is nourished for a time, and times, and half a time, from the face of the serpent.*

FORTY AND TWO MONTHS (Two references in Revelation)

(iv) Revelation 11:2 *But the court which is without the Temple leave out, and measure it not; for it is given unto the Gentiles: and the holy city shall they tread under foot forty and two months.*

(v) Revelation 13:5 *And there was given unto him a mouth speaking great things and blasphemies; and power was given unto him to continue forty and two months.*

A THOUSAND TWO HUNDRED AND THREESCORE DAYS (Two references in Revelation)

(vi) Revelation 11:3 *And I will give power unto My two witnesses, and they shall prophesy a thousand two hundred and threescore days, clothed in sackcloth.*

(vii) Revelation 12:6 *And the woman fled into the wilderness, where she hath a place prepared of God, that*

they should feed her there a thousand two hundred and threescore days.

Quite clearly, *A time, times and dividing of a time, forty and two months* and *a thousand two hundred and threescore days* can be accepted and recognised as different descriptions of a period of three and a half years, the first half of the final week of Daniel's 70th week, and, of course, the second half of the final week.

Then there are three other periods from Daniel's prophecy, which evidently from their context (and being measured in *days*) have associations with these same times (applying to the first and second halves of the

final week, and also to the middle of the week) in the last days and these need to be considered here.

(viii) Daniel 8:14 *And he* said unto me, "Unto TWO THOUSAND AND THREE HUNDRED DAYS; then shall the sanctuary be cleansed."* (* from v13 Margin, Hebrew Palmoni = the wonderful numberer.)

(ix) Daniel 12:11 *And from the time that the daily sacrifice shall be taken away, and the abomination that maketh desolate set up, there shall be A THOUSAND TWO HUNDRED AND NINETY DAYS.*

(x) Daniel 12:12 *Blessed is he that waiteth and cometh to THE THOUSAND THREE HUNDRED AND FIVE AND THIRTY DAYS.* (These revelations were given to Daniel by the angel Gabriel; see 9:1, 21; compare 11:1.)

[It deserves notice that the final week, or the seventieth week, is only so called; it is never expressed in terms of *times, months* or *days*; therefore it must necessarily be considered as two halves, distinctly separated by the mid week period. This was established in the words of the angel Gabriel.]

There are seven verses [(i) - (vii)] involved in the three different ways that the three and a half year periods are described; so it is reasonable to split the final week (seven years) into two; then the three different groups are

a time, times & half a time (i) (ii) (iii)

forty and two months (iv) (v)

1260 days (vi) two witnesses (first half of final week) (vii) woman in wilderness (first half of final week)

(viii) 2,300 days *then shall the sanctuary be cleansed* (first half and middle of final week)

(ix) 1,290 days from *the time the daily sacrifice removed and abomination of desolation set up* (first half plus 30 days)

(x) 1,335 days *blessed is he that waiteth and cometh to* (latter part of middle of week, and second half of final week.)

[The inclusion of (viii) (ix) (x) is because quite clearly all these periods (in *days*) can be associated, scripturally.]

1,260 days is 3½ years (of 360 days), or one half of the final (seventieth) week of the prophecy.

Now let us examine and apply **all these periods of *days*,** as follows:

First half of final week 1260 days | Middle of Week | Second half of final week 1260 days

| 2,300 days *then shall the sanctuary be cleansed* necessarily includes middle week. It might be expressed:

|2,300 days = 1,260 + 1040 and therefore, |the middle of the week 1040 days|

|1,290 = 1260 + 30 days for *removal daily sacrifice and setting up abomination*; but this is irrelevant as explained below*.|

75 + |1260 = 1335 days| *blessed is he that waiteth until*

Concerning the final week, *Blessed is he that cometh to the 1,335 days;* so 75 must be added *previous* to the second half of final week (which is obviously the time when blessing is restored.) The "middle of the week days" are therefore *the days that are shortened* (by 75 days,) otherwise the elect would not survive the appointed time 2,300 days, of the Beast's rule.) [See footnote 50, page 143.]

Whoever survives until the commencement of the 1,335 days reaps the benefit of the shortening of the Beast's allotted time; and the Beast (and the false prophet,) are removed before he (they) can totally exterminate the Jews.

[*The period of `1,290 (1,260 + 30) days, does not require inclusion, because for the whole period (2,300 days) the Jews are under the control of the Beast. By virtue of the fact that 75 days are added to the final half week (to make 1335), this confirms that the "blessed period" (is extended backwards into the *end* of the middle of the week,) so what happened at the *beginning* of the middle of the week does not count in the time involved.]

The first half of the final week can be identified from its commencement (Daniel 9:27) *And he* (the Beast) *shall confirm the covenant with many for one week: and in the midst of the week he shall cause the sacrifice and the oblation to cease, and for the overspreading of abominations he shall make it desolate, even until the consummation, and that determined shall be poured upon the desolate.* The week commences with the confirmation of the covenant, the *prince that shall come* (from v26) will have taken the city Jerusalem and the sanctuary and he ratifies, or signs a covenant, (a treaty, or agreement,) which permits the Jewish worship to commence. The same covenant has been previously agreed in principle by other nations, but the beast (and presumably the nations he controls) are preventing its becoming effective; because the beast only needs to confirm his agreement, when it becomes operative, and commences the final week. This is the time when they shall say, "Peace, peace" (between Jews and Arabs or Muslims) (Thessalonians 5:2, 3.)

After serious consideration all the particulars ((viii), (ix) and (x)) given appear to apply to the first half of the week. This is interesting, and raises the question, "Why then is that same period listed in three different measures *times, months and days?* Such definite distinctions must have a purpose, not related to the time involved, which is the same (effectively three and a half years) in each case. It might be observed:

Time, times and dividing of a time. The first description, which would be meaningless to mortal men without the other measures. Quite evidently these measures originate with the *Most High,* or *Him that liveth forever* and most clearly reveal from the outset, concerning the *times* relating to the Beast that the care of the Woman is entirely under the Most High's divine control. This truth must be applied throughout these considerations, for the vile extremes of blasphemy, wickedness and evil manifest in the words and deeds of the man of sin, empowered by Satan will cause many weak believers to seriously doubt whether GOD exists. It is essential to grasp and remember from the outset, that the activities of the man of sin and the False Prophet are for a strictly limited time, divinely ordained. [1040 days in Middle of week less 75 days = 965 days.]

(i) Daniel 7:25 *And he shall speak great words against the MOST HIGH, and shall wear out the saints of the MOST HIGH, and think to change times and laws: and they shall be given into his hand until a time and times and the dividing of time.* The saints of the Most High are believing Jews, and the Beast's extremes of blasphemy and profanity, and his changing *times and laws* (making their ritual offerings very difficult to observe,) quite understandably *wear out the saints.* Their worship is made very difficult, even impossible.

(ii) Daniel 12:7 *And I heard the man clothed in linen, which was upon the waters of the river, when he held up his right hand and his left hand unto heaven, and sware by Him That liveth for ever that it shall be for a time, times, and an half; and when he shall have accomplished to scatter the power of the holy people, all these things shall be finished.* These are the times of the Jewish tribulation, which eventually succeeds in scattering *the power of the holy people*; presumably they will be unable to form any groups to offer resistance or (more importantly,) to worship effectively. As the LORD's teachings revealed concerning these times, this will be a time when the top priority for Jewish men and women is simply to survive.

(iii) Revelation 12:14 *And to the woman were given two wings of a great eagle, that she might fly into the wilderness into her place, where she is nourished for a time, and times, and half a time, from the face of the serpent.* Provision (wings) for her to fly to the wilderness *into her place* confirms the divine care for her.

During this same time, expressed as *Forty and two months*, clearly pointing to the divine control of man; the gentiles are permitted to walk in the holy city for this time. This privilege will not apply to Gentiles once the Kingdom of GOD is established. The Beast will be given power to continue *speaking great things* for the same period, this makes no difference to his overall allotted time.

(iv) Revelation 11:2 *But the court which is without the Temple leave out, and measure it not; for it is given unto the Gentiles: and the holy city shall they tread under foot forty and two months.*

(v) Revelation 13:5 *And there was given unto him a mouth speaking great things and blasphemies; and power was given unto him to continue forty and two months.*

Finally expressed as <u>1,260 days</u> the same period covered in each case, but particularly for His people,

(vi) Revelation 11:3 *And I will give power unto My two witnesses, and they shall prophesy a thousand two hundred and threescore days, clothed in sackcloth.*

(vii) Revelation 12:6 *And the woman fled into the wilderness, where she hath a place prepared of God, that they should feed her there a thousand two hundred and threescore days.*

For GOD's people, for His earthly witnesses, His nation (the Woman) every *day* counts; this is proved by the fact that the beast can only kill the witnesses, when their testimony is finished. (Revelation 11:7) *when they shall have finished their testimony, the beast that ascendeth out of the bottomless pit shall make war against them, and shall overcome them, and kill them.* Their dead bodies are allowed to lie in public for all to see, whilst everyone rejoices at the victory of the beast over these two witnesses; this rejoicing must be part of his triumph. The beast's jubilance over the deaths of the witnesses is short lived and the catastrophic consequences mark the turning point in the fortunes of the Beast (Revelation 11:11-14) *And after three days and an half the spirit of life from God entered into them, and they stood upon their feet; and great fear fell upon them which saw them. And they heard a voice from heaven saying unto them, "Come up hither." And they ascended up to heaven in a cloud; and their enemies beheld them. And in the same hour was there a great earthquake, and the tenth part of the city fell, and in the earthquake were slain of men seven thousand:*

APPENDIX 3 The Final Week (continued)

and the remnant were affrighted, and gave glory to the God of heaven.

Most significantly, *The second woe is past; and, behold, the third woe cometh quickly.* The three woes are associated with the three last trumpets and the last woe is declared (Revelation 12:12) *Woe to the inhabiters of the earth and of the sea! For the devil is come down unto you, having great wrath, because he knoweth that he hath but a short time.* This is in perfect accord with the division of the final week, because the rage

and wrath of the dragon (personally) is directed at the woman

(Israel) who is (iii) *nourished for a time, and times, and half a time, from the face of the serpent.* Satan appreciates that his masterpiece, the Beast (and the False Prophet) have been defeated in his (their) efforts to totally destroy the Jews.

In the middle of the week, after three and a half years therefore, the Beast causes the sacrifice and the oblation to cease, sacrifices and freewill offerings are no longer permitted; breaking the covenant that he confirmed. This immediately stops the week (as a time of GOD's blessing for Israel) because at this time the Beast introduces the Abomination of desolation (his image,) so Israel as an idolatrous nation (hence they become *the desolate,* of Daniel 9:27) are out of the will of GOD. This time refers to the 1290 days, for it takes the beast about a month for *removal daily sacrifice and setting up abomination*; but this is all part of the 2,300 days (when beast is in control.) It does mark the end of *the first half* of the final week of seven years (1260 days), and the beginning of the allotted 1040 days for the middle of the week (totalling 2,300 days).

The first half of the week is when the woman flees into the wilderness (iii) and also the two witnesses testify (vi) (because both are marked by the 1,260 days.) The beast's overcoming the two witnesses (who will have finished their testimony,) probably occurs in the 30 days (at the end of the first half of the week (1,290 days.) This is the time about which the LORD warned His people to get out of Jerusalem in the strongest possible terms; those who refuse to bow the knee to the Abomination will be killed; whilst the woman (vii) is cared for in her wilderness sanctuary.

There are two points to make, *firstly,* it was made clear to Daniel that these revelations were for *The End* (8:17, 19 12:4, 9, 13) and therefore such times are not possible to fully understand until their fulfilment, when to the Jews especially these details will be wonderfully significant. *Secondly,* The End itself can only be seen as the end of the Seventy Weeks and the declaration concerning this (Daniel 9:24) explained: *Seventy Weeks are determined upon thy people and upon thy holy city, to finish the transgression, and to make an end of sins, and to make reconciliation for iniquity, and to bring in everlasting righteousness, and to seal up the vision and prophecy, and to anoint the most Holy.*

These are the days of the most savage and desperate measures taken by the Beast and the False Prophet, to totally destroy the Jews (*spiritually* by idolatry, or *physically* by death) this marks the zenith of the ghastly Tribulation. During this period the "clock" stops, for Israel is out of divine favour, the Beast rules, whilst the faithful, scattered Jews (no longer permitted to make their offerings,) are tested to extreme. To succeed the Beast must win totally; let us remind ourselves the Beast is inspired, backed, guided and empowered by Satan, (this must not be lightly esteemed,) and the False Prophet in this merciless persecution.

The periods of time involved (particularly those measured in *days*, (viii, ix and x; see page 141)

are especially significant; because these eventualities occur during the middle of the week, and extend for a predetermined period until the second half of the week; for these are undoubtedly the days *that will be shortened for the elect's sake*[51]. Clearly from the context of these references, the spiritual fate of mankind (not just the Jews) is in the balance; and undoubtedly given the allotted time, Satan could win; but the LORD over-rules for the elect's sake, in the will of His heavenly Father. [From Job's experience we learn that a divine limit was imposed on Satan, as he tested Job to a ghastly extreme; likewise, in these last days, Satan is not permitted to vent his full

---

[51] Matthew 24:21 *For then shall be great tribulation, such as was not since the beginning of the world to this time, no, nor ever shall be.* 24:22 *And except those days should be shortened, there should no flesh be saved: but for the elect's sake those days shall be shortened.*
Mark 13:19 *For in those days shall be affliction, such as was not from the beginning of the creation which GOD created unto this time, neither shall be.* 13:20 *And except that the LORD had shortened those days, no flesh should be saved; but for the elect's sake, whom He hath chosen, He hath shortened the days.*

power and rage on mankind (and particularly the Jews) beyond a certain divine limit.] But the allotted period, for the shortening of those days, is revealed scripturally. This in fact is 75 days before the actual time of the commencement of the second half of the week, during which the Jewish worship is restored (compare viii and x.)

APPENDIX 4 Scriptural Titles and References to the Beast and the False Prophet

OLD TESTAMENT

Isaiah
14:4   King of Babylon
14:25 The Assyrian
16:4   The Spoiler
       The Extortioner
       (margin = The Wringer)
21:2   The Treacherous Dealer

Jeremiah
25:26 The King of Sheshak One

The Massorah (Hebrew notes made in the text margins of the Old Testament, to explain their writings for subsequent scribes,) reveals that SHESHAK is a simple cipher for Babel; the same as A=Z, B=Y, C=Z etc. Both words occur together in Jeremiah 51:41 which the Massorah confirms.

Ezekiel
38:2   Gog (chief prince of Meshech and Tubal)

Daniel
7:8   The little horn
7:11   The horn
8:9   The little horn
8:43   The king of fierce countenance
9:26   The prince that shall come
11:3   A mighty king
11:21 The vile person
11:31 The abomination of desolation

NEW TESTAMENT

Matthew
24:15 The abomination of desolation

Mark
13:14 The abomination of desolation

2 Thessalonians
2:3   The man of sin
      The son of perdition
2:8   That Wicked (One) or, Lawless One

The Revelation
11:7 The Beast (the only title he is given in Revelation, also chapters 13:1, 2, 3, 4 etc. 17:3, 7, 8, 11, 13, 16, 17. 19:19, 20 and 20:10.)

THE FALSE PROPHET

John
5:43 Another shall come in his own name

2 Thessalonians
2:8 That Wicked (= lawless) One

1 John
4:3 The Antichrist (see next page)

The Revelation
13:11   Another beast

11:36	The wilful king	16:13 the False Prophet
		19:20 the False Prophet
Micah		20:10 the False Prophet
2:13	The breaker	

Zechariah
11:17 The idol shepherd

The Antichrist – The actual name antichrist is a transliteration (*Greek antichristos*) meaning an opponent of Christ, and it is found only in John's first and second epistles (five times as indicated in bold.)

1 John 2:18 *Little children, it is the last time: and as ye have heard that **antichrist** shall come, even now are there many **antichrists**; whereby we know that it is the last time.* In this first mention of the antichrist(s), it is revealed that their appearance (as *many*) is a sure sign of the last time. 2:22 *Who is a liar but he that denieth that Jesus is the Christ? He is **antichrist**, that denieth the Father and the Son.* This identifies the antichrist (whoever it is) he not only denies Christ the Son, but the Father also. 4:3 *And every spirit that confesseth not that Jesus Christ is come in the flesh is not of GOD; and this is that (spirit) of **antichrist**, whereof ye have heard that it should come; and even now already is it in the world.* 2 John 7 *For many deceivers are entered into the world, and confess not that Jesus Christ is come in the flesh. This is a deceiver and an **antichrist**.*

As the references show, the word antichrist applies in several ways: particularly, to the Beast himself, (who, in his extremes of blasphemy will deny the Father and the Son without any doubt,) and individually, to those who openly oppose Christ, or to those who deny Him and His Father; and (as Dr Bullinger noted *Companion Bible* Daniel 7:8 margin) collectively, there are twelve named "antichrists", whose opposition was manifest in different ways. In their scriptural order these are:

1 *The King of Babylon* (Isaiah 14:4). 2 *Lucifer son of the morning* (Isaiah 14:12). [In contrast to Jesus, *the Bright and Morning Star* Revelation 22:16.] 3 *The Assyrian* (Isaiah 14:25). 4 *The little horn* (Daniel 7:8). 5 *The King of fierce countenance* (Daniel 8:23). 6 *The Prince that shall come* (Daniel 9:26). 7 *The vile person* (Daniel 11:21). 8 *The wilful king* (Daniel 11:36). 9 *The man of sin* (2 Thessalonians 2:3). 10 *The son of perdition* (2 Thessalonians 2:3). 11 *That wicked (or lawless) one* (2 Thessalonians 2:8). 12 *The beast with ten horns* (Revelation 13:1). It can be recognised that Satan's involvement with these antichrists is manifest consistently (as 1 the King of Babylon, 2 Lucifer, 3 the Assyrian.) Also as the various titles of the Beast (applying to him and Satan) 1, 4, 5, 6, 7, 8, 9, 10, and 12. (10, 11 *The son of perdition* and *That wicked (or lawless) one* are more likely to be The False Prophet.)

APPENDIX 5 The Scriptural Gospels

In general terms the gospels refer to the New Testament records of the life and ministry of the Lord Jesus Christ (Matthew, Mark Luke & John) but scripturally, the word gospel (which means "good news") applies to five distinct and divinely ordained ministries.

These are:

The Everlasting Gospel

The Kingdom Gospel

The Gospel of God

The Gospel of the Grace of God

The Glorious Gospel of Christ

THE EVERLASTING GOSPEL

Scripturally this is the First and in point of fact also, the Last, Gospel. It was proclaimed immediately after Adam's fall, among its heralds were Enoch and Noah (see Hebrews 11:7,

2 Peter 2:5 and Jude 14, 15.)

Its message basically is that GOD the Creator of All is to be feared and that men are to have no other gods in their lives, only Him. He alone, is the Holy and Righteous GOD and He is the ultimate Judge of all mankind (this judgment GOD has delegated to His Son, Who as the Son of man, will judge mankind in His divine power.) This gospel will be proclaimed again (Revelation 14:6, 7) making it the first and last gospel to mankind, before GOD's eternal kingdom is established and men will be called again to "Fear God and give glory to Him". Hence its name Everlasting, for this is the eternal, everlasting gospel.

THE KINGDOM GOSPEL

The second of the scriptural gospels, The Kingdom Gospel was originally proclaimed to Abraham and his seed (Genesis 12:1-3); the heir to this kingdom (The Messiah) was announced later (Genesis 15:4 and Galatians 3:16.) The throne of David was promised to his seed forever, by yet another unconditional promise (2 Samuel 7:12, 13) and The Messiah came to fulfil this, but was rejected (John 1:11.)

The gospel given to Abraham was thus expanded gradually, until eventually, in its fulness, it was proclaimed by Angels sent especially from heaven, who pronounced its terms (Luke 2:10, 11) Their good news concerned a Saviour, a Person, Who would save His people from their sin (see also Matthew 1:21.)

In the LORD's Own proclamation of the good news of the Kingdom, He used parables, because it involves mysteries, which were foreseen (Luke 24:26.) These mysteries, as the parables prove and reveal, concern the rejection of The Messiah by His people and the subsequent postponement of the establishment of the Kingdom that He was intended to rule. The Jewish rejection of John the baptist and the LORD Himself (who were both prophets preaching the Kingdom Gospel[52]) did not alter God's intention (Acts 2:30) and Peter followed their ministries (Acts 3:17-26) by continuing to preach the Gospel of God (see below.)

---

[52] The Kingdom Gospel preached by John the baptist, and the LORD Himself, and also the Gospel of God, apply to the Kingdom of Heaven. This has to be distinguished from the Kingdom of God, for these are scripturally different and separate kingdoms.

The LORD's Sermon on the Mount (Matthew 5, 6 &7) is a discourse associated with the proclamation of the Gospel of the Kingdom of Heaven and has to be applied with respect to the establishment of that Kingdom (when He rules with a rod of iron.)

The Kingdom of Heaven proclaimed in this gospel is established by force, (Matthew 11:11-13) *Verily I say unto you, Among them that are born of women there hath not risen a greater than John the Baptist: notwithstanding he that is least in the kingdom of heaven is greater than he. And from the days of John the Baptist until now the kingdom of heaven suffereth violence, and the violent take it by force. For all the prophets and the law prophesied until John.* This will be the time when evil is rooted out (Matthew 3:7) *But when he saw many of the Pharisees and Sadducees come to his baptism, he said unto them, "O generation of vipers, who hath warned you to flee from the wrath to come?"* (Matthew 3:10-12) *"And now also the axe is laid unto the root of the trees: therefore every tree which bringeth not forth good fruit is hewn down, and cast into the fire. I indeed baptise you with water unto repentance: but He that cometh after me is mightier than I, Whose shoes I am not worthy to bear: He shall baptize you with the Holy Ghost, and with fire: Whose fan is in His hand, and He will thoroughly purge His floor, and gather His wheat into the garner; but He will burn up the chaff with unquenchable fire."*

This Kingdom of Heaven is established by force and ruled with a rod of iron.

In the Jewish rejection of the King, the Kingdom that He will rule is in abeyance. The sermon was given in Matthew's account before the calling of the disciples (Matthew 9:9) but the portions from it quoted by Luke (who uses only about 30 verses, of 107 recorded in Matthew) confirm that He recognised that most of it was no longer relevant because He had been rejected. It is a blunder to attempt to rigidly apply the teachings of His sermon on the mount to this dispensation of grace, not evidence of spiritual understanding.

The LORD's parable teachings are particularly significant in respect of the rejection of the Kingdom Gospel (see The Sower, Matthew 13:3-23. The Marriage Feast, Matthew 22:1-14. The Great Supper, Luke 14:15-24.)

THE KINGDOM OF HEAVEN

This was proclaimed within the ministries of the Gospel of the Kingdom and the Gospel of God; which, had these been accepted, would have resulted in the establishment of the Kingdom of Heaven on earth (in contrast to the Kingdom of God following.) The particular features of the Kingdom of heaven might be summarised:

1 Messiah is King (ruling with a rod of iron.)

2 It is established and situated on earth, therefore it has inherent limitations even though it lasts for a very long time.

3 It is Jewish in character (as the natural seed of Abraham)

4 It was prophesied in the Old Testament.

5 It is dispensational, of limited duration.

THE KINGDOM OF GOD

The Kingdom of God was also preached by the LORD Himself (Luke 8:1-3) and is far more extensive, its features are:

1   GOD is ruler

2   Heaven is its location

3   Unlimited in its character, it involves spiritual and moral characteristics

4   It includes the natural seed (The Jews) and the spiritual seed (The

Church) of Abraham

5   Particularly revealed in the New Testament

6   Eternal, of unlimited duration

Distinguishing between these two kingdoms considerably helps scriptural understanding and from the features noted it should be possible to instantly identify either.

THE GOSPEL OF GOD

Following the LORD's crucifixion and His resurrection, in His great mercy God gave His people opportunity to repent and accept His Son and this was effectively offered in The Gospel of God, first proclaimed by Peter (Acts 3:17-26.) The apostles continued to preach this same gospel and were given divine support in their ministries from the miracles (the power evident in the Kingdom Gospel ministry of the LORD Jesus Christ, but not in the ministry of John the baptist - John 10:41. See also Hebrews 2:1-4.)

The Gospel of God was ministered with the intention of giving the Jewish nation a chance to repent and accept and believe in The Risen Lord. This ministry was brought to its conclusion when that generation consistently rejected this offer and the consequences of this were recognised by the apostle Paul, who knew that the salvation of God would then be offered freely to the gentiles.

The Kingdom of Heaven (which should have been established through the Kingdom Gospel, or The Gospel of GOD,) is postponed (Hebrews 2:8) *"but NOW we see NOT YET all things put under Him."* The Gospel of GOD was preached throughout the period covered by the Acts of the Apostles and had it been accepted by that generation, it would have resulted in the LORD's immediate return to establish His Kingdom. (See Acts 2:23-36, 3:12-18, 4:33, 5:29-32, 10:34-43 & 13:23-41. It is quite clear, see 3:10-26 especially v10, that the Lord would have been sent to the Jews, if they had accepted this ministry.)

THE GOSPEL OF THE GRACE OF GOD

The apostle Paul recognised in their rejection of the Gospel of GOD that the Jews had effectively opened the door for the gentiles. He revealed, what had been committed quite specifically to him, the *mystery kept secret since the world began*, The Gospel of The Grace of GOD, "my gospel" as Paul referred to it. (See Acts 28:25-28 Romans 2:16 & 16:25.) It is this Gospel of the Grace of GOD that is the subject of Paul's prison epistles (Ephesians, Philippians and Colossians;) and it is entirely in this Gospel of the Grace of GOD that the Gentile Church is made the BODY (not the Bride) of Christ.

The mystery was not (as is generally supposed) that the gentiles would be blessed (this was revealed to Abraham, Genesis 22:18 and see also Isaiah 6:9,10 which clearly prophesied the blindness of Israel and Paul showed that this was the means by which the gentiles would be enabled to see - Acts 28:25-28.) The mystery was in the duration, or the time, of this blindness to Israel and this period is effectively "the times of the gentiles" (see Romans 11 especially v25.)

The LORD Himself recognised this offer to the gentiles (see John 10:16,) and in fact gave Peter the first chance to preach this message (John 21:15-17.) This was totally confirmed subsequently by Peter's remarkable vision (Acts 10:9-18) in which case it is noted that *"Peter doubted in himself what this vision which he had seen should mean"*. Although in this instance Peter's experience did result in the conversion of Cornelius, Peter never fully realised the potential of this ministry; a fact which Paul later confirmed beyond all doubt (Galatians 2:7,8.) It is wonderful to recognise that GOD had clearly anticipated Peter's failure in this respect and in spite of the vision given to Peter (which he evidently doubted, a fatal mistake on his part,) GOD had already provided for this lack in the apostle, by converting the most unlikely candidate of all the Jews, to become the apostle to the gentiles (Acts 9) the zealous Saul of Tarsus.

The point has to be made however, that for most of his ministry as recorded in Acts, Paul preached the Gospel of GOD, to the Jew first.

It was only when Paul finally acknowledged the Jewish rejection of this, that he turned his ministry exclusively to the gentiles.. There are two occasions (Acts 18:1-6 & 19:8-12) when Paul, frustrated by Jewish rejection in their synagogues, preached to the gentiles. But these were isolated incidents, through local opposition and in each case (18:19ff & 19:10) Paul resumed his ministry by preaching to the Jews and ultimately came to trial in Jerusalem for this work. These two exceptions reveal Paul's superb stewardship in containing what had been committed to him, until the Jewish rejection was final; then Paul revealed this wonderful Gospel of The Grace of GOD. It was most probably at this time too that he added his postscript to his Roman epistle (16:25-27) which he had written originally for believing Jews (Hellenists) in Rome.

THE GLORIOUS GOSPEL OF CHRIST

The Glorious Gospel of Christ (mentioned by Paul, see 2 Corinthians 4:4) particularly refers to the LORD Jesus Christ's exaltation over all things, as The Head of His Church (His Body.) (See also Ephesians 1:21-23 Philippians 2:9-11 Colossians 1:14-19).

His exaltation also includes the ultimate defeat of Satan and the total overthrow of all spiritual powers, forces and beings who oppose GOD. This was foretold from the beginning (Genesis 3:16) and its fulfilment is also prophesied (Revelation 20.) His Church, as His Body, shares this wonderful experience with Him.

APPENDIX 6 ARMAGEDDON

The name Armageddon occurs only once (Revelation 16:16) in scripture as a Greek transliteration of two Hebrew words, HAR = mountain/ height/range, and MEGIDDO = gathering/company/ assembly/rendezvous/ slaughter. But the name Armageddon needs to be considered in three respects to understand what is involved, Geographically, Scripturally and Prophetically (which is how the word is used in Revelation. See also Figure 6.)

Geographically

The vale/valley/plain of Megiddo (whence comes the name Armageddon = heights of Meggido) commences on Israel's coast at the exit of the river Kishon into the Mediterranean. The Kishon and its tributaries flow across the plain of Acco, which is immediately north of Mount Carmel, the familiar and only hook shaped promontory on the coastline, just south of the border of Lebanon. The main port Haifa is built on Mount Carmel. Moving eastward, the valley is marked on maps as "the vale/valley/plain of Megiddo or Esdraelon" Esdraelon is not a scriptural name, but was the name given to this portion of the plain/valley in the Apocryphal book of Judith (3:9.) its meaning is uncertain. The principal town is Meggido, scripturally. The eastern third or so of the valley drains into the Jordan and its streams, rivers are not named in scripture, this is called the valley/vale of Jezreel and is named after its principal town. The eastern extremity on the Jordan itself is Beth Shan.

If Armageddon needs to be located accurately, its name would apply to a height slightly east of the town Meggido, (Hebrew = Ar-Meggidon = city of Megiddo) which is roughly central to the whole valley range. The valley separates Galilee from Samaria and it lies just south of Nazareth, where the LORD Himself was brought up. Its total length is approximately 25 miles (40 Kilometres.) Jerusalem is about

35 miles due south of Megiddo. About 5 miles north east of Megiddo is Mount Tabor, not mentioned by name in the New Testament, but traditionally the Mount of the Transfiguration. It was also the place at which Deborah and Barak gathered their forces (Judges 4, 5 see below.)

South of the valley of Megiddo lie the central highlands, and near Shechem (about 15 miles from Megiddo) lie Mount Ebal and Mount Gerizim both of which were regarded as sacred by the Israelites, as the mounts of cursing and blessing when they entered Canaan. The founding of the temple in Jerusalem overshadowed the traditional respect for these mountains, but the Samaritans continued to regard them as sacred, building their temple on mount Gerizim. It was to the woman of the city of Samaria (about 2 miles north of these mountains,) that the LORD spoke when she questioned Him about these rival claims for places of' worship.

Scripturally

Various places along the valleys of Megiddo and Jezreel have considerable scriptural importance and these are considered in their geographical order (west to east) rather than chronological.

Mount Carmel (= vineyard of GOD,) is famous as the place on which Elijah made his spectacular debut, confounding the 400 prophets of Baal when the searing blast of heavenly fire consumed Elijah's drenched offering. The mount itself begins to rise about 10 miles inland on the plain of Esdraelon/Megiddo until it reaches its height on the coastline. A place is still called Mukrakah (= place of burning) which is the traditional location of Elijah's sacrifice, a perennial well in close proximity would have supplied the water required to saturate Elijah's offering, in spite of three years drought (1 Kings 18:19-40).

The plain/valley of Esdraelon/Megiddo drains into the Mediterranean through the Kishon and its streams, which flow out across the plain of Accro immediately north of Carmel. A flash flood turned this whole area into a quagmire *"that discomforted Sisera and all his chariots and all his hosts"*, (Judges 4 & 5 especially 4:15) when his army and chariots were routed under the hands of Deborah and Barak. The details of their destruction are implied in the song of Deborah and Barak, but if any should doubt the possibility of such destruction, from what are normally reasonably small rivers, any good library will furnish evidence of the terrible power of flash floods in world wide localities, but they are already becoming fairly common.

The valley of Jezreel (its eastern end drains into the Jordan,) was the location of the hosts of the Midianites and Amalekites (Judges 6 -8) whom Gideon overcame in the strength of the LORD, Who had reduced Gideon's original force to three hundred men.

The city of Jezreel (a city means a walled town in scripture) became the dwelling place of Ahab and Jezebel, where she eventually was slain, and it was to Jezreel that Elijah ran, (from Mount Carmel,) in the power of The Spirit, in advance of Ahab's chariot. It was Naboth's vineyard in Jezreel that Ahab coveted

(1 Kings 18:46, 21:1-24. 2 Kings 9:30-37.) In the valley of Jezreel the good king Josiah died in battle against Pharaoh Necho, who in his defence warned Josiah not to get involved in the fighting (2 Kings 23:29. 2 Chronicles 35:20-24.)

The valley of Jezreel was never totally conquered by the Israelites and the Canaanites and later the Philistines, maintained their hold (Judges 1:27). Beth Shan (= house of rest) was a city of Manasseh even though it was west of the Jordan (Joshua 17:11-16). In the days of Saul it was the Philistines who hung Saul's body on the wall of Beth Shan (1 Samuel 31:7-10)

Prophetically

The name Jezreel is a homonym, it has two meanings: "GOD scatters" or "GOD sows", and both meanings need to be considered in the use of the name. Jezreel features in the prophecy of Hosea (1:4, 5&11 2:22, 23 and compare Jeremiah 24:6 31:28 & 32:41 and also Amos 9:15.) From Hosea's prophecy, Jezreel is the place in which first, GOD judges His people Israel, or *"breaks the bow of Israel"* ie the power or army; and then scatters them or sows them among other nations. But, in His final mercy Israel will be sown, or sown again, in her own land.

The name Armageddon is found only in Revelation (16:16) which is prophecy, but it must be seen in its total context.

Revelation 16:12-16

"And the sixth angel poured out his vial upon the great river Euphrates; and the water thereof was dried up, that the way of the kings of the east might be prepared. And I saw three unclean spirits like frogs come out of the mouth of the dragon, and out of the mouth of the beast, and out of the mouth of the false prophet. For they are the spirits of devils, working miracles, which go forth unto the kings of the earth and of the whole world, to gather them to the battle of that great day of GOD ALMIGHTY. Behold, I come as a thief. Blessed is he that watcheth, and keepeth his garments, lest he walk naked, and they see his shame. And he gathered them together into a place called in the Hebrew tongue Armageddon."

Armageddon is referred to in the context of the outpouring of the sixth vial [182] of the seven last plagues, *"in them is filled up the wrath of GOD"* (1 5: 1) [176-183]

Nowhere in scripture does it declare that this is a final mighty conflict between nations in a war that totally destroys the world; although this is a generally accepted view of what Armageddon means. (There is no need at all to pursue the ridiculous themes or situations, which are given an "Armageddon" label, in science fiction or film fantasy; these are too absurd for words.)

Armageddon is a place, probably encompassing the whole valley from Carmel to Beth Shan (quite possibly visible from the "height of Meggido, a mountain top near the town,) but it is the rendezvous for the gathering of the nations, who *"are called to the battle of the great day of GOD ALMIGHTY."*

To appreciate what is involved, the scriptures have to be rightly divided - and the seven vials were the fruits of the world, which had been reaped by the Son of man (Revelation 14:14-20)

"And 1 looked, and behold a white cloud, and upon the cloud one sat like unto the Son of man, having on His head a golden crown, and in His hand a sharp sickle. And another angel came out of the temple, crying with a loud voice to Him that sat on the cloud, 'Thrust In Thy sickle, and reap: for the time is come for Thee to reap; for the harvest of the earth is ripe.' And He that sat on the cloud thrust in His sickle on the earth; and the earth was reaped. And another angel came out of the temple which is in heaven, he also having a sharp sickle. And another angel came out from the altar, which had power over fire; and cried with a loud cry to him that had the sharp sickle, saying, "Thrust in thy sharp sickle, and gather the clusters of the vine of the earth; for her grapes are fully ripe.' And the angel thrust in his sickle into the earth, and gathered the vine of the earth, and cast it into the great winepress of the wrath of GOD. And the winepress was trodden without the city, and blood came out of the winepress, even unto the horse bridles, by the space of a thousand and six hundred furlongs."

After which come the seven vials, which it is explained, *"in them is filled up the wrath of GOD"*. The events concerning these vials (and the sixth vial involves the gathering of the armies of the nations,) are described, including the fall of Babylon, and the announcement of the marriage of The Lamb (19:7). Then John takes up the theme involving the winepress of the wrath of GOD. Note the full context in which this appears (Revelation 19:11-21) *"And I saw heaven opened, and behold a white horse; and He that sat upon him was called Faithful and True, and in righteousness He doth judge and make war. His eyes were as a flame of fire, and on His head were many crowns; and He had a name written, that no man knew, but He Himself. And He was clothed in a vesture dipped in blood: and His name is called The Word of GOD. And the armies which were in heaven followed Him upon white horses, clothed in fine linen, white and clean. And out of His mouth goeth a sharp sword, that with it He should smite the nations: and He shall rule them with a rod of iron: and He treadeth the winepress of the fierceness and wrath of ALMIGHTY GOD. And He hath on His vesture and on His thigh a name written, KING OF KINGS, AND LORD OF LORDS. And I saw an angel standing in the sun; and he cried with a loud voice, saying to all the fowls that fly in the midst of heaven, 'Come and gather yourselves together unto the supper of the great GOD; that ye may eat the flesh of kings, and the flesh of captains, and the flesh of mighty men, and the flesh of horses, and of them that sit on them, and the flesh of all men, both free and bond, both small and great.' And I saw the beast, and the kings of the earth, and their armies, gathered together to make war against Him that sat on the horse, and against His army. And the beast was taken, and with him the false prophet that wrought miracles before him, with which he deceived them that had received the mark of the beast, and them that worshipped his image. These both were cast alive into a lake of fire burning with brimstone. And the remnant were slain with the sword of Him that sat upon the horse, which sword proceeded out of His mouth: and all the fowls were filled with their flesh."*

The rulers have been deceived by the unclean spirits, they have not gathered to fight The LORD but to wipe out Jerusalem and the Jews but in the outpouring of the wrath of GOD, the world reaps their reward for the fruits of their ways, their ungodliness.

Other scriptures apply to this time (Zechariah 14, see also Ezekiel 38, 39) for prophecies can have more than one fulfilment or application.

Armageddon is not the end of the world, it is deliverance for His people and the beginning of His rule over all nations and it marks the commencement of *"the great day of GOD Almighty."*

Appendix 7 DANIEL'S SUPPLICATIONS and The Persian Kings

INTRODUCTION: The Persian Kings are a neglected feature of last days' studies and after some deliberation, it was decided to add an additional appendix to cover this aspect of Bible prophecy, as a separate issue, in the context of Daniel's Supplications (9,) and Daniel's Vision (10 -12, especially 11:1, 2.)

Daniel's prayer and supplications to the LORD were his response to what he had learned from what the LORD had given the prophet Jeremiah (who was in Jerusalem,) when Daniel was in Babylon, or possibly Shushan, in captivity.

9:1, 2 *In the first year of Darius the son of Ahasuerus, of the seed of the Medes, which was made king over the realm of the Chaldeans; in the first year of his reign I Daniel understood by books the number of the years, whereof the word of the Lord came to Jeremiah the prophet, that He would accomplish seventy years in the desolations of Jerusalem.*

9:3-15 *And I set my face unto the Lord God, to seek by prayer and supplications, with fasting, and sackcloth, and ashes: and I prayed unto the Lord my God, and made my confession, and said, "O Lord, the great and dreadful God, keeping the covenant and mercy to them that love Him, and to them that keep His commandments; we have sinned, and have committed iniquity, and have done wickedly, and have rebelled, even by departing from Thy precepts and from Thy judgments: Neither have we hearkened unto Thy servants the prophets, which spake in Thy name to our kings, our princes, and our fathers, and to all the people of the land. O Lord, righteousness (belongeth) unto Thee but unto us confusion of faces, as at this day; to the men of Judah, and to the inhabitants of Jerusalem, and unto all Israel, (that are) near, and that are far off, through all the countries whither Thou hast driven them, because of their trespass that they have trespassed against Thee. O Lord, to us (belongeth) confusion of* face, to our kings, to our princes, and to our fathers, because we have sinned against Thee. To the Lord our God belong mercies and forgivenesses, though we have rebelled against Him; neither have we obeyed the voice of the Lord our God, to walk in His laws, which He set before us by His servants the prophets. Yea, all Israel have transgressed Thy law, even by departing, that they might not obey Thy voice; therefore the curse is poured upon us, and the oath that is written in the law of Moses the servant of God, because we have sinned against Him. And He hath confirmed His words, which He spake against us, and against our judges that judged us, by bringing upon us a great evil: for under the whole heaven hath not been done as hath been done upon Jerusalem. As (it is) written in the law of Moses, all this evil is come upon us: yet made we not our prayer before the Lord our God, that we might turn from our iniquities, and understand Thy truth. Therefore hath the Lord watched upon the evil, and brought it upon us: for the Lord our God is righteous in all His works which He doeth: for we obeyed not His voice. And now, O Lord our God, that hast brought Thy people forth out of the land of Egypt with a mighty hand, and hast gotten Thee renown, as at this day; we have sinned, we have done wickedly.

9:16-19 O Lord, according to all Thy righteousness, I beseech Thee, let Thine anger and Thy fury be turned away from Thy city Jerusalem, Thy holy mountain: because for our sins, and for the iniquities of our fathers, Jerusalem and Thy people (are become) a reproach to all (that are) about us. Now therefore, O our God, hear the prayer of Thy servant, and his supplications, and cause Thy face to shine upon Thy sanctuary that is desolate, for the Lord's sake. O my God, incline Thine ear, and hear; open Thine eyes, and behold our desolations, and the city which is called by Thy name: for we do not present our supplications before Thee for our righteousnesses, but for Thy great mercies. O Lord, hear; O Lord, forgive; O Lord, hearken and do; defer not, for Thine Own sake, O my God: for Thy city and Thy people are called by Thy name."

9:20-27 And whiles I (was) speaking, and praying, and confessing my *sin and the sin of my people Israel, and presenting my supplication before the Lord my God for the holy mountain of my God; Yea, whiles I (was) speaking in prayer, even the man Gabriel, whom I had seen in the vision at the beginning, being caused to fly swiftly, touched me about the time of the evening oblation. And he informed (me,) and talked with me, and said, "O Daniel, I am now come forth to give thee skill and understanding. At the beginning of thy supplications the commandment came forth, and I am come to shew (thee;) for thou (art) greatly beloved: therefore understand the matter, and consider the vision. Seventy weeks are determined upon thy people, and upon thy holy city, to finish the transgression, and to make an end of sins, and to make reconciliation for iniquity, and to bring in everlasting righteousness, and to seal up the vision and prophecy, and to anoint the most Holy. Know therefore and understand, (that) from the going forth of the commandment to restore and to build Jerusalem unto the Messiah the Prince (shall be) seven weeks, and threescore and two weeks: the street shall be built again, and the wall, even in troublous times. And after threescore and two weeks shall Messiah be cut off, but not for Himself: and the people of the prince that shall come shall destroy the city and the sanctuary; and the end thereof (shall be) with a flood, and unto the end of the war desolations are determined. And he shall confirm the covenant with many for one week: and in the midst of the week he shall cause the sacrifice and the oblation to cease, and for the overspreading of abominations he shall make (it) desolate, even until the consummation, and that determined shall be poured upon the desolate."*

In this remarkably succinct account of Daniel's supplication (in English translation the whole account totals 971words, of which the reply given to Daniel amounts to 239 words;) it was explained to Daniel what the seventy years in the desolations of Jerusalem involved; and *the man Gabriel* referred to the whole time involved in periods of a total of seventy weeks (each week comprising seven years.) This whole passage has been brilliantly examined and explained by Sir Robert Anderson, whose scholarship and research were remarkably vindicated as he explained in his book *The Coming*

Prince[53]; in which he proved the literal fulfilment of the first sixty nine weeks (of seven years each) of this prophecy. To explain it briefly:

Essentially, the starting date of the seventy weeks (490 years in total,) was calculated from Nehemiah 2:1 *the twentieth year of Artaxerxes,* from which Sir Robert Anderson proved that the commandment to rebuild Jerusalem was fulfilled in the Jewish month Nisan, (14th March) of the year BC 445. This marked the commencement of the epoch of the seventy weeks. On 10th Nisan in AD 32 Christ's entry into Jerusalem took place (6th April AD 32.) The intervening period was a total of 476 years and 24 days:

Then,

476×365 = 173,740 days

Add 14th March to 6th April both dates inclusive = 24 days

Add for Leap Years = 116 day

———

173,880

And 69 weeks of prophetic years of 360 days (69 X 7 X 360) = 173,880

[For the full presentation of Sir Robert Anderson's calculations see *The Coming Prince,* Chapter 10 page 128 footnote.]

This leaves the seventieth week of Daniel's revelation on Jeremiah's prophecy yet to be fulfilled, the prophetic "clock" having stopped at the cutting off of Messiah (AD 32.) There is as Sir Robert Anderson clearly showed a scriptural precedent and explanation for this

---

[53] *The Coming Prince* by Sir Robert Anderson, was first published in 1881, and is still in print after 15 new editions and countless reprints.

feature of prophecy. Scripturally, Solomon began to build the temple in the 480th year after the children of Israel were come out of the land of Egypt[54]; this verse has been seriously challenged and dismissed by chronologers and professors and students of Bible prophecy. This appears to contradict other scriptures, most notably Paul's sermon at Antioch[55]. Paul's figures were: 40 years in the wilderness, 450 years under the Judges, 40 years reign of Saul, 40 years for David's reign, and the first 3 years of Solomon's reign (40 + 450 + 40 + 40 + 3 = 573 years.) Clearly the accounts differ, and the problem is how to reconcile them scripturally. During the times of the Judges, there were five periods in which as punishment for their idolatry, the nation Israel were put under bondage to various nations. The Israelites were slaves to the king of Mesopotamia (8 years), to the king of Moab (18 years), to the king of Canaan (20 years), to the Midianites (7 years) and to the Philistines (40 Years.) 8 + 18 + 20 + 7 + 40 = 93 years total; if this is deducted from 573, the remainder is 480 years. The important thing is that Paul's figures were not challenged in the slightest, which shows that the Jews themselves regarded the times of their captivity under their Judges, as outside the will of GOD *and* the context of prophecy. It is therefore quite admissible to apply the same principle to a prophetic era such as the seventy weeks.

Again from Daniel's interpretation of the dream of Nebuchadnezzar, (Daniel 2) it was prophesied that a succession of four Gentile Empires (Babylonian, Persian, Greek and Roman,) would have dominion over Jerusalem during what is called the *Times of the Gentiles*; and within

---

[54] 1 Kings 6:1 *And it came to pass in the four hundred and eightieth year after the children of Israel were come out of the land of Egypt, in the fourth year of Solomon's reign over Israel, in the month Zif (= May) which is the second month, that he began to build the house of the LORD.*

[55] Acts 13:16-21 *Then Paul stood up, and beckoning with (his) hand said, "Men of Israel, and ye that fear GOD, give audience. The GOD of this people of Israel chose our fathers, and exalted the people when they dwelt as strangers in the land of Egypt, and with an high arm brought He them out of it. And about the time of forty years suffered He their manners in the wilderness. And when He had destroyed seven nations in the land of Canaan, He divided their land to them by lot. And after that He (gave unto) them judges about the space of four hundred and fifty years, until Samuel the prophet."*

this dispensation, the Jews lost their Temple and land and thereby their status as a nation, when in their rebellion they were expelled by the Romans (from AD 70 until fairly recently 1945.) Now more importantly, they cannot conduct their worship in Jerusalem, because the Jewish Temple site (which is the only divinely permissible place for Jews to offer sacrifices,) is at present occupied by the Muslim Shrine, the Dome of the Rock.

[Realistically, it is possibly the existence of this Muslim Shrine, which has prevented the rocket bombardment of Jerusalem by extremist Muslim groups (or even Saddam Hussein,) who would be in real trouble themselves if they damaged or destroyed the Dome of the Rock; for the Jews would seriously challenge their right to rebuild it.]

Discussing the replacement of the Dome of the Rock with a Jewish Temple is unrealistic, and even unnecessary; a concession allowing Jewish access to the site to make their sacrifices or offerings on an altar would be all that was required and such a prospect might even be negotiable with a man having the power of the Beast; the Jews would of course be expected to make equivalent concessions. This is only a suggestion; there are endless situations for such eventualities to become possibilities.

These things have all been discussed at length (in *The End* study,) but there is one aspect of these last days' prophecies, which deserves more attention, for it is very seldom discussed or mentioned. In Daniel's final vision (Daniel 10-12) the hierophant (heavenly messenger,) included the following prophetical facts:

Daniel 11:2 *"And now will I shew thee the truth. Behold, there shall stand up yet three kings in Persia; and the fourth shall be far richer than (they) all: and by his strength through his riches he shall stir up all against the realm of Grecia."* Our purpose is to consider these four kings, to see what significance they had in the history (or prophecies,) concerning Judah (particularly during the period of the Seventy Weeks.)

First, it needs to be appreciated that what is termed *the (Jewish) Captivity in Babylon,* was not a simple straightforward event, but actually involved three successive (and increasingly severe) seventy year terms of judgment called (in succession,) *the Servitude, the Captivity,* and finally *the Desolations.* The Jews were initially warned to accept the conquest of Jerusalem by Nebuchadnezzar, and to accept their punishment of seventy years *Servitude* to Babylon (whilst the Jews remained in their own land under his dominion.) Nebuchadnezzar captured the city BC 606, and took Daniel and his companions captive, but the king Jehoiakim regained his liberty by swearing his allegiance to Babylon, and Nebuchadnezzar withdrew, taking some of the holy vessels as spoil, which he put in the temple of his gods in Babylon. Three years later Jehoiakim foolishly revolted, but it was another five years before the Babylonians under Nebuchadnezzar could return (they were conducting wars elsewhere) to reinstate his authority and exact his revenge on Jehoiakim for breaking his pledge. Jehoiakim had been taken captive (by Pharaoh Necho, on his return journey to Egypt after his defeat at Carchemish by Nebuchadnezzar) and Necho had replaced Jehoiakim with Jehoiachin. Nebuchadnezzar also took Jehoiachin captive to Babylon, (with Ezekiel and Mordecai and Esther,) leaving Nebuchadnezzar's choice of Zedekiah as King in Jerusalem.

THE SERVITUDE (70 Years)

Dates: From BC 605 (3rd year of Jehoiakim, 1st year of Nebuchadnezzar)

To BC 535 (Decree of Cyrus[56])

Scripture References: 2 Kings 24:1 Jeremiah 27:6, 8 & 11. Daniel 1:1, 2

---

[56] Under the decree of Cyrus, (BC 536) the Jews returned to Jerusalem, immediately set up their altar (Ezra 3:3, 6). They did lay the foundation of the temple (Ezra 3:8–11) but were unable to continue to build and the foundation had to be re-laid (Haggai 2:10-18 in BC 520) this delayed by sixteen years the commencement of the Seventy Weeks of Daniel.

Remarks: The Servitude resulted from the first invasion of Jerusalem by Nebuchadnezzar. Originally the LORD intended that Judah should remain in their land in servitude to Nebuchadnezzar. It was from this invasion that Daniel and his companions were taken captive to Babylon.

THE CAPTIVITY (62 Years)

Dates: From BC 598 (8th year of Nebuchadnezzar)

To   BC 536

Scripture References 2 Kings 24:10 Esther 2:5-7 Jeremiah 27:6, 17; 28:14; 29:10

Remarks Second invasion by Nebuchadnezzar when he took Jehoiachin into captivity with Ezekiel, and including Mordecai and Esther his niece. The message to those in captivity in Babylon was that the LORD would let them return to Jerusalem. (Ezekiel began to prophesy in Babylon, in the fifth year of the Captivity Period BC 594.) The *Captivity* commenced eight years after the *Servitude.* The Captivity was stated to be for seventy years (Jeremiah 29:10-14.)

[The vision was given to Cyrus 538 BC and the restoration under Cyrus began in 536 BC.]

THE DESOLATIONS (70 Years)

Dates: From BC 589 (17th year of Nebuchadnezzar)

To   BC 520 (2nd year of Darius Hystaspes)

Scripture References 2 Kings 25:1-17 Daniel 10:1 Jeremiah 25:8-11 & 32:1-5 Haggai 2:18

Remarks Third invasion by Nebuchadnezzar. Desolations prophesied. The Desolations ended with the laying of the foundations of the temple the second time (see Footnote 4 under Servitude.)

[NOTE: The Seventy Years of the Servitude, or The Captivity or the Desolations have nothing to do with the Seventy Weeks of Daniel's Prophecy, (which commenced 73 years after the Captivity in BC 445.) But the consideration of these periods is essential for calculating and comprehending the dates for the commencement and end of the Seventy Weeks of Daniel. (See note The 70th Week below.) Note also: Daniel 10:1, the third year of Darius is the latest date mentioned in Daniel.) There is a further consideration to make; BC 589 was the date when Jerusalem was besieged by Nebuchadnezzar (commencing the Desolations,) but the city was taken and destroyed (BC 587.) Forty years previous to this date (in BC 627,) Jeremiah commenced His prophetic ministry in Jerusalem for forty years to Judah, commencing in 13th year of Josiah (Jeremiah 1:2, 3; 25:3; and compare Ezekiel 4:6.)]

NOTE: The scriptures clearly differentiate between the SEVENTY WEEKS (of years, i.e. 490 years,) of Daniel's Supplications, (based on the prophecy given to Jeremiah,) and the three successive SEVENTY YEAR periods of judgment (called the *Servitude*, the *Captivity* and the *Desolations*) which were imposed on the Jews for their increasing disobedience to the prophet Jeremiah.

In Gabriel's explanation to Daniel, *The Seventy Weeks* were divided into a period of seven weeks of seven years (i.e. forty-nine years, which ended with the closure of the scriptures with the prophecy of Malachi,) then, a period of sixty and two weeks (of seven years) totalling 434 years to the cutting off of Messiah (total = 483 years (of 360 days each.= 173,880 days. See page 2.) The three separate (and overlapping) successive judgments of seventy years (the *servitude, captivity* and *desolation*) occurred within the period of The Seventy Weeks covering a total of 85 years (from BC 606 to 520), because of their overlapping;) but these times of judgment had no bearing or influence on the fulfilment of the Seventy Week prophecy itself they merely revealed the LORD's increasing anger with Judah.

SUBSEQUENT EVENTS

BC 515 (Ezra 6:15) Temple dedicated

(Seventy years interim period)

BC 445 (Nehemiah 1:2 2:5 6:15) Jerusalem restored, Daniel's 70 Weeks of years commenced.

BC 397 Prophecy of Malachi completed the Old Testament canon, and this ends the first seven weeks

(49 years) of Daniel's 70 Weeks, (leaving 62 weeks times 7 = 434 years.)

AD 32 Messiah cut off (The Cross) End of Daniel's 69th Week, (leaving the final week unfulfilled.)

The Times of the Gentiles

It is necessary at this point to explain *the Times of the Gentiles,* which was the term the LORD Jesus Christ Himself used to describe the whole period of the Gentile domination of the holy land and particularly Jerusalem. Note especially His words (Luke 21:24) *"and they* (the Jews) *shall fall by the edge of the sword, and shall be led away captive into all nations: and Jerusalem shall be trodden down of the Gentiles, until the times of the Gentiles be fulfilled.*[57]*"*

---

[57] The fulfilment of the times of the Gentiles means effectively the end of Gentile power over the Jews (which happens when the final week of the Seventy is completed;) at which time the sceptre for world rule passes back to the King of Kings; and representing Him will be the appointed Son of David in Jerusalem ruling Israel and Judah as one nation (see Ezekiel 37:20-28.)

Nebuchadnezzar, who ruled Jerusalem at the time from Babylon, had to be humbled and reduced in his madness to an animal state for seven years, *"till thou know that the MOST HIGH ruleth in the kingdom of men, and giveth it to whomsoever He will."* (Daniel 4:25.) Nebuchadnezzar was in fact the first of the gentile kings (and the only one with absolute power in his own right,) to have domination over the Holy Land and Jerusalem, the commencement of the *times of the Gentiles* was from Nebuchadnezzar's first conquest of Jerusalem (BC 606.) This domination passed through his successors and then various empires in turn (the Medo-Persian, the Greek and the Roman Empires) during which periods; authority in the Holy Land was maintained by the sword of whatever conqueror had established himself as ruler.

Within the times of the Gentiles the Seventy Weeks (of years) occurred, which period was first revealed to Jeremiah, and explained to Daniel as a result of his supplications, by the heavenly messenger, who explained:

"Seventy weeks are determined upon thy people, and upon thy holy city, to finish the transgression, and to make an end of sins, and to make reconciliation for iniquity, and to bring in everlasting righteousness, and to seal up the vision and prophecy, and to anoint the most Holy. Know therefore and understand, (that) from the going forth of the commandment to restore and to build Jerusalem unto the Messiah the Prince (shall be) seven weeks, and threescore and two weeks: the street shall be built again, and the wall, even in troublous times. And after threescore and two weeks shall Messiah be cut off, but not for Himself:"

The first seven weeks of years (49 years) covered the period from the time of the laying of the foundation of the Temple (BC 445) to the completion of the Old Testament canon (the Jewish Scriptures) with

---

This must not be confused with the *fulness of the Gentiles* (Romans 11:26) which refers to the eventual total of Gentile believers in the LORD (i.e. added to His true Church) during this dispensation of grace, whilst blindness in part has happened to Israel.

the prophecy of Malachi (BC 397). The second period of sixty-two weeks of years (434 years) was completed with the cutting off of Messiah (AD 32.) This leaves the final week (of seven years) to commence and be fulfilled. But, with the Jewish rejection of their Messiah, and their failure to repent as a nation, during the period of grace given them covering the ministry of the Gospel of GOD by the Apostles (described in Acts;) after which the Jews were expelled from their land totally by the Romans. Ever since the Holy Land and Jerusalem has been totally dominated by gentiles (but mainly Muslims) until 1945.

The failure of the Christian Churches mainly the Roman Catholics (in gentile nations,) to appreciate that the Holy Land (and therefore Jerusalem) was prophetically destined to be ruled by Gentiles (not necessarily Christians) resulted in the Crusades. This was an absolute waste of time (and many lives were lost) accomplishing nothing; for until the Jews are enabled to return to their land, there is no possibility of any covenant reinstating their worship (in Jerusalem, for no other place on earth would be acceptable for a Jewish capital, and particularly as a centre for their worship.)

The *Times of the Gentiles* therefore effectively extends from Nebuchadnezzar's first conquest of Jerusalem (BC 606) to the (yet future) establishment of the covenant between the Jewish nation and the Beast of Revelation; at which time the final week of Daniel's Seventieth Week commences.

This final week will fulfil the ultimate requirements of the prophecy *determined upon thy people, and upon thy holy city* which were: *to finish the transgression, and to make an end of sins, and to make reconciliation for iniquity, and to bring in everlasting righteousness, and to seal up the vision and prophecy, and to anoint the most Holy.* His breaking his covenant (the final, and ultimate act of betrayal of the LORD's people,) completes, what might be called, "*the desolation of the desolate*"; the final outpouring of GOD's wrath upon His people for rejecting His Son. *And he* (the Beast) *shall confirm the covenant with many for one week: and in the midst of the week he shall cause the sacrifice and the oblation to cease, and for the overspreading of abominations he shall make (it) desolate, even until the consummation, and that determined shall be poured upon the desolate."*

It is on the authority of the LORD's Own teachings[58] (and there can

---

[58] *Luke 21:7-24 And they asked Him saying, "Master, but when shall these things be? And what sign (will there be) when these things shall come to pass?" And He said, "Take heed that ye be not deceived: for many shall come in My name, saying I am (Christ;) and the time draweth near: go ye not therefore after them. But when ye shall hear of wars and commotions, be not terrified: for these things must first come to pass, but the end (is) not by and by." Then said He unto them, "Nation shall rise against nation, and kingdom against kingdom: and great earthquakes shall be in divers places, and famines, and pestilences; and fearful sights and great signs shall there be from heaven. But before all these, they shall lay their hands on you, and persecute (you,) delivering (you) up to the synagogues, and into prisons, being brought before kings and rulers for My name's sake. And it shall turn to you for a testimony. Settle (it) therefore in your hearts, not to meditate before what ye shall answer: for I will give you a mouth and wisdom, which all your adversaries shall not be able to gainsay nor resist. And ye shall be betrayed both by parents, and brethren, and kinsfolks, and friends; and (some) of you shall they cause to be put to death. And ye shall be hated of all (men) for My name's sake. But there shall not an hair of your head perish. In your patience possess ye your souls. And when ye shall see Jerusalem compassed with armies, then know that the desolation thereof is nigh. Then let them which are in Judaea flee to the mountains; and let them which are in the midst of it depart out; and let not them that are in the countries enter there into. For these be the days of vengeance, that all things which are written may be fulfilled. But woe unto them that are with child, and to them that give suck, in those days! For there shall be great distress in the land, and wrath upon this people. And they shall fall by the edge of the sword, and shall be led away captive into all nations: and Jerusalem shall be trodden down of the Gentiles, until the times of the Gentiles be fulfilled.*

21:25-33 And there shall be signs in the sun, and in the moon, and in the stars; and upon the earth distress of nations, with perplexity; the sea and the waves roaring; men's hearts failing them for fear, and for looking after those things which are coming on the earth: for the powers of heaven shall be shaken. And then shall they see the Son of man coming in a cloud with power and great glory. And when these things begin to come to pass, then look up, and lift up your heads; for your redemption draweth nigh". And He spake to them a parable: "Behold the fig tree, and all the trees; when they now shoot forth, ye see and know of your own selves that summer is now nigh at hand. So likewise ye, when ye see these things come to pass, know ye that the kingdom of GOD is nigh at hand. Verily I say unto you, this generation shall not pass away, till all be fulfilled. Heaven and earth shall pass away: but My words shall not pass away."

be no higher authority than His,) that we accept that the Times of the Gentiles ends with the covenant established by the Beast. As already stated (page 143): The end of the seventieth week marks the end of Gentile domination of Jerusalem (the Jews); when the sceptre of world domination passes to the LORD, (Who rules from the New Jerusalem.)

Turning our attention now to Daniel 11:1, 2 *"Also I in the first year of Darius the Mede, (even) I, stood to confirm and to strengthen him. And now will I shew thee the truth. Behold, there shall stand up yet three kings in Persia; and the fourth shall be far richer than (they) all: and by his strength through his riches he shall sir up all against the realm of Grecia."* The words of the heavenly messenger to Daniel in his vision drew particular attention to these succeeding kings of Persia.

It is essential to recognise also that scripturally Mordecai and Esther, his niece were taken captive by Nebuchadnezzar (Esther 2:6) ...*a certain Jew, whose name was Mordecai, ... who had been carried away from Jerusalem, with the captivity which had been carried away with Jeconiah king of Judah, whom Nebuchadnezzar the king of Babylon had carried away. And he brought up Hadassah, that is, Esther, etc* their Captivity dated from BC 598 (as shown above.)

Scripturally the kings of Media and Persia played a most important role in the history of Israel, for they were directly involved with the prophecies (commencing with Isaiah) concerning the judgments on Israel and the subsequent restoration of that nation to their own land. The various scriptural accounts (Daniel, Esther, Ezra and Nehemiah) in which these kings are mentioned can be quite

---

21:34-36 *"And take heed to yourselves, lest at any time your hearts be overcharged with surfeiting, and drunkenness, and cares of this life, and (so) that day come upon you unawares. For as a snare shall it come on all them that dwell on the face of the whole earth. Watch ye therefore, and pray always, that ye may be accounted worthy to escape all these things that shall come to pass, and to stand before (the son) of man."*

confusing, because all these kings had several titles and names, and it is very difficult to ascertain which kings are meant in different circumstances. These considerations are based on the premise that the scriptures have to be right (as will become evident) and the events and dates obtained from secular history (in association with fulfilled Bible prophecies and events,) have been carefully compared with the scriptural narrative to determine as accurately as possible, which kings are referred to in scripture.

Secular sources including the names given on the Cyrus Cylinder and the Behistun Rock, (which have been published) and the efforts of several authors have been examined to unravel these difficulties. However errors or discrepancies have been found in most cases and it was felt that the only way to resolve the matter satisfactorily was to use the scriptures as the basis for such considerations. Then to consider every king involved from every aspect possible to make an accurate assessment of which king is being spoken about scripturally. The names of the kings in scripture are given in bold type, but their historical name is given in full where appropriate: e.g. **Artaxerxes** Longimanus.

Concerning the *scriptural* kings of Media and Persia, it is necessary to commence with

Ahasuerus or Astyages, (BC 585-538) for he was undoubtedly the scriptural Ahasuerus (and the first king scripturally so called) of the book of Esther. Mordecai and Esther were taken into captivity by Nebuchadnezzar into Babylon with king Jeconiah of Judah (BC 598.) All the references to the king Ahasuerus in Esther must apply to Astyages. To suggest that any of the other kings also called Ahasuerus could be married to Esther is absurd; at the lowest estimate this would make Esther over a hundred years old [Xerxes (486-465), Artaxerxes Longimanus (464-423) or Artaxerxes Mnemon (404-358.)]

Ahasuerus (Astyages,) was also the father of Darius the Mede for he was the last of the Median kings.

[Sir Robert Anderson was in error suggesting that the Ahasuerus of Esther 3:7 was Xerxes (*The Coming Prince,* Appendix II page 256.) For the reasons already stated; the Ahasuerus of Esther has to be Astyages.]

Darius the Mede or **Cyrus** (both names are used for him scripturally.)

Daniel 5:31 *And Darius the Median took the kingdom, being about threescore and two years old.* Daniel 9:1 *In the first year of Darius the son of Ahasuerus, of the seed of the Medes, which was made king over the realm of the Chaldeans, etc*

Daniel 10:1 *In the third year of Cyrus king of Persia a thing was revealed unto Daniel, whose name was called Belteshazzar; and the thing was true, but the time appointed was long: and he understood the thing, and had understanding of the vision*

Daniel 11:1 *Also I in the first year of Darius the Mede, even I, stood to confirm and to strengthen him.* One of the heavenly beings came and strengthened Daniel, and explained things to him (from 10:18). But clearly this is the same Darius the Mede in every case, or Cyrus king of Persia.

The date on which Darius took the kingdom of Babylon (off Nabonidus, although it was his nephew Belshazzar, who was reigning in Babylon at the time,) was BC 536. Since Darius or Cyrus was about sixty-two at that time (he was born in BC 598) it means he could not have been born of Esther. For Ahasuerus did not marry her until the seventh year of his reign (BC 578, Esther 2:16.)

This does not mean of course that Esther and Mordecai had no influence on Cyrus; it was probably Mordecai and Esther, who were used to make Cyrus aware of the Jews as a nation. This would explain why a Persian king would make the proclamation that Cyrus made the first year he ruled in Babylon concerning the LORD's house in Jerusalem.

Mordecai would have known the prophecy of Isaiah (45:1-4) *Thus saith the LORD to His anointed, to Cyrus, whose right hand I have holden, to subdue nations before him; and I will loose the loins of kings, to open before him the two leaved gates; and the gates shall not be shut; I will go before thee, and make the crooked places straight: I will break in pieces the gates of brass, and cut in sunder the bars of iron: and I will give thee the treasures of darkness, and hidden riches of secret places, that thou mayest know that I, the LORD, Which call thee by thy name, am the GOD of Israel.*

Critics detest this prophecy and they have invented *Pseudo-Isaiah* or *Deutero-Isaiah* (or even more corny, *Second Isaiah*,) claiming that Isaiah the son of Amos could never have prophesied the name of Cyrus a hundred years or more in advance. Effectively they do not want to admit that the prophet Isaiah was that good (or rather that the LORD could give him such a prophecy.) So they invented another Isaiah (born after the Captivity), who they claim wrote the last part of the book of Isaiah, for which they have no evidence whatsoever. Whilst the Jews never challenged Isaiah's prophecy previously in this respect, it is sad to say that in these times some Jews do go along with this view. However, the LORD Jesus Christ spoke of Isaiah as one prophet, and the New Testament contains quotations from the whole book, nowhere remotely suggesting that there were two Isaiahs. (Isaiah 1:1 effectively settles the matter most effectively of all.).

Cyrus BC 559-530 he ruled originally over the Medes and Persians, (he ruled in Babylon from BC 536). Ezra commenced (1:1-4) *Now in the first year of Cyrus king of Persia, that the word of the LORD by the mouth of Jeremiah might be fulfilled, the LORD stirred up the spirit of Cyrus king of Persia, that he made a proclamation throughout all his kingdom, and put it also in writing, saying, "Thus saith Cyrus king of Persia, The LORD GOD of heaven hath given me all the kingdoms of the earth; and He hath charged me to build Him an house at Jerusalem, which is in Judah. Who is there among you of all His people? His GOD be with him, and let him go up to Jerusalem, which* *is in Judah, and build the house of the LORD GOD of Israel, (he is the GOD,) which is in Jerusalem. And whosoever remaineth in any place where he sojourneth, let the men of his place help him with silver, and with gold, and with goods, and with beasts, beside the freewill offering for the house of GOD that is in Jerusalem."*

This proclamation in the first year of the reign of Cyrus in Babylon (BC 536) was the incentive for some of the Jews to return to Jerusalem, to rebuild the Temple and the city, and *Cyrus brought forth the vessels of the house of the LORD,* (which Nebuchadnezzar had taken to Babylon,) for their restoration to the Temple of the LORD in Jerusalem. (The quotation from Isaiah 45 naming Cyrus has already been given.) Cyrus was referred to several times also in:

Ezra 4:5 *And hired counsellors against them, to frustrate their purpose, all the days of Cyrus king of Persia, even until the reign of Darius king of Persia.* Whilst Cyrus started off a Mede, (*Darius the Mede*) he established himself as Cyrus king of Persia.

Ezra 5:13-17 *But in the first year of Cyrus the king of Babylon the same king Cyrus made a decree to build this house of GOD.* Etc. Such munificence by an eastern monarch to former enemies was unheard of, in this respect Cyrus was a most notable and unusual king.

Ezra 6:3 *And there was found at Achmetha, in the palace that is in the province of the Medes, a roll, and therein was a record thus written: 'In the first year of Cyrus the king, the same Cyrus the king made a decree concerning the house of GOD at Jerusalem etc.* The interesting thing here is that the roll found at Achmetha clearly confirmed that Cyrus was a Mede originally. On the death of Cyrus, his son Cambyses took the throne.

Cambyses II (BC 530-522) Initially he was a successful king and conquered Egypt (BC 525) but later he went insane and committed suicide. On his death a character, who called himself Smerdis, usurped and held the throne for eight months, but neither the impostor Smerdis nor Cambyses are mentioned by these names in scripture. (The real Smerdis was the brother of Cambyses II, whom Cambyses II is alleged to have disposed of to take the throne. His body was never found so his death remains a mystery.) The impostor Smerdis held the throne as "Artaxerxes" for eight months and he was slain by Darius Hystaspis. Nevertheless the impostor Smerdis or Artaxerxes (which is the name he was given scripturally) stopped the building in Jerusalem, when he was appealed to by the adversaries of the Jews. This explains the Artaxerxes mentioned in Ezra (4: 7, 8, 11, and 23) who stopped the work until the second year of Darius Hystaspis, who actually slew his brother Smerdis and was the next ruler.

Darius Hystaspis (522-486) (sometimes spelled Histaspes, but this is usually avoided to prevent confusion with his father Histaspes[59], who was the son of Astyages (the original Ahasuerus) and Vashti, Ahasuerus's first queen (Darius Histaspis was a brother or more accurately a step-brother to Cyrus.)

Darius Hystaspis thoughtfully decided to record his genealogy and the major events of his reign for posterity, and he had these carved (in three languages) on the Rock at Behistun (see pages 161, 162.) He totally omitted any reference to Cyrus or Cambyses II (the son of Cyrus) but mentioned his own father *my father is Hystaspes*, (so he was alive although Darius Histaspis was king,) *whose father was* Arsames (Astyages), *whose father was* Ariyaramnes, *whose father was* Teispes, *whose father was* Achaemenes. Whilst his inscription only gave six names, Darius nevertheless declared himself to be the ninth king. [This total could only be accurate if Cyrus, Cambyses II, and Smerdis (or Artaxerxes as he was called scripturally) were included; so these omissions must have been deliberate.] Nevertheless without the inscription of Darius Hystaspis, in the Behistun Rock, [which was discovered, copied at considerable risk to himself, and translated by Major (later Sir Henry) Rawlinson] scholars

---

[59] Whilst Darius Histaspis included his father Histaspes (son of Astyages & Vashti) on the inscriptions, there is no record of Histaspes ruling as king. (Cyrus was most certainly not the son of Astyages and Esther as some claim.)

would have had a very difficult job working out the lines of Persian monarchs. The difficulties the historians faced were enormous, because apart from language difficulties, all of these rulers had several appellatives (which were mistaken for names,) and these were sometimes transliterated. What is important for these considerations is that on the Behustun rock inscriptions, Darius Hystaspis claimed to be effectively the (grand)son of Arsames or Astyages (the Ahasuerus of Esther.) But he omitted Cyrus (or Darius the Mede,) Cambyses II and impostor Smerdis (Artaxerxes.) It has to be the impostor Smerdis, because the real Smerdis had been murdered.

Darius the king as he is referred to, appears several times in scripture:

Ezra 4:5 *And hired counsellors against them to frustrate their purpose, all the days of Cyrus king of Persia, even until the reign of* **Darius king of Persia.**

Ezra 4:24 *Then ceased the work of the house of GOD, which is at Jerusalem. So it ceased unto the second year of the reign of* **Darius king of Persia.** (BC 521.)

[From the second year of Cyrus ruling in Babylon (BC 536) to the second year of Darius (BC 521) was fourteen years, which was the delay caused by local petty opposition, to the written proclamation of a Persian king. A most remarkable occurrence for such disobedience was normally intolerable and dealt with very harshly.]

Ezra 5:6, 7 *The copy of the letter that Tatnai, governor on this side the river, and Shethar-boznai, and his companions the Apharsachites, which were on this side the river, sent unto* **Darius the king:** *they sent a letter unto him, wherein was written thus; "Unto* **Darius the king**, *all peace. Etc.*

Ezra 6:1 *Then* **Darius the king** *made a decree, and search was made in the house of the rolls, where the treasures were laid up in Babylon.*

And there was found at Achmetha, in the palace that is in the province of the Medes, a roll, etc.

Ezra 6:2-12 Darius's reply insisting that they offer fullest co-operation and assistance to the work, concluded: *I Darius have made a decree; let it be done with speed.*

Darius Hystaspis was succeeded by Xerxes (BC 486-465) of whom there is no mention in scripture. Xerxes was murdered by Artabanus, (465) who reigned only seven months and was slain by Artaxerxes Longimanus, the son of Xerxes. Artaxerxes Longimanus did not even consider Artabanus a king, and reckoned his own reign from his father's death.

Artaxerxes Longimanus (464-423) was mentioned several times in scripture and again his reign had considerable significance. His involvement was with Nehemiah (as will be shown, clearly not Esther.)

Ezra 4:4-8 *Then the people of the land weakened the hands of the people of Judah, and troubled them in building, and hired counsellors against them, to frustrate their purpose, all the days of Cyrus king of Persia, even until the reign of Darius king of Persia. And in the reign of* **Ahasuerus,** *in the beginning of his reign,* (Obviously, this cannot have been the Ahasuerus of Esther, for the decree of Cyrus came after his death; so it has to be Smerdis who called himself Artaxerxes and whom the Bible calls Ahasuerus.) *wrote they unto him an accusation against the inhabitants of Judah and Jerusalem. And in the reign of* **Artaxerxes** *wrote Bishlam, Mithredath, Tabeel, and the rest of their companions, unto* **Artaxerxes king of Persia**; *and the writing of the letter was written in the Syrian tongue, and interpreted in the Syrian tongue. Rehum the chancellor and Shimshai the scribe wrote a letter against Jerusalem to Artaxerxes the king in this sort, etc.*

Ezra 4:11 *This is a copy of the letter that they sent unto him, even unto* **Artaxerxes the king**; *"Thy servants the men on this side the river, and at such a time. Etc*

The context is most important in deciding who these kings Ahasuerus and Artaxerxes were.

The king as requested searched out the records, which confirmed to him that Jerusalem was a troublesome city, and he commanded that the work should cease.

Ezra 4:23 *Now when the copy of king Artaxerxes' letter was read before Rehum, and Shimshai the scribe, and their companions, they went up in haste to Jerusalem unto the Jews, and made them to cease by force and power.*

This was the disruption of the work that was caused during the reign of Cyrus to the second year of Darius (4:24 as above.) This Ahasuerus cannot be the original Astyages (of Esther) as already shown, he was dead before the decree of Cyrus was made. It is most unlikely that it was Cyrus himself, for as a Persian king and ruling in Babylon he would have been most offended to learn that his decree was being challenged. It is suggested therefore, since the scripture specifically stated *in the beginning of his reign,* (4:6) that this king Ahasuerus was not the son of Cyrus, Cambyses II (BC 530-522) because he went insane at the end of his reign and committed suicide. Artaxerxes king of Persia (of Ezra 4:7, 8, 11, & 23) must therefore be the impostor Smerdis, the immediate successor to Cambyses II, by claiming to be his brother Smerdis. Darius Histaspis had no illusions concerning "Smerdis" and slew him after eight months to take the throne. (Darius Histaspis did not include (the impostor) Smerdis in the list of monarchs on the Behistan Rock.)

Ezra 7:1 *Now after these things, in the reign of* **Artaxerxes king of Persia***, Ezra the son of Seraiah, the son of Azariah, the son of Hilkiah, etc*

Ezra 7:7, 8 *And there went up some of the children of Israel, and of the priests, and the Levites, and the singers, and the porters, and the Nethinims, unto Jerusalem, in the seventh year of* **Artaxerxes the** *king. And he* (Ezra) *came to Jerusalem in the fifth month, which was in the seventh year of the king.*

Ezra 7:11-28 This whole chapter refers to the decree from Artaxerxes the king giving Ezra authority to go up to Jerusalem *to beautify the house of the LORD which is in Jerusalem.*

This clearly happened in the seventh year of **Artaxerxes** (BC 458) confirming the scriptures refer to **Artaxerxes Longimanus**, and this decree restored the worship of Israel, their *spiritual* identity.

Ezra 8:1 *These are now the chief of their fathers, and this is the genealogy of them that went up with me from Babylon, in the reign of Artaxerxes the king. Etc.*

This is the last reference to any king in Ezra, but Nehemiah provides further references.

Nehemiah 1:1 *The words of Nehemiah the son of Hachaliah. And it came to pass in the month Chisleu,* (= December) *in the twentieth year, as I was in Shushan the palace, etc.* (The twentieth year is explained in the next chapter.)

Nehemiah 2:1 *And it came to pass in the month Nisan,*(= April) *in the twentieth year of* **Artaxerxes the king,** *that wine was before him: and I took up the wine, and gave it unto the king. Now I had not been beforetime sad in his presence. Wherefore the king said unto me, "Why is thy countenance sad, seeing thou art not sick? This is nothing else but sorrow of heart." Then I was very sore afraid, and said unto the king, "Let the king live for ever: why should not my countenance be sad, when the city, the place of my fathers' sepulchres, lieth waste, and the gates thereof are consumed with fire?" Then the king said unto me, "For what dost thou make request?" So I prayed to the GOD of heaven. And I said unto the king, "If it please the king, and if thy servant have found favour in thy sight, that thou wouldest send me unto Judah, unto the city of my fathers' sepulchres, that I may build it." And the king said unto me, (the queen also sitting by him,) "For* *how long shall thy journey be? And when wilt thou return?" So it pleased the king to send me; and I set him a time.*

Nehemiah obtained favour in the sight of Artaxerxes Longimanus, who in the twentieth year of his reign, provided the letters of authority for Nehemiah to go and build the city [BC 445, this is the most important date scripturally, it commenced the Seventy Weeks of Jeremiah's prophecy (Jeremiah 29, Daniel 9).] His previous command *to beautify the house of the LORD* was itself a milestone, (it restored their national worship) but in this instance the foundation was laid that commenced the fulfilment of the prophecy. *"Know therefore and understand, that from the going forth of the commandment to restore and to build Jerusalem unto the Messiah the Prince shall be seven weeks, and threescore and two weeks: the street shall be built again, and the wall, even in troublous times."* (Daniel 9:25.) This decree restored their *political* identity; Israel became a recognised nation, capable (in theory) of defending itself.

Nehemiah 13:6 *But in all this time was not I at Jerusalem: for in the two and thirtieth year of Artaxerxes king of Babylon came I unto the king, and after certain days obtained I leave of the king: and came to Jerusalem, and understood the evil that Eliashib did for Tobiah, in preparing him a chamber in the courts of the house of GOD.*

In the thirty-second year of Artaxerxes, Nehemiah returned (this meant he must have requested twelve years, from the twentieth year of Artaxerxes, to complete his work in Jerusalem. Note also Nehemiah 5:14 *Moreover from the time that I was appointed to be their governor in the land of Judah, from the twentieth year even unto the two and thirtieth year of Artaxerxes the king, that is twelve years, I and my brethren had not eaten the bread of the governor.*) However Nehemiah requested that he might return again to Jerusalem, which he did, and he was grieved because Eliashib had made room for Tobiah one of their enemies in the house of the LORD. There were other problems too, which Nehemiah detailed.

Darius the Persian Darius Nothus (BC 423-404) There is another scripture from Nehemiah to consider, (12:22) *The Levites in the days of Eliashib, Joiada and Johanan, and Jaddua were recorded chief of the fathers: also the priests, to the reign of* **Darius the Persian.** If this is considered in the context in which it is found in Nehemiah, i.e. *after* the references to Artaxerxes, with the exception of the final reference (13:6 as above). It will be seen that the final reference could have been included by Nehemiah quite easily before this verse, but he just chose to insert it after, (it clearly applied before this verse.) Then this verse concerning **Darius the Persian**, cannot be applied Darius Hystaspis, who was usually scripturally called *Darius king of Persia*, or *Darius the King* (Ezra 5:6, 7.) There remains only Darius Nothus to whom this verse (Nehemiah 12:22) can apply.

The other scriptures to settle concerning scriptural Persian kings come from Daniel's prophecy.

Daniel 11:1, 2 *Also I in the first year of Darius the Mede* (already considered, and shown to be Cyrus, page 2) *even I, stood to confirm and to strengthen him. And now will I shew thee the truth. Behold, there shall stand up yet three kings in Persia; and the fourth shall be far richer than they all: and by his strength through his riches he shall stir up all against the realm of Grecia.*

The problem is who were the future three kings in Persia? (See page 11 Chronology of Persian Kings)

Following Artaxerxes Longimanus were two insignificant kings (BC 425) Xerxes II who reigned for two months, and Sogdianus (no time specified.) Ptolemy made no mention of them in his canon. This leaves as possibilities for the three kings (of Daniel 11:2): Darius Nothus (BC 423-404 Nehemiah 12:22, above) Artaxerxes II Mnemon of Persia (BC 404-358) who was also another king named Ahasuerus, but he was not named in scripture. Ochus Artaxerxes III of Persia (BC 359-338) not mentioned by name in scripture.

Arogus (or possibly Arsaces) (BC 338-336?) ruled briefly, but he was clearly insignificant.

The fourth king of Daniel's prophecy must be the last Persian king, who did have the accumulated wealth of all the previous kings and *his riches* were what attracted the attention of the Greeks, as prophesied by the heavenly being to Daniel.

Darius III Codomanus of Persia (BC 336- 331) was the last king of Persia; he was defeated at the battle of Arbela by Alexander the Great, which marked the end of the Persian Empire.

[NOTE: There are only two kings named Ahasuerus mentioned in scripture: Astyages (BC 585-538), who was the first so-called. (The Ahasuerus of Esther etc.) Smerdis, the imposter, (who called himself Artaxerxes) but was addressed as Ahasuerus by the Jews in their correspondence (Ezra 4:6, 7, 8, 11, 23.)

Finally Artaxerxes II Mnemon of Persia (BC 404-358) who was also known historically as Ahasuerus; but he is not mentioned in scripture.]

Confusion existed among historians for a long time over the succession and names of Persian kings and this was due to the fact that titles or appellatives were being mistaken for proper names and these were transliterated into other languages. The sources of information were the historians Herodotus, Xenophon, Ctesias and Nicolas of Damascus (all BC) and Arrian (2nd century AD.)

Writers and scholars were unable to agree totally in reconciling the different accounts by these historians. In 1846 AD Major (later Sir Henry) Rawlinson published his translation of the trilingual Persian texts found on the isolated *Rock of Behistun* (or Bahistun). This is a massive rock escarpment, which rises out of the plain on the high road from Baghdad to Teheran, on the face of which Darius Hystaspis had his genealogy and history engraved. At considerable risk, Major

Rawlinson had himself lowered to the face and somehow copied the inscriptions. There was also the Cuneiform Cylinder of Cyrus, which provided further confirmation of the various names and enabled the problem to be unravelled.

The appellatives or titles are:

Ahasuerus = the Mighty, this is used of four Median and Persian monarchs.

Artaxerxes = Great king, it is synonymous with *Artachshast* from *Arta* = great and *Kshatza* = kingdom (whence

comes modern title *Shah*)

Darius = Restrainer or Maintainer.

The Persian text (in three languages) on the Behistun Rock translated as:

1 I am Darius the great king, the king of kings, the king of Persia, the king of the provinces, the son of Hystaspes, the grandson of Arsames the Achaemenian.

II (Thus) saith Darius the king: My father is Hystaspes; the father of Hystaspes was Arsames; the father of Arsames was Ariyaramnes; the father of Ariyarammes was (Teispes); the father of Teispes was Achaemenes.

III (Thus) saith Darius the king: On that account are we called Achaemenians; from antiquity are we descended; from antiquity hath our race been kings.

IV (Thus) saith Darius the king: Eight of my race were kings before (me) I am the ninth. In two lines we have been kings.

[The *two lines* probably referring also to the line of the kings of Lydia, for Darius Hystaspis was the son of Hystaspes, the son of Vashti (the queen of Lydian descent, whom Astyages married before Esther,) and Astyages (*Arsames* on the Behistun Rock.)]

The line of kings with the different names given to each by Herodotus (a contemporary historian,) the Behistun Rock and the Cyrus Cylinder are given below, with (from Herodotus only) the line of the Kings of Lydia.

The Persian Kings

From all sources	Behistun Rock	Cyrus Cylinder	Herodotus
			Lydian Kings[60]
(1) Phraortes I			*Atys*
(2) Deiokes	(2) Achaemenes		*Lydus*
(3) Phraortes II	(3) Teispes	(3) Teispes	*Candaules*
(4) Cyaxares	(4) Ariyaramnes	(4) Cyrus I	*Gyges*
(5) Astyages	(5) Arsames	(5) Cambyses	*Ardys*
(BC 585-538)			*Sadyattes*
Ahasuerus Esther 1:1 & 2:17			*Alyattes*(father
(3rd & 7th years, Esther 1:9)			of A*ryenis*=
[Jehoiachin's captivity, with Mordecai & Esther commenced BC 594.]			*Vashti.*)
(6) **Cyrus**		(6) Cyrus II	
(BC 559-530)			
Ezra 1:1-6 & Ezra 6:3 (BC 536)			
Daniel 5:31, 9:1 10:1 11:1 Darius the Mede			
(7) Cambyses II		(7) Cambyses II	
(BC 530-522) Ezra 4:6 (Ahasuerus)			
(Smerdis, an impostor, reigned 8 months.)			

[*The Magian impostor, calling himself Smerdis was slain by Darius Hystaspis, who it is believed had slain his brother the real Smerdis to take the throne. (Smerdis the impostor must not be confused with Artabanus, who murdered Xerxes, (below) and who was slain by Artaxerxes Longimanus.)*]

---

[60] The Lydian Kings were recorded only by Herodotus, who also recorded Hystaspes and Darius Hystaspis as shown.

[*Through the marriage of Astyages to Vashti came Hystaspes, who never ruled; but Darius included him as his father:*]

Hystaspes	Hystaspes	Hystaspes	Hystaspes
(9) Darius (Hyst.)	(9) **Darius** I Hystaspis* Ezra 4:5 5:6, 7 6:1-12 Haggai [61]1:1 2:18	(9) Darius (Hyst.)	(BC 522-486)

[*Darius I Hystaspis was the king who ordered the inscriptions on the Behustan Rock.]

From other sources:

Xerxes (BC 486-465)
Murdered by Artabanus, who reigned seven months, and was slain by Artaxxerxes Longimans
Artaxerxes Longimanus (BC 464-423)
Decree to beautify the Temple (BC 458). Ezra 7:1-28 & 8:1
Nehemiah 2:1 (20th year to Jerusalem) 13:6 (32nd year, returned to Artaxerxes, & then Jerusalem)
BC 445 Era of Seventy Weeks begins, Jerusalem restored.
Xerxes II (BC 424 -423)
Darius II Nothus of Persia (BC 423-404) Nehemiah 12:22
Artaxerxes II Mnemon of Persia (BC 404 -358)
BC 397 Malachi closes dispensation of The Prophets. Ends first week (49 years) of Daniel's seventy weeks.
Ochus of Persia (BC 358 -336)
Darius Codomanus of Persia (BC 336-331)
Alexander the Great etc

After BC 397 the other sixty-nine prophetic weeks (of years = 483 years) of Gabriel's prophecy finished in AD 32, when Messiah was cut off[62].

(Refer to text for further explanations.)

---

[61] Haggai 2:10, 15-19 & Zechariah 1:1, 7:1 gave the prophecies, which Ezra (4:24 & 5:1-5) cites as incentive for the Jews to work.
[62] The remarkable proof of this is found in Sir Robert Anderson's *The Coming Prince*

Appendix 7 DANIEL'S SUPPLICATIONS and The Persian Kings
Chronology of Persian Kings

BC

?   Phraortes I

?   Deiokes

?   Phraortes II

633   Cyaxares king of Media

585   Astyages his son, (585-538) last king of Media, also called Cambyses I, (the **Ahasuerus** of Esther.)

559 **Cyrus** king of Persia, rise of Persian Empire (559-530) 2 Chronicles 36:20-23,

Ezra   1:1-6. 4:3, 5 6:3.

546   Cyrus defeated Croesus King of Lydia

538   Babylon taken by Medes & Persians

536   Cyrus reigning at Babylon (succeeded by Darius Hystaspis) Ezra 1:1

535   Decree of Cyrus (end of Servitude)

530   Cambyses II (530-522)

525   Cambyses II conquered Egypt, later he went insane and committed suicide.

522   Smerdis, held throne eight months, he was an impostor who pretended to be Smerdis, the brother of Cambyses II, (but Cambyses is believed to have disposed of his brother, the real Smerdis.)

522	**Darius** Hystaspis (522-486) the son of Hystaspes, (who was probably a son of Vashti and Astyages, but Hystaspes never ruled,) Ezra 4:5, 5:5 Haggai 1:1 2:18. Darius Hystaspis disposed of Smerdis (the impostor) and he also ordered the inscriptions on Behistan Rock.
520	End of Desolations (2nd year of Darius) Temple foundation was laid and building completed in five years (Ezra 3:8-11 & 6:15. Compare Haggai 2:10, 15, 18.)
515	Temple completed Ezra 5, 6
490	Battle Marathon
485	Xerxes succeeds Darius (another Ahasuerus) (485-465)
480	Battles of Thermopylae and Salamis
475	Artabanus (seven months reign, he assassinated Xerxes, and Artabanus was slain by Artaxerxes Longimanus, who did not even count his reign, but reckoned his own from his father's death.) Artabanus must not be confused with the other impostor Smerdis, who usurped the throne after suicide of Cambyses II (BC 522.)
465	**Artaxerxes** Longimanus (464-423) (another Ahasuerus) Ezra 4:6, 7:1-28 Nehemiah 2:1
458	Decree to beautify Temple Ezra 7:12-28 (note v7, 8 in seventh year of the king)
449	Persians defeated by Greeks at Salamis
445	Era of Seventy Weeks begins (20th year Artaxerxes) (Jeremiah 29 Daniel 9)
425	Xerxes II (two months)
425	Sogdianus

424	**Darius** II Nothus of Persia (423-404) Nehemiah 12:22	*Behold there shall stand up yet three kings in Persia and the fourth shall be richer than all.* Daniel 11:2
405	Artaxerxes II Mnemon of Persia (404-358) (Ahasuerus)	
359	Ochus Artaxerxes III of Persia	
338	Arogus (or possibly Arsaces)	
336	Darius III Codomanus of Persia] *The fourth king* (Xerxes II, Sogdianus and Arogus can be ignored.)	
335	Battle of Issus	
334	Battle of Granicus	
331	Battle of Arbela defeat of Darius III end of Persian Empire	
323	Death of Alexander the Great	

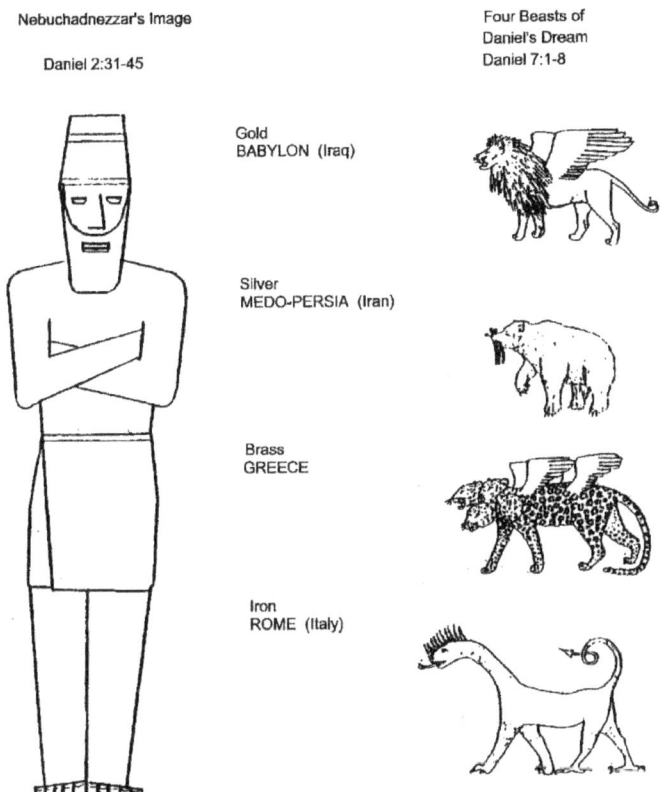

Figure 1
The Image of Nebuchadnezzar's Dream compared with the
Beasts of Daniel's Dream (See [12])

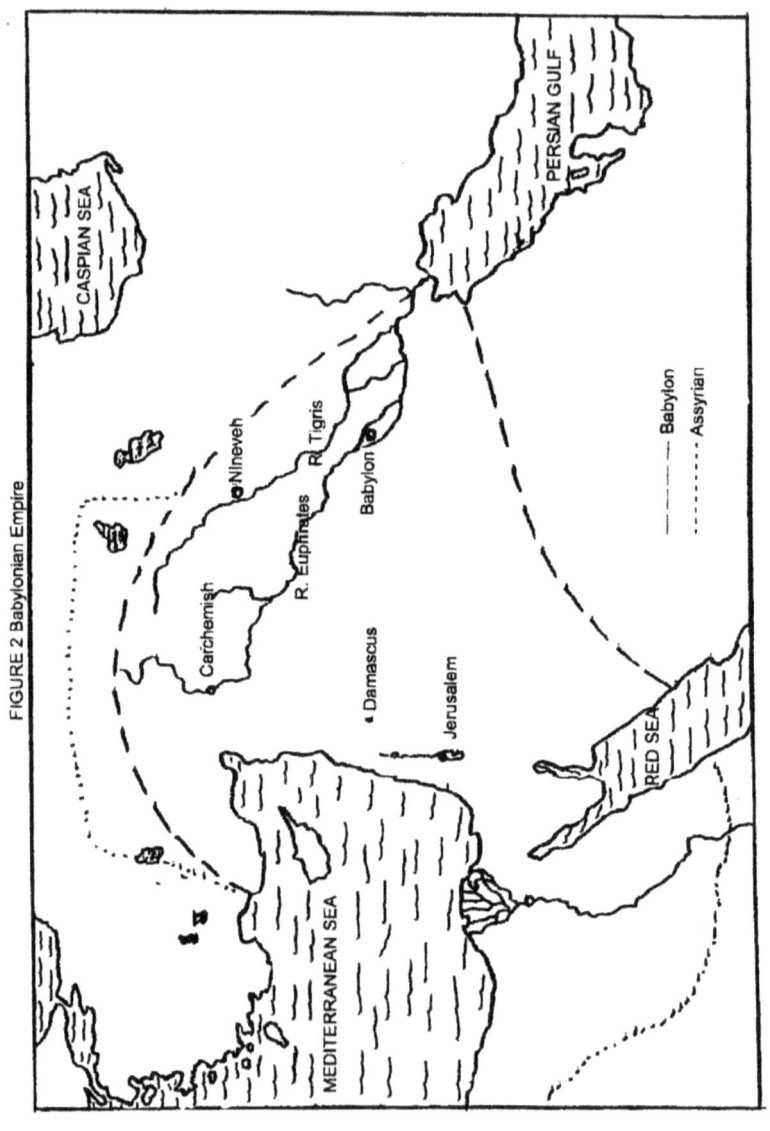

FIGURE 2 Babylonian Empire

FIGURE 3 Persian Empire

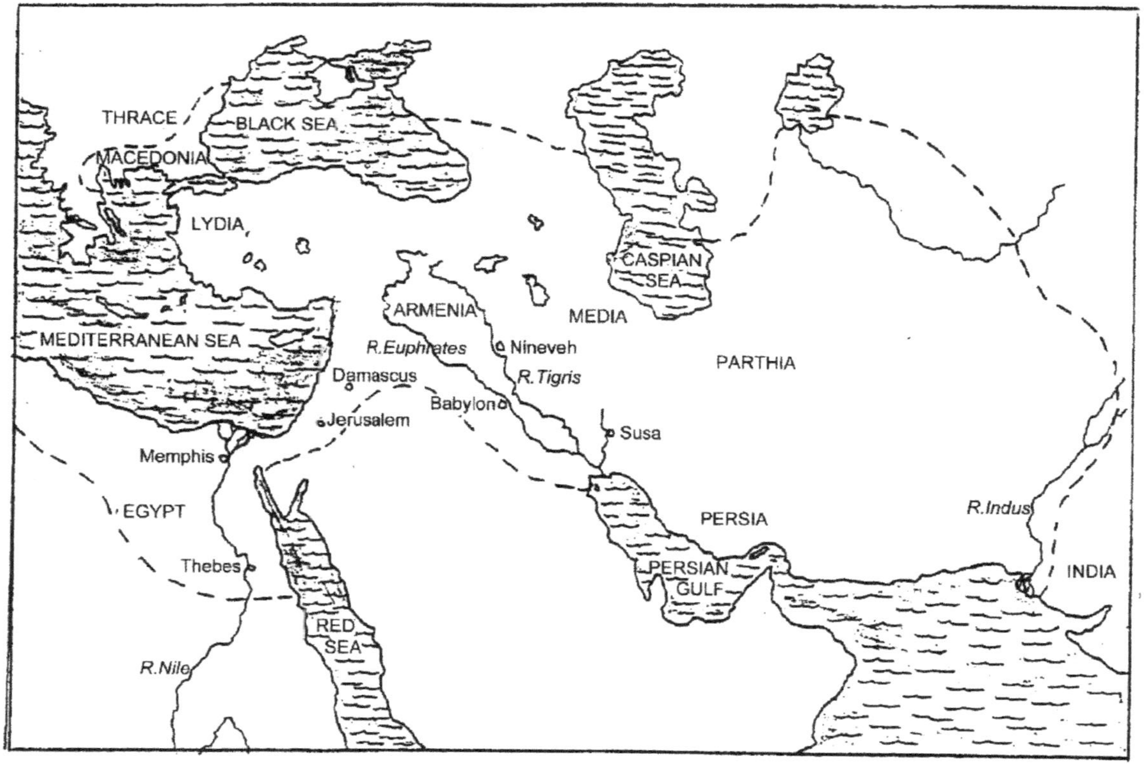

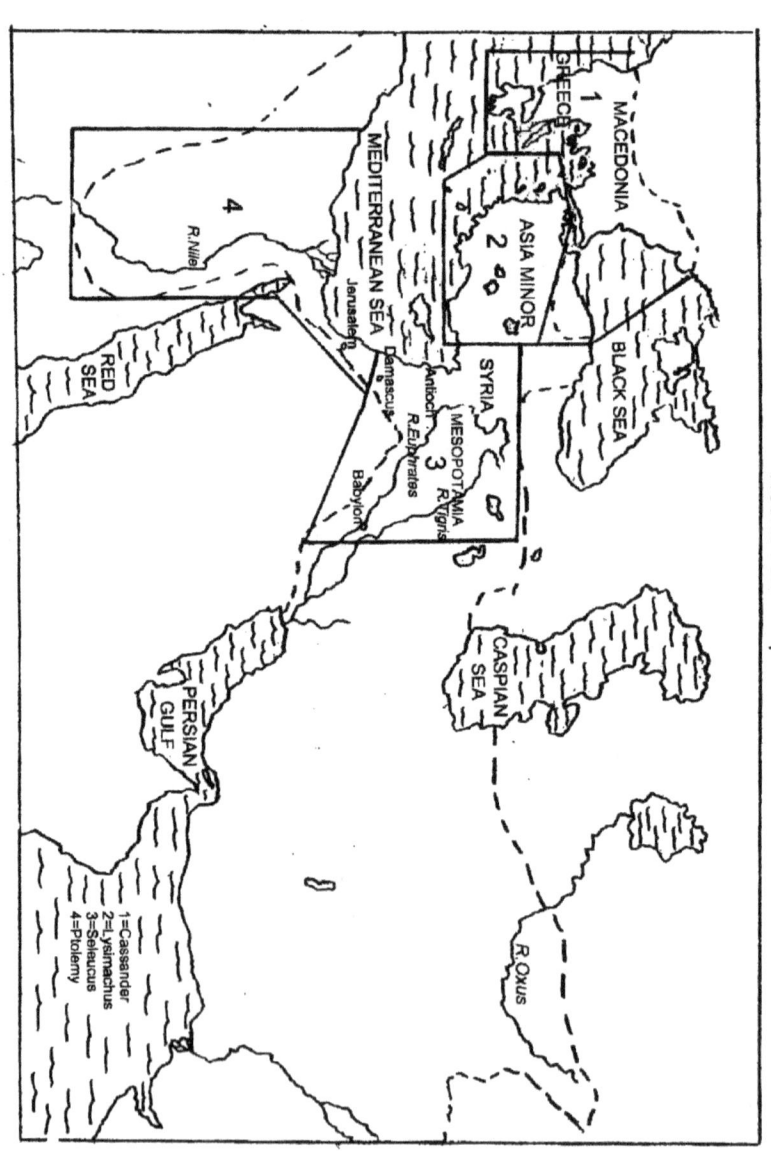

FIGURE 4 Greek Empire

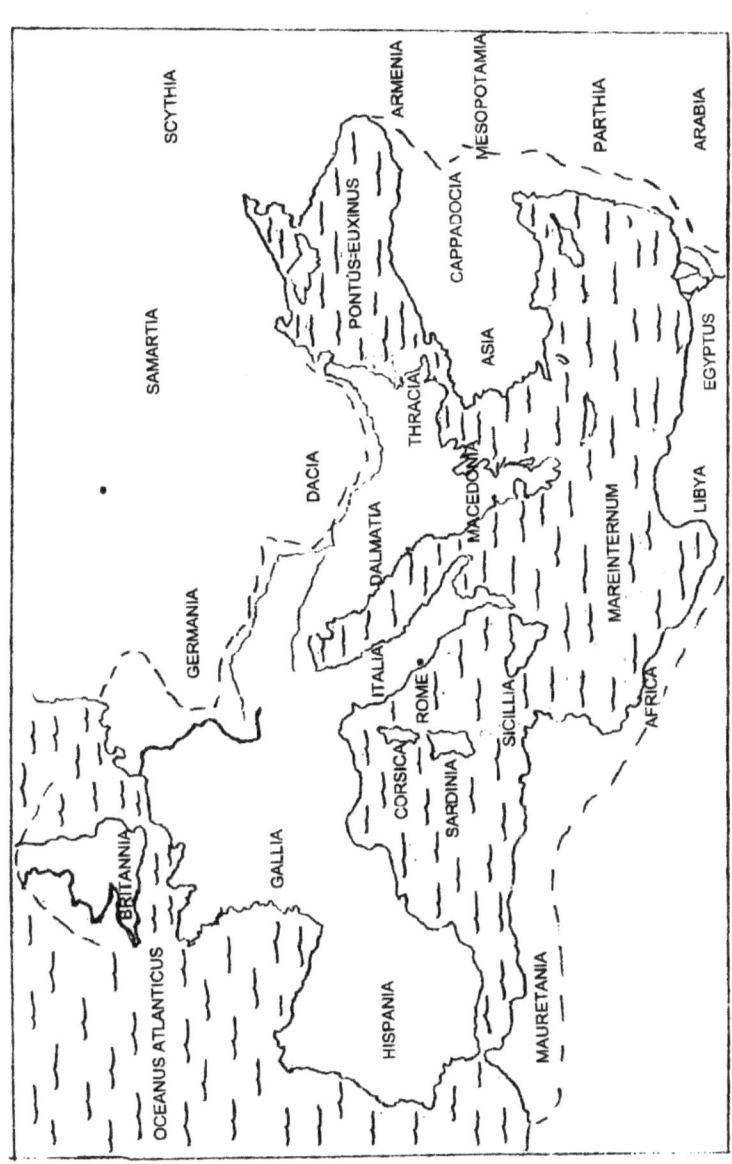

FIGURE 5 ROMAN EMPIRE

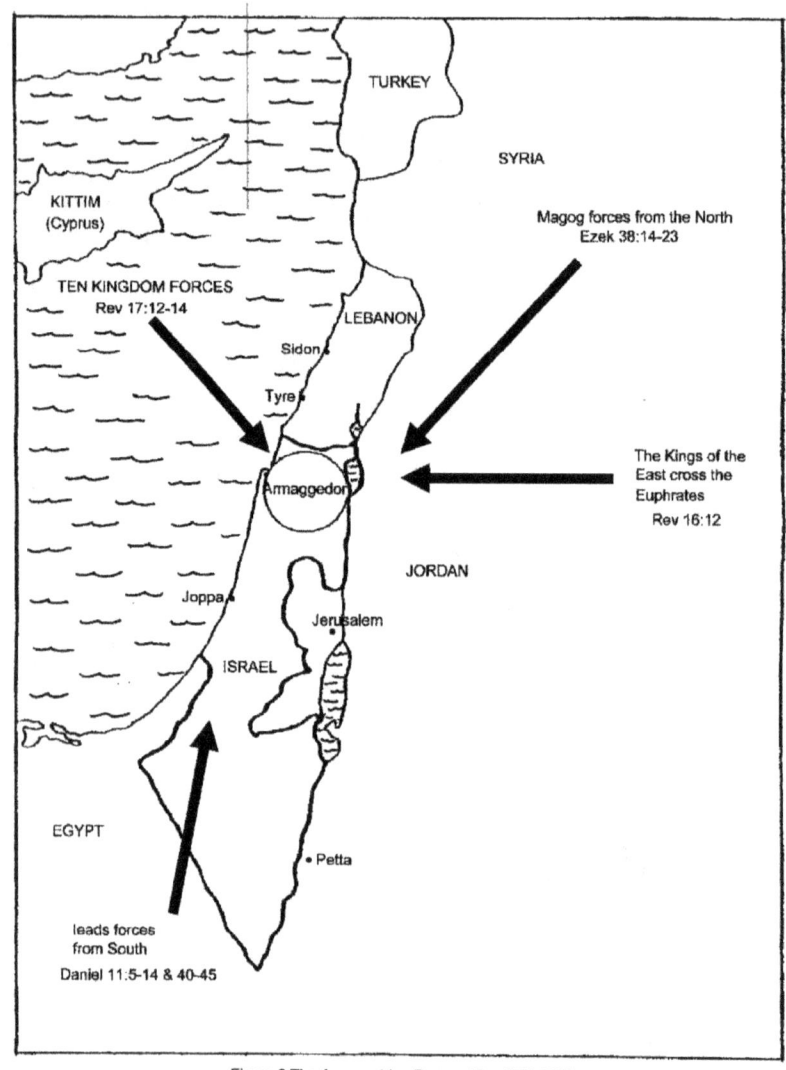

Figure 6 The Armageddon Forces (See [266-269])

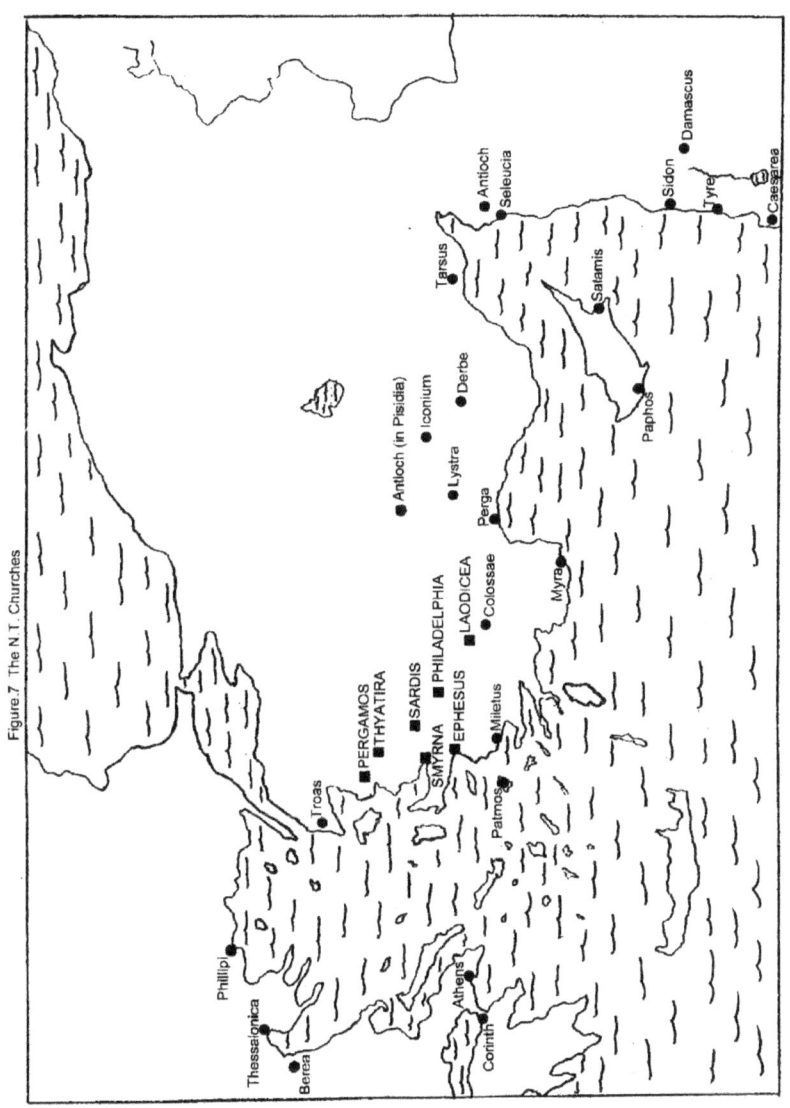

Figure.7 The N.T. Churches

www.ingramcontent.com/pod-product-compliance
Lightning Source LLC
Chambersburg PA
CBHW070457120526
44590CB00013B/670